Americanization of the European Economy

A compact survey of American economic influence
in Europe since the 1880s

by

Harm G. Schröter
University of Bergen, Norway

Springer

A C.I.P. Catalogue record for this book is available from the Library of Congress.

ISBN 1-4020-2884-9 (HB)
ISBN 1-4020-2934-9 (e-book)

Published by Springer,
P.O. Box 17, 3300 AA Dordrecht, The Netherlands.

Sold and distributed in North, Central and South America
by Springer,
101 Philip Drive, Norwell, MA 02061, U.S.A.

In all other countries, sold and distributed
by Springer,
P.O. Box 322, 3300 AH Dordrecht, The Netherlands.

Printed on acid-free paper

For my family

For my friends

And for all who read history in order
to learn for our future.

CONTENTS

PREFACE

For several reasons I worked on this book for a number of years. As a historian, I am not only interested in what happened, but also why it happened. Economics has been claimed to be a "value-empty discipline" (Hampden-Turner & Trompenaars 1993, p. 4), but this is only partly true. It is fascinating to investigate why economic decision-makers opted during certain periods for a change toward an American model, and in other periods for models from different countries. McCreary, an early writer on Americanization, suggested that all economic action rests on culture (1964, p. VIII). Thus, it strives to find out more on the impact of culture on economic action.

Another reason for taking up this topic was the general downturn in demand for economic history; a trend which could be noticed in many countries during the last decade. Proven concepts and methods lost their attractiveness to a great extent. Economic and business history seldom came up with its own theory, but instead applied theories developed in economics, social science, and other fields.

At the background of a large demand in cultural studies, it was fairly easy to imagine a trail of these approaches in the field of economic history. Studies on economic Americanization can be of interest for economists, historians, social scientists, managers and those interested in cultural studies. Surely the reception of such a study will be mixed, because it does not fit in the conventional way of dividing disciplines. However, the interdisciplinary approach of this book can be used to bridge the divides between different disciplines.

I want to wholeheartedly thank my friends and colleagues for reading parts of the manuscript, for information and advice, and for helpful and critical discussion; all of which influenced the project significantly: Rowland Atkinson, Franco Amatori, Gerold Ambrosius, Gerben Bakker, Dominique Barjot, Andrea Colli, Conny Devolder, Margarita Dritsas, Paul Erker, Eduard Gaugler, Ola Grytten, Terry Gourvich, William Hausman, Susanne Hilger, Riitta Hjerppe, Christhard Hoffmann, Edgar Hovland, Matthias Kipping, Christopher Kobrak, Nils Kolle, Christian Kleinschmidt, Akira Kudo, Even Lange, Isabelle Lescent-Gilles, Verena Schröter, Alice Teichova and Mikulas Teich, Kersti Ullenhag, Clemens Wischermann as well as many others. I also received much stimulation, new ideas, and insights from discussions at conferences and workshops. I thank the participants of such meetings in Athens, Bergen, Berlin, Bordeaux, Buenos Aires, Düsseldorf, Fredrikstad, Göteborg, Greifswald, Helsinki, Lille, Lowell, and Tokyo.

Above all, I want to thank my friend and colleague William H. Hubbard for discussion, information, questioning, expertise, and, last but not least, for his engagement in transforming my writings into readable English. Since he is Canadian the text became not "Americanized" but surely "Hubbardized" – which was good!

LIST OF ABBREVIATIONS

AAAA	American Association of Advertizing Agencies
AWV	Algemene Werkgevers Vereninging
AEI	Associated Electrical Industries
BA	British Aerospace
GEC	British General Electric
BR	British Rail
BT	British Telecom
BWL	Betriebswirtschaftslehre
CPA	Centre de Préparation aux Affaires
CAB	Civil Aeronautic Board
CBI	Confederation of British Industry
HE	École des Hautes Études Commerciales
EEC	European Economic Community
EPA	European Productivity Agency
ERP	European Recovery Program
EWC	European Works Council
FS	Ferrovie dello Stato
FDI	Foreign direct investment
GFK	Gesellschaft für Konsumforschung
HBS	Harvard Business School
HTML	Hyper Text Mark-up Language
IT	Information technology
JWT	J. Walter Thompson
LID	League for Industrial Democracy
LSE	London School of Economics
MBA	Master of Business Administration
MTM	Method-Time-Management
MGM	Metro-Goldwyn-Mayer
MNE	multinational (or transnational) enterprise
NAM	National Association of Manufacturers
NBER	National Bureau of Economic Research
NCSA	National Center for Supercomputer Applications
NIRA	National Industrial Recovery Act
NYSE	New York Stock Exchange
ÖKW	Österreichisches Kuratorium für Wirtschaftlichkeit (Austrian Productivity Agency)
OR	Operational research
OEEC	Organization for European Economic Cooperation
PPP	public private partnership
RCA	Radio Corporation of America
RFF	Réseau Ferré de France
RKW	Reichskuratorium für Wirtschaftlichkeit (German Productivity Agency)
SJ	Statens Järnväger

TNS   Taylor Nelson
TCW   Trust Company of the West
TUC   Trade Union Congress
TUC   Trade Union Congress (UK)
Ufa   Universum Film AG
USTA&P   US Technical Assistance and Productivity Mission
VSt   Vereinigte Stahlwerke

INTRODUCTION

AMERICANIZATION AS A COMPREHENSIVE CONCEPT OF ECONOMIC DEVELOPMENT DURING THE 20th CENTURY

"Living in a US-dominated world is more a threat to our ideas than to our interests."

(Hubert Védrine, French Foreign Minister[1])

A CONCEPT AND ITS QUESTIONS

"Culture matters!" This is the latest insight of distinguished economists such as Michael E. Porter, Jeffrey Sachs, Francis Fukuyama and others.[2] We not only agree, but try to provide an answer to the question which is asked in the under-title of the book: "How Values Shape Human Progress". More precisely, we ask how American values have influenced European economic performance during the 20th century.

"The World Welcomes America's Cultural Invasion" was the headline of a series of articles in the *International Herald Tribune* in late autumn 1998. At the end of the century American ideas again triumphed in many areas and many ways. Many characteristics have been suggested for the 20th century, such as the century of socialism, or of totalitarism or the century of atomic power. Though partly true, they do not cover everything. However, if we think of the influence of the USA, its growth in wealth and power throughout the last century until it became the world's hegemon, the term 'the American century' is surely appropriate.

This book tries to describe and to interpret the economic Americanization of Europe in the 20th century, that is the radiation of American practices and attitudes in European economic life. According to Jonathan Zeitlin it represents "the largest and to date most significant example of global phenomenon..."[3] In history we find several examples of such a radiation: for example, France in the 18th century. Radiation implies an attractiveness that is widely accepted in other countries. Because of this attractiveness they are willing to learn from the leader and even to adopt its values, practices, and institutions. Although the radiation of the US model has become in recent decades a global phenomenon, this work focuses on Europe, which was the first area to undertake the learning process of Americanization.

Many very different books have been published on Americanization as a transfer of cultural values or lifestyles, such as youth culture, popular taste, or consumption patterns.[4] However, the economic transfer—one of the "most significant phenomena" of the 20th century—was not seriously taken up in economic history-writing before the 1990s. How can we explain this lag? It is at least partly due to the fact that the concept of Americanization was originally culturally based

1

and therefore did not have a quantifiable sharpness that would make it accessible to cliometric economic analysis. And since cliometrics was the preoccupation for a whole generation of economic historians from the 1960s, this methodological diffuseness may help to explain their initial hesitation to take up Americanization. The neglect, however, has been overcome in recent years, and today there are more than 200 case studies of this important economic transfer. At the same time many other studies by sociologists and economists have taken for granted that transnational enterprise and globalization will change the world and have hence underscored the differences between individual countries.[5] This book does not take convergence for granted, but presents and discusses the available empirical evidence for and against it.

The concept of Americanization raises many questions; above all, how could the US exert such a pressure, such a power, on other states, organizations, and people? Did it *consciously manage* the radiation of its model—in other words, was Americanization a reflected policy or was it rather an unexpected by-product, or both? What means of influence were used? Why were the US patterns of behaviour so widely accepted in other nations? Who were the actors in this process? How did the transfer take place? What channels and conduits were used, and how did they influence the message? What changes and adaptations were applied? How extensive or how important was Americanization? Did it change over time and what phases can we identify? Where are its limits? What methods can be employed in finding and identifying cases of Americanization? How can we exclude reasons for a change which are not related to Americanization but ran parallel to it? Such questions must be tackled with before we can properly judge the usefulness, scope, or invalidity of the concept.

All societies are subject to a certain change; capitalist societies are even based on dynamic change, as economists from Marx to Schumpeter have shown. In this book I investigate the extent of Americanization and the reasons for it: why so many economic actors in so many states decided in their preferential choices to look for American patterns instead of indigenous or other ones. The sum of these preferential choices forms the trend towards Americanization. In all societies the number of areas that change is usually considerably smaller than those that remain stable. None the less, this book focuses on change, not on stability. Yet it must be remembered that all cases of Americanization affected only parts of the respective economic institutions, leaving other parts—indeed the greater number—little changed. Additionally it must be remembered that the very concept of a country or continent—the USA and Europe—is a generalized construction that obscures potentially great variation. But that specific regions, or even countries, might show a different reality at a given time should not obviate the recognition of general trends.

The study of Americanization as a transfer process mirrors current research on multinational or transnational enterprise (MNE). Nearly all such firms still are deeply rooted in their home country with respect to central areas such as personnel, production, or research and development (R&D). Yet in spite of this predominant national characteristics, research on MNEs focuses on specific changes, because foreign direct investment might entail a change of their national character in the long run. Therefore it is change, not stability, which dominants the analyst's attention.

In many ways Americanization is to be compared to technology transfer. There the transfer is concentrated on technology which, at a closer look, used to be embedded in certain everyday practices and values—in short, in culture. Similarly, Americanization deals with transfer of organizational features, management and financial practices, etc.: issues which are culturally even more closely interwoven. Since the international transfer of technology and technological culture is such a well established and important field of study, it is rather surprising that a corresponding phenomenon-the transfer of economic institutions and economic culture—is far less developed.

DEFINITIONS OF AMERICANIZATION AND RESEARCH METHODS

The many questions just mentioned indicate the need of a definition. Various meanings of Americanization have been employed in the literature. They have frequently changed over time, reflecting the necessities of research and the questions asked. At the turn of the 19th century the term was used in the United States itself to describe America as the big "melting pot" for the multitude of immigrants, who through a process of Americanization became Americans.[6] This understanding was focused on the identity of people, which expresses itself in the modes of feeling and thinking, and in usually non-reflected everyday actions. Thus the term referred to the acculturation of the foreign born into the dominant values of American society. At the same time it was a defensive concept against any possible influence of a foreign economic power. For example, shortly before the First Word War the British Marconi Ltd. became so strong in the field of radio transmission that some Americans feared it would dominate the US market. The concern provoked the founding of the Radio Corporation of America (RCA). RCA was to be not only an economic counterweight against Marconi, but also a channel to communicate American influence and feeling to the American people.[7] Politicians and businessmen were clearly well aware of both the political and marketing potentials of this new medium and its cultural consequences.

In this book I reverse the perspective and look for evidence of American economic influence outside the United States. Such influence was felt already during the second half of the 19th century, and many Europeans were impressed by a distinctive American approach to economic affairs. France provides one of the earliest examples of a take-over of American business practices. In the 1880s the Parisian daily, Le Figaro, introduced what they called a new way of running the newspaper–business, derived from leading US papers. It departed from the European approach of relying on freelance journalists and hired permanent reporters, who were sent out on to cover specific stories. This revolutionary practice was extremely expensive; only large newspapers could afford the méthode américain. Le Figaro's adoption of American professional and commercial standards required capital investments of a level previously unknown. In its early phases Americanization often entailed such professionalization and commercialisation of a specific business sector.

To be precise, I define Americanization as an adapted transfer of values, behaviour, institutions, technologies, patterns of organization, symbols and norms from the USA to the economic life of other states. This definition excludes an imagined transfer such as: "The American way was what the French thought it was."[8] I try to be more precise and concrete; an assertion of Americanization needs reality on both sides of the transfer. Misunderstandings of reality, however, are included because these are always part of transfer processes. Furthermore, I would argue against the assertion that "Americanization...has become increasingly disconnected from America."[9] If a principle is taken over and re-worked, I suggest calling the process modernization rather than Americanization. Otherwise the concept of Americanization becomes quite useless, since nearly all American principles—cultural and economic—can be derived in the end from Western or European civilization. In consequence, if we pursue the notion of disconnection to its logical limits, Americanization would become Europeanization, a worthless tautology.

A study of Americanization cannot give a general overview of all transfers of economic culture during the 20th century; for example, it has to leave out other transfer movements such as Japanization. In this respect this study concentrates on the predominant trend from the most advanced to the less advanced. The reverse case of cross-fertilization—how the US learned from Europe or Japan—will be touched upon only occasionally.

In dealing with Americanization a couple of methodological questions have to be observed: How is Americanization to be evaluated? How can we distinguish Americanization from modernization? Is it distinct from "Coca-Colaization" (Kuisel) or "McDonaldization" (Ritzer)? What is the relationship between qualitative and quantitative data?

Americanization should never be understood simply as an unaltered importation from the US, but rather as a national or even regional adaptation to an American-originated influence.[10] Importations of non-native behaviour or institutions have always been adapted to local needs and customs in the process of transfer. The reality of economic Americanization is no exception; American economic culture has sometimes been substantially changed through the process of transfer. Perception, selection, and adaptation to specific needs, traditions, and circumstances play a crucial role in Americanization. Because of the possibility of misunderstandings Mary Nolan speaks of *Visons of Modernity* in her account of American influences on German business.[11] The perceptions might actually deviate from US reality, but as long as the actors involved were convinced of the American origins of the adoptions, we can interpret them as a subjective Americanization. But such a subjective Americanization has to be expressed clearly by the actors. One has to be extremely careful about this special concept, because it is by no means a robust one. A similar consideration applies to the process of selection. In all cases the actors selected what they perceived to be the most suitable and/or the most important item for a transfer from the US to their respective country. The items selected inevitably reflected a certain subjectivity of those involved. In our sector, the economy, this subjectivity might have been smaller than for example in arts, fashion, or music, since businessmen are customarily down-to-earth persons, whose decisions are governed to some extent by financial criteria as well as by other persons sitting on supervisory boards and the like. Yet in spite of such controls and filters, their perceptions will not always mirror exactly the reality in the US.

As Ove Bjarnar, Matthias Kipping, and others have shown, a transfer of values does not take place like the importation of a piece of machinery.[12] There are specific transfer channels, translations and transformations which are part of a process of adaptation. Furthermore, all transfers of culture require time, proceed stepwise, and are subject to roll-backs. It is possible to speak of Americanization if local behaviour, rules, values, organization, etc. have changed in the direction of how such issues are found in the US. However, the assertion must not be made uncritically, because the sources of putative American influence can be quite diffuse. Especially after the Second World War most features of the US economy and society were modern compared with conditions in the rest of the world. The desire to become more competitive and more modern was felt nearly everywhere, and many political and economic leaders acted to achieve these ends. But a substantial part of the push for modernization does not necessarily represent Americanization, since it may have emerged from indigenous sources. Very many cases of Americanization can be understood as modernization, but not all modernization can be claimed to have been an Americanization. In order to be sure of Americanization one needs to find not only a move by indigenous actors into the direction of US-American patterns, but also information on the means and forms of the alleged influence. That is, one needs to know about the concrete process of transfer.

The simplest model of a cultural or institutional transfer comprehends the identification of three elements: a sender, a conduit, and a receiver.[13] The institution, practice, or mentality in question has to be found first in the US, then transferred deliberately, and subsequently re-established somewhere else.

During certain periods, such as the 1920s, travelling was a main means of transmission, while at other times other media (booklets, lectures, etc.) contributed significantly. In the long term the role of radio, film, television, and other electronic information technology has grown in importance. In addition to such direct transfers, indirect ones have also played a crucial role. The behaviour of managers of American firms exemplified how to run an enterprise in a different way. When this example came from an American firm located in a foreign country, indigenous managers could see to what extent the American approach worked in their own country. And if they perceived the American way to be superior to theirs, they acquired an incentive to learn from the US transnational firms.

Generally, Americanization can be expected to occur especially in those economic sectors where the US is strong, for example oil products or distribution of goods. Thus European petrol stations would seem to be a prima facie case of Americanization: that is, the understanding of a filling station, what is sold there and in which way, how a station is constructed, owned and managed, how customers behave, and so on. Indeed, we do have evidence of substantial changes over time; petrol stations look very differently today compared with the 1960s or 1930s; and today many of them earn more money by selling goods such as newspapers or fast food that are not directly related to the automobile. However, most of these changes occurred simultaneously in the United States and in Europe. Behind the simultaneity stand presumably the large, multinational oil companies that have decided centrally how, when and where things should be done. Such cases represent modernization, but not Americanization.

All institutions are culturally bounded, and all transfers of economic institutions from one society to the next are subject to the preconditions and limits of economic life in the recipient society. Two central preconditions are consent and comprehension. Comparisons of Americanization and Sovietization have revealed very different results. After 1945 both the United States and the Soviet Union tried to export their institutions, first to their European allies and satellites and later to Third World countries. While Americanization showed lasting effects everywhere, Sovietization diminished very quickly and virtually vanished once the direct, political influence of the USSR was removed. Americanization became deeply rooted, while Sovietization resulted in no more than an organizational cover in the respective economy. This crudely summarized comparison confirms that a lasting transfer of economic institutions depends upon freely given consent by the receiving partner.[14]

Transfer means adaptation and change. People adapt and change in the hope of gaining something, such as a better economic performance or a better reputation within their group, etc. The adaptive action may or may not be deliberately reasoned; but without hope for gain, there is no incentive to change. The comparison of Americanization and Sovietization shows that organizational patterns can be exported by force, but unless they meet with genuine consent they are doomed to break down once the power that forced the export is removed.[15] Furthermore, at least some of the value of the institution to be transferred must be understood beforehand at the receiving side. Understanding is facilitated if the institutional frameworks of the countries involved have a degree of similarity. If there are no similarities, the meanings of the specific American values can not be decoded and prepared for transfer. If the potential receiving country has a totally different system of values, it will not perceive any advantages in a transfer. The more similar institutions are, the more likely and easy the transfer. American-like institutions are more widespread in the UK than in the rest of Europe, and they are more widespread in Europe than in the rest of the world. In this respect Ralf Dahrendorf (see below) was right in pointing out that Americanization in Europe is a process whereby values that originated in Europe were developed and processed in the United States and then re-imported back to Europe. The historical ties of between the two continents were of great importance in the development of American institutions, and in turn were a helpful conditioning for the Americanization of Europe.

As mentioned earlier, the transfer of economic institutions does not take place like the importation of a piece of machinery. There are specific transfer channels, translations, and transformations that are an integral part of the process of adaptation. All this makes the concept of Americanization on the one hand extremely flexible and potentially powerful, but at the same time it means that a transfer of economic culture can rarely be measured quantitatively.

Yet several potential ways to quantify the extent of Americanization are imaginable. For example, Bourdieu and others have established that language reflects general cultural values and modes of thinking. Thus a count of meaningful American expressions used in another language could give quantitative evidence of Americanization in the society using that language.[16] The expressions to be counted would have to be representative for a new idea, concept, or trend in the United States. A long-term analysis of the use of such expressions in official business communications, e.g. in annual reports or press statements, could provide considerable insight into the diffusion of Americanization.[17]

Another possible quantitative study would be a survey of the implementation of American forms of business organization, of which the multidivisional form—the so-called M-form—is the most prominent example. Alfred D. Chandler has shown that the M-form became the superior type of organization in American large enterprise in the interwar period. The M-form was taken over by many large European firms during the 1960s and 1970s. The transfer was usually carried out with the help of one of the well-known US consultancies and became part of the "American management mystique" (Robert Locke).[18] The number of firms that reorganized in this way could provide a clear indicator of this aspect of Americanization.

But a quantitative survey of surface indicators of Americanization would be misleading, as the following example shows: In 2000 74 per cent of the US working-age population had a job; the corresponding figure for the Euro-zone was only 64 per cent.[19] At the first glance, then, a high percentage of paid work seems to be a characteristic of the American economy. Such data can mislead, however; in this case a high labour force participation rate cannot by itself be claimed as an American characteristic, since this would mean that the former socialist states in Eastern Europe—with rates up to 90 per cent—were more Americanized than either Western Europe or the United States. In all cases of comparison qualitative and quantitative evidence must be gathered to support conclusions.

LITERATURE ON AMERICANIZATION

Scholarly literature on Americanization is not yet extensive, but several books dealing with various aspects of economic Americanization have been published. *Americanisation and its Limits*, edited by Jonathan Zeitlin and Gary Herrigel, focuses on the 1950s, especially on technology and management.[20] Matthias Kipping and Ove Bjarnar explore the change in management education in *The Americanisation of European Business*, and in *Americanisation of West German Industry* Volker Berghahn concentrates on developments in Europe's largest economy with an emphasis on heavy industry and economic policies. *Une Américanisation des entreprises?*, edited by Eli Moen and Harm G. Schröter, is a volume of case-studies of individual companies and economic sectors, whereas the volumes edited by Dominique Barjot, *Catching up with America: Productivity Missions and the Diffusion of American Economic and Technological Influence after the Second World War* and *L'américanisation de l'Europe occidentale au XXe siècle. Mythe et réalité*, look at aspects of Americanization during the 1950s. The most recent book on the topic, edited by Akira Kudo, Matthias Kipping, and Harm G. Schröter, compares Americanization in Japan and West Germany. Marie-Laure Djelic's *Exporting the American Mode. The Post-war Transformation of European Business* is to date the only overall survey and provides so far the most comprehensive view of the phenomenon, drawing on several well-known sociological models of industrial organization. Finally, in preparation for the World Economic History Congress in 2002 Dominique Barjot, Isabelle Lescent-Giles, Marc de Ferrière le Vayer, Matthias Kipping, and Nick Tiratsoo edited two volumes of studies that cover the entire twentieth century, though again with emphasis on the economic boom years of the 1950s and 1960s.

This book differs from the existing literature in various aspects: I will examine how economic *culture* changed, not only economic systems; I do not limit coverage to the post-war years but deal with the entire twentieth as well as with the last decades of the nineteenth century; I will not restrict my view to entrepreneurial activity only but consider both micro- and macroeconomic behaviour. In addition I will look at developments throughout Europe and not just in the major countries. And finally I will use a historical perspective, highlighting the most important institutional changes rather than reciting current statistical information on all countries and issues.

The studies just mentioned revealed important cases of Americanization, but they refrained from putting their findings into a wider context of a general and lasting trend of Americanization of the economies during the twentieth century as a whole. This book attempts to do just that. Its purpose is to provide a deeper insight into the manifold, ever changing and partly contradictory processes that are lumped together under the concept of Americanization. The various cases and stages of Americanization can be properly understood only when considered together. They represent stones fitting into a large mosaic. If the many independent transfers are put together like single stones of a mosaic, contours of a larger picture emerge. The picture drawn here remains necessarily unfinished and rather sketchy in various parts. But at the same time it gives us a better understanding of a long-term process in the economy during the last century that has seldom been fully grasped. This book, however, does not attempt to draw an entirely new picture of modern economic history, rather it argues that during the twentieth century many innovations—from production to distribution, from deregulation to consumption patterns—are related to each other and should be seen not only as single events but also as parts of a general pattern.

THE ROOTS OF AMERICANIZATION

Though Americanization has tended to occur in waves characterized by specific groups of institutions and policies, such as rationalization, decartelization, new management methods, or deregulation, it also took place piecemeal. The end of a transfer wave did not mean the end, or suspension, of Americanization. The different waves were not only connected to each other, but grew out of common roots. This common ground has regularly generated new versions of distinctly American institutions, which in time become so attractive that they are taken over abroad. The idea of a common heritage for Americanization in all its aspects has up to now not been adequately considered.

Jacqueline McGlade raised part of this question when she located the specific American character of Americanization during the 1950s in the "consensus-style politics" that infused American policies immediately after the Second World War.[21] Unfortunately, she did not elaborate on the issue and provided neither evidence nor concrete examples. Consensus-style politics or not, no commentator has suggested the existence of a grand design or a comprehensive master plan drawn up by the US government or by the country's enterprises, foundations, and other institutions to transfer American values abroad. Hegemonic reform imposed by the United States occurred only in the occupied countries of Austria, Germany, and Japan after 1945. There direct US rule did indeed force the dissolution of such practices as cartels and *keiretsu* that had characterized the German or Japanese economies up to then. And it is true that American political and military leaders forced the British and French administrations in occupied Germany to de-cartelise their zones of occupation, even though that went directly against British and French economic policies.[22] But even in the countries mentioned, such directly administrated intervention was only partly responsible for the changes which actually took place.

In his "McDonaldization Thesis" (the spread of American fast food all over the world) the American sociologist George Ritzer suggests that McDonaldization is driven by basic trends such as rationalization and consumerism.[23] Rationalization emphasizes quantification, speed, accountability, simplification or even unification, ranking, control, de-humanisation, and de-skillisation; consumerism demands above all simplicity and value-for money. Such practices can easily be recognized in a MacDonald's fast-food restaurant. Consumerism and rationalization in turn demand high productivity. Indeed, John Gillingham used "productivism as American ideology" as a headline in order to underline its central role.[24] Connected with productivism is the pre-eminent influence of a business-oriented mentality in modern American life. In her essay on the development of business history in the US since 1950, Maury Klein has highlighted the emergence of this mentality, which she has called the most basic change since the Second World War:

> "Finally, business historians have virtually ignored what may be the broadest and most profound movement of this half-century: the amazing irresistible tendency to transform every aspect of American life first into a business and then into a larger business. No institution, activity or value has escaped this relentless organising into some form of commerce. Some of the most obvious examples include the arts, politics, religion, education, sport, sex, entertainment, the family, childhood, and, of course, history."[25]

Americanization, of course, was by no means confined to the post-war period. And, as suggested by McGlade, Klein, and others, many of its underlying roots can be found in general characteristics of American civilization. Since at least Tocqueville's generation, commentators have proposed various basic values, assumptions, and beliefs as defining the American way of life.[26] A number of them are also found in varying degrees in other national cultures, but they have typically been more important and more widespread in the United States than elsewhere. They include:

> 1. *An extremely strong and positive role allocated to the economy in society as well as in a person's life;*
> 2. *a (sometimes naive) belief in the abilities of competition, that advantages for single persons will add up to the best for all members of society;*
> 3. *a strong feeling for individualism (in contrast to communalism, or shared values);*
> 4. *a trend towards a commercialisation of human relations (in contrast to non-money-related behaviour);*
> 5. *a trend to exchange the traditionally given social bonds and controls for contract- and market-based bonds of one's own, deliberate choice.*

The relative importance of these five fields of values varied during the last century. Generally, they became stronger towards the century's end. Collectively, they represent the seedbed for Americanization. Their spread and intensification caused the United States itself to become "more American" during the twentieth century. For example, at mid-century the position of American trade unions in society and economy was much stronger than at the end of twentieth century. Unions as a form of the collective organization of the labour force have given way to individualism. Another example is old-age pensions. As in other countries, after the Second World War American families have become less and less able or willing to care for their aged members. The question thus emerged how the elderly should be cared for, and who should pay for the care. Universal state-financed pensions were the response adopted in most of the European and Asian states. Their underlying principle is that the young and employed members of society pay for the upkeep of the retired, regardless of branch of industry and type of earlier participation in the labour force. In contrast, private occupational or company pension schemes are the predominant answer in the United States, with the state pensions playing a relatively minor role for most persons. Furthermore, over time the importance of collective provision has fallen while the individual provision has risen. In 1980 6 per cent of American households participated in investment funds and 22 per cent owned shares the stock market; in 2000 the percentages were respectively 52 and 47.[27] The move reflected the increased importance of capital markets in the US, not only for businesses but also for private individuals. This shift is also seen in the greater prominence of business and financial news in American mass media. Such information was of course presented earlier, but from the 1980s and 1990s the latest news from the financial markets around the world has come to occupy a prominent position on radio and television; the airtime spent on it is much larger compared with that devoted to issues in employment or innovation in manufacturing. In short, the American century caused an ongoing Americanization of "America" itself. This is why the United has been able to teach the rest of the world economy not once or twice, but again and again. For Americanization's central part in the universal process of societal modernization has been perhaps its most important role in the last hundred years. Societal modernization brings a more effective use of limited resources and opens up more choices for the individual person. More choices mean more possibilities to define one's own optimum, though this can be at times at the expense of the social and economic coherence of society at large. American society has been able to generate the new economic institutions whose transfer entails Americanization because its basic cultural values dovetail with the fundamental tenets of modernization better than those found in other countries. This linkage with modernization is what makes the study of Americanization is so exciting: It means not only exploring "the broadest and most profound movement" (Maury Klein), or "the largest and to date most significant example of global phenomenon..." (Jonathan Zeitlin) of the last century, but also looking into the potential future of world development!

AMERICANIZATION AND SOCIAL SCIENCE THEORY

The methodology of the social sciences can be likened to working with paint rollers, while the methodology of the historian uses a small bristle. Thus Ritzer's McDonaldization thesis can give inspiration and direction, but the picture remains crude. Historians are trained to come up with concrete details and reasoned evidence. Evidence derives from the ordering of bits of relevant information. To be coherent the ordering must follow consistent rules, or theoretical perspective. In our case Douglas C. North's theory of institutional change and economic growth provides an appropriate perspective. Its central thesis is: "The main force underlying dynamic economic change is the continuous interaction between institutions and organizations."[28] North distinguishes between organizations—such as states, universities, companies, churches—and institutions, which are much more comprehensive than organizations: "Institutions are the rules of the game in a society, composed of the formal rules (constitutions, statute and common law, regulations), the informal constraints (norms, conventions and internally devised codes of conduct), and the enforcement characteristics of each. Together they define the way the game is played."[29] This institutional framework provides the incentive structure for economic actors, since it allocates reward and punishment for all behaviour. According to North, economic change is caused by interplay of institutions, reality and perception: Institutions shape reality; reality shapes the perceptions of actors, who in their turn gradually change the institutions of the respective society.

North's theory thus provides us with a useful framework for the interpretation of the specific institutional change called Americanization. It helps to explain why the same incentives do not always produce the same results. Reality is perceived by individual men and women; in other words, it is filtered and interpreted by actors. The interpretation of reality by a specific group of persons can also vary from that of another group. Players in different institutional settings will react differently in various societies because the respective cultural heritage of a given society, to the product of that society's institutional framework, will force actors to optimise their decisions according to their own specific rules. North emphasizes the strong path-dependency of all institutional change, a path-dependency which reflects differences determined by the respective cultural heritage. Thus, the responses to the pressure of Americanization will be different in Sweden from those in Italy.

Perceptions of reality are mental constructs, and mentality is not to be changed over night. Institutional change takes place only when the actors concerned are convinced of its necessity, and this usually takes some time. Many of the Americans involved in the organised transfer-processes connected to the Marshall Plan hoped for substantial changes in Europe within a short period. They soon became disappointed: "In the end ... Western Europe was only 'half-Americanised'"[30] and American hopes for a total transfer, or as Jacqueline McGlade put it, for a "hegemonic reform" were surrendered. They should have known better. As North has shown, the complexity of cultural transfer precludes instant and fundamental institutional change. But the persons mentioned, of course, could not have known Douglas North's theoretical insights.

The process of Americanization varied in both timing and mode. Cultural transfers can be done through open discussion and decision-making, as in the case of a new law. Alternatively, it can be the result of an un-reflected feeling for a desirability of new preferences, such as the wish by single actors or groups to present themselves in a modern and distinguished way. Americanization has taken both paths, the reflected and the un-reflected. Path-dependency sets barriers to all fundamental change, but it does not exclude it.

While North tells us why and how things change, Alfred D. Chandler informs us why it was the United States that developed a persuasive economic model for others to follow. Chandler has marshalled substantial evidence to argue that the American way of running a capitalist economy was superior to all alternatives.[31] Based on an extensive survey of how large firms were organised, governed, and embedded in society, he proposed three organizational prototypes of the modern industrial economy: "competitive capitalism", "personal capitalism", and "cooperative capitalism". He identified the models historically with respectively the USA, the UK, and Germany during the period from 1850 to 1970. In doing so Chandler bridged the gap between micro- and macro-economics, showing how profoundly business systems influenced the development of the society and vice versa. Chandler showed that the three prototypes developed distinctive types of organization, different types of incentives, of learning, and of capabilities. A survey of the diffusion of these prototypes around the world revealed traces of personal capitalism in Belgium, while most of the other European countries, plus Japan and Korea, exhibited strong signs of the cooperative prototype.[32] Their institutional settings were generally less competitive and thus differed from the American prototype of competitive capitalism. These differences, which existed in varying degrees throughout the twentieth century, are the starting point of this study. Chandler's approach argues that the organizational capabilities of a country's economy represent the core of its competitive advantage. In the North's terminology they are to be understood as a substantial part of the respective country's institutional setting. The correspondence between Chandler's organizational capabilities and North's institutions can be used in identifying traces of different capitalist prototypes and their consequences.[33] Such identification is essential to the finding of evidence of change that can be attributed to Americanization.

TEMPORAL SWINGS IN AMERICANIZATION

Economic Americanization is the result of pressure exerted by the USA on "economic" institutions elsewhere in the world. Two types of pressure can be identified: deliberately intended pressure, and informal, unintended pressure arising from economic competition. Conditions varied across countries regions as well as over time. Generally speaking, Americanization increased over the last century, though with substantial swings and even periods of backlash.[34] Before 1914 it was felt only in a couple of branches such as the production of watches or bicycles. During the interwar period it was expressed in trend towards *rationalization*, which was the catch-word of the first massive wave for institutional change along American lines. This wave ended with the coming of the world economic crisis in 1929. The American way of doing things suddenly stopped being a model. All over the world economists, businessmen, and statesmen suggested regulation and planning as the appropriate remedy for economic problems. During years of Roosevelt's New Deal a version of this kind of economic thinking, which can be understood as a kind of Europeanization, even gained support in the US. The transfer of economic institutions was thus not a one-way street during the last century, though the flow from the US was much more important than all others. In the aftermath of its victory-bringing performance in the Second World War, the US model of competitive capitalism exerted massive pressure on the world economy during the 1950s, but its leading influence faded in the 1960s. In the 1970s and 1980s first European, and later Japanese, patterns of economic management expanded worldwide. From the late 1980s, however, the revolution in information technology, the break-through of a new economic paradigm (supply-side oriented ideas and monetarism of the Chicago School), and the break-down of socialist planned economies rejuvenated the leading status of American economic institutions as the world's model for the achievement of economic growth, wealth, and power.

Americanization was not only accepted positively, of course; it was also criticised and resisted. The connotation of the expression *Americanization* differed widely over time and from place to place. At the beginning of the twentieth century little criticism was to be found. Also in the 1920s there was nothing particularly negative in the term. However, the more the United States attained a dominant economic position in a particular country or area, the more critics raised their voices. Yet criticism of Americanization could be set aside in the face of even greater threats. One of the quickest reversals of opinion took place in West Germany, when, during the Soviet blockade of Berlin 1948/49, the Americans became fast friends after having been enemies only a few years earlier. According to an US witness, in just a couple of weeks the "Americans moved from the status of 'lesser of two evils' to somewhat less than angels."[35] In Europe generally the Marshall Plan and the United State's guarantee to protect Europe against Soviet communism generated a lot of goodwill among ordinary people as well as political leaders, opening the doors to Americanization of various kinds. In contrast, business leaders were not as easily convinced to give up the way they had acted before. Moreover, outside Europe, especially in Latin America, the light of the USA did not shine brightly. The picture painted by William Lederer and Eugene Burdick in their 1959 best-seller *The Ugly American* was all too well known for many readers there.[36] In the following years criticism of Americanization increased in many European countries: "Americanization is like mass and mass society, often used as a symbol for 'bad' or 'unsympathetic'."[37] This negative attitude provoked the German sociologist, Ralf Dahrendorf, to intervene on the side of Americanization. He pointed out that "Americanization" was not "the penetration of Europe with 'foreign values',"[38] but rather a return of European values that had been further developed in North America. Dahrendorf considered such phenomena as mass culture and mass consumption consequences of European traits, which had advanced further in the United States than in Europe for the simple reason that the US at the time had the most advanced economy in the world.

In the following decades the pressure of Americanization receded, and the controversy it had once aroused faded. Upon its resurgence in the mid-1980s, its supporters advocated it with using positive or neutral keywords such as 'modernization', 'market liberalism', 'consumers' society', 'democratisation', or 'entertainment'.[39] In the developed countries of the world, Americanization was thereafter usually positively received; by contrast, in large parts of the Muslim world it has typically been met by reserve, distaste, and protest. The implied contest between continuity and change is evident in all countries. All over the world, conservative circles are sceptical of substantial change in indigenous institutions, and critical of their "hybridisation" (Zeitlin) in the direction of an American model. Meanwhile the promoters of change are proud of creating something new and modern, whether or not it had an American origin.

PART 1

THE FIRST WAVE OF AMERICANIZATION
1870-1945

CHAPTER 1

FORDISM AND TAYLORISM COME TO EUROPE

"I suppose you've seen on the hoardings all about this `Smythe's Silent Service'? Or you must be the only person that hasn't. Oh, I don't know much about it, it's some clockwork invention for doing all the housework by machinery. You know the sort of thing: `Press a Button--A Butler who Never Drinks.' `Turn a Handle--Ten Housemaids who Never Flirt.'
"Mr. Flambeau's semi-official flat was on the ground floor, and presented in every way a marked contrast to the American machinery and cold hotel-like luxury of the flat of the Silent Service."

In his Father Brown detective story, "The Invisible Man", published in 1911, the British author Gilbert K. Chesterton called an automat ("some clockwork invention" or in today's terminology an automatic machine) "American". There was no indication that it was made in the USA, nor was any other information given. On the contrary, in the story the inventor of the Silent Service was Scottish and the story placed in Edinburgh. So why was the machinery "American"? At that time the British reader did not need more: automats simply connoted America. Even before the First World War America was recognized as having a different economic organization from Europe.

Was this an arbitrary perception, or was it grounded in economic reality? A brief, comparative look at the factors of productions in the United States and Europe shows that Chesterton's association was not simply poetic invention. Thus labour in Europe was abundant and cheap; in the United States labour was scarce and expensive. For raw materials the situation was reversed: they tended to be limited and expensive in Europe, and plentiful and inexpensive in the US. These fundamental differences lay behind the emergence of a specific American regime of production and innovation, characterized by mass-production, labour-saving machinery, and inter-changeable parts. Labour-saving machines—in agriculture and in industry—emerged first in the United States. Yet American agricultural machines did not sell well in Europe even though they were much more productive than European counterparts. The chief reason for the poor sales was that American mowers, reapers, and threshers were designed for the large, relatively flat fields of the Midwest. And such fields are rare in western Europe. They did exist in eastern Europe, especially in Russia, but there the structures of landownership and labour supply combined with a shortage of capital long inhibited the introduction of American-style agricultural machinery. This brief example underscores our study's guiding thesis: the central importance of technological and institutional adaptation for the transfer of American innovations.

Despite such early weaknesses the performance and characteristics of the American economy attracted the increasing attention of European business. On the Continent the British economic model faded from the 1870s. Though British industry was then at its height—truly "the workshop of the world"—the summit meant relative decline thereafter. The Philadelphia World Exhibition in 1876 was a turning point after which more and more Europeans began to take American industry and technology seriously. In some industries such as steel production engineers and entrepreneurs no longer travelled to Britain to see the latest achievement, but to the United States. In the second half of the nineteenth century a different system of the modern industrial economy developed in the United States— the American system of competitive capitalism—that soon showed its superiority.

The following chapter explores how this system of production first affected Europe from afar and later was partly taken over by it. The emergence of the United States as a world power in the course of the First World War clearly assisted the acceptance of American ideas on business organization by European enterprises. These ideas had many dimensions, and we can not deal with all of them in detail. Here the focus will be on the most comprehensive issues: the processes of economic concentration, rationalization, and the implementation of Scientific Management. A case study of the early film industry then shows how American business principles outcompeted European ones. The growing attraction of the American model suffered a severe reverse in the world economic crisis of 1929–1933. The many fascist regimes in Europe in the 1930s viewed the United States and its economic system with a combination of contempt and respect.

STANDARDIZATION AND INTERCHANGEABLE PARTS

Standardization of production was first developed systematically in the United States. The historian of technology Thomas Hughes has called the innovation of producing machines with interchangeable parts a revolution in production technology. At first the innovation was limited to basic machines such as pumps, railway engines, or sewing machines. It had two advantages: one technological, the other entrepreneurial. The technological advantage was the increased accuracy of components—all parts had to be more precise in *all characteristics* (size, material, mounting) in order to be interchangeable, which resulted in machines with superior performance. The entrepreneurial advantage was derived from economies of scale: standardized products were cheaper to produce—thousands of copies of individual components were produced by exactly the same process—and therefore could also be sold at a cheaper price, thus increasing their attraction in a competitive market.

The consequences of the innovation of standardization were readily apparent in the machine tool industry. Traditionally machines were made individually. Though there was a common design of a specific type, the various parts were made to fit into a specific machine assembled on a given day. Hand-made parts were constructed for that single machine. This meant that without additional adjustment the parts could not be used in another machine even of the same series. The American machine tool industry broke with this tradition of handicraft and produced standardized parts. These parts were interchangeable: it did not matter which one was put into which machine. The achievement of interchangeability required machines capable of close precision as well as a structured organization of the work-process. Acceptable technical norms also had to be developed. In contrast to the myriad variety of custom-made machines produced by the European handicraft method, the number of types of machines produced by the American standardized method was relatively low. This in turn reduced production costs and losses due to spoilage. In Europe highly skilled craftsmen were needed in order to adapt the parts to a certain machine. And to carry out the work they had to have far-reaching control over labour, tools, and raw materials as needed according to their evaluation of the work-process. Close supervision of production was difficult, and managerial control was limited. The American method facilitated managerial control and entrepreneurial calculation. Thus the whole process—planning, production, control, and accounting—became cheaper, while at the same time the product became more useful for the customer, since spare parts could be taken from a broken machine and put to work in another. The European method had advantages for special items, but the American method was clearly superior for ordinary products. Many consumer goods could in fact be standardized, so it was in this area that Europe first felt the competition of American production methods and hence the pressure of Americanization.

For example, the Swiss watchmakers long had had a world-wide reputation for the quality and reliability of their products, which dominated the world market from the 1840s. But in the 1880s American watchmakers entered the competition with standardized products, and a decade later the Swiss watch industry seemed doomed. Using precision-made, interchangeable components the American watch companies produced a comparable quality of watch for a considerably cheaper price; handicrafted Swiss watches became simply too expensive. The whole region of the Swiss Jura was economically endangered. The remedy came from the USA itself. The Swiss watchmakers imported American machinery and adopted the American method of standardized production. The combination of the superior machinery and organization together with the craft-experience in the Jura soon propelled the Swiss industry into its old position of dominance. In the 1890s the British shoe industry faced the same problem as the Swiss watch industry a decade earlier. The massive influx of American-made, high-quality, inexpensive standardized shoes forced the British shoe producers to undertake a massive technological overhaul, after which they re-established their competitive position in the domestic market.

In the case of the bicycle American competition was felt all over Europe. Bicycling was all the rage in the 1890s. In Paris a cyclodrome was constructed where cyclists could practice their skills under cover, and appear socially. Throughout Europe machine builders of all sizes and shapes got into the construction of bicycles. And, as in the watch industry, it was not long before lower-cost American-built brands appeared. With their basis of interchangeable parts the American bicycles were not only cheaper than European brands, they were also easier to maintain. To survive, European bicycle producers had to adopt the same remedy as Swiss watchmakers and British shoe manufacturers, namely Americanization.

In the three examples just related, the prime mover for the adoption of American methods by European producers was the market place: competition compelled the transfer. But an alternative prime mover is the deliberate action of individual entrepreneurs, both American and European. One of the world's leading inventors and technological innovators in the nineteenth century and early twentieth century was the American Thomas A. Edison. To produce and to market his many inventions—among them, the gramophone, the incandescent light bulb, and power-generating equipment—he founded the Edison Electric Light Company, which in 1890 became General Electric Co. (GE). In the early 1880s Edison sold patent licenses to various European firms and thus provided the foundation for the rapid growth of French, British, and German electrical industry. The largest of these licensees started in 1883 as the *Deutsche Edison-Gesellschaft* (German Edison Company) in Berlin, using not only Edison's American patents, but also importing all its machinery from the United States. After a few years the close ties loosened and the firm reorganized as Allgemeine Elektricitäts-Gesellschaft (AEG), which grew into an international giant that in 1914 was even a match for GE. The British and French licensees—British General Electric (GEC), which was not owned by GE, and Thomson-Houston—did not attain the same stature as AEG but did became major players in their national markets.

The transfer of electrical technology was initiated by the American side and received and adapted by the European. In another example the initiative came from Europe. Ludwig Loewe initially was a successful textile merchant in Berlin. In 1869 he visited the United States and was captivated by the system of manufacturing he saw there. Soon after his return to Berlin, although he had no previous training in engineering, he established a machine-tool factory. Loewe based his entire enterprise on the American ideas which he had studied intensively during his voyage.

> "The idea which forms the fundament of our enterprise from the very beginning and which has not yet been realised anywhere in Europe we found there (in America) on a grand scale. All important factories (in the USA) occupy themselves only with the production of a single system and try to do this in an excellent and massive way by producing automatic ("durchaus selbsttätige Einrichtungen") devices for the special purpose of their machines...From the biggest machine to the smallest tool every working material belongs to a standardized system."[40]

In his first annual report he added that he had fully understood the American system, and underlined the necessity of "scientific management" (see below), cost accounting, exact calculation, and precision manufacturing. In order to achieve a full and correct transfer Loewe even hired several American engineers. In order to maintain both the American mentality and American methods, he later sent the company's German engineers on study trips to the United States. Loewe built his American-style factory from scratch; it would have been very difficult, if not impossible, to buy an established firm and Americanize it. Loewe's efforts were rewarded by his company becoming one of the largest enterprises for machine tools and small arms in Germany before 1914.

Such success was not self-evident. Other German factory owners, such as auto-parts manufacturer Robert Bosch or farm-equipment maker Heinrich Lanz, who tried to Americanize their production process around 1900, met with vigorous strikes. Their employees objected to the new form of work-organization that took command and control out of the hands of the traditional masters and foremen. Such worker-supported resistance to the Americanization of production was widespread and long-lived throughout Europe.

Resistance came not only from the workforce but also from owners and managers who did not understand the challenge or the benefits of the American mode of production. The Swiss firm *Aktiengesellschaft für Unternehmungen der Textilindustrie* (AGUT) is a good example of this incomprehension. Before 1914 AGUT was the second largest firm in Switzerland. One of Europe's foremost silk weavers, it had early become a transnational (multinational) enterprise (MNE) with investments in all major European countries as well as from the 1880s in the USA. The American branch quickly became the most dynamic one in the enterprise. But this unbelievable dynamism was met with mistrust and misunderstanding by the Swiss owners.

AGUT was one single firm, owned and managed by a single family located in Thalwil, Switzerland. The rift that arose between the American branch and its European directors was not caused by disunity among competing part-owners but by an inability to perceive the advantages of a different mode of business operation. The Swiss owners considered its European operations superior by default; the company's American operations were after all set up from Europe and constantly nourished by the European side. Specifically, the Thalwil headquarters sent capital, skilled workers, and machinery to the company plants in New York and Philadelphia. Swiss–made silk-waving machines, specially designed for AGUT, were more reliable than American-made ones. Swiss female workers could manage three looms at once, Americans only two. But what caused consternation was that the American branch, in spite of making good profits, constantly asked for more capital. In the eyes of the Swiss owners, the Europeans made the money, while the Americans consumed it. The managers of American branch saw matters differently. Since AGUT was a family firm, the family should provide the necessary capital for growth. The American market was growing tremendously, and if AGUT was to maintain its leading position in that market, the branch's operations had to expand. The firm's owners had not anticipated such a situation.

AGUT's American branch had been started as a modest trial balloon, yet within two decades it had became the firm's most dynamic operation, with as many production sites as in all European branches together. By 1900 the time of Swiss-sent skilled workers had long past, and the original Swiss-built looms had also been reconstructed and even improved in American-built models. Besides economic growth the American branch could present its owners with two marketing innovations. The first was an activist system of distribution. In Europe AGUT's production managers waited for customers to come to them; additionally, they attended the large trade fairs and kept in contact with their established clientele in the wholesale business. In contrast, the American branch had built up an active sales force that visited even small towns all over the USA, using its own cars; it sold not only to wholesalers but also to retailers and even to individual tailors. The second innovation was cost accounting, which monitored the costs of all aspects of distribution. Although new to AGUT, these innovations and similar practices were well known in US business, both among other textile companies and in other types of industry. Nevertheless, when the "American" son tried to explain to the annual family meetings the tremendous advantages of this distribution system, he met only scepticism and disbelief.[41] Since the level of competition was lower in Europe than in the United States, neither the Swiss owners nor his European managerial colleagues could perceive the worth of the American practices.

AGUT's case is representative of the long-standing inability of European business to learn from the US. European entrepreneurs tended to overestimate their own abilities and to underestimate those of American counterparts. Although there were a few European writers who published books with alarming titles such as *The American Invaders* (1901), or *The Americanization of the World* (1902), or even *The American Invasion* (1902), such dire warnings were not take seriously. In 1914, European business still basked in the conviction that it was Europe—with its culture, diplomacy, military and naval power, colonies, financial wealth, and global exports—that dominated the world. Who else but Europe itself could change that?

Yet indeed Europeans were mad enough to dismantle their dominance, not by intention but by engaging in the disastrous war of 1914–1918. By 1914 the USA already was the world's largest industrial nation in fact; its financial support of the Entente during the war-years transformed it from a debtor state into the world's supreme creditor. Its direct involvement in European affairs was, however, short-lived. Despite President Wilson's leading role in the Paris peace negotiations in 1918–19, the United States did not ratify the Versailles Treaty, nor did it ever join the League of Nations, which the treaty had established. The country's proclaimed foreign policy throughout the 1920s and most of the 1930s was to stay out of Europe. The isolationist attitude also dominated economic policy. For example, Herbert Hoover, the former international mining engineer who was secretary of commerce in 1921-1928 and president in 1928-1932, advised strongly against US foreign direct investment (FDI) on the grounds that it would strengthen foreign industrial production and thereby reduce US exports.

In spite of the American withdrawal, most Europeans were deeply impressed by the USA. The war had taught them how important and how powerful the country had become. Yet acknowledgment of American power did not necessarily ease approval or acceptance of American ways. On the one hand, Europeans could be captivated by American technological and personal achievements, such as Lindbergh's solo crossing of the Atlantic by air in 1927. On the other hand, they were perplexed by Prohibition and repelled by reports of organized crime and judicial monstrosities such as the Scopes and Sacco-Vanzetti trials.

AMERICAN BIG BUSINESS AND INDUSTRIAL CONCENTRATION

In general, then, Europeans had a very mixed perception of the United States after 1919, but almost all admired American big business, which was seen as the epitome of US economic, political, and military prowess. Especially two aspects of big business were emphasized: the sheer size of individual enterprises, and their superior productivity.

The first aspect—large-scale enterprise—was quickly adopted in many European economies. Both political and economic leaders in individual countries undertook to organize national champions: industrial giants that would safeguard the country's trading position in a particular product or group of products and collectively uphold the economic independence of the country. The First World War had revealed the strategic importance of items previously regarded as insignificant, such as dyestuffs. To counteract Germany's worldwide dominance in this field, the British Government in 1926 pressed the country's chemical industry to consolidate into one large enterprise: Imperial Chemical Industries (ICI). Other giant firms in Europe were formed primarily by private economic actors without direct state intervention. But in all cases the respective government supported mergers as a positive contribution to the strength of national industry. Backed by such encouragement, the wave of industrial fusions in Europe did not peter out until the world economic crisis hit in 1929–30. The mergers took place in all countries and in all branches of industry; some of the most illustrious and well-known ones are Kuhlmann in France, IG Farben and Vereinigte Stahlwerke in Germany, IRI—the giant holding for state-owned enterprises in Italy, and Kreuger & Toll, which controlled the world's match industry, in Sweden. And these firms represented only the tip of the iceberg: big had become beautiful in Europe as well as in America.

Not only beautiful but powerful, too. Powerful were especially those enterprises which by their size could influence not only their home market but also foreign markets as well. The most suitable tool for a company's economic influence abroad was foreign direct investment (FDI). Until it was overtaken by the United States after 1945, the UK was the world's leader in FDI. But British FDI was traditionally concentrated in the Commonwealth and in North and South America. On the Continent, meanwhile, US enterprises had become the largest suppliers of FDI during the 1920s. Though it had no such deliberate intention at the time, American FDI in due course became a major conduit for the transfer of American habits and norms to Europe.

And despite official discouragement by successive US administration, American FDI grew substantially throughout the interwar years. In 1914 the book value of American FDI in Europe amounted to 573 million dollars, in 1919 to 694, in 1929 to 1340, and in 1940 to 1420 million dollars.[42] As Hoover had feared, American FDI concentrated on production facilities in manufacturing and the oil sector. It thus enabled European business to experience and learn from American practices within their own countries. But these chances were unevenly distributed. Thirty-five per cent of interwar American FDI went to the UK, 18 per cent to Germany, and 11 per cent to France; all others each received less than 5 per cent. The concentration becomes even more striking when we look at the distribution by industrial branch. The investing enterprises, in all cases a small number of giant firms, represented only five areas: electrical products, automobiles, office equipment, oil, and rubber. A brief inventory of American FDI in Europe at the end of the 1920s gives these figures concreteness. General Electric Co. (GE) had acquired substantial holdings in the UK giant, Associated Electrical Industries (AEI), as well as in AEG, its German competitor. International Telephone & Telegraph Co. (ITT) directed 22 subsidiaries throughout Europe. General Motors

Corp. (GM) owned Vauxhall Motors in England as well as the leading German car maker Opel AG, while the Ford Motor Co. had turned its Dagenham production facility near London into the world's largest automobile plant outside the United States. International Business Machines (IBM) and its rival Remington Rand Corp. each produced office equipment in France, Germany, and the UK. The large American oil companies, such as Standard Oil of New Jersey, Chevron, and Texaco, had refineries in the major European countries, and their distribution networks covered the whole of Europe. Especially in electrical products, business machines, rubber products, and automobiles the US enterprises were acknowledged to be technically superior to their European competitors, so the FDI could be construed as an invitation to European business to learn from the Americans.

        The response to this invitation was mixed. In many cases indigenous industry was afraid of, or at least concerned about, the increased competition that FDI implied. For example, the German electrical-equipment giant Siemens & Halske competed with ITT both in and outside Germany. It was therefore extremely embarrassed when ITT acquired operations inside Germany and in this way "invaded" Siemens' own backyard. Especially during the hyper-inflation of the early 1920s, industry in central and eastern Europe feared hostile takeovers by foreigners. Under the circumstances, a few dollars offered at the right moment could wrest control from the existing owners. To prevent such action, exposed companies introduced defence mechanisms such as multiple-vote shares. Yet in fact few hostile takeovers were ever attempted. It appears that businessmen in Austria, Germany, Poland, and Hungary—the major countries experiencing hyperinflation—had an exaggerated, even hysterical, fear of the financial potential of their American competitors.[43] And fear seldom facilitates learning. Though there are a handful of exceptions, it was only after hyperinflation had ended that the majority of European enterprises were open for the most important economic message the American system offered at that time: namely, rationalization.

RATIONALIZATION AND SCIENTIFIC MANAGEMENT

        The catchwords of rationalization are Taylorism and Fordism, which in fact are quite different things. In his 1911 book, *Principles of Scientific Management*, Frederick Taylor summed up two decades of empirical studies and practical work by himself and others. He argued that there was a single best way to organize a certain work-activity and that the purpose of rationalization was to find that way and implement it. To this end he and his assistants studied carefully the single movements of a worker, measured them, optimized them, and then allocated a defined period of time to each, including interruptions for miscellaneous activities and for relaxation. Comprehensive management of the working process was the fundamental principle: "Earlier man stood at the first place; in future the system must have priority."[44] Taylor's intention was not to increase the economic exploitation of workers, but rather to increase working efficiency and output productivity to the advantage of both labour and capital. Taylor's initial practical impact on American industry was limited; in 1914 only about one per cent of industrial working places had been redesigned along Taylorist lines.[45] But Taylorism quickly influenced the discourse on industrial management and had immediate international repercussions: within two years of publication Taylor's book could be bought in Dutch, French, German, Italian, Japanese, Russian, Spanish, and Swedish! Taylor's pupil, Frank G. Gilbreth, who pioneered time-and-motion studies, was hired as a management consultant in the UK and in Germany before the outbreak of war in 1914.[46] And Taylor's was not the only American system of scientific management at the time. The Italian engineer, A. Morinni, studied the Emerson system in the US, and brought it to Europe.

Whereas Taylor was concerned with the minute organizational structure of the working process, Henry Ford focused on the product and production techniques from a practical point of view. Fordism embodied the epitome of the American system of production: precision-made standardization. Ford reduced the number of car types on offer to a single model, the Model T, and on top of that in only a single colour, black. The "Tin Lizzy" was indeed basic, but it was also extremely cheap, which made it the world's first mass-owned automobile. Ford's application of the conveyor belt in production was another example of taking a known practice or principle to its logical consequences. Work-lines with automatic transport were known at the time in the slaughterhouses of Chicago. Ford applied the practice to the much more complex process of car assembly. In doing so, he revolutionized car production as well as nearly all assembly processes in manufacturing. His conveyor belt assembly line represented the first true system of mass production of a complicated good. Fordism stood for the total control of the flow of material and energy in a system of mass production.

Technological and institutional transfers seldom occur on totally unprepared ground. The transfer of rationalization and scientific management from the United States to Europe is no exception. Even before 1914 several European firms had experimented with time-and-motion studies, notably Krupp and Bosch in Germany, and Berliet and Renault in France. At Bosch and Renault the introduction of Taylorist methods was stopped by workers' strikes. The Swiss shoe company, Bally, reorganized its organisation according to Taylor's principles during the war. However, the peak of the European rationalization movement came in the 1920s. The movement became so general and important that in some countries semi-state organizations were set up for its promotion, such as the *British Higher Productivity Council,* the *Work Efficiency Organization* in Finland in 1924 or the *Reichskuratorium für Wirtschaftlichkeit* (RKW) in Germany in 1921. The Austrian *Österreichisches Kuratorium für Wirtschaftlichkeit* (ÖKW) was modelled after its German counterpart in 1928. In all countries workers opposed Taylorism, because they saw it as a means to speed up work and to increase managerial control. Moreover, as Taylor had witnessed himself, achieved productivity gains were not automatically shared between capital and labour, but pocketed by the owners alone.

As workers correctly perceived, Taylorism did establish a much more comprehensive control over all steps of the production process than previously achieved. And changes in workplace control meant changes in workplace power. In general the winners were managers and production engineers; the losers were shop-floor workers and their foremen. Such implied shifts of authority affected the reception of rationalization. In Great Britain the negotiators between management and shop floor, the shop stewards, had become strong during the First World War. British management was largely unable to recoup its position after 1918, and its relative weakness has been seen as a reason for the limited scope of rationalization in interwar UK.[47] For the most part the British business community rejected Taylorism as inappropriate for its situation.

The major exception to the British reluctance towards rationalization came in the automobile industry and was the result of American FDI. Ford succeeded in implementing Taylorist working procedures in its Dagenham plant with very minor deviations (such as smoking privileges), but no indigenous car maker followed its lead. Car makers on the Continent, especially in France, were more positive. As mentioned earlier, Renault's pre-war attempt to rationalize had been stopped by strikes. So it is not surprising that soon after the end of the First World War the most important French car companies reorganized production facilities to American-style assembly lines: Citroen in 1919, Berliet in 1920, Renault in 1922, and Peugeot in 1924. In the German car industry, by contrast, it was only Opel that installed American fabricating and assembling facilities, between 1924 and 1928.

In France, Taylorist rationalization had to compete against an indigenous theory of management formulated by Henri Fayol. The practical organization of the firm formed the core of Fayol's ideas, and since this focus paralleled that of Fordism, the transfer of American practices to France was limited.

In most cases European managers picked out pieces from whatever was on offer; comprehensive transfers were rare. One such example was the leading German rubber producer and tire maker, Continental-Cautchouc-Compagnie AG. After 1918 Continental needed an infusion of new technology to regain its pre-war position in the world market. Therefore, in 1920 it signed a far-reaching contract with an American ally, B. F. Goodrich of Akron, Ohio, that provided for a massive technological and organizational transfer. Continental became one of the rare examples where nearly all that could be transferred was indeed copied and implemented—after suitable adaptation to local conditions. Continental did not get this massive assistance for free, of course; since it was short of foreign exchange, it awarded Goodrich a 25 per cent participation of its stock-capital. In addition to supplying best-practice technology, Goodrich also taught Continental American marketing techniques, and the German company designed its business strategy accordingly. As a result of this alliance Continental was one of the most Americanized companies in Europe during the interwar period.[48]

In both the USA and Europe the principles of scientific management were applied not only to industry but to all kinds of bureaucracies. Scientific management probably had as deep an impact on white-collar salaried employees as on blue-collar workers. This is shown by the well-documented activities of RKW, the German rationalization agency.[49] The agency was founded by the country's most influential industrialists in cooperation with representatives from government and, surprisingly, the trade unions.

"Interestingly each group saw in America what it wanted to see. Industrialists stressed the homogeneous domestic market, relatively low taxes and the willingness of the American worker to submit to higher labour intensity. Trade unionists pointed out to the high wages and the high purchasing power of the American worker. All agreed, however, that much of what America had, Germany needed."[50]

An institution for time-and-motion studies (REFA) was set up, which in due time advised nearly all major firms and bureaucratic institutions in the country on the organization of working procedures. In most cases the advice was taken seriously and even implemented. Carl Friedrich von Siemens, CEO of the eponymous industrial giant, became president of the RKW and his right hand, Carl Köttgen, its main executive officer. Both were deeply impressed by American economic achievements. After a tour of the USA in 1924, Köttgen published a laudatory account under the title *Efficient America (Das wirtschaftliche Amerika)*. Yet neither advocated taking over everything from the United States. Siemens warned against an uncritical *"Americanism"*, a standardization and simplification that contradicted German individualism. Yet he also recognized that this individualism had unhealthy aspects which should be resisted in the areas of industrial production and consumption.

The differentiated approach of Köttgen and Siemens was quite representative of European business attitudes. There were, of course, persons such as Hugo Prager, head of the first Swiss Rotary Club, who admired the USA without any trace of criticism. More widespread, however, was the position of Ernst von Streeruwitz, the president of the Austrian rationalization committee (ÖKW), who found in the Soviet and American societies a similar "exploitation" that amounted to a "Russo-American mechanization of man..." Streeruwitz regarded the United States as a country "where technology drags the inner civilization as an appendix behind itself."[51] Such persons were willing to learn from America, to be sure, but not too much. And they refused to recognize that rationalization, once applied, would not only increase economic productivity, but inevitably would also change social and cultural habits at the same time.

A special variant of scientific management was the Bedaux-system. Charles Eugène Bedaux was a Frenchman who emigrated to the United States in 1906. While working as an interpreter for the Italian engineer Morinni, who had come to the USA to study scientific management, Bedaux developed a passion for the subject himself. In 1916 he set up a management agency that applied his own version of time-and-motion measurement: the Bedaux system. It was based on a time-unit called "B", which represented forty seconds of work and twenty seconds rest. All work could be measured in the number of Bs it required. The Bedaux system was the very essence of quantification, accountability, and control, as well as de-humanization, which many attached to the rationalization movement. Bedaux's agency became the most widespread purveyor of payment-by-result advice on scientific management in the US. By 1924 Bedaux had established bureaus in five major American cities. In 1927 he exported his business to Europe, setting up subsidiaries in four countries.

What we see from the table below is that the Bedaux system, which was fairly widespread in the USA, met a varied reception in Europe. It was quite known in the UK and in France, but it had limited presence in Italy and especially in Germany. A closer look at how the system was spread helps to explain the variations. Bedaux was charismatic person who could easily persuade potential customers of the advantages of his system of time management. He also engaged heavily in social activities and threw impressive parties at his Chateau de Candé in the Loire valley, by which he could attract important individuals. In this way he was able to convince prominent personalities to sit on the board of directors of respective Bedaux subsidiaries. Bedaux also secured customers via American FDI. Several firms that had adopted the Bedaux system in their US plants transferred the time-management practice to subsidiaries abroad. One of these was the tire maker B. F. Goodrich; it not only reorganized its British plant according to Bedaux rules, but also recommended the adoption of the system to its German ally, Continental. Other American management consultancies, such as Wallace Clarke's, entered the European market the same way: from US clients to American FDI.

The Diffusion of the Bedaux-System

Number of enterprises using the Bedaux System

Country	Office opened in	1931	1937
US	1918	52	500
UK	1926	30	225
Italy	1927	21	49
France	1929	16	144
Germany	1927	5	25

Source: Kipping (1999), p. 198

Taylorism and Fordism were more than just ideologies of management; they were also ideologies of American modernism. As such they were the sources of inspiration for the most important developments in European architecture during the 1920s. Le Corbusier, Gropius, Mies van der Rohe, and others of the German school of design, *Bauhaus*, were deeply impressed by American architecture and even more by American technology. Their artistic ideas varied, but they shared a commitment to Fordist methods of construction. In Dessau-Törten Walter Gropius designed and built 300 houses using only a few basic models. The construction was rationalized according to Ford's and Taylor's precepts, using pre-fabricated parts, transported to site by rail, and assembled in place. At the time (1926–27) the German construction industry was still dominated by artisanal labour, so Gropius's modernist building site constituted a managerial and technological revolution. The French-Swiss architect Le Corbusier had even more revolutionary ideas; he published plans of houses to be assembled within three days! The characteristic appearance of this modernist architecture—lack of ornament and simple geometric shapes—came to be labelled *international style*, and it represented an amalgam of American and European aesthetics and technology. During the 1930s, when resurgent nationalism made any connections with internationalism suspicious, the international style lost ground, especially in Germany. When the Nazis came to power, many of the Bauhaus group were forced to emigrate; most wound up in the United States, where their modernist credentials and international contacts enabled successful reestablishment in a new country.

The reception of Taylorism and Fordism varied considerably from country to country. Some were more open than others. The country's position at the end of the First World War was often decisive in this respect. Generally speaking, the losers—e.g. Germany, Austria, and Hungary—as well as the newly established states—e.g. Czechoslovakia—were more receptive, for the war had challenged the effectiveness and legitimacy of their economic and political institutions. Countries on the winning side or that had been neutral tended to be less receptive; their institutions had, after all, largely been confirmed by the war's outcome. On the Continent the war's foremost winner was France, and it should be no surprise that during the 1920s French political and economic leaders were very cautious and reluctant to take over new ideas from anywhere, including the USA. Indeed, France was perhaps the most outspoken critic of the American model in interwar Europe. The French automobile industry achieved great success following American production practices, but in the majority of French industry the application of managerial rationalization was less widespread than in most other countries. One hindrance was the continuing business confidence in the classical management theory of Henri Fayol. A second and perhaps more important hindrance was cultural anxiety: "the dominant reaction of France to the American system of industrial production was one of dismay and fear."[52] The French political and business elites rejected and even despised the implications—social, economic, political, and cultural—of the American model. The spirit of the French—and the Continental—manufacturing industry was considered to be originality, variety, polish, and perfection. This was exactly what Carl Friedrich von Siemens had had in mind when he criticized the American trend toward simplification. The French writer André Siegfried enlarged on this attitude, claiming that in the USA people were happy to adapt to goods while in Europe goods had to adapt to people. According to Siegfried, the Americans "moulded as easily as clay" and "lose sight of the fact that goods were made for man and not man for goods."[53]

The rationalization movement, Taylorism, and Fordism all represent versions of Americanization whose content and modes of transfer can be documented reasonably clearly. Other potential instruments of Americanization, such as American social and professional associations, are more difficult to follow and interpret. In 1922 the American Rotary club movement, an organization of business and professional men for the promotion of high vocational standards and community service, adopted the name Rotary International and proceeded to set up clubs all over Europe. The movement's stated purpose was to advance international understanding and peace through a world fellowship of service. The high-flown rhetoric emphasizing integrity, rationality, individualism, and competition bore a striking resemblance to the gospel of the American economic ethic. Generally, Rotary's expansion into Europe was quite successful. In some countries it could build on predecessors. For example, in Switzerland a couple of businessmen founded the *Swiss Friends of the USA* at the end of the First World War. When Rotary International's "special commissioner", F. W. Teele, arrived in Switzerland in 1923 to establish a club, he could build on this group. In only four years Rotary

International had established 18 clubs in the country with more than 600 members in all. In Germany Rotary's association with both American and international values led to the clubs being prohibited by the Nazis as soon as they achieved power in 1933. The effects of Rotary clubs on the reception of Americanization in Europe can hardly be measured, but at the least they surely opened up the minds of their members, exclusively business and professional leaders, to American ideas.

MOTION PICTURES AND AMERICANIZATION

In 1936 the fledgling field of marketing research scored its most spectacular triumph to date. On a basis of a small but representative sample of registered voters, the American journalist and advertising researcher George H. Gallup correctly predicted the outcome of the US presidential election. The previous year Gallup had founded the *American Institute of Public Opinion* (AIPO), which became so successful und its methods so trusted that the kind of opinion survey he developed is still today called a *Gallup poll*. In 1937 AIPO established subsidiaries in France, Sweden, and the UK. Marketing research in Europe, however, stopped almost completely after 1939 and did not recover until the 1950s. Gallup was the most sophisticated practitioner of opinion polling and marketing research in the formative years of the field, but he was not the first. Measuring customer preferences had for some time played a major role in the American motion picture industry. Today the world's film industry is clearly dominated by the giant Hollywood studios, but in the beginning the situation was quite different. Before 1914 European films and film-makers were more prominent and famous than any in the USA. France was the world's leading film nation with its series of Phantomas and other detective stories as well as the "Max" comedies, whose central character was a model for Charlie Chaplin. The Danish Nordisk company, one of Europe's larger producers at the time, was known for making films with alternative endings: a "happy end" for western European audiences, and a dramatic ending for east European.[54] In contrast to the inventiveness and variety of European cinema, contemporary films in the United States appeared to be unimaginative. According to European film critics American film-makers were satisfied with showing bravery and agility; seen one seen them all was a typical comment. In 1921, under the ominous headline "The Foreign Invasion", the indigenous American critic Kuttner criticised his countrymen that the Americans "made movies for underdeveloped adults at the level of nine-year olds."[55] But if the quality of its film-making was so inferior at the outset, how did the American film industry achieve its world-dominance?

One reason was size and accompanying economies of scale. From the late 1910s American film-making was concentrated in Hollywood, California, and consolidated in a few large studios: Universal, Paramount, MGM, United Artists, etc. European film-makers, by contrast, were geographically fragmented, modest in size, and financially weak. The difference in resources inevitably had consequences in a branch so dependent on modern technology. American cinema soon excelled in many of the technical aspects of cinema—set design, lighting, and editing, including artistic issues, such as design. Also the acting performances in American films seemed to be more natural, and the narrative more compelling. In the USA film acting developed as a distinctive type of artistic performance that accommodated the special demands and potentialities of the medium. In European films, however, actors and actresses alternated between film, opera, and theatre, and their performing techniques were derived from the latter two. But film catered to a mass audience, whereas opera and stage played mainly for the educated population, and in more intimate surroundings. In cinema, even more than in opera and theatre, the individual performers play a decisive role in the success of the product and the company. The film industry has a great structural problem in that its product cycle is extremely short, namely the production and showing of a single film. Such product transiency means that a film-maker must find a way to hold the audience and move it consistently from film to film. The American motion-picture industry was quicker than the European to recognize that the name of the studio was a weaker drawing card than the name of individual actors and actresses. Thus was born the film-star system. Film stars were more than mere performers; they were a film studio's key assets, for they could attract the audience again and again.

Identifying individual film stars and their respective strengths and limitations in the eyes of audiences was the function of the studios' marketing activities. American film producers pioneered market research in monitoring audience response to individual films and performers. Key figures in the early years of the industry started as 'Nickelodeon' operators in respectively Chicago (Carl Laemmle) and New York (Adolph Zukor), where they learned to coordinate offerings and audience. Later Laemmle founded *Universal Pictures Corp* and Zukor *Paramount Pictures Corp*. Both applied an unabashed business approach to cinema. While European film-makers tried to produce art, a meaningful story, or a memorable performance, the Americans produced what would sell. Simply put, they produced what the audience was willing to pay for, namely, entertainment. Audience research was again a primary source of information. Not only were the best times and best places for showing a film investigated, but also the differences between large and small towns, age of the audience, as well as the specific appeal of individual film stars. The consequences could be far-reaching. Not even divas such as Greta Garbo were immune. When Garbo attempted a come-back in 1947, she could not obtain a role, for the simple reason that Gallup polls showed that the American audience could not imagine her return to the screen. No studio doubted her ability, but the market had spoken, and for American film companies it was the market that decided, not artistic quality. In the eyes of many Europeans American film branch kowtowed to commerce and sacrificed art, something European producers claimed they would never do.

After the First World War the German film industry was one of the strongest European challengers to the growing power of Hollywood. In spite of its territorial losses Germany still had the largest potential audience in Europe, and it had one of the Continent's largest motion-picture companies, Universum Film AG (Ufa). Ufa was founded in 1917 to counter Allied cinemagraphic war propaganda. Ufa was as big as any Hollywood competitor and commanded studios in Berlin-Babelsberg that matched those in southern California. But its concept of film-making was utterly different. Whereas European film critics considered American movies to be simplistic, if not childish, their American colleagues evaluated European movies from a business standpoint and came up with a telling conclusion: "It is a curious fact about many German pictures. They deal with great stories but have no romance, being entirely for men."[56] In business terms such an assessment was devastating, for American market research had revealed that in most cases it was not men but women who decided whether or not to go to the cinema and who chose the movie to be seen. Then, as today, women's opinion determined success or failure of films. According to the *New York Times* in 1921:

> "In Germany many of the important films are too gruesome for the American public.
> The actresses who appear in many of the films are not young and beautiful enough to
> satisfy Americans."

In addition to its potential misreading of viewer interest, Ufa lacked capital. When Adolph Zukor bought up 25 German films during the 1920s to keep them off the US market, Ufa could not retaliate. In 1925 Ufa was in financial trouble, and in order to obtain a loan, it was forced to sign an agreement—the Parufamet Treaty— with Paramount and MGM. Ufa was thereby required to show annually 25 films made by the two American partners in return for their distributing 10 Ufa films per year.

The emergence of the talking film in the late 1920s might have reversed the situation. The French film company Gaumont had demonstrated talking films and equipment since the 1910s, but technical quality of its system was inadequate for ordinary commercial use. This deficiency was overcome by the invention of the electric microphone by the Bell Laboratories in the mid-1920s. Like Gaumont, German companies had developed a sound-track technology in 1919, but could not find any buyers. Still, the technology's patent protection seemed to be strong. Yet when Warner Brothers introduced its first sound film in 1926, this event shook the industry worldwide. In the USA Radio Corporation of America (RCA) and Electrical Research Products Incorporated (ERPI) acquired the US patents for soundtrack, while the German ones were with Tobis-Klangfilm. After a short fight, an agreement was reached. The outcome was an international cartel in 1930 that divided the world market for sound film equipment between the three companies mentioned.

The small Greek film industry shows that American-style movie-making was possible in interwar Europe. Using an indigenously developed sound-track technology, Skouras Film produced films in the 1920s and 1930s that were followed the Hollywood formula: a focus on entertainment and box-office success with no deliberate cultural ambition.[57] The example, however, is rather special both because of the peripheral location of the Greek market and the persons involved. The three brothers who owned Skouras Film had emigrated to St. Louis, Missouri, as teenagers and from 1914 built up a chain of cinemas there before starting operations in their native country. In the early 1930s all three joined Hollywood studios as executives, and the youngest, Spiros Skouras, became president of Twentieth-Century Fox in 1943 and headed the company until 1962. Given such close involvement with film-making in the United States, it was logical that the Skouras company would adapt American practices to Greek cinema in as far as possible.

There were several reasons for the worldwide success of American film-making; but the key one was the better understanding of the nature of the motion-picture business. The cinema was not a substitute for the opera, ballet, or theatre; it was mass entertainment, not high culture. To thrive, it had to be driven by a business approach, not an educational one. And people from business, not from the creative arts, had to run it. Movie-making required large sums of capital, which were scarce in Europe after the First World War, and it required a great deal of highly sophisticated and exactly executed issues that combined handicrafts and arts—art alone was not enough. The European film industry expended efforts in these directions. But its adaptation of Americanization was restrained both by less expansive economic conditions and by a continuing difference of vision about the nature of the product.

1929: THE COLLAPSE OF THE AMERICAN-STYLE CAPITALISM

The world economic crisis that started with a crash on the New York Stock Exchange on 24 October 1929 spread immediately to all other countries. Several economic problems came together: a burst speculative bubble; overproduction in industry; as well as a long-standing structural overproduction in agriculture and raw materials. The crisis deepened in 1931 when a financial- and international transfer crisis broke out, which led to devaluation of currencies, deflation and regulation of payment in foreign exchange. For three years world exports contracted month after month; when the bottom was reached in mid-1933 the size of exports amounted only to one-third of the 1929 level. In the USA and in Germany at least a third of the workforce was unemployed.

The Great Depression not only rocked the economy in real terms but profoundly affected ideas about how the economy should be organized. The dominant nineteenth-century idea of free-market capitalism with a substantial international division of labour was upheld only by a tiny minority without political influence. All major states tried to safeguard their national economy. Everyone looked for something new; the old system was bankrupt, and nobody defended it. All countries tried to recover economic prosperity not by laissez-faire mechanisms of foreign trade and open markets, but by mercantilist-style policies of concentrating on national resources, which included formal and informal empires. Remedies were no longer sought on the basis of Adam Smith's open international market but on Friedrich List's national protectionism. State intervention, planning, cooperation (cartels), and organization were the new keywords of the day. The American prototype of competitive capitalism, which European business and political leaders had found increasingly attractive since the beginning of the century, forfeited its allure by the crash of 1929. Indeed, the flow of economic ideas reversed itself: Americans became attracted to European-style cooperative capitalism.

As a result a number of American firms took part in international cartelization. US antitrust legislation outlawed such practices inside the USA, but there was no legal impediment to participating in cartels on the world market. Thus, General Electric was the most important player in the international light bulb-cartel,

Aloca in the international aluminium cartel, and so on. In the face of the world economic crisis American enterprise was no longer convinced that competition was always the best business principle and conceded that some cooperative practices could be warranted.

Such opinions also gained currency in American political circles. State intervention, planning, and order were the principles characterizing the economic recovery programmes implemented by the Roosevelt administration from 1933. Government assumed a certain responsibility for housing and other economic services that had previously been controlled entirely by the market place. The Tennessee Valley Authority (TVA), which constructed a chain of huge dams in that region and brought electricity to farmers there, was responsible directly to the President and Congress in Washington. The New Deal also intervened in production and competition. In June 1933 the US Congress passed the National Industrial Recovery Act (NIRA), establishing the National Recovery Administration (NRA) with a sweeping mandate to organize the American internal market. The NRA not only monitored the economic performance but actively suggested levels of production and prices. The NRA also formulated branch-specific codes for the regulation of working hours, wages, prices, and competitive practices. Such interventionist activity was unprecedented and contentious. In 1935 the US Supreme Court declared the NIRA unconstitutional, thereby dissolving the NRA, which counted more than 5000 employees at the time. The setback forced the Roosevelt administration to pursue a more flexible version of its interventionist economic policy. During the 1930s the American economy became more European than ever before—or since. Broadly speaking, the Roosevelt administration acted along lines suggested by the British economist J. M. Keynes. Keynes established that a deep and prolonged business crisis could leave a country's economy at such a low level of supply and demand that free market forces would lose their expansive potential and instead establish a low-level equilibrium. To circumvent this development Keynes proposed the subsequently famous policy of deficit spending, the antithesis of the balanced budget of Gladstonean liberalism. Though it cannot be claimed that President Roosevelt followed Keynes's suggestions directly, he did spend state funds on borrowed money, and Keynes hailed him for doing so in an open letter to Roosevelt, printed in the *New York Times* on 31 December 1933.

FASCISM AND AMERICANIZATION

In Europe of the 1930s the economic crisis coincided with and abetted the establishment or consolidation of many fascist and semi-fascist dictatorships. The attitude of these regimes towards the USA and Americanization was ambivalent. On the one hand, they uniformly rejected and despised the core American principles of free speech, individualism, and popular election of representative governmental authorities. Yet they were impressed the productive power and technological prowess of the US economy, as embodied in the country's big business. Many distinguished American businessmen observed approvingly that the firm actions of a Mussolini, a Salazar, a Franco, or a Hitler were necessary to restore order and prosperity to the countries involved. Henry Ford's openly expressed sympathies for the Nazi government and its anti-Jewish policies were notorious. But such expressions of entrepreneurial sympathy were less important to the dictators than America's industrial might.

This material might was attractive, but the institutions it represented repelled. Both Italian Fascists and German National Socialists considered America a materialist society that was efficient but soulless. This mixed perception is demonstrated by two small incidents. During the Nazi years the American soft drink, Coca-Cola, became very successful in Germany. Coke's marketing accommodated the political situation and presented its trademark label together with the swastika or a picture of the Führer. When the Nazi Four-Year-Plan designed trips to the United States to study production techniques, Coca-Cola's main plant in Atlanta, Georgia, was on the itinerary; other Nazi organizations carried out similar study tours for engineers and specialists, in 1937 no less than forty.[58] However, the Nazis resisted implementation of a systematic economic or managerial rationalization even in such a key sector as war-related materials, which were beset by a chaos of competing authorities until the end. Though it had a much smaller productive capacity than American industry, German industry turned out many more different models of trucks and planes. The "efficient" American economy was thus more a rhetorical reference than a guide to practice.

Hitler himself pointed to the example of Henry Ford and the motorization of America. To promote this in Germany, the Nazi government introduced tax exemptions for cars and motorbikes, and constructed a highly publicized national network of dual-carriage motorways (Autobahnen). It also embarked on a large project of producing a car for everyman: the *Volkswagen* or people's car. The entire basic production design (ground plan, press shop, body work, mechanical workshop, and so on) was carried out by American experts. Yet at the same time Hitler is said to have enjoyed showing off German technological superiority by overtaking American cars on the Autobahn. When after a private race on the autobahn at 170 km per hour the American car overheated and broke down, while Hitler's large Daimler-Benz continued to purr along, the German dictator felt good and proud. Such small incidents, even rather ridiculous to mention, nevertheless show a widespread European dilemma: even if despised or rejected, America's shadow was everywhere; it was impossible to ignore it.

THE UNITED STATES VERSUS EUROPE TO 1945:
INDIVIDUAL VALUES AND NORMS

How did European contemporaries explain the differences between the American model of economic organization and their own? A widespread thesis was that a different relationship between work and social position was the key reason. In 1927 Axel Enström, the director of the Swedish Academy of Engineers, devoted an entire article on this issue, headlined "Americanization".[59] He suggested the European works to earn his living, while the American works to stand out from the others. Therefore the American looks more to what he earns than the European, since his salary defines his place in society. Thus a high payment was understood as a distinguishing reward for outstanding work. In America a prominent position in society was not ascribed at birth, but had to be earned through competence and achievement. In Europe it did not matter where the income came from, as long as the person owned property. In the end, Enström concluded, that Europeans had to learn from the USA for their own benefit. Enström's ideas were undifferentiated and overdrawn, but at a time when nobles still counted in Europe, and authority was handed out by the state, the engineer's view and his wish to entrust competence with power was what Europe needed.

Individualism was understood in very different ways in Europe and the USA. Both agreed in its high value, but its meaning differed greatly. Both claimed to be much more individualistic than the other. Both were right when measured by their own definition. While in the United States individualism was not diminished by uniformity of consumption——everyone drinking coke, driving tin-lizzies, or watching the same film——in Europe such behaviour was considered to be the denial of all individual taste, thought, feeling, being. "You are what you eat" was a widespread proverb on the Continent. At the same time Europeans were ready to hand over their lifetime to a single employer. Europeans stuck to their own, socially and geographically; group-loyalty was a highly regarded value. Americans expressed their individualism by showing independence from such ties, be it the enterprise, the hometown, or the social group they were born into. Europeans understood groups as a means of individual protection. Members of a group were entitled to protection in important and basic issues, such as workplace, respectability, and so on. Thus protected, Europeans lived their individual lives, which were distinguished from those of other group-members by slightly different habits and slightly different consumption (different types of clothing, food, drinks, tobacco, cars). The group could prosper or fail; it could move up or down the social scale, but as long as the group itself stayed intact, its members were largely ready to play their part within it and thereby preserve reputation and individual worth. Americans were less committed to groups; they derived their individual worth to a much lesser extent from group membership. Freed from group-defined constraints, their food consumption did not matter. What mattered was the hope of a higher income. These deep and fundamental differences in the meaning of individualism underlay another cultural divide: Americans were much more prepared than Europeans to accept the power of the economy over personal lives. While Europeans understood the economy as a means to construct a good and just society, Americans considered the economy itself to be the best available society. Thus, whereas Europeans wanted to govern the economy, Americans wanted to be governed by the economy.

THE UNITED STATES VERSUS EUROPE TO 1945:
CONCEPTS OF WORLD ECONOMIC ORDER

The differences between what the USA and Europe considered right, beneficial, just, and good extended beyond the individual to the world economic order. The contrast is revealed by an examination of how an American enterprise— the electrical-equipment giant General Electric (GE)—and a European enterprise— the German chemical trust IG Farben—pursued the same strategic business goal, namely an orderly world market. GE was larger than IG Farben—its turnover in 1929 was 327 million dollars compared with 247 million, but each was the world's most important company in its field.

GE's sought to achieve an orderly world market by means of its FDI, by securing "a tranche in the electrical industry of the world."[60] It had business investments on all continents, but its most important were in Europe. In England it suggested a merger of the major UK firms and played a crucial role in bringing it about. GE thereby secured minority but decisive holdings in the largest and second largest UK electrical-equipment companies (Associated Electrical Industries and General Electric Ltd). It was also a minority shareholder in the French Comp. Générale d'Électricité and in the German AEG. In 1929 only three firms of world significance in the sector had no financial connections with GE: Siemens (Germany), BBC (Switzerland), and ASEA (Sweden). GE secretly bought shares in ASEA and BBC, but after publicly disclosing the move, it sold them to the major shareholders, who vowed to maintain a friendly relationship with GE. In terms of technology Siemens was GE's strongest competitor, and at the same time it was one of the four largest companies in the world. And despite the German company's long-standing partnership with Westinghouse, GE managed to establish a close working relationship. In 1927 it proposed to acquire a minority interest in Siemens, which needed capital at the time, but retreated when Siemens declared its lack of interest. Instead GE bought 11 million dollars worth of Siemens debentures, more than 90 per cent of the entire issue. What made the financial move special—almost a gift from the American company—was that the debentures were not to be redeemed until after 99 years! Siemens honoured the generosity with a special working relationship.

In all the investments just mentioned, GE promised not to intervene in the day-to-day business of the companies; its representatives rather assumed a watchful attitude. To achieve its goal of an orderly world market in electrical equipment, GE wanted to reduce competition and raise prices, stabilize demand, enforce patent rights, and enhance technical progress by exchange of technology. It did not aim to eliminate competition outright; it considered competition a crucial stimulus for the sector's R&D. The capstone of GE's world economic strategy was the signing of the International Notification and Compensation Agreement in 1933, which divided the oligopolic sector into marketing territories and required that the successful bidder on a major project compensate the losing companies. By dint of its overwhelming financial power, GE achieved its goal of market stability. Yet GE's concept of world economic order also upheld the American model of competitive capitalism in principle. Competition among the major producers was to be controlled and negotiated, but it was not to be eliminated. In GE's view a guided competition was beneficial for all, producers and consumers.

GE's world economic strategy built on its typically American advantages of financial power and technical-managerial competence; IG Farben's was based on the company's strong market position and technological leadership. IG Farben also sought to establish an orderly world market in its sector, but its approach was characteristically European. Market stability was to be achieved not indirectly by guided competition but directly by cooperation among producers. This cooperation would be formalized by international cartel agreements that would allocate market shares to cartel members. It took IG Farben several years to construct these agreements, of which the nitrogen and dyestuff cartels are the most famous. We will concentrate on the example of the dyestuff cartel. In 1927 IG Farben and the major French producers of dyestuffs agreed to form a cartel; two years later the Swiss dye-producers joined, followed in 1932 by the British ICI. The result was known as the Four Party Cartel.[61] Other dye-producers were added directly and indirectly. Ultimately the cartel controlled nearly all European sales and between 80 and 90 per cent of world sales in dyestuffs. The cartel was constructed like an onion, with a hard core to which new members were added one after the other. This organizational arrangement insured that the German/Swiss group would control the cartel's decisions, and in doing so the group also controlled world sales in the sector. This naturally benefited the major producers, but the cartel also guaranteed that the output of even very small dyestuff companies would find a buyer; nobody would be squeezed out of the market. Indeed, when some of the French producers had difficulty selling outdated products, IG Farben found them customers. At the same time the cartel strictly barred the transfer of technology, and outsiders were fought with all available means. The Dutch outsider "Schiedam" was forced to buy its intermediate materials from the USA, and the British outsider "Holliday" was to be bought out. In 1938 ICI came under pressure from the cartel's inner core, the so-called Three Party Cartel, to cleanse the British market by buying Holliday; the cartel would even pay part of the price. The referring letter, signed by the German, Swiss, and French representatives, read:

> "We hope that by the foregoing proposals and suggestions we are offering a constructive contribution towards the solution of the Holliday problem, which has occupied our minds more or less since the formation of the Four Party Cartel."[62]

In most cases participation in the industrial cooperation was freely consented, but some smaller firms had to be compelled. IG Farben's strategy for a stable world market depended on a solid, predictable network of cooperation among major producers.

In the end both GE and IG Farben realized their common goal of an orderly world market, but in very different ways. GE's American strategy was flexible and open, but fairly unreliable: its strategy of financial participation collapsed during the 1930s. In contrast, IG Farben's European strategy was rigid but stable. Its solution not only survived the world economic crisis but even grew in strength to reach a peak in 1939. The American strategy counted on the invisible hand of the market, the European on the visible hand of organization.

CONCLUSION: ADOPTING FORM, REJECTING CONTEXT

Before the First World War only a few Europeans perceived the emergence of the American economic model and its dynamics. The ability of American industry to manufacture large quantities of standardized products and precision-made interchangeable parts at low prices impressed European observers but seldom motivated concrete response. Since at the time American industry as a whole had yet to emerge as a major exporter, its direct confrontation with European competitors was limited.

But there were exceptions on both sides of the Atlantic. Some US firms, especially in watch-making and bicycles, engaged heavily in foreign trade, and their successes forced European competitors to take over or adapt American manufacturing practices. At the same time, a few European entrepreneurs, such as Germany's Ludwig Loewe, did understand the fundamental implications of the American system and applied them to their companies. A small number of European firms also experimented with Taylor's ideas of rationalizing the production process. Yet all told the American impact on the European economy was quite limited up to 1914.

The First World War changed the European attitude towards the US profoundly. All countries wanted to learn from America, though the amount of what was to be perceived as both good and at the same time suitable for an adapted transfer differed greatly. Big business was one of the items all European countries wanted to have, and everywhere big firms were constructed, often with government help. While in America big business stood for oligopolistic competition, in the limited national markets of Europe it often meant a monopolistic position. Thus, Europeans took over the American form, but not its context. Europeans had nothing against monopolies as long as they were perceived to be beneficial. A similar attitude supported the widespread use of cartels and pressure groups in European industry and services: cartels, monopolies, and the like were acceptable regulators of the market. Their function was to reduce waste and energy as well as to guarantee a steady supply of goods and the economic existence of members. The American doctrine of the inherent superiority of market competition had few adherents in interwar Europe. Still, the acceptance of big business as a principle entailed a certain commercialisation of society, which we identified earlier as one of the roots of Americanization. And the experience of modern mass warfare and economic blockade in 1914–1918 burned in the lesson of the <u>direct</u> link between political power and economic strength. Consequently, European politicians were increasingly willing to cede to the economy a much larger role in society than previously, this, too, a feature of Americanization.

But a substantial gap remained as shown by the differing world economic strategies of GE and IG Farben. Both firms dominated the world in their respective fields of electrical equipment and chemicals, and both wanted to achieve an orderly, stable world market. GE pursued this goal by financial means. It bought minority holdings in competing firms and used this investment power to control competition but not to eliminate it. IG Farben adopted the radically different approach of building a system of interlocking cartels of producers. Inside the cartel, competition between members was very limited; outsiders, however, faced cut-throat competition. GE's model was built on information, competition, and managerial freedom, but it included no guarantees. IG's model was constructed on planning and direction. There was little freedom, but it contained a guarantee of supplies for customers and a guarantee of survival for member firms. In the protective environment of the interwar period, the European model proved to be more suitable. While GE's system collapsed during the 1930s, IG Farben's prospered until war began in 1939.

Despite the differences just described, there was a considerable European willingness to learn and transfer from American business in the 1920s. "Rationalization" was the keyword that summarized much of the transfer. Both individual enterprises and national governments participated in the rationalization movement. To promote rationalization several states set up cooperative agencies, which acted as intermediaries between governments, business pressure groups, and labour unions. In Austria, Finland, and Germany these agencies achieved considerable influence. In other countries, such as France and the UK, American advising firms, above all the Bedaux group, were especially important in implementing scientific management. Rationalization and scientific management introduced a strong dose of commercialization to relations between individuals and groups in both business and government. Tradition, power, and mutual respect no longer played the decisive role in inter-personal relations, but a specific kind of formal logic. Rationalization was considered by its detractors to be de-humanising, but its defenders argued that it was good for business.

The principles of scientific management also encouraged the commercialization of the relationship between producer and consumer. In the interwar period this development was best demonstrated by the application of market research in the film industry. The American film studios developed sophisticated methods of assessing audience opinion and tailored their products and film-making operations according to the results. Already during the 1920, Hollywood's success over its European competitors rested on these business techniques, not on the intrinsic quality of its films. Often European-produced films were superior in terms of story, make-up, and the like, but the American companies excelled in distribution and the box-office assessment of film-goers' tastes—good products did not sell themselves!

In the 1930s the Great Depression upheaved the international economic context that had enabled and even encouraged the early waves of Americanization. Europe introduced all kinds of protections concerning foreign trade and exchange. America, too, introduced extremely high tariffs, but Europeans applied a even wider arsenal of protective measures, such as barter-trade. Other measures of economic control were implemented by business organisations, whose cooperation enabled them to direct trade.

Given this background of tolerated heavy state intervention in the economy, right-wing and fascist governments in Europe were able to orchestrate their country's industry to a large extent. These governments not only criticized the political liberalism of the United States, but also the commercialisation of everyday life there, claiming their ideals to be superior to American values. This included the complex of values designated individualism. While these European governments devalued the individual human being by preaching the priority of the collectivity— "you are nothing – your group/people is all", the American model held fast to an insistence on individual choice and competition. In spite of these (and other) fundamental differences, even fascist governments were not able to totally ignore the United States. America was always in the background, providing a comparative yardstick, economically, socially, politically.

PART 2

THE SECOND WAVE OF AMERICANIZATION: THE GREAT POST-WAR BOOM, 1945-1975

CHAPTER 2

AMERICANIZATION AS A MISSION, 1945-1955

> "Do you want a shirt - a washing machine - a
> breakfast food? Competition gives you a choice.
> Competition improves products and increases
> values. You are part of the competitive power
> PRODUCE *BETTER* – LIVE *BETTER*"
> (US propaganda poster, used in the 1950s)

In this chapter we will explore how the Marshall Plan and the following American initiatives, the Productivity Mission, and the engagement of the Ford Foundation promoted Americanization. A special part of the chapter will concentrate on Germany and Austria, which, as countries under military occupation, were exposed directly to American administration. The chapter is of particular interest because not only the US Government but also other American institutions believed they had a mission to Americanize Western Europe. Never before or after this exceptional period did the United States try actively to Americanize Europe.

AMERICAN INTERNATIONAL COMMITMENT AFTER 1945

The United States and its government did not fully recognize the country's role as a world power until the Second World War. Up to then the country's international engagement had been fitful. After keeping his country out of the First World War for three years, President Wilson joined the fight against the Central Powers in 1917, calling for a great crusade to make the world safe for democracy. Yet in 1919 Wilson's idealistic internationalism was defeated by opponents in the US Congress. The United States never ratified the Treaty of Versailles and never joined the League of Nations that this treaty had created. Although it emerged from the war as by far the strongest country in the world in terms of economic and financial resources, the United States largely distanced itself from European affairs throughout much of the interwar period, retreating behind high tariffs and low immigration quotas. The isolationist policies, however, could not seal off the country from economic and political interaction with the rest of the world. The intertwined repercussions of the world economic crisis in the 1930s showed clearly the vulnerability of the American economy in a world economy without proper playing rules. The attack on Pearl Harbour underscored that isolationism and neutrality did not necessarily provide military security either. In response to these developments President Roosevelt and his advisers not only reoriented domestic policy (the New Deal), they also committed the United States to an activist internationalism. Simply put, this new American world policy was based on the conviction that the application of American political and economic values—representative democracy and competitive capitalism—to world affairs would bring

45

peace and prosperity for all. The new internationalism was doubly motivated: on the one hand, it was founded on pragmatic self-interest; on the other hand, it was fed by a crusading, messianic spirit. Especially the latter motivation was much in evidence in early post-war period. The oft-repeated message was that the United States— 'God's own country'—had a mission to care for the world's well-being; to this end the world's countries must be taught the virtues of the American model and persuaded to adopt it.[63]

Even before the end of the war representatives from the United States and 43 other countries negotiated the establishment of institutions that would insure the future stability of world currencies and international trade. The Final Act of the international finance conference at Bretton Woods (New Hampshire) in July 1944 that after the war all currencies should be fixed in a defined relation to the US dollar, which in turn was fixed to gold. The Bretton Woods agreement thus established the US dollar as the world reserve currency and the United States as the lender of the last resort. The conference proposed as well the establishment of an International Monetary Fund (IMF) and an International Bank for Reconstruction and Development (the World Bank). While the IMF was assigned the task of international short-term lending in the management of exchange rates and short-term trade imbalances, the World Bank was to give out long-term credits to finance economic development. The intention was to make sure that world trade should never again be blocked and sent into a downward spiral as during the Great Depression. In 1948 these two institutions were joined by the General Agreement on Tariffs and Trade (GATT), which aimed at promoting international trade by lowering or removing barriers such as tariffs and quotas. All three institutions became formally agencies of the United Nations, but all three were founded on American principles and values. And to this day the US government occupies a preeminent position:

> "to the extent that some nations use their government to intervene in favour, restrict
> foreign investment or seek unfair advantage it is the American 'referee' who blows the
> whistle, who knows what is fair and unfair."[64]

Soon after the end of the Second World War the systemic conflict of interest between the West and the Soviet Union broke out openly and gave American post-war internationalism a largely unintended military dimension. At first the US shipped back large parts of its army; for it had no intentions to stay long in the liberated countries. In contrast, the Soviet Red Army stayed in all states it had reached during hostilities. Its presence fostered the growth of communist parties there and promoted and guaranteed their take-over of power. The danger of Soviet expansion into western Europe was confirmed by the blockade of Berlin (including the US-, British, and French troops stationed there) in 1948/49. These developments convinced contemporary American leaders that communism posed a fundamental and permanent threat to the American model of democratic, competitive capitalism. For the United States it would be a disaster if the whole of Europe came under the domination of the USSR. Thus, American engagement in Europe and the official promotion of Americanization in the immediate post-war years were not only intended to enhance the exchange of goods and finances for a better world, but were also understood to be in the deepest political and military as well as economic interest of the United States.

REBUILDING EUROPE: THE MARSHALL PLAN

After the war economic and social conditions were extremely bad in Europe. Production and transport capacity had been severely damaged and disrupted by military operations. There was a great shortage of energy, and an even greater shortage of American dollars, the only currency which could buy all goods, given the severe foreign exchange restrictions that prevailed everywhere. Remedy was sought by applying tried and tested tools: planning and organization. Since the breakdown of international market economy during the world economic crisis, all countries had a greater trust in publicly controlled organizations, such as state-owned companies or cooperatives, than in private enterprise. In all Nazi-occupied countries private firms had collaborated, either out of the fear of expropriation or in search of profits. Against this background various European governments expanded the organized or controlled sector of the economy. For example, the UK nationalized the Bank of England, civil aviation, coal mining, railways, and public utilities such as gas and electricity. France nationalized banks, insurance companies, the coal sector, etc., and enterprises which had collaborated too openly with the Nazi occupation forces, such as Renault, the country's largest car maker. Even neutral countries expropriated German-owned assets in 1945. Sweden used these means to construct an economic sector of cooperative enterprises, which was designed to keep private companies in check. As in many other European countries, political leaders in Sweden believed that private ownership needed to be counterbalanced by cooperative ownership. The dominant economic ideas in immediate post-war Europe focused on publicly owned or at least publicly controlled enterprise; private property or private initiative was suspect. European and American economic ideas thus differed substantially and openly.

In this context of economic and political reconstruction the Truman administration proposed the European Recovery Program (ERP), better known as the Marshall Plan, in 1947. The programme started in April 1948, and it formally ended in June 1952. The ERP was designed not only to stimulate economic growth and foreign trade but at the same time to turn western Europe into a bulwark against communism. Full employment and economic growth, it was believed, would stop the virulent communist movement. "Paul Hofman, who from 1948 led the Marshall Plan administration, summed up his strategy very clearly by opposing the 'American assembly line' to the 'communist party line'".[65] All European states, including the USSR, were invited to participate in the ERP on the condition that their markets will be gradually opened to the world economy. The USSR declined the offer and forced the east European countries under its control to do likewise. The American leaders had never really expected the USSR to join, for they knew that foreign trade was one of the "commanding heights" (Lenin) of a socialist economy; in Marxist-Leninist terms a socialist economy is by definition a closed economy. During the four years of its operation, the Marshall Plan transferred 12.5 billion dollars in aid to 16 states in Europe (excluding Finland and Spain but including Turkey). Nearly half of the aid was given within the first year. One-quarter and one-fifth of the total amount were ear-marked for Great Britain and France respectively. The former enemies West Germany, Austria, and Italy received per head a relative small part in the beginning, a situation that changed as the confrontations of the Cold War persisted. Most of the aid was given in goods, such as wheat, and raw materials; only a small portion was transferred in dollars.

What did the ERP achieve? With the exception of France and the UK, the transfer represented a tiny fraction of the recipients' GNP, so the direct, measurable economic impact was actually quite small. The main effect of the ERP was qualitative: 1) it provided European industry with much needed raw materials, badly needed to start production; 2) it provided Europe with food, badly needed for workers in key sectors such as coal mining; and 3) it provided Europe with confidence, badly needed by indigenous investors. The Marshall Plan underwrote the promise of the US not to leave Europe unprotected and not to let the Soviet Union make further incursions. It reduced European business's fear of communist-inspired expropriation and increased its confidence that new investments would indeed pay.

Of course, the ERP generated generally positive feelings of gratitude towards America among European investors and general public. But American behaviour and values were expressed by more than material aid. Five per cent of ERP funds were earmarked for the advertising of the Marshall Plan and its functioning. Denmark, for instance, experienced three major pro-Marshall-Aid campaigns between 1949 and 1951. One of the several marketing instruments was the 'European Train'. Between 1951 and 1953 this seven-carriage train explained how participating countries improved their situation through European cooperation and American aid. The exhibition clustered around topics such as "European resources", "European cooperation", "OEEC", and so on. Films and sculptures showed how Europe—by cooperating—could construct a house or climb the peak of a mountain, with American support. The train visited Norway, Sweden, Denmark, West Germany, West Berlin, Belgium, France, and Italy; in the end some six million people had seen the exhibition. Of course, such activity was not welcomed in all quarters. Some disliked the replacement of the old European wisdom of 'do well and keep quiet about it' by the new American style of 'do good and trumpet it around'. Some "Europeans viewed companies such as Coca-Cola and JWT as warriors inside the Trojan horse of the Marshall Plan aid – in fact, JWT-Paris had an account with the U.S. government to promote the Marshall Plan."[66]

Besides the marketing efforts, the ERP used other, quite substantial, means to promote American views. Marshall Plan authorities distributed the aid in tranches or instalments and not as a one-time payment. And the tranches had to be earned by economic and political good behaviour. To organize and monitor the transfer payments, two institutions were set up: on the donor side the Economic Cooperation Administration (ECA), which controlled the flow of funds and goods, and on the receiver side the Organization for European Economic Cooperation (OEEC). The OEEC was to suggest the economic requirements of the receiving countries and above all to facilitate European economic integration. In 1950 the ECA commanded a large workforce of 3701 persons, three-quarters of whom were situated in Europe. Most of them were stationed at OEEC headquarters in Paris, but there were a number of representatives in every participating country. The ECA was the organizational core of the Marshall Plan and its tendency to act on its own authority provoked a number of clashes with its European counterpart, the OEEC. While the British government successfully contained respective initiatives of the ECA, the French complained officially.[67] Each tranche of ERP aid was accompanied by the 'advice' to carry out steps to lower trade and financial barriers between the countries. As a result of this 'persuasion' west European countries had substantially lowered restrictions to foreign trade by the end of the ERP in 1951. After the experience of the 1930s and the war, this liberalization would surely not have happened without the US intervention. That this intervention was both supportive and cooperative created a new trust in the American way of thinking, and in US policy and habits.

The tying of Marshall Plan aid to economic and political behaviour caused several governments, such as the Norwegian, to hesitate in accepting it. But all countries were exhausted and in desperate need. Moreover, the Truman administration repeatedly responded to European hesitation with a willingness to conclude accommodating special deals. This flexibility encouraged several governments, such as the Attlee Government in Britain, to press their industry to cooperate with American aid officials. At the same time the Americans made it very clear that communist participation in government, such as existed in France and Italy up to 1947, would hamper the flow of its aid.

> "All these conditions combined, in the end, to make the American economy and system of industrial production the only available and acceptable model for the modernisation of French structures; the only possible answer to the national crisis as it had come to be defined after the end of the Second World War."[68]

This evaluation provided by Mary-Laure Djelic in her book on the Americanization of France, Germany, and Italy during the post-war period holds true not only for France, but for the majority of west European countries.

US intervention in early post-war Europe also had a specific military dimension that reinforced the cooperative goals of the ERP. The threat of military confrontation with the USSR led to the establishment of the North Atlantic Treaty Organization (NATO) in April 1949, which joined the United States, Canada, and many western European countries in a mutual defence alliance. The treaty guaranteed the continued presence of American troops in Europe, and this buoyed business confidence that economic recovery and reconstruction could continue on capitalist terms. NATO also contributed directly to European economic growth. In October 1949 the US Congress passed the Mutual Defence Assistance Program, which delivered weapons to European military forces and distributed economic aid for the restructuring of the European armaments industry. After the start of the Korean War in 1950, the Mutual Security Programme was launched, which increased American support for arms manufacturers in Europe. From this time on American military aid played a larger direct role in the European economic recovery than the economic aid provided under the Marshall Plan.

AMERICAN AID AFTER THE MARSHALL PLAN: THE PRODUCTIVITY
MISSION

The Marshall Plan lasted four years. In each of these years the amount of aid transferred was reduced by about 40 per cent.[69] Even the United States, the world's richest economy, did not have the means to sustain such a large financial transfer over many years. At the same time some American administrators expressed disappointment over the selectivity and hesitation with which the, in their minds, superior American principles were taken over by Europeans. They did not, however, argue that the United States should give up its commitment in Europe but rather that the system of aid had to be adjusted to changing possibilities and needs.

A very small part of the Marshall Plan was the US Technical Assistance and Productivity Mission (USTA&P).[70] It represented no more than 1.5 per cent of all aid and acted independently within the ERP. The core of the program was the idea to make European industry and administration as productive as American. By the end of the Marshall Plan requirements in Europe had changed. The main problem of the European economy was no longer low absolute level of production, but low productivity. Of course, there were differences. While the British Labour Government started activities to improve productivity right after the war, and French decision makers, such as Jean Monnet, considered productivity a key problem of the economy, others, such as the Belgians, showed little concern. Belgian industry was traditionally concentrated in energy and semiprocessed products, and general demand in both areas was so strong that the Belgian industrialists were most concerned with increasing output as such and not with improving productivity. The idea of promoting productivity was a centrepiece of the USTA&P; and from the early 1950s it became the centrepiece of US economic assistance generally. The American proposal to create productivity centres in all states was met with varied enthusiasm. While the Germans and Austrians were very willing to revive their prewar productivity agencies (RKW and ÖKW), the Italians and the Dutch initially declined. However, as with many other American suggestions at the time, the proposal was put forward so persuasively, not to say pressingly, that in the course of 1952 all countries had set up such an agency. Next came the American demand to create a European Productivity Agency (EPA) as part of the OEEC. The Swiss opposed it, and the British representative within the OEEC, Hugh Ellis-Rees, admitted later: "the creation of the agency was not entirely a matter of free will"[71], but in March 1953 the EPA was in place.

The Productivity Mission was much more focused on the transfer of American proceedings, habits, and values than the Marshall Plan had been. American businessmen and trade union representatives were sent to Europe to inform their European counterparts about American organisations and methods. But in terms of quantity and quality the other direction of travel was much more important. As Djelic has shown, thousands of European decision makers from business, trade unions, social organizations and administration travelled to the United States in order to learn, among them 1,600 Italians, 4,500 French, and 5,000 Germans. The learning was organized in coherent groups according to industry and nations; there were only a few mixed groups. In the beginning union representatives were supposed to be included, a condition later dropped. Usually the participants came from different enterprises. Officially such groups organized themselves, submitting a suggestion to their national productivity centre, which after evaluation formally transmitted the suggestion to the ECA in Washington. In fact, in nearly all cases the initiative was taken by the ECA, which suggested a certain project to a national productivity centre, which in its turn advertised it and assembled a group of interested persons. Thus, the initiative rested in American hands. Very important for the success was the free will of the participants. Nobody was ordered to go. All expenses were paid by the ECA, and the only obligation was to submit a written report in the end. The reports, some of which have been published, confirm two general impressions: The first impression was how much more advanced American industry was compared with European industry. Here not so much the larger size was underlined—this was predictable—but rather organizational styles and the attitudes towards materials, energy, and transport. The second impression was even more profound: the openness with which American businessmen answered the questions, showed procedures, and handed over operational data. In Europe all this was traditionally regarded as strictly confidential. Part of the motivation for such openness can be traced to the confidence of American business in its superiority, and this confidence as well as the honest desire to help made its representatives willing to give nearly all information asked. Nearly all reports by visiting European businessmen underlined this overwhelming openness. Such an attitude of lofty generosity for needy colleagues was unusual. (A similar case could be found in the 1990s, after the run-down GDR joined West Germany).

The European participants of these study tours obtained an additional, unplanned benefit. They did not always know each other at the beginning, but there was ample time during the ocean crossing by steamer to exchange views and questions, to discuss the impressions received, and to ponder the tour's usefulness. These journeys thus presented the opportunity to construct networks of people promoting new ideas within their branch of industry. Regarding Portugal, Spain, Yugoslavia, and Greece, Puig and Alvaro have shown that national networks played a crucial role in the process of Americanization and, vice versa, that American aid stimulated the formation of such networks:

> "After 1945, however, overall USA assistance plus the natural effects of USA technological leadership and the post-war world order (particularly the emergence of an international technological market) created many opportunities, which were seized upon be these and other, more recent, networks. USA aid can be considered, therefore, as a catalyst for the constituent elements of networks, playing a relevant role in the transfer of technology and the creation and seizing of business opportunities. ... In a sense, these networks reflect the absorptive capacity of each national entrepreneurial community for, rather than suffocating local initiatives, encouraging entrepreneurship in institutionally limited environments."[72]

In the more industrialized countries of northwestern Europe, these networks had different character, since many of the tasks they filled in southern Europe were provided by other institutions. However, this does not mean that similar networks did not exist there nor had no influence. Networks were used above all for the exchange of views, which is important for the structure of meaning among decision makers, and for the change of habits.

A number of European businessmen were in the advantageous position of having old ties to the United States. By tradition and language the British especially had such connections, which had not been much interrupted between 1939 and 1945. Others, such as the Van der Grinten brothers from the Dutch Océ firm, stepped up their connections, which they had been able to maintain during the war on a reduced scale. Many others renewed close prewar contacts with the US, for example, Jean Monnet, who became a high-ranking administrator in France and was one of the fathers of the European Community for Coal and Steel. A third group had more diffuse prewar ties—friends or former business partners—that were rekindled by simple correspondence. Two such examples are the German CEOs, Otto A. Friedrich from Phoenix rubber works and Ludwig Vaubel from Glanzstoff, a chemical firm producing artificial fibre.

In spite of the considerable growth of direct and indirect contacts between American and European businessmen, the extent of American influence varied greatly. In France, the American influence became decisive in one area: macroeconomic planning. The disastrous defeat of the French army in 1940 meant that all traditional institutions and attitudes were questioned. American military and industrial supremacy suggested that better alternatives might be found in the USA. The French *Commissariat Général du Plan*, set up in 1946, was modelled after the successful American War Production Board. Jean Monnet, a person who knew the USA well, had lived there, and was a close friend of Robert Nathan, sometime chairman of the planning committee of the War Production Board, was appointed as its president (*Commissaire*). Thus, American-style planning influenced strongly one of the most important of the French authorities even before the establishment of the Productivity Mission. Consequently, the French took up the Productivity Mission most enthusiastically. Summing up the achievements between 1948 and 1958, the official report underlined the French had constructed "the largest and the most varied productivity program in Europe."[73]

Proceeding on the same idea, namely, a transfer of the organizational principles the War Production Board, several European states introduced new means and standards of accounting and statistics. Common standards in national income statistics were adopted, which made meaningful comparisons between European countries possible. In this way the take-over of such standards promoted the US goal of increased European cooperation. As with all such cases, there were exceptions. While many countries changed their systems, a few did not. For example, Ireland at that time was strongly opposed to European cooperation; the Irish government realized that the standards would facilitate European comparison and cooperation, so it stood back. Technological transfer, however, was not comprehensive, at least up to the mid-1950s. Christian Kleinschmidt has stressed the reluctance of German engineers to take over US patterns; and the same is reported for Britain.

The achievements of the Productivity Mission were indeed mixed. In some countries, especially those with social-democratic governments, its activities were promoted. The British, Norwegian, or Swedish government recognized that the goal of a welfare state could be achieved only with a better productivity. In most cases the managers and engineers sent to the United States were deeply impressed, and back home, were ready for a change towards American principles of production and organization.[74] Even though many Italian decision makers took part in ECA study tours, Luciano Segreto has argued that the country's participation in the mission was a failure. Italy was one of the last country's to set up a national productivity agency; political and economic leaders viewed it with suspicion and made little use of it. The Dutch centre was said also to have worked in a vacuum with little relation to enterprise. Mathias Kipping has claimed that the British centre was ignored by industry, while an American official complained in 1954 about Germany:

> "Confining my observations to Germany, I doubt whether any industrialist or top management person in the country has not been approached on the subject (of productivity). Yet positive results in terms of our intent and purpose are almost negligible. European industry, and certainly German industry, has reverted to its age-old 'business as usual' form of management."[75]

Was the Productivity Mission a failure then? Yes, if one expects, as some Americans involved did, a quick and easy adoption of American principles and habits. Such an expectation, of course, would be naive. The Europeans who travelled to the US were by definition open for American ideas, while those sitting back to be approached by US representatives in Europe did not necessarily see any advantages. Segreto looked into public policy and found much resistance to American ideas, but at the same time Italian industry sent 1607 senior managers to the United States to learn about those very ideas. Dutch industry, traditionally one of the most export-oriented in the world, had many established ties with the American economy. These were renewed and intensified, which means that even if the Dutch productivity centres in fact were "living in a vacuum" (Keetie Sluyterman), this did not signify little exchange with the United States. The south European study on networks also emphasized the importance of pre-war networks. It would indeed be difficult to comprehend why thousands of European businessmen, year after year, should get a paid leave of absence for a month or two in order to travel to the USA, one year after the other, if little or nothing came out of such an investment. In addition to Segreto's study of Italian managers, there is a contemporary official evaluation of the French experience. It reported that 90 per cent of the managers and 100 per cent of the executives who had travelled to the United States had acquired new knowledge. More than 80 per cent explained that the information obtained was useful for their particular enterprise. Still, only 40 per cent claimed that productivity gains were made directly as a result of such visits.[76] Barring contradicting information, we can reasonably suppose that other countries had similar experiences. Furthermore, contemporaries looked for something more profound than a mere machine: Kurt Pentzlin suggested the "secret of success of leading American enterprises... (was their) ... different technique of thinking."[77] Judging from the number of exchanges, the Productivity Mission had its main impact in the early 1950s. Officially it continued to the end of the 1950s, after which some of its activities, such as the exchange of teachers of business schools, were taken over by the Ford Foundation.

OCCUPATION POLITICS: THE US-ZONES IN GERMANY AND AUSTRIA

A special case of Americanization through official mission [through directive] was the occupied countries of Germany and Austria, because there the United States had the possibility of direct intervention. And the Truman administration, and later the Eisenhower, was determined to use its authority. The focus of US policy was initially on Germany as a whole and then, after the deadlock of the Allies Control Council, on the western zones of occupation. Before 1948/49 Germany had no central government and there was limited coordination between the zones of occupation, so the individual occupying powers rebuild political and economic structures largely according to their own designs. (When we write of Germany henceforth, we refer exclusively to West Germany (FRG); East Germany (GDR) was a separate state in the orbit of the Soviet Union before it joined West Germany on 3 October 1990.) Austria was from the beginning in a special position, since it had been part of the German Reich only from March 1938. In May 1945 a provisional government, set up by the Soviet military, declared the country's independence and claimed that it had been one of the victims of Hitler's aggression. Moreover, even though the country, like Germany, was divided into four zones of occupation, Austria had from December 1945 an all-party national government that regularly asserted its authority against the occupying powers. In consequence, US occupational authorities did not have as free a hand here as in Germany.

Austria and Germany received Marshall Plan aid, too. And the American carrot-and-stick policy was applied here as well. But there were important differences. In these two occupied countries, and particularly in Germany, the US administration could act much more directly than in the independent European states. Austria's and Germany's share of Marshall Plan aid measured per head was rather moderate, but the assistance given under the Government and Relief in Occupied Areas (GARIOA) programme should be included in the total. This aid was distributed largely before the Marshall Plan came into existence. GARIOA aid made no direct connection between politics and relief, and helped to give a human face to the military occupation. Formally, the military occupation lasted ten years in each country. All foreign troops departed Austria when the country negotiated its full sovereignty on condition of perpetual neutrality in 1955. In the same year West Germany was also recognized as a sovereign state, but it joined NATO, so US troops remained stationed in the country, though now as official allies rather than occupiers. The transition from occupier to ally was inevitably not without rough edges on both sides, but it was an important background factor in the process of economic Americanization in Germany.

The American desire to rebuild Germany and Austria by teaching new values was not limited to economic education. The idea was to export as much American culture as possible, for US policy makers were convinced that this cultural knowledge would enable Germany and Austria not only to increase economic output and productivity, but also to develop democracy and to improve the quality of life in general. About the efforts encountered a massive ignorance and a considerable indifference. The German universities were not interested in the US system, and persons attached to high culture (opera, theatre, literature, lectures by authors, etc.)

showed a cold shoulder. The most comprehensive undertaking in cultural education was carried out via the US cultural outposts, the America Houses (*Amerikahäuser*). The initiative peaked in 1951, at which time there were 27 America Houses, running 135 reading rooms in different towns throughout Germany. Small towns and villages were served by "bookmobiles", trucks filled with books for loan. Between 1948 and 1953 10,000 leading persons from all walks of American society—politicians, professors, journalists, trade union representatives, clergymen, representatives of women's movements—travelled the Atlantic in order to educate Germans on American culture. In 1952 alone one million Germans attended activities of the America Houses. The intention was to address primarily the elite. But this group turned a deaf ear. Those who attended were young urban people, two-thirds being university students or *Abiturienten* (graduating class of academic secondary school). Thus it was tomorrow's elite which showed interest, not the contemporary decision makers that were the intended audience. Surely this US initiative broadened the minds of many Germans, but to what extent it changed later behaviour is hard to judge. On the whole, the American attempt to reach the contemporary German cultural elite was largely a failure.

The central idea behind American policy in Germany was to change some basic structures of German society and to replace them by US designed institutions. In this way democracy would be implanted into the country and all possibilities for the emergence of another aggressive government excluded. E. Hadley, one of the American antitrust specialists, expressed this belief:

> "In both Germany and Japan the victors attempted to revamp the social structure, to establish democracy. ...Nothing less than basic reconstruction was needed if democracy, which would be peaceable, were to take root....
> The programmes for democratization in Germany and Japan were essentially similar. In both instances they called for a new constitution, new leadership, and change in the structure of the economy."[78]

Opinions differed on how this goal was to be achieved. The American leaders envisaged an economic organization of Germany like that in the US: no monopolies but rather oligopolies which would compete against each other and thus create a balance of economic power. In one very important area US intentions succeeded entirely: the central banks in Austria and Germany were re-constituted as organizations totally independent of government. In Germany the central or federal bank (*Bundesbank*) headed the conference of state banks (*Länderbanken*), which were themselves independent of the respective state governments (*Länderregierungen*). The votes of the *Länderbanken* determined the central bank's decisions. The construction broke with long-standing German banking and fiscal traditions, but it proved to be very important in the long run for the strength of the country's currency. The introduction of a new currency, the German mark or *Deutsche Mark* (DM), in 1948 was decided unilaterally by the US occupational authority; the Germans were hardly informed. And yet, this dictated Americanization became one of the foundations of German economic life. The advantages of a politically independent central bank were soon recognized, and all attempts by the West German government to influence central bank decisions were immediately rebuffed. Later the DM even became the foremost symbol of German national pride, much more than the flag, the national hymn, the constitution, or other possible institutions.

In other matters the Americans were not so successful. For example, the effort to de-concentrate specific large enterprises largely failed. At first the large commercial banks—Deutsche Bank and Dresdner Bank, the chemical trust IG Farben, and the United Steelworks (VSt.) were divided into several smaller units. The banks, however, remerged within a decade, while in the steel sector it took Thyssen about two decades to re-assemble the 13 VSt. firms (and more) under one roof. Only the chemical firms—BASF, Bayer, and Hoechst—stayed apart. At first sight it might be strange that the United States did not intervene to prevent the re-concentration. But world political and economic conditions had changed between 1945 and the early 1950s. For the US government the new enemy, communism, was more dangerous than yesterday's, the Nazis; so the Americans tolerated not only German economic concentration in general but even the re-mergers in the sectors of banking and steel. Writing on the Americanization of Germany during the 1940s, Ralph Willet concluded:

> "…much more could have been done to transform the German economy into a system of decentralized, competitive firms and to encourage a new class of entrepreneurs untainted by monopoly capitalism and a Nazi past."[79]

Although they initially agreed to carry out economic de-concentration, the British and French authorities followed their own lines in their respective zones of occupation. Both were under economic strain and therefore preferred entities which could continue work without interruption. For example, BASF, situated in Ludwigshafen in the French zone, accounted 15 per cent of all chemical goods produced in territories under French rule. In desperate need of fertilizer and other industrial chemicals, France avoided all action that could interrupt the flow of goods from the BASF facilities, and therefore rejected US demands to break up the firm. The same happened with respect to the changeover of leading management personnel. The policy of denazification called for the replacement of the CEOs of large German firms. Many German companies anticipated this policy and had installed a new CEO with no open Nazi affiliation soon after May 1945. The Americans were not to be fooled and often installed a third person, but in the British and French zones the occupying authorities often were more interested in preserving or restoring the output of goods than in denazifying and educating. In Austria the situation was even more difficult, as far as American intentions were concerned. There the large firms had been nationalized as early as 1946/47. This step was partly undertaken to prevent expropriation by Soviet occupational authorities, but it also precluded any US-sponsored de-concentration.

De-cartelization also occasioned a clear-cut clash of interest among the Allies. The UK and France, at that time heavily cartelized themselves, had nothing against cartels—as long as goods were produced and distributed. Achieving such economic performance was, after all, the purpose of cartels. In contrast, Americans considered cartels not only as detrimental to economic development, but also the power base of right-wing German politics. Thus the United States was very strict in applying its anti-cartel policy: all cartels were interdicted in its zone of occupation.

The governments in London and Paris regarded this policy as an American quirk. The British representative, Sir Henry Percy Mills, described the US policy of de-cartelization as a special hobbyhorse of the Americans. In 1947 the United States compelled the French and British occupational authorities, against their expressed protest, to carry out the American anti-cartel policy in their zones of occupation. The Truman administration perceived de-cartelization to be a cornerstone of economic development as well as of democracy. And in the late 1940s the Americans really wanted to reconstruct a new Germany. The French and British, however, viewed de-cartelization as appropriate only for a prosperous economy and world economic leader like the US. They just could not afford such a policy; they were economically pressed both at home and in their zones of occupation, a situation that necessitated pragmatic muddling through rather than the application of idealistic principles.

Another major difference was the attitude towards private property, especially the private ownership of means of production. The differences emerged clearly in 1947, when the British Labour government nationalized the country's coal mines. It also had plans to nationalize the steel and coal industry in its occupation zone in northwestern Germany. Since this zone contained nearly all German heavy industry, the plan's realization would have had enormous consequences for the structure of the German economy. The British plans mirrored the demands of German trade union leaders and a wide spectrum of German politicians. Like their counterparts in many other European countries, both British and German leaders were convinced that it was the capitalist organization of society and private property of means of production that ultimately had led to fascism and war. State ownership, therefore, was considered an insurance against the recurrence of both. The Americans, however, strictly opposed the idea:

> "In the American view, private property was, at its most basic level, a constitutive
> feature of a market economy, without which there could be no exchange. By protecting
> its sovereignty in market competition, and yet at the same time opposing monopoly,
> Americans believed that an ensuing healthy competition among private capital would
> drive innovation in the economy, expand the spectrum of opportunity for individual
> private actors, and create the social power of organization to limit the unhealthy growth
> of state power. This view of property assumed an equality of property holders and
> understood social order to be a competitive equilibrium among plural sources of social
> and political power. Private property was constitutive of the American conception of
> liberal-democratic pluralism."[80]

Thus convinced, the US administration was unwilling to tolerate any attack on private property. It compelled the British to retreat from their nationalization plans in North Rhine-Westphalia. As with the issues of central banks and cartels the United States insisted its policy be taken over for the whole of the western occupational zones.

The diffusion of Americanization in the occupied Germany and Austria also occurred in less obvious ways. The massive presence of American soldiers confronted the local populations from early on with American habits and institutions, not only chewing gum and jeans but also US banking. Before 1945 US banks had been largely absent from Europe, conducting their business on a contractual basis with partner banks. In 1947, however, Chase Manhattan Bank and

American Express Company received the status of military banks in the American zones. They served the armed forces as well as their entourage. This brought Austrian and German commercial banks into contact with US banking practices. Banking is only an example; there are many ways by which a large army of occupation and local population come into contact—road traffic, food, organizational principles, holiday stays, sports contests, and so on.

There were also indigenous initiatives to spread American values. Perhaps the most influential one of these in Germany was the *Wirtschaftspolitische Gesellschaft* (economic-political society), founded in Frankfurt in 1947. Its founding members were German executives with good connections to the United States. The idea of the society was to improve the image of business and businessmen, free markets and competition, and a trust-based cooperation between management and trade unions. In all these points the explicit reference institutions were American ones. The society quickly gathered support from top personnel in business, politics, academia, media, and even the churches. In 1949 it had a membership of 3000, and its most prominent member was Ludwig Erhard, the West German minister of economics and later the country's chancellor. From the beginning the society received financial support from the US government. Its main channel of influence was its newsletter which was addressed to high-level managers.

A similar initiative was taken by the president of the Chamber of Commerce in Köln, Franz Greiß. He founded the association *die Waage* (the balance) in 1952. It promoted the ideas of market economy, rationalization and fairness in the balance between employers and employees, private enterprise and private property: all core American values. New was the way the association undertook the promotion: it paid an advertising agency which placed advertisements in newspapers and cinemas.

Thus, by a combination of direct interference and popular promotion the US military occupation in Germany and Austria prepared for a quicker adaptation of American institutions compared with other states in Europe. Hence the two countries had a structural advantage over the rest of Europe as far as the deepening of Americanization during the 1950s and 1960s was concerned.

CONCLUSION: THE LIMITS OF DIRECTED AMERICANIZATION

"The method of the oppressive conqueror is to force upon others the acceptance of his own philosophies. At the very least, he says 'Copy us; do as we do and uses his economic power to secure compliance. But the method of America is to show by example, to give others an opportunity to see and adapt American methods to their own very different conditions."[81]

(Sir Norman Kipping, Director General, Federation of British Industries, 1951)

Sir Norman Kipping neglected to mention that many conquerors have been quite satisfied with receiving tax-payments and that the Americans did not conquer Europe but liberated it. But it is interesting, indeed, to see how the Americans proceeded. After the Second World War they definitely wanted to transfer their—to them obviously—more efficient and superior solutions to Europe. By means of a sequence of aid programmes—the Marshall Plan (early 1950s), the Productivity Mission (second part of the 1950s), and the Ford Foundation (during the 1960s)— US political and economic leaders tried to convince Europeans of the superiority of the American system by demonstrating the American way of life, and by facilitating transfer processes. Demonstrating superiority and offering a helping hand was the preferred method, but this preference did not preclude the use of hidden or, if necessary, open pressure. By means of the Marshall Plan the United States compelled European governments against their will to open national markets to free exchange and international competition. While the Europeans wanted to continue their traditional view of a national supremacy of the political sphere over the economic, the Marshall Plan forced them to accept that both, the economy and international economic exchange, had to play a much larger role than originally designed. This enlarged role of the economy represents one of the dynamic forces of Americanization. France and Italy dismissed communist ministers from their governments after the United States had communicated that this step would facilitate the flow of American aid. The United States opposed socialization of private property. It could not prevent British, French or other countries from doing so, but it exerted so much pressure within the three occupied western zones of Germany that planned socializations (e.g. German collieries) were not implemented. In these cases the cooperative European view clashed with the American value of individualism. The United States valued individual ownership and responsibility much higher than cooperation and the anonymous responsibility of a large state-run organization. This different appreciation of individualism is a perpetual touchstone of Americanization

At the enterprise level Marshall Plan aid helped not only to re-construct but also to re-shape processes and proceedings. The wide strip mills in steel processing or the construction of the *Tignes* dam are examples that will be presented in the next two chapters. The Productivity Mission had a different impact in the various countries. The Netherlands and the UK showed little interest, while France, Germany, and Scandinavia were eager to learn. The reasons were manifold, and not all were rooted in economic considerations. The Germans were defeated and knew they had to change much. The French had been defeated earlier and wanted to catch up to become a world power again. The Scandinavians intended to construct a welfare state, and that required a thriving economy. The Spanish were largely excluded and had to rely on prewar connections, while the Italians were torn between innovators and traditionalists, of which the latter were backed up by an influential and suspicious Catholic church together with the communists in an un- holy alliance.

Especially in the early 1950s Europeans were very interested to learn how Americans had achieved their substantial higher productivity. And yet the US more or less had to force European governments to establish national productivity centres, which then directed the distribution of information about the American model through transfer of both persons and ideas. The Europeans seldom wanted to copy the American model directly, but selected from it what they perceived not only as good and superior but also as suitable to their national settings. The tours to the United States by European managers effected fewer direct changes than expected by Americans, largely because the time was not ripe. Throughout much of the first decade after the war, many branches of European industry devoted all energies to rebuilding their business and putting it on solid ground. Only after that was achieved, typically from the early 1950s, did firms start to expand. Marshall Plan aid stopped in June 1952 by which time the European economic recovery had become robust. After that Americans no longer aided with goods and financial means but with advice and military aid. European managers could learn about the new trends in their business area and the tools by which to exploit these trends. These tools—proceedings, networks, systems, and habits—were applied later. The actual transfer of raw materials, food, and, of course, business confidence, did not immediately cause deep-going change in Europe. In many cases Americanisation was not always an immediate result but a long-term one.

Many of the Americans actively involved in promoting the transfer processes were disappointed that immediate, measurable results were limited. They believed the Europeans could have achieved much more, simply by taking over much more of the American model. These evaluations overlooked that substantial cultural-structural changes, such as Americanisation, always require time, and are selective as well as adaptive. During this period many Europeans began to adopt a number of American-style habits and values, but they did not become Americans.

The occupied countries Austria and West Germany were in a special position, for they were subject to direct intervention by the US administration. And the United States was so powerful in the immediate post-war years that it determined the basic lines of the British and French occupation policies as well. The US prevented the nationalization of German heavy industry and interdicted all cartels, in both cases against the will of its two main allies. It broke up several crucial sectors of German big business, and introduced a new German national currency. The American occupational authorities also re-constructed the Austrian and the German central banks by direct intervention and established new structures that separated central banking and state finances. Although these changes were imposed without consultation with or consent of the Austrian and German governments and broke with long-standing national traditions of economic-political organization in the two countries, they were largely retained after the end of the military occupation. As a result, West Germany and Austria had a head start over the rest of Europe in key aspects of an eventual Americanization of basic economic institutions. Neither cartels nor heavy industry nor the central banks could be manipulated as political instruments, at least not to the same extent as previously. Thus the autonomous role of economic institutions in society—a prominent feature of the American model—was considerably strengthened.

CHAPTER 3

MASS PRODUCTION, MASS DISTRIBUTION, AND NEW TECHNOLOGY

This chapter explores how central institutions of macroeconomic development changed in Europe during the "thirty glorious years" (Jean Fourastié) of post-war economic expansion. The recast of "the rules of the game" (North) took place partly as a comprehensive design and partly as a series of steps that were not formally related. Designed was decartelization, while the new regimes of *mass*-production and *mass*-distribution were achieved stepwise. Similarly, American foreign direct investment (FDI) in Europe played a direct and an indirect rule in the transfer process. For instance, it initiated self-service in Italy, while several business habits of American enterprise were taken over by European competitors. A massive, direct transfer of American technology took place in connection with large issues, such as nuclear power generation or the assembly of advanced aircraft, but at the same time incremental transfers of a less spectacular nature occurred in all industries. This technology transfer, together with the introduction of mass consumption and mass distribution changed traditional European mentalities about the consumption of goods and natural resources.

> "What is happening is that portions of the economic structure of the countries of Europe are changing and growing, and from this flows much more change. The status and value systems, the arts and social attitudes, the very 'cultural essence' of a people are in large part a reflection of their economic part and present. The world of ideas and cultural traditions does much to shape the manner and style by which men think and live. But the substructure on which a culture rests is the way in which men earn their daily bread and organize their workaday lives. New developments at this level create and spread new ideas and relationships throughout the whole structure. Sometimes these changes are so profound that the participants only vaguely realize what is under way. At other times, as at present, at least some of the effects are immediately obvious."[82]

It is hardly possible to characterize the situation better than by these words by the American contemporary Edward McCreary, who, after having interviewed 300 business and government representatives, in 1964 published his book *The Americanization of Europe. The Impact of Americans and American Business on the Uncommon Market.*

The macroeconomic development during the long post-war boom, roughly between 1950 and 1975, was unique in history. Never before nor since has Europe achieved higher rates of economic growth. The average annual growth rate in Western Europe during these decades was about 4.5 per cent. This was not only an absolute growth, but a substantial growth per head; and all citizens experienced a hitherto unknown improvement of living conditions. This economic expansion provided the purchasing power which was necessary for mass distribution and mass production. The boom also provided the economic foundation for the growth of the

European welfare state and its consequences, such as trust in government administration, in trade unions, and in other collective organisations. At the same time the prolonged prosperity sheltered the European economy from the competition of the world market and the American economy. European enterprises could thus preserve many traditional practices and reconstruct their economic positions until they were strong enough for international competition. Additionally, in a number of cases government subsidies enabled individual companies and entire sectors to postpone necessary adjustments over an extended period. Heavy industry, agriculture, and public utilities in many countries became notoriously heavily subsidized, and without protest from taxpayers. The boom ended with the first oil-price shock in 1974, when the trebling of oil prices sent both the European and the world economy into depression. The long post-war prosperity gave European business an unusual room for manoeuvre, and yet the pressure of the American model was so strong that a second wave of Americanization, even larger than that of the 1920s, occurred.

FOREIGN DIRECT INVESTMENT AND ITS EFFECTS

From a European perspective US enterprise was not only more productive, but impressively larger. Around 1950 only about 20 German and 20 British firms would have entered the largest 200 in the United States ranked by assets. Only a few French companies would have been included. The traditional French tax system was an obstacle to concentration since it penalized mergers. Already under Jean Monnet the legislation had been amended and tax exemptions became a tool in the hands of the government to promote mergers. Electronics and steel were understood as key sectors for a future economy and consequently the French government pushed concentration in these sectors. Beginning with eleven significant steel companies, the number was reduced to six by 1953 and in 1967 to the only two, *Unisor* and *Sidelor* (later *Sacilor*). In the UK and Italy nationalized firms became to represent whole branches of industry. In other countries concentration was driven by private initiative, e.g. in Switzerland and the Netherlands large enterprises such as Unilever and Nestlé bought firms in the food industry; and of the 20 firms producing vehicles in Germany only seven survived until the 1970s.

In our context the various mergers as such are less interesting than the impression that concentration was the only way in order to compete against American firms. The idea was to achieve more-or-less a quantitative equality with US firms before competition was taken up, especially on foreign markets. These mergers took place in their national setting; fusions across country borders were rare and the few ones insignificant. European integration on the level of enterprises, as had existed before 1914, did not generally emerge.

How impressed the Europeans were by the US economy was illustrated by the famous outcry, *Le défi américain,* published by the French politician, Jean-Jacques Servan-Schreiber in 1967. It was immediately translated into various languages and about ten million copies were sold. Servan-Schreiber understood massive foreign direct investment not as an enrichment of the host country, but as an economic threat. Large American firms could undermine the sovereignty of European countries and the independence of their enterprises. He did not blame the USA, but rather the European governments and firms. He predicted that within a few years American FDI in Europe would constitute the world's second largest economy, not natively owned European industry. Servan-Schreiber reasoned in the traditional European way: the state and its power and policy were the most important issues, while the economy had the role to serve the state. The perceived threat lay as much in the amount of economic command foreign ownership would convey as in the foreign cultural influence on European habits.

Behind the fears expressed by Servan-Schreiber was the perception that American FDI in Europe behaved differently from other European enterprise. An investigation of British conditions by John Dunning showed that the perception was not unfounded. In 1953 Dunning and his research team examined the behaviour of 205 US subsidiaries in the UK, which represented over 90 per cent of the labour force of all American companies active in Great Britain. He established a) that the management behaved in typically American ways, with little difference between individual firms, and b) that substantial differences emerged when American subsidiaries were compared with British enterprises. Dunning summarized: "…there is sufficient evidence to suggest that the principles of management adopted by the great majority of US parent and branch plants are substantially the same."[83]

Although from a Continental perspective British economic habits were much closer to American ones, there remained enough differences between them: "The explanatory reasons are complex, but the fact remains, that, in the 1950s, given identical or near identical conditions, the outcome of the final decision often depended on whether a British or a US businessman was making it."[84] On the question of the impact of US subsidiaries in Britain on indigenous industry Dunning concluded:

> "the evidence strongly suggests that UK industrial productivity in the 1950s was advanced by the implementations of USA managerial philosophy and practices, both by the UK affiliates of USA firms and by the impact of these affiliates on the strategies and policies of their UK competitors, suppliers and customers."[85]

Since American FDI could have been a major source of Americanization, it is worth while to look into its actual quantity. Until the early 1950s, American FDI was of no great importance in Europe except for some branches of industry such as oil and cars (GM with Vauxhall, Opel, and Ford under its own name in several countries). There was even divestment as a result of official American policy. As Mira Wilkins has shown, there were a number of important prosecutions lodged against US firms in the United States by the US trade department, which charged them with collusion with foreign enterprises and even with their own subsidiaries! For example, US courts ruled that the US firm Timken Roller Bearing Company had to compete with its own subsidiaries in the UK and France in bidding for public contracts! Timken complied, with the result that the competition reduced its export earnings at the same time as the transfer of profits from its British and French subsidiaries slumped. Such a situation was clearly bad business for individual American enterprises and reduced incentive to invest directly abroad.

American companies that were not subjected to trade-department interference often took up FDI extremely quickly. Coca-Cola was known in Europe before 1945, but it was the combination of the victorious US army and Coke which made it an American icon in Europe. The US army command believed that the morale of US troops was directly affected by the supply of Coke. The beverage was considered so important that bottling plants were set up right behind the frontline, first in north Africa, then in France and finally in Berlin.[86] In 1954 Coca-Cola had 96 bottling plants in West Germany alone.

In 1950 American FDI in Europe accounted only for 14.7 per cent of its world total; until then bulk was in Latin America. But Europe's share grew; in 1960 it stood for 21.0 and 1970 for 31.4 per cent. The amount of FDI was distributed very unevenly. Up to 1963 more than half of the invested sums went to the UK alone, from then on especially France and Germany received a substantial amount. During the decade between 1965 and 1975 the number of US banks busy in Germany rose sevenfold. They took up new opportunities with new institutions, primarily the Eurocurrency and Eurobond market, as well as medium-term corporate financing, which represented a gap in European banking system.

At the same time the quality of FDI changed, too. Not only sales outlets but more and more production units, services, and even R&D were set up in Europe. For example, the pharmaceutical firm of Merck established its first foreign R&D centre in Spain in 1954. This meant that Merck thought the Spanish personnel good enough to cooperate with its American facilities. Good enough meant not only scientific reputation, but also that structures of exchange and communication met American standards.

American FDI was a major means of American influence, and contemporaries understood it in this way as surveys on west, central, and south Europe stressed.[87] There were many channels by which the transfer took place, competition at the open market, cooperation with partners, private talks, American clubs for executives such as Rotary or Lions, periodicals such as Reader's Digest, and many more. Yet in spite of these adaptations, basic differences remained. The following two quotations illustrate the views by each side. American industry used to be hierarchic. Therefore management of US firms in Europe communicated very closely with its headquarters in US. It caused European managers to muse: "Americans in Europe cannot seem to make decisions on their own, are always on the phone to New York or Chicago, and insist by doing things by the book." At the same time Americans shook their heads as well: "…summing up the essence of five years experience in Europe, an American production chief warns U.S. headquarters personnel and all newcomers. 'In Europe, everything takes longer.'"[88]

The following example illustrates how American business habits changed the European ones. Together with American enterprise came a special business institution which was hardly known on the Continent: consultancies for management, marketing, and advertising. Firms offering such technical business advice existed in Scandinavia and the UK, but were almost absent on the Continent. A few firms existed which placed advertisements in newspapers but offered little else. In the central European business practice, for example, advice was traditionally provided primarily by banks, because they stood close to their clients and were considered to have appropriate information. The banks could indeed help quite often with informed business advice; especially when they represented the type of universal banks (see below). The respective advice covered not only financial issues; it also included strategic suggestions. Small and medium-sized companies received advice from their tax adviser, who very often also acted as a general business consultant. Specialist advice on management, however, was a strange concept. The common view was that managers, especially sitting on boards of directors, were paid for the very reason they commanded all the necessary advice. They could orientate themselves and talk to each other; but asking for advice, or even worse—to buy it!—was considered intellectual bankruptcy. Such a manager showed himself to be unworthy of the post and should be dismissed. There simply was no open market for consultants and consequently no significant firms specialized on this field. The American attitude was totally different. American managers at home and in Europe felt free to consult outsiders whenever they needed advice and specifically when, by using a third party, problems could be identified and solved more quickly. In matters of consultation European firms turned to their traditional business contacts—banks or tax-advisers, while US firms went to independent professional consultancies.

Since there were no suitable indigenous firms, and since American FDI was bound to the same consultancy as the parent company, US firms in Europe sought advice from US consultancies for advice. Thus, this new kind of activity—and enterprise—came to the Continent, like American banks, trailing behind other US organizations such as companies, the armed forces, and diplomatic corps.

Naturally some effort was needed to change the traditional European attitude. In 1956 the German productivity centre, RKW, set up a programme to subsidize a consulting service. Two years later the programme was extended to small- and medium-sized enterprises. The subsidy had two dimensions. One was outright financial support, covering up to 45 per cent of the programme's costs. The other was to promote the acceptance of professional advice among German business. There was a natural demand for such advice, but it was hidden, for the reasons explained above. The RKW thus functioned as a mediator. The RKW was accepted in the business world as the traditional national centre for technical aid and general financial advice (such as courses on bookkeeping). This acceptance was transferred to professional consulting. It was acceptable to German business to ask the RKW for advice, which then forwarded the request to a consultancy. The exchange worked as follows: A manager would ring up the regional centre of the RKW, which in turn would send one of its employees to the firm. These two would discuss the issues involved and define the necessary tasks and estimate the probable cost. After these discussions the RKW would send the manager a service contract, but actual advising service would be carried out by a consultant who cooperated with the RKW but was not employed by it. The service contract was between the firm and the RKW, so the consultant was paid by the RKW and not the firm. This arm's-length model was attractive business for both financial and psychological reasons, and worked extremely effectively. After its success became better known, several European countries created similar constructions.

In this way American consulting companies expanded operations into Europe. By 1963 Booz Allen, Arthur D. Little, and McKinsey each had one establishment in Europe, employing 70, 30 and 15 personnel respectively.[89] In each case this meant about one-tenth of their employees were busy in Europe. All of the persons involved had had at least some training in the US. But while three of four employees with Booz Allen were US citizens, at Arthur D. Little the respective percentage was already down to one in ten. In 1969 Booz Allen owned two subsidiaries in Europe, employing 111 persons; Arthur D. Little had four with 53; and McKinsey employed no less than 160 in six different companies. Though they all offered the whole variety of management consulting, their experience gave them different profiles. Booz Allen had a special reputation in the producing and manufacturing area. Arthur D. Little was known for its marketing advice. McKinsey concentrated on top management, and it played a crucial role in internal re-organizations of enterprise towards the multidivisional enterprise in Europe (see below). This may explain the jump in employment of this firm up to 160, since company re-organization was a frequent occurrence during the second part of the 1960s and 1970s. European enterprises clearly valued the advice highly, for they were ready to pay fees between 150 and 450 dollars per man and day, an amount only the most famous lawyers could command at that time. As McCreary maintained in 1964:

> "These European companies pay the Americans to import technologies, and – possibly even more important – to impart and explain some attitudes and points of view (ways of thinking about business) that are increasingly germane in the new Europe."[90]

The rapid growth of these US consultancies stimulated the emergence of similar home-grown services. There were a few traditional companies, which usually concentrated more on shop floor efficiency than on organization and higher management. But the bulk of the native European business consultancies were founded by persons who had been employed for a time by one of the American companies. European consultants tried not only to imitate the service but the whole entourage: appearance, clothing, life style, etc.:

> "...there is little doubt that the success of U.S. consultancies had a profound impact on the existing service providers in Europe. They became trendsetters for their European counterparts in terms of life style and appearance. German consultants tried to imitate the 'McKinsey look of successful young professionals' – the attributes of which included a Porsche sports car, a house in a fashionable suburb, ski vacations, and regular visits to art galleries. Similarly, at the British consultancies, , an observer noted in the 1970s, the 'American image' had also become all-important: 'If you are not just back from the States, or just going, you must at least drop the odd Americanism, the perceptible hint of an American accent.'"[91]

It took some time, but they became in due course as successful as their American teachers. From the 1960s onwards consultancies became an ordinary part of the European economy, used not only by industry but by governments, administrations, and non-profit organizations, too. Today the American habit of consulting outside specialists is no longer considered to be a take-over or something special but is rather an ordinary aspect of everyday business. Europeans have taken over the habit, and it is no longer reflected as something special. In this area Americanization has clearly taken hold and been internalized as European practice.

The business of consultancy was not only born and raised in the US, it is still today an area in which Americans excel and American habits and values predominate. Consultancy is a task. When that task is completed, there is little commitment to the future of the contracting firm; that future, or the implementation of the consultant's recommendations, rests with the firm's management. If the advice turns out not to achieve the desired effects, the firm simply calls in another consultancy and confront it with the problems created by the first.

DECARTELIZATION

Decartelization was an extremely important issue in the course of Americanization. While Americans opposed cartels in principle, the Europeans were convinced not only of their utility but of their necessity.[92] The case of Norway provides a good example for the general European view up to the Second World War. Norway was one of the few states which had passed special legislation on economic concentration during the 1920s. The laws of 1922 and 1926 established the *trustkontroll*, an organization to formally approve and control all cartels. The legislation in principle limited a cartel to one year, after which it had to be approved anew. However, Wilhelm Thagaard, who became president of the trustkontroll, was strongly in favour of the kind of economic cooperation that cartels represented; in his view cartels were positive forces that assisted the accumulation of national wealth. With Thagaard's support the one-year limitation was often overlooked. For example, in 1929 the Norwegian canned food industry applied for an exception from the one-year rule on the grounds that with the prosperity of the industry would be better served by a long-term cartel contract. The trustkontroll duly approved the request, giving the justification that "in its scrutiny the usefulness had been revealed, which by merger and cooperation, by strict planning and economic security in production and export of canned food was sought after."[93]

Nearly all European decision makers in industry and governments as well as economists understood cartelization as a positive benefit to the national economy. A few states, such as Denmark, Poland, and Yugoslavia, viewed this institution a bit less enthusiastically, though still positively. By structuring production, sales, etc., cartels had a rationalizing effect, reducing waste and mis-investment. At the same time cartels helped less competitive enterprises to stay in business, an important side-effect not only for those directly concerned, but also for politicians. In hard economic times, cartels help to maintain employment and tax revenues. They were an important part of the European habit of business cooperation. The accusation that cartels hampered competition and slowed economic dynamism was known, but the positive aspects weighed more. For instance, it was well known that the Norwegian milk cartel set higher prices than economically necessary. Norwegian consumers had to accept the high prices, so it was argued, in order to keep the dairymen on the farm. If farmers abandoned the countryside, the number of unemployed in towns would increase. Furthermore, a diminished rural population would it make it relatively more expensive to keep up the existing rural infrastructure. Thus, governments could value cartels not only for general political reasons but also, and perhaps above all, for reasons connected to the well-being of special groups or populations. In general terms, cartels offered advantages to groups, whereas competition offered advantages to private persons. Europeans were not as convinced as Americans that competition in the end seeks out the best for all, and tended therefore to prefer a mode of organizing economic activity that offered concrete advantages to specific interest-groups.

During the 1940s the discussion on cartelization focused very much in the question of the political power of cartels and its abuse by Nazi Germany. Since pre-war Germany had played the leading role in various European and international cartels, decartelization was also a means to reduce Germany's political and economic potential in the future. For this reason decartelization was one of the cornerstones of US policy towards Germany. Furthermore, Germany's defeat implied that the type of cooperative capitalism it had traditionally stood for was also put in question. All over Europe cartelization was on trial. There were two approaches; critics of cartelization suggested a ban—though with exceptions, while cartel advocates pleaded that only the abuse of power should be prohibited.

In (West) Germany cartelization was prohibited by the Allies from 1947, and the verdict stayed in force until German legislation came into effect in 1957. German industrialists exerted heavy pressure to legalize cartels again, but the campaign failed; cartels remained interdicted. Only slowly did German business truly accept the decartelization of the country's economic system. Volker Berghahn has described this process of acceptance as a cornerstone of Americanization of West Germany.[94]

In contrast, in the UK many leaders of industry and distinguished economists, such as J. M. Keynes, openly opposed cartels. Therefore the British anti-cartel movement became strong earlier than in most European countries. In 1956 Parliament passed the Restrictive Trade Practices Act. The act did not outlaw cartelization as such but only agreements detrimental to "public interest". Yet, what looked to be a lukewarm anti-cooperative law turned out to be a strong weapon against cartelization in British courts.

In several north and west European countries the anti-cartel climate arrived soon after 1945. In Sweden one of the country's leading economists, Arthur Montgomery, won over official opinion with his insistence that open competition was of central importance for the country's welfare. From 1946 all Swedish cartels had to be registered. A governmental committee was set up to investigate the extent of cartelization in the country, and published several reports at the beginning of the 1950s. They were the background for a 1953 law prohibiting any abuse connected with cartelization. These activities put Sweden along side the UK in the forefront of decartelization in Europe. The Dutch and Danish cases had many similarities with the Swedish. Up to the Second World War the Dutch government had strongly favoured cartels and similar forms of economic cooperation, but the tide of opinion turned afterwards. In 1951 an "act on the suspension of economic regulation" was passed, which was applied more strictly in the course of time. At the same time a parliamentary committee on monopolization was established in Denmark to evaluate the extent of economic cooperation. From 1952 it published several volumes of evidence that led to the passage of legislation in 1955, which focussed on controlling the abuses of economic cooperation.

Finland and Norway were considerably more reluctant to sharpen controls on cartels. In Finland the Economic Planning Commission, comprising representatives from employers' organizations, trade unions, and senior government officials, assembled a survey on national cartels already in 1945, but it had no political result. In 1952, the committee still saw no reasons for any change in policy; it was convinced that cartelization was of economic advantage for the country. The reluctance later gave way and a draft for an anti-cartel law was submitted to parliament in 1954; however, it lay dormant for several years, before it finally was passed in the late 1950s. Nonetheless, cartels continued to exist in Finland for a long time; the cartel on Finnish paper exports was not dissolved before the second half of the 1990s!

Equally reluctant was Norway. The country already had an official register of cartels, and the government had the legal power to dissolve cartels. In 1953 government control in the area were extended: penalties up to the liquidation of enterprises could be imposed in cases of abuse of economic position. However, serious initiatives to prohibit cartelization were not politically feasible so long as Wilhelm Thagaard, the pro-cartel president of the country's trustkontroll, remained in office; and he did not leave until the early 1960s.

France, Italy, and Belgium were even slower to move directly against economic cartels. On the one hand, France was among the first European states to enact legislation on economic cooperation after 1945. And in 1953 it prohibited price-fixing but not cartels as such. This established a pattern of ambiguous decartelization that was widely adopted on the Continent: Cartels as such were permitted, but they were not allowed to abuse their economic position. To control French cartels, the state bureaucracy regularly monitored market prices, especially of those goods and services that were subject to cartel agreements. Generally the French government was not against economic cooperation as long as it did not eliminate national competitive advantages. This ambiguous attitude was long sustained. Not until 1986 did France formally prohibit economic cartels. Italy followed the French pattern; legislation interdicting cartels was not passed before 1990.

The process of decartelization proceeded even more slowly in Belgium. The first bill on the issue, presented to parliament in 1954, was not even debated before 1957. However, cartelization in the country's centrally important heavy industry sector had been regulated since the establishment in 1952 of the European Coal and Steel Community (ECSC) with its cross-national organizational structures. And the founding of the European Economic Community (EEC) in 1958 imposed additional super-national regulations regarding cartelization on Belgium as on other members of the Common Market. In contrast, the Belgian national legislation of

1960 was still limited to the control of potential abuses arising from cartels. A national interdiction of cartels was not enacted in Belgium until 1993.

Switzerland remained long the last bulwark of cartelization in Europe. Supporters of this form of cooperative economic organization even claimed that cartelization was guaranteed in the country's constitution. A tough control law was not passed before 1996.

In this area, however, supranational legislation became increasingly relevant, even predominant. The treaties of the EEC and ECSC prohibited cartels. International cartels used to recognize members' home markets, a segregation that was contradictory to the idea of European integration. The EEC and the ECSC were set up with staunch anti-cartel views derived from the United States. With respect to cartel policy they were more quickly and more thoroughly Americanized than their individual member-states. However, the EEC conceded the possibility of legal cartels in specific situations, e.g. to reduce structural over-production and to re-construct markets. And such exceptions were applied several times. Hence the possibility of organized economic cooperation among competitors remained alive in the minds of European businessmen and administrators.

Still today most Europeans think more in terms of structured cooperation than do Americans. But by the 1980s European business opinion on the relative benefits of market competition as opposed to those of organized cooperation had shifted substantially. An example from Germany, long a bastion of pro-cooperative opinion and practice, illustrates this: in 1902 a cable cartel established by the then main customer for cables, the Post Office, and the cable producers. This contractual agreement was dissolved by the Allies after 1945. In 1965, however, it was re-introduced at the suggestion of the Post Office, still the main customer for cables. Twenty-six cable producers belonged to the cartel and membership enabled each firm to specialize in certain types of cable. Two decades later, in 1987, the Post Office terminated the arrangement even though cartel members claimed that the resultant rationalization saved one billion dollars altogether. The reason for the dissolution was thus not economic but political-cultural: an anti-cartel attitude had come to dominate official economic thinking in Germany and in the European Community (EC) and this attitude persuaded bureaucrats in Germany's state-owned Post Office to regard cartels as no longer an appropriate form of economic organization. The decision represented a milestone in the shift from European cooperative to American competitive habits. A long-standing institution that all participants had perceived as economically beneficial, or at least as not detrimental, was dismantled simply because of a change of opinion: Competition had become the predominant principle of economic organization.

Cartelization as an important instrument of economic cooperation was closely connected to traditional values. Europeans had traditionally believed more in the benefits of direction and organization according to interest-groups than in the 'invisible hand' of market forces. To abandon cartels—the institutional embodiment of these beliefs—represented a transformation that signalled the adoption of American preferences, practices, and values regarding the economic organization of society. The adoption was a process with considerable variation in time, not a once-only big step but many small ones. Generally speaking, opinion in northern Europe shifted earlier than in southern Europe. Around 1990 the Americanization of European attitudes on social-economic organization led to a toughening of national legislation on cartelization in ten countries that largely reversed the relative positions of north and south.[95] While northern Europe maintained the pattern of cartel control based on anti-abuse laws, southern Europe enacted much tougher anti-cartel legislation that placed them in the forefront of decartelization. Yet in spite of some 50 years of decartelization, such organized economic cooperation still counts many supporters in Europe, and a few branches, such as the cement or the chemical industry, are notorious for forming illegal cartels.

MASS PRODUCTION

By the interwar years mass production was a widespread characteristic of the American economy, but it was much less known in Europe. This does not mean, however, that European industrial production was small-scale. During the years up to 1930 the Austro-Hungarian furniture company *Thonet* had sold no less than 50 million of its well-known chairs. This is just one example of production in large quantities, which could easily be supplemented by Belgian bricks, British steel rails for railways, Finnish sawn timber, French embroideries, Swedish ball bearings, or Swiss condensed milk. Historians have a penchant for pushing beginnings ever farther back in time, and there certainly existed European production in very large series and even a few examples of genuine mass production, for example, in the French car industry. But what was new in Europe after 1930 was American-style mass production: a way of generally understanding and organizing the process of manufacturing, including a systematic preparation for work and execution of work by machines to a large extent. The early European traces of mass production enabled European producers to understand the concept and prepared their readiness to adopt it and its consequences. "Throughput" became a key word in the discourse of industrial organization, reflecting the principle of movement of material inside a factory as well as the massive inflow and outflow of a plant.

As in the United States, the car industry became a major symbol for mass production in Europe. Perhaps the most outstanding example of European, and even worldwide, mass production has been the Volkswagen beetle. Originally designed as the Nazis' 'People's Car' (*Volkswagen*), its wartime production was limited to a military version, the *Kübelwagen,* which proved markedly inferior to Chrysler's multipurpose military vehicle, the 'Jeep'. The combination of poor performance, outstanding ugliness, and Nazi associations meant that no American or British car manufacturer was really interested in taking it over: who on earth would buy Hitler's little favourite? Yet, today Volkswagen is one of the world's largest car producers. A large extent of the success story can be explained by Americanization, the application of American techniques of mass production in car manufacturing.

Heinrich Nordhoff became the first CEO of Volkswagen AG (VW) in 1948. He was a strong personality and an outstanding industrial manager. Before his appointment at VW, Nordhoff had served in the middle management of Opel, the

German subsidiary of GM; so he was well acquainted with on American methods. His idea was to create something similar to Henry Ford's famous Model T, which had been sold more than 10 million times. Nordhoff, too, concentrated on one model, the beetle. In the end he succeeded beyond imagination; the beetle became the largest selling single model in the history of the automobile, more than 25 million cars; and the last beetle was produced after the millennium. This enormous success could not have been achieved without the transfer of American machines, organization, methods, principles, and habits to VW. Nordhoff visited Detroit in 1949 and left convinced that he would take over whatever possible for the design and lay-out of production in his Wolfsburg plant. Initially, American machinery was bought with Marshall Plan aid. This was followed by a systematically organized transfer of technology from the United States to VW. In 1952, for example, a VW delegation investigating the latest technology in metal hardening visited 27 American firms and research institutes, "in order to get an idea how our works should and can look like in ten years."[96] From 1954 the automatization of production was carried out stepwise with the help of American specialists. By the mid-1960s Carl Hahn, Nordhoff's successor, claimed VW to be at the level of American technology. For example, industrial robots were developed in the United States in the 1960s, and GM introduced robots for welding in 1970. One year later VW tested the same brand of welding robot but was not satisfied with its performance. Consequently, VW started to develop its own robots.

As in a number of other cases, the time for simple take-overs of American technology had ended with the 1960s. The early 1970s represent a watershed after which European products were of similar quality as American and sometimes even a better value-for-money. Consequently, thereafter there was little that was appropriate to take over from the United States, the transfer process largely petered out.

Fiat, the Italian arch-rival of VW in the production of small cars, was as ready as its German competitor to learn from the US. Millions of its famous *cinquecento* cars (500-series) were sold in the 1950s and 1960s. Fiat regularly sent out delegations to American automobile plants; it even signed a contract with Chrysler regarding technological and managerial assistance in 1947. Fiat's managers were not so much impressed by the machinery Chrysler used as by its approach of keeping everything in the production line on the move. This movement was exactly what had impressed Nordhoff so deeply that he coined his own expression for it. Nordhoff understood this permanent movement as a key element of economic success in mass production and impressed its importance on his staff.[97] At first Fiat's management thought this huge amount of transport within a plant overdone and unnecessary, but when its main plant at Mirafiori grew larger and larger, employing more than 50,000 workers, the doubts disappeared, and Fiat embarked fully on an Americanized assembly line during the 1960s: production was automated and steps of production directly linked to each other. Unfortunately, Fiat ran into deep troubles during the 1970s. The economic historian Duccio Bigazzi has charged that Fiat's management did not perceive the American model correctly. He pointed out that Fiat took up the American assembly line just as the US auto industry had started to sectionize automation to give production and workers a greater flexibility.[98] The size of Fiat's plant and the company's employment of unskilled labour made Fiat an easy target for social unrest during the 1970s. Yet VW's plant at Wolfsburg was even larger and ran on the same American principles that Fiat had implemented. What was different was that the German car manufacturer employed skilled labour; moreover, its workforce was organized in a single trade union, whereas Fiat's workforce was divided among several trade unions. In a technical sense Americanization at VW and Fiat ran quite parallel, but in contrasting socio-political environments. German workers had largely abandoned socialist demands by the 1970s; their Italian comrades had not. American technologies and organizational practices were clearly much more compatible with central-European-style cooperation between labour and capital than with the confrontational labour-capital relations of south Europe.

Other car manufacturers in Europe—Vauxhall, Opel, and Ford Europe—would seem to have had the best preconditions for the adoption of American-style mass production, since they were US subsidiaries. And they did import American machines and principles of organizations, but their potential advantages turned out in fact to be a burden because of lack of direction from the respective parent company. Ford's FDI in Germany nearly went bankrupt in 1958 and was saved only after a new American CEO and top managers assumed full control and introduced management methods, cost-control, labour standards, design-for-manufacture, vendor-assistance, modern production facilities, and American tooling. Vauxhall and Opel stayed very independent. Substantial technical and styling assistance came from GM, but all changes in these US-owned enterprises were far less than what could have been achieved:

"In Britain, France and Germany, it was arguably the domestic companies, such as Citroen, Renault, VW, Austin and Morris, which were better able to draw selectively upon American experience and apply it in the European context."[99]

This judgement can also be applied to Sweden's Volvo. Though small compared with Fiat or Renault, Volvo's management was fascinated by the American approach. In the early 1950s it introduced the famous Method-Time-Management (MTM) technique and the assembly line, in spite of considerable resistance from the usually cooperative trade unions. However, Volvo's management soon abandoned some of MTM's basic principles, such as strict control and rigid hierarchy, in favour of pragmatic, high-trust labour relations. Finally, during the 1970s Volvo changed its production philosophy towards a more European, traditional arrangement, giving groups of workers more to decide themselves.

Large firms could relatively easily take up mass production, whereas small and medium-sized enterprises (SMEs) were in a position of disadvantage. How they, too, could benefit from the American principle was shown in the Norwegian county of Møre-Romsdal. With the help of the Norwegian National Productivity Institute (NPI), set up during the Productivity Mission, networks of independent firms emerged, which opened up new possibilities of cooperation, which in turn generated economies of scale. The NPI's initiative was crucial as shown by the lack of a

similar development in a comparable Italian region. The economic structure of
Emilia-Romagna was characterized by SMEs and had a strong likeness to that of
Møre-Romsdal. But the province was a stronghold of the Italian Communist Party,
so for political reasons no American-sponsored assistance was forthcoming. A
cooperative network of SMEs akin to that in Møre-Romsdal based on American
principles never got off the ground in Emilia-Romagna, leaving most of the
province's industrial companies out of the larger European or world market. Still,
companies in Emilia-Romagna constructed different networks, focussed on learning
and knowledge.[100]

Another major candidate for Americanization was the European steel
industry, especially regarding the use of the continuous wide strip mills. In 1939 the
United States had 28 of such installations, Europe just one with two more to come in
1940. The wide strip mill had a very high production capacity and needed a
corresponding high investment. In its continuous version both capacity and
investment were enormous, while labour costs were low. The giant mills could
produce sheet steel continuously, automatically cut it into the right size, and roll it
into large coils. Previously, all these steps had to be carried out one after the other,
thus requiring not only much more man-power but also much more energy, since the
sheets had to be warmed up to 1200°C before work could resume. Thus, the
continuous strip mill embodied the central, distinctive features of the American
economic model: high capital investment, low labour costs. The strip mill was just
the first step of further innovations to come, such as the cold-rolling continuous mill
and later coating the plates. The Europeans were reluctant to adopt strip mills,
because they were not used to operating in such large capacities. One of the most
important buyers of thin steel plates, the car industry, was gearing up for mass
production and projected high demand, but when steel producers had to decide on
the construction of the strip mills, the demand was still only a prediction and not
real. The hesitation of steel producers to undertake the massive investment required
provoked threats by Renault and Fiat to build their own strip mills. The threats had
the intended effect on European steel producers. Between 1951 and 1953 nine strip
mills came on line with a total capacity of 5,600,000 tons. Although they were
located in seven countries—the UK, France, the Netherlands, Austria, Italy,
Belgium, and Luxemburg—they had a common basis in American design and
entirely US-made machinery.

But the overall reception of American practices by the European steel
industry differed considerably from country to country. The Italians were most open
and enthusiastic about the transfer. The large, state-owned steel producer Finsider
reconstructed itself entirely after the American model by using to a large extent
Marshall Plan aid. Oscar Sinigaglia, who had become Finsider's CEO in 1945,
strongly believed in competition. His vision was an economically much more open
world economy in which a country's industry required standardization, mass
production, and cost controlling in order to survive. In other words, though a
nationalist and planning for the benefit not only of the Finsider enterprise but of the
entire country, he shared basic American values regarding business and the world
economy. Signiaglia proposed to concentrate Finsider's mass steel production in
three large coastal plants with a worldwide supply of raw materials and energy, each

concentrating on one main field of steel industry: Bagnoli near Naples for steel rods and bars, Piombino near Livorno for rails and heavy products, and Cornigliano near Genoa for sheets and plates.

Sinigaglia's robust reconstruction raised Finsider's share of Italian steel production from 44 per cent in 1952 to 60 per cent in the mid-1960s. Cornigliano became the largest and most modern industrial plant in Italy, modelled entirely along American lines. Not only design and technique was imported but also the organization. During the 1950s there was a steady flow of Finsider personnel, from shop floor to management, to the United States for on-site information gathering. Teams of American experts came to Genoa not only in the beginning for design and implementation of equipment, but later to improve product quality, teach marketing, and raise productivity. The US consultancy Booz Allen helped with the implementation, a participation that in itself represented an adoption of American ways. Specifically, Cornigliano copied the organization of the American Rolling Mill Corporation (ARMCO). Production and sales departments in ARMCO were closely linked with an emphasis on marketing. Internal organization was centralized and strictly functional: management incentive plans, standard costs, job analysis, and evaluation. The performance of each production unit was monitored according to standard costs and profit-and-loss accounts. In the late 1950s a computerized central monitoring system was introduced, the first of its kind in Italy. The success of Cornigliano had a significant impact on other steel producers in Italy and even on other enterprises, namely on Fiat, Olivetti, and ENI. But there were also limits. The enthusiasm with which American patterns were introduced into the green-field investment of Cornigliano was not shared in traditional steel plants at Terni and elsewhere. Production sites with a higher proportion of skilled workers tended to resist American hierarchization.

The experience of Cornigliano was mirrored in other countries. Generally, the preparedness to adopt American technology, methods, and practices was most widespread in those plants which were totally new, e.g. in Port Talbot (UK) or in Hayange (France). Recent research showed that French sites were in the end usually more open to Americanization than British ones.[101] During the 1940s French steel producers hesitated to construct continuous strip mills, because of the high investment involved and the ensuing high economic risk. Their solution was typically European for the time: they sought and received a guarantee from the French state for a certain amount of sales, which was distributed among the firms by means of a cartel. On this basis they formed joint ventures in order to reach American standards of size, which were the precondition for the new technology. Though the firms were reluctant in the beginning, they became enthusiastic during the implementation of the new technology in the 1950s, because demand for their product was very buoyant. Compared to their European competitors the French steel industry was late in switching to American standards in size, rationalization, and management. Matthias Kipping has claimed that this belated switch to Americanization is the reason why the French steel industry had such difficulties extricating itself from the American model during the 1970s and 1980s.

Another example of the problem of severing ties with an old technology is found in the German tire industry. During the war German-made tires lost their competitive edge in the world market. In 1950 American tires were superior in quality and produced more quickly—and therefore more cheaply—than German tires. This was not only due to the inferior design of German tires but also to the new American technology of making *"cold rubber"*, a superior sort for tire rubber. German pre-war leadership in the making of artificial rubber was gone. However, structural know-how had not been lost; and it enabled German producers such as Hüls, Continental, and Bayer to grasp the American advantages and to implement them rather quickly with the help of cooperating American tire producers. Mass production of cold rubber was introduced into Germany during the early 1950s, in time to benefit from the boom in car ownership.

Mass production of tires of high quality was needed to meet the demand of mass-produced cars such as the VW beetle. For the German tire producers it was a question of Americanizing or closing down in the foreseeable future. Consequently, the two largest German tire manufacturers, Continental and Phoenix, linked up with General Tire (later with Goodyear) and Firestone respectively. Otto A. Friedrich, the CEO of Phoenix, even considered that his company's contract, which secured massive American help in exchange for a 25 per cent participation in Phoenix, could serve as a model contract for the German industry in general. Both companies Americanized thoroughly in business organization and technology, including the preference for tires reinforced with artificial fibres. An alternative technology, reinforcement with steel belting, was being developed and promoted by Michelin, the leading French tire producer. Though Michelin's market share grew steadily throughout the 1950s, American and German tire producers remained committed to cross-ply fibre cased tires. The turning point came in 1967 when Michelin's triumph could no longer be ignored; a success which was founded on a new type of tire—the steel-belted radial tire—in which the rubber was reinforced by a radial-ply steel casing. Steel-belted radials cost more, but they gripped the road better and lasted longer. Phoenix, Continental, and their American partners believed that car owners would not pay the substantial difference in price. But European drivers on the whole valued quality and security over price and shifted to Michelin radials in large numbers. In due course, to remain competitive all European and American tire producers had to buy the new technology from Michelin. The German tire industry had been so fixed on the American way that it had overlooked the emergence of a superior European competence.

It has been observed that a French manager's "depiction of the US example was not always an accurate reflection of American reality..."[102] The assertion could easily be applied to other countries as well; indeed, a gap between appearance and reality is a general characteristic of the processes of economic habits. The Italian debate about how to modernize the country's steel industry after 1945 exemplifies well how depiction and reality function as tools in a process of decision making. The Italian discourse contrasted two models of industrial behaviour: the American model represented the way of the future, whereas the German model stood for tradition, or the past. The American model meant mass production and an automated assembly line manned by semi-skilled or unskilled workers. The German model was characterized by small-scale batch or niche-production, high added value, an educated labour force, and geographically dispersed sites of production. This Italian perception, it should be noted, was in considerable variance with German self-perception. Germans regarded their steel industry as very much concentrated in several respects: concentrated geographically in the Ruhr district (in the 1950s the world's largest industrial area), and concentrated at the level of enterprise in a small handful of very large firms. All perceptions of both models—American and German—exaggerated reality, but they also reflected major aspects of reality. In the Italian discourse those characteristics that were needed for the sake of one's own argument were brought to the fore. What was proposed as the German model actually described the private Italian steel producers: small and medium-sized enterprises that were scattered throughout the country. The proposed American model generally described Finsider, the state-owned steel giant. The private firms and Finsider were locked in a struggle about the future direction of the Italian steel industry in which the American and German models were code words for contrasting visions and interests. The smaller private owners wanted to go on with their special products (the "German model"). They rejected mass production, because they simply could not afford it. At the same time their vision was short-sighted: they could not imagine that mass production of steel would ever be profitable in Italy. In the end Finsider and its American model won out. Finsider extended its market share at the expense of small and medium-sized steel companies. Both sides in the debate exaggerated historical development and contemporary reality. Finsider's winning model was also a lop-sided representation of the American realty. Distortion in political-economic debate is not, of course, a specialty of Italian steel producers, but is generally a part of most processes of technological transfer and adaptation.

MASS DISTRIBUTION

Mass production goes logically hand in hand with mass distribution. One cannot have either-or; yet this was exactly what many Europeans seem to have wanted. The principle of mass production was widely accepted rather quickly, but the principle and reality of mass distribution met considerable resistance. In Europe, the UK included, the basic feeling that 'quality sells itself' was very tenacious. The attitude was that customers should come in for their needs and desires, and that it was not honourable to run after them and press them to buy what they in the end did not 'really' want. In short, production was good, sales inferior. The attitude reflected a centuries-old tradition of regulating business. Many countries, such as Germany and Austria, were not only heavily cartelized, which eased sales tremendously for contracting companies, but also had regulated labour markets for professionals and professional services. In the latter case the country was divided into a certain number of districts, each reserved for a single representative of the profession. The district had to be large enough to support the practitioner and his or her family at a level appropriate to the profession. The attitude reflected a pre-industrial idea of a minimum "living" or "place". Markets for such diverse services and goods as medical doctors, chimney sweeps, and pharmacists were regulated in this way. In such an organized economy, distribution—especially of quality items—is a much smaller problem than production. The Americans had become typically good at both, mass production and mass distribution. Since Europeans lagged behind in distribution much more than in production, their potential to learn and to transfer was much greater in the sector of distribution.

From the 1950s the nicely regulated European world was challenged by the growing need to balance mass production with mass distribution. But—to the relief of European traditionalists—the long economic boom after 1950 turned the European and the world markets into sellers' markets. In some sectors such as ships, steel, or automobiles, customers had to queue to obtain the goods desired. The sellers' market relieved pressure to deregulate distribution, and in many European countries retail trade was regulated in one way or the other into the 1960s. Even today certain aspects of distribution, such as shop opening hours, remain controlled in many places. Long-standing European traditions combined with daily experience emphasized the value of production, as opposed to distribution. However, as growth rates began to decline, the internal value of companies' sales departments began to rise.

According to Robert Nieschlag, the change amounted to nothing less than a "revolution in trade".[103] By using the term revolution, Nieschlag wanted to underline the dramatic change which took place not only in the form and size of distribution systems but also in the attitude towards them. At the beginning of the boom in the 1950s Burkardt Röper, a leading German economist, contended: "the desire of retailers to compete with each other on prices is surprisingly small."[104] Less than a decade later Nieschlag had changed his opinion: "While formerly a defensive attitude was widespread among retailers, there now is a remarkable change in the younger generation towards a truly trader's approach."[105] Before the Second World War all changes in distribution were looked upon with disapproval by established shopkeepers, in the belief that innovations generally threatened their existence. When a conservative attitude, such as 'we do not want any novelties' changed into a business orientation like 'how can I exploit this innovation for my own business?' the word 'revolution' does seem appropriate. At an international symposium in 1962, Max Gloor, at the time director of the marketing department of the Swiss transnational firm Nestlé, encapsulated the 'revolution in trade' under the headline:

> "Today in the USA - tomorrow in Europe?": "Basically I could tackle my task very easily - I would not be the first - by simply saying what is going on in the USA today will be the tomorrow in Europe."[106]

In other words, for Gloor what happened in Europe largely meant an Americanization of distribution.

DEVELOPMENT OF SELF-SERVICE

One of the first and most consequential American innovations in distribution to arrive in Europe was self-service retailing. The concept of self-service was invented in the United States about 1912. The new system of sales grew substantially during the interwar period and took off after 1945. From the late 1940s more and more retail shops, especially foodstores, changed to this system, and in 1958 self-service shops accounted for 95 per cent of retail food sales in the United States.

In due course, self-service as a method of distribution has almost entirely replaced clerk-serviced, over-the-counter sales in nearly all areas of sales. Food retailing was the first to adopt self-service, and at the same time it is the largest single sector in sales and distribution. Therefore we will concentrate on the development of self-service in European food retailing.

In 1938 Herbert Eklöh, a shopkeeper in the small north German town of Osnabrück, opened the first self-service shop in Europe. It was neither a great success nor a total failure. Consumers simply showed little interest, and in the course of the war the shop was destroyed. After the war the first German self-service shop was opened in 1949 by a food cooperative, and by 1950 there were 38 such stores. In retrospect one can sense a trend, but at the time the number was miniscule compared with the more than 150,000 ordinary foodstores. In 1954 the European Productivity Agency evaluated self-service and wrote in its report *Productivity in the Distribution Trade in Europe*:

> "When Europe is taken as a whole the tendency for self-service seems to be more an experiment than a development, which takes place on the basis of conviction and generally accepted principles."[107]

Europe was not yet ready for self-service. Throughout the 1950s the whole distribution sector debated self-service intensely. An evaluation of the few existing self-service shops revealed that the switch to the new system was accompanied by a 90 per cent increase of turnover. Sales per head of personnel grew 50 per cent and turnover per square meter of shop floor 25 per cent. Such positive figures could not be ignored. In Europe the break-through of self-service occurred in the different countries between 1955 and 1965; in an individual country the process usually took about one decade. Germany was the early leader in self-service, but it was soon overtaken and was only in middle position in 1957. Sweden, Norway, and Switzerland led Europe with respectively 5000, 1300, and 1120 self-service foodshops, with the UK, Denmark, and the Netherlands were at about the same level, while the rest of Europe lagged far behind. The geographic distribution showed a clear north-south divide. In 1957 the percentage of self-service shops among foodstores as a whole was 10.1 in Norway, 2.2 in Germany, 0.2 in Austria, and 0.003 in Spain. Two years later, in 1959, Germany led Europe with 11.8 per cent, closely followed by Norway with 11.5 (the Netherlands 7.4, Switzerland 7.0, UK 4.3, France 0.9, Spain 0.14, and in Italy 0.11). By the end of the post-war boom in 1975 self-service shops provided 96 per cent of food turnover in Germany, two-thirds in Belgium, and much less in southern Europe. In other words, self-service food retailing in even the most receptive European countries took two decades to achieve the levels of market penetration that had prevailed in the US in the 1950s, while in southern Europe the small, counter-service foodshop even today defends a sizable market share.

To what extent can Eklöh's "triumphal march of self-service" be understood as Americanization? Representatives of the distribution sector and customers alike regarded self-service shopping as a transfer of American values and behaviour that had to be learned. There was no immediate vision of a new and more productive organization with larger sales or of more accessible consumer choice, but instead reservations were found among all groups of society. First of all, shopkeepers feared theft. They considered it an invitation for shoplifting that goods were to be taken from the shelves by the customers themselves. Free access to goods would tempt customers to steal them. And indeed widespread shoplifting was (and still is) an inherent problem in self-service stores. It posed a much greater problem— psychologically and economically—for small shopkeepers than for supermarket managers, for shoplifters were not always the hungry or the poor but also ordinary customers. For a small shopkeeper this translated into: 'What shall I do in case a regular customer steals something? My alternatives are rotten: If close my eyes I lose the item; if I say something, I lose my customer.' Secondly, many foodshops were simply too small to allow self-service. During the 1950s even new shops for local supply were frequently built with no more than 25 square metres of sales floor. Thirdly, the switch to self-service meant a costly reconstruction of a shop's interior. Small shopkeepers seldom had the requisite capital; and banks, both because of the lack of tradition as well as lack of vision of what self-service could mean, were extremely reluctant to lend money for such refurbishing. Even Herbert Eklöh, the well-known pioneer of self-service, could not obtain credit to enlarge his shops. Fourth, food wholesalers were not used to supplying self-service shops. Very few food items were prepacked, a necessary part of self-service food sales. Fifth, the selection of goods on offer was rather limited for a long time. And sixth, it was widely contended that self-service shopping suited the American mentality, but not the European.

Indeed, the shopkeepers had good reason to hesitate. The switch to self-service really was revolutionary; it turned what happened in shops upside down. For example, it redefined the shopkeeper's role. In the direct-service shop the shopkeeper concentrated on the contact with customers. His job was not only to hand over goods and add up the bill but also to give advice about products. In so doing he could not only perhaps sell a bit more but also—more importantly—he could build up customer loyalty. Good advice for a customer was differentiated advice; a wealthy person had to be advised differently from less well-to-do ones. The precondition for such differentiated service was personal information about the various customers. Often the shopkeeper could address customers by name, and knew their personal tastes. Especially in villages and small towns, where the majority of Europeans lived until the 1970s, shopkeepers used to inherit job and shop from their fathers, who in turn had inherited them from parents. Dynasties of shopkeepers thus sold to dynasties of customers, each knowing the other from cradle to bier. The key to success in such a situation was customer knowledge. Self-service shopping devalued and even invalidated this type of business knowledge. The central idea of self-service is that goods should sell by themselves or via advertising but not because of the intervention of sales personnel, the strong point of the traditional shopkeeper. The presentation of goods, the window displays, the interior design of the shop, the packaging, and so forth arc all-important. At the same time business accounting needs changed: detailed financial matters such as tax reductions and write-offs, small percentages of rebates, and credit margins became crucial. Yet, none of these things had ever been taught to traditional shopkeepers. Thus, hundreds of years of retailers' tradition became worthless within a decade. Under such conditions many traditional retailers reflected gloomily on their predicament: "This bedevilled 'triumphal march of self-service' holds us in its claws." Others, however, were upbeat: "we will adjust to the (growing - H.G.S.) speed of coming years and we will learn to swim, even in the whirlpool."[108]

Shopkeepers were also anxious about how customers would react when confronted by the new and strange features of self-service: 'Wouldn't they feel neglected? Would they accept the shopping basket or trolley?' Indeed, it took some time until customers learned to distinguish between their own bags and the shopping basket. In the early days of self-service, German customers were known to jam up at the entrance to the shop because they were insecure about what to do. There was a story told about a man who refused to take a shopping trolley, arguing that pushing a cart which resembled a pram would hurt his male pride! But such teething problems occurred only at the very beginning, and after the practice of self-service became more widely known even new in remote villages had no difficulties adjusting. The predominant presumption of traditional retailers that customer mentality was conservative and would therefore reject self-service turned out to be wrong. Consumers liked self-service; and surveys of customer attitudes, assembled in several European countries during the late 1950s and early 1960s, produced the following positive list: uninfluenced and undisturbed choice, open display of goods, easier comparison of price and quality, better information on goods, better hygiene, timesaving, and better after-sale control of prices. Negative issues were hardly mentioned, perhaps for social reasons. Who would admit that it was hard to read the name of the cheese and its price without glasses, and who would admit to loving served shopping because it facilitated chatting and exchange of the neighbourhood gossip? In the end it was not customers who had the most problems with self-service shopping, but rather the shopkeepers.

Self-service retailing represented a massive take-over of Americanization. Eklöh, who had visited the United States for the first time in 1935, deliberately patterned his first self-service shop on his impressions from New Jersey. When he built up a chain of stores after 1945, he continued to draw on American practices. Altogether he travelled to the United States 33 times. The frequency of Eklöh's trips was presumably exceptional, but in the 1950s and 1960s many managers regularly travelled to the US to acquire specific information and to imbibe the American retailing spirit. Employees in distribution departments even called such journeys "the pilgrimage" and referred to the United States as "Mecca", which besides a certain mockery reveals how frequently such trips were carried out and how importantly they were taken.

Werner Otto, for instance, the founder of the world's largest mail-order firm today, went to the United States in 1955. He returned home full of new impressions which he used in the organization of his own enterprise. Rudolf Wanzl, who provided the first carts for self-service shops, travelled to the US in the early 1950s to meet Mr. Goldmann, the inventor of the shopping cart. Though Wanzl also produced such carts at the time, his intention was not to exchange specific product information. Instead he wanted to draw inspiration from the pioneer's experience. He evidently learned a lot indeed; today Wanzl's company is the largest supplier of shopping carts in Europe. Clearly, these business travels were not simply unthinking pilgrimages. The impressions and possible transfers were critically screened; acceptable American practices were then adapted to local conditions.

Another channel of transfer of business practices and attitudes was trade journals and books. Nearly all trade publications on distribution in Germany referred at least generally to American patterns concerning style, salesmanship, or organization. Since few German businessmen could read English easily in the 1950s, relevant books were generally translated and published under a German editor known in business circles. Such works usually presented the United States as the model to be copied. A prominent example is *Verkaufsdynamik* (original: *Selling Forces*), published in 1955, by Donald M. Hobart, vice-president of Curtis Publishing Company, and J.P. Wood, chief of the information section of the same enterprise. The introduction, in this case provided by the well-known economics professor Carl Hundhausen, pointed out proudly that some of issues mentioned in the book had already been carried out in one or the other German business. Often the words used were "as in America, only smaller…"

In Italy American influence in introducing self-service retailing was especially decisive. There were no such shops until 1957 when the International Basis Economy Corp. (IBEC) opened five, all in Milan. IBEC was established by Nelson A. Rockefeller in 1946 to aid the economies of developing countries. It was mainly active in Latin America, but came to Europe in order to introduce self-service in Italy. This was one of the few transfers that occurred with very little adaptation. Although 49 per cent of business capital came from Italian sources, *Supermarkets Italiani* were operated as and looked like US stores. They were just a bit less luxurious, and the shopping carts were smaller. The shops turned out to be a roaring success. In the beginning customers even queued to gain entry, and profit margins were extremely high. The big problem was obtaining wholesale suppliers. These were under pressure from their normal customers, the over-the-counter shopkeepers, not to provide the new stores with goods. In response to the ensuing boycott by wholesalers, Supermarkets Italiani (today Esselunga) integrated vertically and undertook to roast its own coffee, produce its own pasta, ice cream, etc. In 1961 IBEC sold out to its Italian partners. The owners as well as some business commentators considered the transfer of American self-service retailing a great success. It provided a model for rationalization of the Italian distribution sector, and simultaneously awarded the IBEC-foundation a profit of about 650 per cent in only four years.

However, a quick spread of the self-service system in Italy was barred in several ways. Media campaigns and public demonstrations, supported by the socialists and communists, accused it of ruining small shops. At the same time many Italian housewives were reluctant to buy in self-service foodstores. The processed and prepacked food on offer there could not be scrutinized using all the senses, and Italian tradition required that proper housewives prepare a 'real meal', made from 'good food'. Not doing so expressed neglect of housewifely duties, and what wife and mother would want to be exposed to such accusations? A third reason that allegedly helped traditional shops to stay competitive was a casual attitude in collecting taxes from small businesses.

SELF-SERVICE ON A LARGE SCALE: THE SUPERMARKET

The supermarket is an extension and enlargement of the self-service shop and, like it, an American innovation. Supermarkets emerged in the early 1930s when, because of the world economic crisis, large, open locales such as garages stood unused and empty. Goods were just put on display, and in order to keep prices low no service was offered. In fact, the innovation initially resembled more what is now called a discount shop than a supermarket; however, out of this initial idea the US supermarket developed, whereas the discount shop emerged later. A supermarket is understood to be a self-service foodstore that offers not only tinned goods and processed or semi-processed foods but also fresh meat, fresh vegetables, fresh fruit, and sometimes even some non-food items. The idea behind the supermarket is to concentrate all requirements of everyday shopping in one shop. The implantation of this idea spread rapidly in the US from the 1940s. By the early 1960s two-thirds of food sales in the US took place in supermarkets. As the better is the enemy of the good, the supermarket soon out-competed most small self-service shops. A 1962 study showed that the standard rule of the thumb of self-service—one cash point per 50 square metres of shopping floor—did not apply to supermarkets; they could get by with a cash point every 84 square metres. The difference reflected the jump in productivity brought by the new store-type. In Europe the supermarket spread first in the north-west; especially the UK, Belgium, and Denmark acted as forerunners during the 1950s.[109] Adopting the American-style supermarket also entailed taking over American principles for the locations of sales. Small self-service shops—in both the US and Europe—typically replaced the traditional shop at its original location. But supermarkets needed a considerable amount of space. In contrast to downtown department stores with several storeys, supermarkets usually had only one floor. At the same time they needed a car park, for a central part of supermarket shopping was using the family car. The large space requirements coupled with high property prices in city centres meant that supermarkets were located not in the city centre but along main access routes in urban outskirts. The supermarket thus advanced the geographical division of modern industrial society. At first only work was separated from residence, now shopping became separated as well.

Although the supermarket was based on the principle of self-service, it went much further. Self-service was one step in the destruction of the traditional personal commitment between shopkeeper and customer, but in relatively small shops such a relationship could be preserved to a certain extent. In contrast the supermarket created a huge gap between these two groups; the organization of the shop prevented any personal contact. The traditional European idea that the shopkeeper cares for the provisioning and well-being of his known customers hence was terminated not so much by self-service but by the establishment of supermarkets. In the supermarket, the alienation between management and customers was much more profound than in ordinary self-service shops. While in the latter the shopowner often continued to carry out all necessary tasks: work the cashpoint, arrange goods at the display, talk to customers, the manager of a supermarket had little or no contact with the store's customers. His task was to take care of the entire operation—supervise the heads of divisions (e.g. for fresh meat or non-food), look after the flow of supplies, or evaluate staff performance—in short, to organize and to manage. He no longer needed to be a good seller himself; his success was based on management skills. Logistics became much more important, as the following figures for a rather moderate-sized US supermarket in the late 1960s show: With an annual turnover of 1.5 million dollars, it handled 1500 tons of goods; the goods arrived in 2800 different deliveries; and four persons were needed to operate this part of the shop alone.

The supermarket not only revolutionized shopping, it also affected the structure of employment. Part-time work was not widespread in Europe before the arrival of the supermarket. In traditional shops full-time employment was the rule; in supermarkets often half of the personnel worked part-time. Owning and running a supermarket successfully clearly required a very different type of person than a traditional shopkeeper.

On their study trips to the US, European delegations and private persons were impressed by the wide range of products on offer in shops. It was much bigger than in Europe, and the number increased even further. In 1955 a typical US supermarket stocked 2200 different products, in 1960 4500, and by 1974 9000. The traditional shopkeeper offered a rather small range of goods with little or no choice for customers. The advantages of the limited assortment were obvious: less capital was tied up and less work needed for supervision, orders, accounting, and so forth. The conviction was that customers would cover their needs by buying what was on offer. Why offer a variety of brands of the same product? The European shopkeeper envisioned a customer as a person who bought necessities, and the shopkeeper's responsibility was to provide these required goods. The following personal experience in England as recently as 1979 illustrates this mentality. At the time my wife and I lived in a small village in East Anglia, and became known customers at the village grocery. When a nation-wide shortage of sugar occurred because of a transport strike, the village grocer behaved as just described. The normal storage location for sugar was empty, but the grocer informed us that he could provide us with "our pound of sugar" since we were regular customers. In other words, the grocer felt responsible for the provisioning of "his" people and consequently took direct control of his sugar supply. He refused to sell out his stock to whatever casual

customer might have entered the store in search of sugar. The traditional European
principle of food retailing was the shopkeeper's responsibility for the basic needs of
regular customers. The US principle of food retailing was much more dynamic: sell
the customer—regular or no—what can be sold, and satisfy the customer. It was the
approach of a market economy, in contrast to a system of allocation. It took quite a
long time before the European distribution sector understood that competition
between parallel brands did not lead to what was called *cannibalism* but to
additional sales in quality and quantity.

Supermarkets by definition included fresh vegetables, fresh meat, and other
fresh food. While today we take such products for granted, this was not always so.
In the 1950s many Europeans questioned whether fresh meat should be sold by self-
service, since the product's nature seemed incompatible with such a sales system.
Fresh meat, after all, had to be cut, prepacked, and displayed. Shopkeepers agreed
that fresh meat acted as a "magnet" for customers, but it could also generate
substantial losses because of its perishability. Food retailers were divided on the
issue. While the managers of some large foodstores considered the drawing power
of fresh meat was so important that they were prepared to write off constant losses
on the item, others maintained that the meat department had to fulfil the same
requirements of commerciability as other store departments, and consequently
hesitated with the introduction of fresh meat. In any case, all agreed that fresh meat
was by far a store's "most dangerous" department. The "danger" grew out of a)
fluctuating demand, b) quality and quality control, and c) packaging. The first
problem is illustrated by an admittedly extreme case.[110] In the 1960s there were
reports from Germany that Monday's turnover in meat was less than five per cent of
Saturday's. Such extreme swings in demand resulted in two large problems:
preserving the freshness of meat and organizing the working schedules of the
department's personnel. Even using part-time personnel such an uneven demand
was difficult to accommodate.

A second difficult for the sale of fresh meat in the early European
supermarket was the quality of the meat. In the 1950s the greatest demand was for
medium-quality meat. This placed the supermarket retailers in a quandary: their
system was based on sales by appearance and naturally medium-quality meat was
not as attractive as premium quality. Hence, even those retailers who were
convinced that fresh meat would be offered in the future were long reluctant start the
item. It is revealing that even enthusiastic pioneers such as Eklöh hesitated:

"... we think it is not entirely sound and fair to the handicraft of butchers, if we as
owners of large shops use our possibilities to subsidize the meat division from others,
and force down those prices on which a respected and competent profession has to live
on."[111]

Eklöh retreated to the traditional retailing mentality of *do not compete too
much*, and *live and let live with your competitor*. His remarks reveal the tenacity of
old habits and modes of behaviour even in persons deeply influenced by American
ways.

In the end all the difficulties just described were overcome in large part by the general rise in the standard of living. By the end of the 1960s many Europeans could afford to eat meat on other days than Sundays, and the day-to-day variation of meat sales of meat evened out. They also demanded higher quality meat, which looked better and thus was more appropriate for self-service sales.

The spread of American-style supermarkets also brought new items such as frozen food. In the United States frozen foods were introduced commercially in the 1930s and by the 1950s were widely available and encompassed both luxury and everyday items. Such foods entered European foodstores a decade later, in the first half of the 1960s. Though frozen food needed another new investment, the deep-freeze appliance, it had the great advantage of tolerating long periods of storage without spoilage. For the food retailer, then, the decision to stock frozen food should have been easy and straight-forward, just a question of investment and space. Yet many European shopkeepers were reluctant to take in frozen foods. The reason was that their customers hesitated to buy the product. First, it was a largely unknown method of presenting food and required somewhat different cooking procedures; second, frozen food was widely considered to be of lower quality than fresh food; and third, only very few customers had their own freezer at home, which meant that frozen food had to be consumed at once and its advantages for storage were thus unrealized. Under these conditions the majority of European consumers long preferred fresh food. Therefore it took some time for frozen food to penetrate the European food market. Not until the mid-1970s did nearly all groceries offer frozen food, which was a symbol of American food retail.

Subsequent developments in self-service retailing occurred roughly simultaneously in the United States and in Europe. On both continents large shopping centres in the suburbs became typical in the 1970s, and enormous hypermarkets first emerged in France. But there is no real European equivalent to Wall-Mart, the world's largest retailing enterprise, and there are still few European examples of the full-scale American shopping mall. At least in terms of the sheer size of self-service retailing the United States is still ahead of Europe.

OTHER DISTRIBUTIONAL INNOVATIONS: CHAINS, FRANCHISE, AND MAIL-ORDER FIRMS

Unlike self-service retailing, chain stores were not entirely American in origin; they were also known in Europe before 1945. For example, in 1934 the German chain *Thams & Garfs* commanded 1185 retail shops from its headquarters in Schwerin. While this common type of chain stores, owned by one person or institutional investor, was known, the Americans innovated the so-called voluntary chain. A voluntary chain is constituted by a group of shopkeepers who join together to enjoy the advantages of a large enterprise, without selling their own shop. Such voluntary chain stores have been typically initiated by wholesale traders. In creating a chain a wholesaling company could organize its own market, creating a network of shops to be delivered exclusively by itself. The shopkeeper-members of the chain are bound to buy only from the chain-wholesaler.

In the United States voluntary chains emerged in the 1920s, and their numbers increased especially during the depression of the 1930s when competition in retailing was especially tough. America's first voluntary chain—and up to the 1950s the country's biggest—the Red and White Corporation, was founded in 1921. It would appear that the time was just ripe for such an idea, for three persons in three states—S. M. Flickinger in New York, H. A. Marr in Colorado, and A. M. Scokum in Minnesota—arrived at the same idea independently. At first each set up his own chain, but when they learned of each other they merged to set up the Red and White Corporation. Other grocery chains soon followed; for example, the Independent Grocers' Alliance of America and Clover Farm Stores were both founded in 1926. In 1940 chains accounted for 24 per cent of food sales in the US, in 1955 55 per cent. The business advantages of such chains to individual members were substantial. It could act as its own wholesaler and thus could save much money in the purchasing of sale stock. Combining efforts in marketing and advertising, starting with a standardization of the shops' exterior, also reduced operating costs for individual owners. Further savings arose from adopting identical methods of calculating costs and income, coordinating job training, bookkeeping procedures, and so on. In addition a chain created a transferable customer loyalty that benefited all member stores.

The concept of the voluntary chain store did not take long to cross the Atlantic. One of the first European voluntary food retailing chains was founded in 1932 by a Dutch wholesaler, Adriann van Well, who explicitly followed the American model. In order to reduce start-up costs he used a previously registered trademark for the new chain. His original notion had been to sell just tea under the trademark, and the chief reason for extending the name to a retailing network was to save money. And "Save!" was indeed the trademark's key word. Thus began the SPAR grocery chain, now well known throughout Europe and the world. *Spar* is the Dutch word for fir tree, but it also means "*save!*" The symbol of the chain is still a fir tree, but for customers the term "*save!*" is of course more appealing. The trademark had wider advantages that were discovered later just by chance. When the SPAR chain expanded outside the Netherlands, it was discovered that the original Dutch word *spar* had the same meaning also in German and in the Scandinavian languages, which generated immediately common brand recognition in a market that was six times larger than the chain's home. The German and Scandinavian SPAR organizations were founded in the 1950s as independent networks; the Dutch parent organization did not invest in them, but gave advice for a long time. While the Dutch SPAR was designed after American models, the Scandinavians and Germans focused on the Dutch experience. But many internal operating procedures, such as the so-called "cost-plus" system of calculation, were taken directly from the United States, as were the common initiatives in public relations. The SPAR chains in toto are an example of a combination of direct and indirect Americanization in European merchandizing.

The same could be said for mail-order retailing. Such enterprises existed in Europe before 1945, but the United States was far and away the world's leader. In 1950, for example, Sears Roebuck's main warehouse in Chicago handled an astonishing 100,000 orders per day, more than many traditional shops carried out in their owner's life-time. In the United States even the most unlikely items, such as fresh eggs and horses, were successfully sold by mail-order! In connection with the Marshall Plan's Productivity Mission Europeans involved in mail-order retailing toured the US in the early 1950s. It is well documented how much the German mail-order company *Otto* or the Finnish *Kalle Anttila* learned on these visits, especially regarding organization and ways to lower operational costs. Other aspects of mail ordering, such as telephone order, were matters of the future, for in the 1950s many European homes lacked a telephone. For some time the European mail-order houses themselves lacked important technical apparatus such as punch card machines and later computers. The core of any mail-order business is detailed information about customers, their tastes and habits. American mail-order companies used the most advanced machinery available in order to react to changes in demand and even to anticipate them. Still more important than the expensive machines were the ideas, standards, proceedings, and routines on which they were constructed. In these areas European mail-order firms learned a lot from their American counterparts, even if they could not immediately implement it. Their visiting representatives gained insight into the future of the branch and into the thinking and behaviour needed to exploit the trend. Although the possibilities of instant transfer were small, the long-term impact was profound.

Strangely, British mail-order houses showed little interest in learning from the American experience. Three reasons may explain their reluctance. In the 1950s the British firms enjoyed growth rates of about 15 per cent; there was thus neither a pressing incentive to learn about new ideas nor a capacity to do so, since all organisations which grow at such a rapid pace have problems securing enough trained personnel. Furthermore, the British mail-order system was very differently organised than that of other countries. Easy transfers of non-British practices were consequently excluded. UK mail-order firms sold nine out of ten orders to agents, not to end customers. Agents were usually women, themselves customers of the enterprise, who generated sales by showing catalogues or sample products at their own home or in meeting halls in the neighbourhood. They also collected payment for mail-order shipments. These persons were experts in the technique of social selling. British mail ordering functioned as a social system based on personal contacts between the company's representative and potential customers. In contrast, American mail ordering was based on direct contact with each customer, with the company sending catalogues and goods directly. These profound differences presumably lay behind the long-standing British lack of interest in the American system. This attitude changed only when working-class clientele—the backbone of agent-mediated social selling—faded and the mail-order business sagged. Continental mail-order houses implemented American procedures in the 1960s; the British firms did not do so until the 1980s. The Continental companies learned the lessons of Americanization very well, and after perfecting it, some became more dynamic than their former teachers. In 2004 the previously mentioned German company, Otto, is the largest group of mail-order houses in the world.

In the late 1960s information about a new system of distribution reached European trade journals: franchise. The system of franchising was developed in the

United States in 1898 by the car manufacturer General Motors Corp., which sold individual dealers a license to sell and service the company's products. In the course of a few decades it became a widespread practice in American retail trade; and by the 1950s many chains such as McDonald's hamburger restaurants were based on it. In the franchise system one contractor, usually an individual person, provides the operational business site, while the other, usually a known company with recognized brands, gives an exclusive license to manufacture or sell and serve a named product or use the specific trademark for a designated period in return for a royalty on sales. Both firms stay independent and can, after the expiration of the contract, go their separate ways. The core idea of franchising is a long-term binding contract which can save both sides substantial amounts of capital. Although some American firms (e.g. Coca-Cola) had introduced franchising into Europe even before 1939, it was generally a little-known practice. Franchising contradicted traditional conceptions of ownership, responsibility, and longevity. In Europe similar contracts, such as those in voluntary chains, had no set time limits, and were often backed up by ownership. In 1969 the German trade journal *Blätter für Genossenschaftswesen,* in evaluating the concept of franchise, summed up a widespread European reserve: "Another step towards a contract-oriented market economy," which meant in other words, 'another step towards Americanization'.

One special sector, the distribution of petrol, became dominated by franchising—and thereby Americanized—right after the Second World War. Before 1945 European filling stations typically sold several competing brands of petrol simultaneously. Often a cheaper no-name brand was also offered. In the late 1940s the Standard Oil Company of New Jersey decided to break this practice by introducing franchising, which it had long practiced in the US. It offered certain filling stations in the UK special rebates, which bound the stations to sell only Standard Oil's "Esso" brand of petroleum products. The initiative succeeded and was immediately imitated by competing oil companies. Franchised petrol stations quickly spread through the Continent. Since most of the oil companies were American, franchising made it fairly easy to transfer practices first developed in US petrol stations. Today, filling stations in Europe, as in the US, sell newspapers, coffee, hamburgers, etc.; and it is commonly said that they make the least money from the sale of petrol and oil.

NEW HABITS, NEW MATERIALS, NEW TECHNOLOGIES

The traditional European mentality towards the consumption of materials emphasized saving and preserving. In most European residences up to the 1960s only the kitchen and perhaps the living room were heated during winter time, generally by coal-fired stoves. Sleeping rooms did not normally even have such facilities; instead hot-water bottles were used to warm the beds. All this meant that the consumption of energy per head or home was much lower than today. Workers lived near their working places in order to walk there; before the Second World War, for many workers even a daily use of the tram was beyond financial means.

Used glass jars were washed and kept to put home-made jam in. Holes in socks were darned. Worn-out pullovers were unravelled in order to re-use the wool to knit something new. Though the expression "to recycle" was not in use, the activity was in fact carried out many times each day. Farmers worked with horse-drawn machines and fed their animals home-grown fodder. Industry clustered near railway lines or canals in order to have easy access to coal supplies. All this was in tune with an economy where labour was relatively cheap and goods relatively expensive. Twenty-five years of rapid economic growth from 1950 changed all this profoundly. Labour became scarce—as in the US; after 1958 the EEC/EC/EU created a large internal market—as in the US; mass production and mass consumption developed— as in the US; and the world market offered cheap raw materials—as in the US. Consequently, European attitudes and behaviour became similar to American ones. Of course, variations and adaptations existed on many levels: European, national, regional, and local; such variations were to be found in the United States as well.

Europeans visiting the United States during the 1950s were impressed— some even shocked—by the profligate attitude of Americans regarding materials and energy. While Europe suffered from energy shortages of all kinds, in the United States even the most advanced fuels, petrol and diesel, were readily available and cheap at the same time. Mass production of goods and mass consumption of energy were linked. The touring Europeans learned that sales were more important than savings. They learned that they had to overcome their thrifty mentality to materials and energy if they wanted to enter the promised land of American-style prosperity. In the 1950s this new abundance could be used as an incentive to workers. Volkswagen's CEO, Heinrich Nordhoff, who otherwise deliberately copied American methods in car production, purposely hoarded raw materials and semi-finished products. But his idea was not to safeguard the production process against shortages; no, he was convinced employees would work faster if they had to pass stockpiles of raw materials as they entered the plant, and simultaneously saw that the parking area for finished cars ready for shipping was empty.

The shifting popular attitude to materials—to buy new rather than to preserve and repair—was soon reflected in the growing amount of waste. Up to the 1950s European dustbins, or ashbins, were typically rather small. Their main content was reflected in the name: dust, in the form of ash plus a few empty tins. The conversion of home heating from one or two individual stoves to central heating or electrical heating—a substantial improvement of living quality few wanted to miss once it was affordable—not only consumed more energy than previously, it also generated more waste. Used paper, wood, and other combustible material, which previously had gone into the stove, now ended up in the garbage. Used glass jars or glassware were increasingly discarded, as well as a totally new material, plastic. The amounts of waste swelled rapidly from year to year, quadrupling between the 1950s and the 1970. Waste represents a true indicator of the change of attitude towards the consumption of material and energy.

Changing energy sources in industry was not as straight-forward as in private residences. In *Opting for Oil*, Raymond Stokes has explained how deliberately and hesitantly the European chemical industry, for example, embarked on the use of oil, for it represented not just a simple change in heating technology;

once done, there was no way back; it meant 'burning the ships'. Up to 1939 the world's chemical industry used coal as both fuel and raw material. During the war and immediately following, the American chemical industry switched to oil. Germany's chemical producers, which earlier had been foremost in the world, had to decide whether to follow suit. Continuing with coal meant continuing known and chemically well-described processes, using known technologies, in well-proven apparatus staffed by a skilled workforce who knew their jobs. Furthermore, using coal obviated supply shortages, since there was more than enough coal in Europe. In contrast, the technology for oil-based processes was new and had to be obtained mainly from American firms. Its implementation required capital investments that were several times larger than comparable coal technology. This in turn meant higher financial exposure, re-training of personnel, and a re-direction of R&D. Switching to oil-based technology also lowered the scientific self-esteem of chemists—all leading managers of German chemical enterprises used to be chemists—and damaged their pride; the chemistry of coal was well known and largely German-based, whereas the chemistry of oil was not yet similarly scientifically established. Moreover, in the 1950s there were few known oil reserves in Europe, so opting for oil meant creating a dependency on overseas supplies, supplies which at the time were largely controlled by the United States. Finally, because the profitability of oil-based technology depended on high output, the German chemical producers would be compelled to compete on a world scale directly against American firms. Their established instruments of cooperation, regulation, and cartelization would no longer be appropriate. Consequently, they felt that opting for oil would place the German chemical industry at the mercy of American competitors. In short, coal stood for security and stability; oil meant risk but also dynamism. Continuing with coal was traditionalist, opting for oil innovative, entailing a total change of technology and mentality. At the beginning of the 1950s the entire European chemical industry stood at these crossroads. In the German case we know that managers understood how far-reaching their decision would be. The tension of the decision was especially high for German, Austrian, and to a certain extent Italian managers, because the switch implied placing their respective enterprises structurally at the mercy of the United States, with which their countries had been at war only a few years earlier. Yet in spite of these uncertainties all major producers went over to the new technology, and those that did not, or changed too late, ceased to be major producers. In short, the European chemical industry opted for Americanization.

Many new technologies were imported into Europe after World War II, and historians of science and technology have published extensively about these transfers. Two of the most promising new technologies after 1945 were nuclear energy for power generation and information technology (IT). IT did not mature until the 1980s, so it will be dealt with in chapter 5. Here the focus will be on nuclear power, or atomic energy.

The first nuclear reactors used commercially combined the generation of electric power and the production of plutonium, which was used for weapons. These reactors were thus under military surveillance, and reactor technology was considered a military secret. But in the course of the 1950s the coupling of civilian and military purposes weakened, enabling transfers of the technology to other countries. All major European firms producing electrical equipment recognized that nuclear power generation would be an important source of future profits. At the same time all were dependent on technological transfer from the US. This applied especially to companies outside Britain, above all to the French Framatome, the Swedish ASEA, the Swiss BBC, and the German firms Siemens and AEG, all of which became main contractors in the construction of nuclear power plants.

The Siemens involvement is the best documented. In the early twentieth century Siemens established a close relationship based on patent exchange with the American Westinghouse company. During the Second World War the relationship was cancelled, but Siemens succeeded in renewing its ties with Westinghouse after 1950, and the two once again signed a contract on the exchange of patents in 1954. At that time patents related to nuclear power generation were not included for political reasons, but some years later they were included in an amendment. Westinghouse concentrated on the development of pressurized water reactor technology. This type of nuclear power generation demonstrated its excellence when in 1957 the first large plant of this kind went critical at Shippingport, Pennsylvania. Siemens embarked on the production of the same type of reactor and transferred substantial technological know-how from Westinghouse. Siemens tested alternative types of reactor, but its commitment to pressurized water technology predominated. By 1970 it no longer needed Westinghouse's assistance in the sector, and cancelled the patent exchange contract. A few years later Siemens merged its power generation division with that of AEG, which had acquired its nuclear power technology from General Electric. Together the two German companies produced nuclear power plants during the 1980s that were world leaders in reliability, measured in kilowatt hours produced and uninterrupted time online.

France became Europe's leader in the development of nuclear power generation. The French government, pushed by political and military considerations, intervened heavily in the sector and concentrated nuclear power generation in the state-owned electricity utility, Electricité de France (EdF). Nevertheless, American influence in the sector was substantial. EdF ordered all its nuclear power plants—the first of which went critical in 1970—from a single constructor, Framatome. In the following decade Framatome constructed no fewer than 34 plants of the same design, a 900 megawatt-version of the pressurized water reactor technology licensed from Westinghouse, which also owned 30 per cent of the French company. When the licensing agreement came up for renewal in 1981, Westinghouse conceded that Framatome was capable of designing its own reactor. This was confirmed in 1984 when EdF ordered its first totally French-designed nuclear power reactor.

As in several other areas, nuclear power technology in the UK initially went its own way and led the world in gas-graphite reactors. In the 1960s it went over to American pressurized water technology, when this technology was more available. In sum, with the partial exception of the British, all major European enterprises engaged in the construction of nuclear power plants initially depended on the transfer from American technology. From the second half of the 1960s this dependency petered out as European-produced technology matured.

Remarkably, the question of Americanization in the armament industry has been little researched. Surely there was a massive transfer, but information about it is scarce. One of the most ambitious projects was the European construction of the American F-104 fighter plane. The Lockheed F-104 was designed as a good-weather interceptor, and the US Air Force originally ordered 722 planes. It cut this order to less than 300, after being disappointed in the plane's active performance. Nonetheless, the F-104 won the contest for a major order for an all-weather fighter-bomber for the German air force in 1958. One of the order's conditions was that 210 planes had to be built in Germany. Similar deals with Belgium and Italy followed suit, and in 1960 a licensing agreement was concluded for international cooperation on a major scale. The Europeans regarded the F-104 as the vehicle to learn about the newest airplane technology in order to build up their own aviation industry. Thus the F-104 became the backbone of west European air forces during the 1960s and well into the 1970s. However, construction ran into deep troubles because the transfer of knowledge needed to produce the aircraft turned out to be more complex than anticipated. An US engineer involved in the transfer process summed up a central difficulty:

> "We need standard parts to a millionth-of-an-inch tolerance for this unit. These people in Europe have fine tools and equipment, they can make parts to tolerance; but for them – up till now – it has been laboratory stunt. They make one part; we are making them by the thousands. But it took us ten years to learn how. The Europeans can learn how, too, but it will take a couple of years."[112]

The Europeans were disappointed with the technology transfer, and later with the plane, too. Up to 50 per cent of all F-104s crashed because of technical problems. Yet for the European aircraft industry the construction of an advanced US fighter plane was a major contribution in developing its own technological competence in aeronautics.

A notable failure of Americanization in this area, on the other hand, was the US-German cooperation in tank design. The German-made tank "Leopard II", which became the standard tank in many west European armies in the 1980s, began as an American-German co-project in the 1960s. A variety of political and technological conflicts led to the termination of the cooperation in 1970, but the German developers continued, retaining many of the earlier project's specifications. Later the Leopard II became the economic main competitor in west European armies against the US-made Abrams tank.

CONCLUSION: THE EMERGENCE OF A EUROPEAN MASS MARKET

On the macroeconomic level Americanization proceeded by a combination of European imitation and American pressure. American firms impressed not only by their technology and organization but by their pure size. European firms attempted to imitate such magnitudes by buying up smaller competitors and consolidating. Fiat's takeover of Alpha Romeo and Lancia is a good example, and similar mergers occurred in the French, German or British automobile industry.

Consolidation took place in nearly all branches of industry, but only on a national scale, and the emergence of the European Economic Community did not change this national preference. Therefore only very few European firms came to match their American competitors in size.

Direct American influence was exerted by US subsidiaries in Europe. Their example taught European firms much, especially in the area of modern business management, e.g. the use of consultancies to implement major changes within the enterprise. By going to external agencies for professional advice European enterprise departed from long-standing business practice in this special area. Severing traditional ties with house banks or tax advisers in favour of a new professional organization represented an important step in the European acceptance of Americanization.

European adoption of American ideas about decartelization, however, occurred only gradually and after considerable US pressure. In the first decade after 1945 only Germany and Austria became strictly decartelized, and that was due to US intervention against their own will. The positive attitude towards cartels dwindled as the European economy recovered and prospered. The founding document of the EEC, signed in 1957, signalled the shift by incorporating a strict anti-cartel provisions, a policy that was taken over by individual states first in northern Europe and somewhat later in southern Europe. Despite its slowness, the shift away from cartels was a profound transformation of the business mentality that had dominated the Europe since industrialization. Cartels and their underlying idea of economic cooperation were long considered beneficial not only for the respective interest group, but also for the country as a whole. To renounce cartels meant giving up a traditional instrument of national economic policy and opening up the national economy to the dominance of competitive market forces. Thus, in abandoning cartels and preferring competition over cooperation European political and business leaders concurred in a fundamental principle of the American economic model.

The spread of American-style mass production from the 1950s did not immediately change the consumer habits of Europeans. There were several reasons for this: 1) mass production was a not completely new practice; it already existed in a few sectors; 2) the production-oriented mentality of mass production was also already present in much European business, so to produce larger quantities and more continuously was not a big change; and 3) the booming demand for goods meant that mass production could be introduced without a symmetrical investment in distribution. Given this background European producers could afford for some time to distinguish between low-quality mass production and high-quality batch production. The American combination of quality product and mass product was strange and had to be learned. For instance, when it opened its first restaurants in England, McDonald's was criticized for lowering food standards; low prices and high sales had to mean a low-quality product. English competitors hated McDonald's not so much for its additional competition but because it spoiled customers' tastes.

American-style mass distribution, however, had a quicker and much more profound impact. A number of the principles of mass distribution, especially in the sale of food, were quite alien to European shopkeepers and consumers. In this area

Americans could teach Europe not only once or twice, but again and again. The introduction of self-service, supermarkets, shopping by car, frozen- and prepacked foods were innovations that brought deep-going changes to the individuals concerned. Self-service and the supermarket re-defined the role of the shopkeeper. It changed from being an individual customer adviser, a full-blooded seller, to being a manager who primarily took care of logistics, finances, and personnel in the respective shop. Self-service re-defined shopping. It was no longer a social activity with an economic purpose, but a purely business activity. The personal and social dimensions of sales contacts were reduced to the economic dimension of the cashpoint—a commercialization of everyday life.

These developments also redefined the role of the housewife. Both she and her family had to learn and accept that investing less time in cooking by using pre-packed, frozen, or even processed food did not mean less affection for her family. The supermarket changed attitudes to shopping even further. Traditionally, most Europeans lived very near to their food shop. It was possible to fetch some salt, sugar, fresh milk, or other items that might be urgently needed for meal preparation by just going around the corner. Buying at a supermarket was different. It entailed planning with shopping lists, the upkeep of a much larger domestic food supply than previously, and most importantly the availability of a car. In bringing a far-reaching commercialization of the roles of both shopkeepers and consumers, the supermarket has been a potent instrument of Americanization.

The strong growth of the European economy between 1950 and 1975 naturally promoted the importation of new technologies from the more advanced United States. These transfers—in nuclear energy, military technology, electronics, numerical control, etc.—entailed a short-term Americanization, which petered out when the transfer slowed down as a result of growing European competence in the respective field. In contrast, the importation of American patterns in the consumption of energy and raw materials has had lasting effects. Europeans traditionally saved both, but the combination of mass production, booming demand, and very low oil prices made this tradition of thrift redundant and the American practice of profligacy attractive. However, American consumption levels were never fully realized in Europe. Energy was relatively cheap, but not as cheap as in the US, and in European as a whole the unconcerned use of raw materials and energy never became really accepted. It was not by accident that the Club of Rome, a global think tank founded in 1968 to raise questions about the relationship between the modern industrial economy and the environment, was created in Europe and not in the United States. The timing of its critique—its first report *The Limits of Growth* appeared in 1972—was not by accident either. By that time Europeans had learned and taken over a lot from the United States; the gap in income and productivity, in know-how and technology had narrowed. In some cases the Europeans even had overtaken their American teachers. At the beginning of the 1970s Michelin's steel belted radial tires, Framatome's nuclear power stations, and VW's home-made robots were superior to what was on offer in the United States. European consultancies, supermarkets and mail-order houses could compete successfully against American companies on the world market. Thus the incentives to adopt the

American way were no longer evident, and the post-war wave of Americanization
ebbed.

CHAPTER 4

MANAGING FIRMS AND THEIR CONSUMERS

The macroeconomic transformation of the European economy in the post-war boom was paralleled by substantial changes at the microeconomic level, that is, the internal running of firms and their relations to their markets. Many of these changes—such as management training, marketing research, and advertising—were logical corollaries of American FDI, mass production, and mass distribution. In short, these changes in microeconomic behaviour were a part of the ongoing Americanization of European economic life.

EDUCATION FOR BUSINESS MANAGEMENT

Formal education in business management is largely the product of modern industrial capitalism. Before the last two decades of the nineteenth century managerial skills were typically acquired by a combination of ad-hoc experience and in-house training. To be sure, secondary-level commercial schools emerged in several countries from ca. 1850s, but their primary purpose was to train clerical staff in bookkeeping, arithmetic, commercial law, business correspondence (including handwriting), and foreign languages. Post-secondary-level schools devoted to the study of economic affairs or business management in its various guises began to emerge in the 1880s, and a rapid expansion occurred in both Europe and the United States in the two decades preceding the First World War. The world's first collegiate/university-level business school was established in 1881 at the University of Pennsylvania: the Wharton School, named after its founding benefactor Joseph Wharton. Similar programmes were started at the University of California and The University of Chicago in 1898, the universities of Wisconsin and Michigan, New York University, and Dartmouth College in 1900–01, followed by Harvard University in 1908, Columbia University in 1916, and Stanford University in 1926, along with many others. The chronology of establishment of European higher education in business management and economics is broadly similar. A single foundation in Paris in 1881 (Ecole de Commerce, the precursor to l'Ecole des Hautes Etudes Commerciales) was followed by a spate of establishments in the two decades after 1898: for example, Leipzig, Vienna, London, and St Gallen (Switzerland) in 1898, Cologne in 1901, Milan in 1902, Solvay Business School (Belgium) in 1903, Helsinki, Stockholm, and Mannheim in 1909, Copenhagen in 1917, and Nürnberg in 1919.

Yet the similarity in chronology and appellation did not mean that these institutions were alike in purpose, content, or method of instruction. In general three different models of educating business managers emerged: the German, the Latin, and the American.[113] Initially the German type was the most influential one throughout north-west Europe and Scandinavia. In the German model of management education occurred at two institutions of higher education, institutes of engineering (*Technische Hochschulen*) and institutes of commercial studies (*Handelshochschulen*), both of which were located outside the traditional universities. The first stressed production technologies, and trained engineers, chemists, and the like. The second trained its students in the systematic science of the business enterprise. Additionally business or trade schools at the secondary level were established to teach future middle-level personnel accounting, business administration, financing, and other basic commercial skills. Whatever the level, all training was focused on the microeconomic level. The guiding idea was that microeconomic production runs the economy.

The Latin model, found in France, Italy, and Spain, focussed on law, economics, and the general administration of organizations. The French version was built on the tradition of the *grandes écoles,* which graduated a small elite who filled top jobs in both the private and the public sector. The model's guiding idea was that the economy runs according to law and political direction. The schools had no permanent staff and did not teach systematic business management. Their main function was to provide a mechanism of social selection, by competitive examination, of the country's future political and economic leaders.

The American model of management education, by contrast, was from the outset a part of the general system of higher education in the United States. It focussed on generalized business leadership and management with a stress on practical decision-making under market conditions. In addition to training students in accounting and business financing, American business schools incorporated subjects such as advertising and marketing into their curricula from early on. The emphasis on educating middle and top management in this system is typified by the establishment of the postgraduate degree of Master of Business Administration (MBA) in the 1910–20s. The MBA became emblematic of American management education, and an entry ticket (nowadays nearly obligatory) to top managerial positions in American industry. The underlying idea of the American system was that good business leadership was best founded on a microeconomic perspective of the enterprise in general and not on specialized technical knowledge. In 1924 the Harvard Business School introduced the system's perhaps most characteristic instructional expression: the case method using real (or simulated) examples of business problems and managerial decision-making. But the American system of management education involved more than practical training; like other university teachers, business school professors were expected to engage in scientific research and publish their results in academic journals and the like. Although scientific management was initially developed outside any formal system of managerial education, the concept became a core of the ethos of the American business school.

The spread of rationalization, Taylorism, and Fordism and the general growth of big business in the interwar period underscored the importance of industrial management in the modern world economy and encouraged representatives from the three models of business school and management education to exchange information about their respective activities. To promote such exchange they founded a *Comité International de l'Organisation Scientifique* in Paris in the early 1930s. The committee ceased work during the war, but in 1947 it resumed its earlier activity of organizing a congress every three years. The information about the practices of American business schools received at these congresses may have been stimulating to European participants but it was not necessarily immediately convincing. As Robert Locke has shown, how individual European countries reacted to and absorbed American ideas on business management education largely depended on their respective educational systems.

American managers and educators had few doubts about the superiority of the US model of management education. In the post-war reconstruction of European economies they eagerly urged their model on European colleagues, a fact which has led Guiliana Gemelli to speak of an "American invasion" and a "big push".[114] During the government-sponsored Productivity Mission of the early 1950s and later with the help of the Ford Foundation American business schools consciously undertook to export their educational and instructional model to Europe.

Business schools in the Scandinavian countries successively took over American ideas, but without doing away with their traditional approach. A key element in the transfer was the attitude of professoriate of the respective schools. During the 1950s nearly all of the teaching personnel, with American financial support, studied in the United States for some time. From this experience teachers introduced alterations in the curriculum in their respective business schools. Yet the old model was not easily overturned. Sometimes completely new institutions were needed. The *Institutet för Företagsledning* (institute of management), founded in Stockholm in 1968, deliberately copied the American model, including case method of instruction. However, specific Scandinavian features soon emerged even at this school. There developed a special cooperation and trust between the school and enterprise. Professors and representatives of companies worked together as teachers in project groups. A lot of firm-specific knowledge, some of which could even be qualified as enterprise-specific advantages directly related to profits, was communicated. Such openness went far beyond the US model and in fact even surprised visiting American instructors.

American managerial practices could also be introduced by individual intervention. In Norway, for example, they were applied directly in individual enterprises, bypassing existing schools of business management. The person largely responsible for this introduction was the American George Kenning, a one-time trade unionist who had succeeded in moving into business management. In 1954 Kenning, who was then personnel manager at the GM factory in Antwerp, was invited to Norway by the Norwegian Productivity Institute as part of the US-funded programme for industrial training. In contrast to other American advisors who often remained no more than a few days, Kenning stayed in Norway for some time and exercised considerable influence among the country's business leaders. He had constructed a system of 35 theses, which represented a coherent system for hierarchical authority within any organization. The system was quite inflexible, if not to say authoritarian: workers had only to obey. Still, it expressed a central tenet of the managerial philosophy behind the American MBA: it is more important to be an expert in general management than to be an expert in a specific functional field. Although Kenning's system was adopted only by a minority of Norway's companies, it was a substantial minority. At first glance it is difficult to understand

Kenning's success in the Norwegian environment, which was largely characterized by cooperation and engineers in top management. However, it was perhaps facilitated by a widespread anti-intellectualism in shipping circles and in the social democratic movement as well as the general conservatism of Norwegian business management. Kenning's system appealed especially to a new generation of managers, who took over decisive posts during the decade between 1955 and 1965.

The impact of American management ideas in Scandinavia can also be seen in the changing terminology of business communications. Linguistic research has clearly established a causal connection between ideas and the use of related concepts and key words. Such an analysis has recently been undertaken in Norway to identify signs of Americanization. The study examined the use of key words, such as scientific management, in the official communications of several firms in different branches of industry (timber, sweets, oil) in the four decades between 1950 and 1990.[115] Individual terms were assigned weights and usage scores were tallied over the period of investigation. The results partly confirmed expectations, but they also gave new insights: 1) All of the firms knew about American management methods; they partly reflected its American origins, and they applied it in their enterprise. 2) The impact of American managerial practices (and terminology) was substantial as early as the 1950s. 3) The influence of American methods fluctuated; it was especially high during the late 1950s and early 1960s and again during the late 1980s. 4) The level of American influence in the various branches of business varied little even though they included export-oriented firms as well as companies selling only on the national market. Unfortunately there are no similar studies for other countries, but from known general structures elsewhere we can presume that these findings are fairly representative, at least in northern Europe.

The first European business school to adopt the American model of management education completely was the *Instituto Postuniversitario di Organizzazione Aziendale* (IPSOA management school) in Italy. It was established in 1952 on the initiative of Adriano Olivetti (Olivetti) and Vittorio Valetta (FIAT), who had become convinced of the necessity of such a school while attending a conference organized by the National Management Council in New York City. IPSOA was an unadulterated copy of the Harvard Business School's programme. It was lively, democratic, action-oriented, and pragmatic. It was also largely isolated in its Italian setting. Attempts to network with the country's traditional-minded universities failed early; even more importantly, it also failed to establish a working relationship with Italian companies. So instruction at IPOSA had to rely on cases taken over from Harvard. IPSOA's isolation forced the school to close in 1964 (it was revived later). The school's initial failure partly reflected the negative attitude of traditional higher education in Italy towards management education, but it was also a classic example of the inherent difficulty of institutional transfer without adaptation. The negativism gradually faded during the 1980s, and in the 1990s American-style MBA training began to flourish. But according to Giuliana Gemelli the real challenge for Italian management education at the beginning of the twenty-first century is not the further spread of the American model but the adaptation of that model to the much more flexible structures of Italian business.[116]

A similar creation in France was much more successful. A few months after the signing of the Treaty of Rome in 1957 the *Institut Européen d'Administration des Affaires*, European Institute of Business Administration, better known as INSEAD, opened its doors in Fontainebleau near Paris. The foundation was to a large extent the brainchild of a single person, Georges Frederic Doriot. Like Kenning, Doriot exemplifies the role of individuals in the dynamics of transfer. The French-born Doriot entered Harvard Business School (HBS) as a student in 1921; five years later, only 27 years old, he was hired by HBS to teach industrial management and simultaneously appointed one of the school's assistant deans. Convinced of France's need for modern management education, Doriot convinced the chamber of commerce in Paris to establish a small training centre in 1930, the *Centre de Préparation aux Affaires* (CPA). During the Second World War he served in the US Army and was an energetic and effective Chief of the Military Planning Division in the Office of the Quartermaster General, rising to the rank of Brigadier General. After the war Doriot successfully lobbied American and French political and economic leaders to establish an American-style school of business management in his native country. The timing and setting were propitious, and within a short time INSEAD became one of the leading business schools in Europe.

Several factors contributed to INSEAD's success. Doriot's long-standing and close connections with both HBS and American government and business leadership enabled the mobilization of financial resources and political goodwill in the United States. INSEAD received substantial donations from American firms, the European Productivity Agency, and the Ford Foundation. But Doriot also succeeded in securing high-level support for INSEAD from French political, business, and educational leaders, thus preventing the isolation that had stymied IPSOA's development. An institution of higher education in modern methods of business management and economic leadership fit in well with the French government's post-war plans to modernize the country and overhaul its central institutions. That several of the young activists in the powerful French planning authority (*Commissariat Général du Plan*), such as Pierre Uri, a trusted co-worker of both Jean Monnet and Robert Schuman, were graduates of the Doriot-initiated CPA undoubtedly also smoothed the acceptance of the new institution. Moreover, INSEAD's stated combination of European as well as French orientation enabled it to benefit from the prevailing enthusiasm for the new European Economic Community (EEC).

Generally, both French universities and their elitist counterparts, the Grandes Écoles, were slow to take up American-style management education. But there was an important exception. In 1957, the same year INSEAD opened, the venerable *École des Hautes Études Commerciales* (HEC), following US visits of several of its staff, decided to transform itself into a school of business administration along American lines.[117] It introduced a three-year curriculum patterned on the American Bachelor of Arts degree (BA): during the first year general studies and introduction into management studies; during the second year more advanced management studies and courses about the nature of the firm; and during the third year a special management project focused on one enterprise. The teaching methods were taken over from the Columbia Business School in New York: 40 per cent lectures; 20 per cent discussion after lectures; 20 per cent case studies; and 20 per cent seminars. From 1967 HEC accepted engineers seeking management education and a year later it introduced computer programming. In 1969 it also initiated an MBA programme. Thus, HEC, in contrast to other Grandes Écoles, produced candidates for top management, educated according to American managerial philosophy and techniques. However, HEC and the other Grandes Écoles lacked the substantial research facilities and tradition found in American business schools, most of which had become postgraduate institutions after 1945. The lack of research meant that presentations were primarily based on second- or third-hand material. The direct connection to enterprises that was an integral part of training in US management schools was lacking for many years.

Up to the Second World War French universities taught economics in the faculty of law, emphasizing institutional studies and trade law. During the 1950s economics was detached from law and in 1960 a separate licentiate in economics was established. In addition, *Instituts d'Administration des Entreprises* (institutes of business studies) were introduced at several universities. The slow growth of these institutes was speeded up by the students' revolt in 1968. As a part of a massive reform of university education the number of staff in business studies was increased, and many of them (210 between 1969 and 1972) sent to the United States to imbibe American methods of management education. Thus, France, which commonly is the European country most critical towards the United States, came to have a system of business education that was heavily Americanized. Still it was a broken Americanization. Graduates of the traditional Grandes Écoles, who were only to a small extent confronted with American methods and philosophy, continued to dominate top managerial positions. HEC and INSEAD, with their smaller number of graduates, could not substantially dint this dominance. Nor could the partly Americanized university institutes of business; their graduates qualified mainly for positions in middle management.

In the UK up to the 1950s the prevailing attitude was that running a business ordinarily did not require a specialized education. This changed with the Robbins Report of 1963 on higher education, headed by the economist Lionel Robbins, which proposed the development of university-level instruction in business management. The report's proposal was supplemented by the readiness of the US Ford Foundation to offer to subsidize the establishment of business schools both inside and outside existing universities. The London School of Economics, Imperial College of the University of London, and Warwick University were among those that took up the offer. The resulting programmes were a mixture of the British industrial engineering and accounting tradition and American management ideas. The impact of the highly selective adoption of the American model was also small for many years. In the early 1990s only two per cent of the directors of British incorporated companies had an MBA.

The case of Belgium illustrates the often difficult relations between the business and university communities concerning the formal education of managers. To 1945 there was almost no contact; the relationship that emerged in the post-war years can generally be characterized as an Americanization. Once again, the change depended largely on the vision and activity of a single person, Gaston Deurinck. Deurinck graduated from the University of Leuven in 1947 and pursued further studies in the United States. During the US Productivity Mission he organized the Belgian Productivity Centre as part of the Federation of Belgian Industrialists. In 1953 he convinced the country's universities to set up the Inter-University Programme of Business Administration, run by five professors acquainted with American methods of managerial training, for the purpose of providing university-level preparation for middle and top managers. Overcoming an initial scepticism towards Deurinck's project, several leading Belgian industrialists created the Industry-University Foundation in 1956 to support management education. But as in Britain, the development of American-style business training in Belgium relied heavily on support from the Ford Foundation. In the mid-1960s of the role of universities in management education was again questioned by a number of prominent businessmen. The universities' response was to redouble their efforts in the area. From 1969 university departments of economics offered complete MBA programmes, taught in English and based on American management literature. The strategy of increasing Americanization succeeded in regaining the widespread support of the country's industrial community.

Before 1945 the German model of business education was the most fully established European alternative to the American model. Thus, it was predictable that it put up the strongest resistance to Americanization; Robert Locke even labelled the resistance "German obstinacy". Down to the substantial re-structuring of German higher education in the late 1960s training for business management remained the preserve of the *Handelshochschulen* (business colleges). One new foundation in the area in 1956, the *Akademie für Führungskräfte* (Academy for Managers) in the small town of Bad Harzburg, organized business seminars for active managers and offered a diploma. But its short and ad-hoc programme, although very popular, was in no way an equivalent of an MBA.

The slow establishment of modern management education in Germany was a product of the traditional view of the place of the university. As in many European countries, German universities defined themselves as centres for scientific research rather than professional training. And for the traditionalists there simply existed no scientific theory of management. This standpoint was (and still is) founded on an exalted notion of what constitutes "theory" or "science", whereas the American notion of these terms tends to be quite pragmatic. This difference hampered and delayed the introduction of American ideas into German university education. It also had practical, economic consequences for the country's higher-education graduates. In the German system a person's career path and salary were largely determined by the type of educational institution attended and graduated from: specialized school, college, or university. These distinctions were lessened by the reforms of the 1960s and 1970s, which redefined most of the colleges (*Hochschulen*) as universities, but they were not entirely eliminated. Both processes, the adaptation of American-style attitudes and procedures and the redefinition of college status took time; even the internationally known business college in St. Gallen, one of the most American-influenced institutions of higher education in Switzerland, did not attain university status until 1994.

In the German tradition management training was not generalized but specialized; it was always strictly attached to a defined task in a specific place. As

Locke and Schöne have shown, it distinguished two types of qualification: *berufsfähig* (capable of work) and *berufsfertig* (ready for work). While the first could be achieved at an educational institution, the latter could be achieved only through on-the-job training. *Betriebswirtschaftslehre* (BWL, or business economics) was taught at colleges and universities in a theoretical way, to school the student's mind. BWL consisted mainly of accounting and the elaboration of a coherent scientific system to describe the enterprise and its environment. Passage of final examinations rendered graduates *berufsfähig*. Training for practical business was left to non-academic personnel, and only after such training, usually within enterprise, did BWL graduates become *berufsfertig*. BWL professors typically cared little about the relevance of their teaching for practical issues as long as their research added to the corpus of scientific knowledge. Neither marketing nor advertising fit in and were therefore neglected. After 1945 operational research (OR) was added to the BWL curriculum, but its weight was minor. Predictably, practicing business managers complained that BWL was impractical, but since they also believed in the central value of on-the-job training, their pressure to modernize the curriculum remained limited. Modernization of the field was also held up by the dismissive attitude of German economists towards BWL. For university economists macroeconomics, the study of national economics and national income, was both more demanding and more important; the microeconomic focus of BWL was considered little more than an assembly of common-sense rules. Hence, the professional status of both professors and students of BWL in Germany was low. The traditional attitudes of business and professional economists combined to block the transition to a more practice-oriented, Americanized managerial education in Germany for many years.

During the post-war boom, then, the transfer of Americanized education for business management to Europe varied considerably from country to country. The transfer of American educational approaches in other fields that had a direct role in business operations, such as the training of engineers, was even more limited. There is, however, one major exception: chemical engineering. Before World War II this occupation—combining equally chemistry, engineering, and industrial management—was little known in Europe. Germany was the leading European producer of chemicals, and the most venerable leader in the industry, Carl Duisberg, openly rejected chemical engineering. Duisberg and like-minded colleagues believed that research chemists should determine the productive operations of the chemical industry; mechanical engineers in chemical firms were subordinated to the chemists. Duisberg's opinion reflected the dominant production processes of Germany's chemical industry at the time. The control of chemical reactions differs according to size and timing of production. Relatively small-scale, discontinuous production of fine chemicals in batch reactors did not need the technical-managerial expertise of the chemical engineer, but mass-scale, continuous output of basic industrial chemicals did. Since the American chemical industry from the 1890s became a world leader in the production of basic industrial chemicals, especially in the application of new electrolytic technologies, it also was quick to embrace the field of chemical engineering. The Massachusetts Institute of Technology (MIT) established the first programme in chemical engineering in 1888 and three MIT professors published the standard text for modern chemical engineering instruction in 1923. Demand for the field grew rapidly; by 1930 it had 30,000 students throughout the country. The field's links with industrial management emerged early. One of the leading advocates of chemical engineering and the codifier of its key concept of "unit operations", the MIT-educated chemist Arthur D. Little, had a simultaneous career as an engineering and management consultant, and his company, Arthur D. Little Inc., is nowadays one of the world's largest management consulting agencies.

The European, and specifically German, neglect of chemical engineering persisted into the 1950s. But the shift from coal-based production to petroleum-based production made the field decisive for the survival of the chemical industry. The value of elegant chemical reactions, the pride and glory of the research chemists, was depreciated; the priority now was maximum throughput. Consequently, American textbooks in chemical engineering were translated, and training programmes adapted to fit the new demands. Into the 1960s a substantial part of American superiority in the chemical industry rested on the education and the availability of chemical engineers.

Although the reception of American management education in post-war Europe was mixed, no country escaped its influence. Huibert de Man's summing up of the Dutch system can be extended to the whole of Europe: the respective faculties took over American subject matter, but did not adopt the educational philosophy on which it rested. Thus, American management education never acquired a cultural hegemony during this period. Moreover, its influence even declined during the 1970s and 1980s. Robert R. Locke has even argued in his *The Collapse of the American Management Mystique* (1996) that American-style management contributed significantly to the relative deterioration of American competitiveness in the aftermath of the post-war boom!

INTERNAL RE-ORGANIZATION OF ENTERPRISE: MARKETING AND DIVISIONALIZATION

One of the core subjects of the curriculum at American business schools was marketing, whose importance and content grew in direct proportion with the development of mass production and mass distribution in the modern capitalist economy. Although the fundamental spirit of marketing has a long heritage, modern marketing as it was developed in the United States involved a new, comprehensive way of defining the enterprise and the relationship between the market and the company. According to the traditional understanding of the producer-consumer relationship, especially influential in European business, a company first manufactured a good and then proceeded to find a buyer for it. The process of production and distribution was dominated by a supply-side point of view. Marketing, however, defines the relationship from the other side: first a potential demand is established, and after that a product is designed and manufactured to meet that demand. That is, the relation between selling and buying is viewed from the demand side. Since the demand has been established through marketing research, it is an easy and logical step to go beyond finding out what consumers want, suggesting to them additional desires by the use of advertising and other means of persuasion. Initially marketing entered business management because it was a more comprehensive concept than sales. But it took decades before marketing was understood to be more than a collection of practices completing production, that it entailed a redefinition of the firm itself. Since American business led this development, the country remained the world centre of marketing throughout the twentieth century.

During the 1950s marketing mainly meant finding the optimal combination of sales instruments within the given firm. At the same time, "American marketing science" started to incorporate the methods of the empirical social sciences, such as depth interviewing, to determine consumer behaviour. European marketing theorists and practitioners have often tried to fix the development of marketing to an earlier date; some even date the beginnings back to the turn of the century. Georg Bergler, a pioneer German marketing specialist at Nürnberg Handelshochschule, asserted in 1958 that the new term "marketing" designated essentially what he and his colleagues had labelled the "primacy of turnover" three decades earlier. What Bergler overlooked was that only a handful of persons with little influence understood the concept in that way at the time. By contrast, the introduction of marketing in the 1950s was a broad movement affecting many enterprises simultaneously. The motto of the First Congress for Sales and Marketing in Germany in 1958—"From sales to marketing"—summed up what was happening throughout Europe. The congress's report stated that "marketing was no longer a foreign word.... Marketing proved to be an adequate link uniting the terms of turnover-thinking which had existed side by side up to this point. It is a simple word, with which all parts of a company can communicate with each other and with the market."[118] The business experts gathered at the congress evidently considered the idea of linking all activities concerning distribution to be innovative.

In fact, few of them fully comprehended the significance of the new approach. For modern marketing revolutionized the perspective of the firm. It defined the firm from market demand, not from production. Up to the 1950s European enterprises focussed on production. Especially during and after the Second World War the central bottlenecks had been procurement and production. Marketing now put sales at the centre of entrepreneurial action, and managements of manufacturing firms were understandably sceptical of the new approach and its implications. The boards of European firms were still dominated by technicians, engineers, chemists, or lawyers, who had concentrated mainly on the problem of producing goods. For them marketing not only demanded a radical change of perspective, but in addition entailed a loss of power inside the firm. Of course, the "working method of practical action" (Peter Burke) in the companies could not be changed from one day to the next. In Germany a wide acceptance of marketing and related methods of Americanized management did not occur until the generational shift at the beginning of the 1960s.

Putting distribution into the centre of all decisions within the firm entailed organizational consequences. Internal bureaucratic structures had to be reorganized and responsibilities redistributed. How little progress the mentioned first German

Congress for Sales and Marketing in 1958 had achieved can be seen in the autumn 1964 special edition of the business journal *Volkswirt* (Economist) with the title "advertising is a management task". Twelve of the 13 essays revealed continuing deficits concerning the place of marketing in German enterprises, the most important being that the decision-making in marketing was placed in middle management rather than in top management where it belonged. The placement mirrored the continuing general European preference for production over distribution. Even though European managers in the 1950s recognized that marketing would become important, they typically established the marketing unit as a small subdivision of the sales department. At that time, however, most American companies had already separated sales and marketing. The marketing department developed the long-term strategy of the enterprise, while the sales department took care of short-term tactics. Marketing defined four interconnected, comprehensive fields of policy in a company's marketing mix: 1) product policy (kind of product, quality, branding, packaging); 2) price policy (definition of market segment, recommended retail price, discounting and credit terms); 3) distribution policy (logistics, direct or indirect sales, stock levels); and 4) communication policy (public relations, advertising). At many American firms, such as The Coca-Cola Company, the marketing department became strategically much more important than the sales department. In the early 1960s European observers were still astonished by the superior placement of marketing personnel in US companies:

> "In America it can be observed ever more often that the marketing department is located underneath a 'vice-president of marketing'. In many cases this means that the marketing manager is at the same level as the sales manager. A remarkable fact!"[119]

But by the end of the decade Europeans had grasped the point. By 1968 79 per cent of German enterprises had drawn a clear organizational line between sales and marketing departments, and the latter was subordinate to the sales management in only in a third of the cases. The same development took place in other European countries, spearheaded by the growth of fast-moving consumer goods.

Marketing was not the only Americanizing change in the internal organization of European firms during this period; divisionalization, or product-based structure, was another. Many enterprises were powered by the post-war boom to an unexpected size. They had increased not only in scale but also in scope. Furthermore, many had branched out into related or new sectors; the expansion offered economic growth, and diversification reduced exposure to swings in sales and thereby stabilized financial results. It also meant that an increasing variety of products and activities came under the purview of the original enterprise, generating considerable difficulties for top management. The remedy for this problem was the multidivisional form (M-form) of company organization.

Traditionally, the internal organization of the firm distinguished between units for production, sales, personnel, purchasing, finances, and so on. In large and diversified companies this meant that very different products were handled by the same means of distribution. The M-form split companies into different divisions according to product groups. Each division had its own unit for purchase, production, sales, and other activities; while a few functions, such as the legal unit, remained common for all divisions. Each company, of course, determined for itself the exact mixture of centralization and decentralization. Consequently, the traditional centralized form and the modern M-form were not mutually exclusive; they represented ideal types with many variations in reality. In the centralized company it was relatively easy for units making little or no profit to live at the expense of the more successful units as long as the company generated an overall profit. Often detailed unit-level accounting was absent, making the identification of failing units very difficult; the firm as a whole constituted a single unit for profit and loss. Under the M-form each division had an individual account; the company's top management could thereby locate less profitable divisions and to put pressure upon their managers to correct the situation. Generally speaking, the M-form improved profit potential but weakened employees' coherence and company loyalty.

The M-form was first systematically applied by large and diversified American firms such as DuPont de Nemours & Co. in the interwar period. In 1949 20 of the largest 100 corporations in the United States had adopted the M-form, by 1969 73. Peter Drucker and Alfred D. Chandler characterize the M-form as the most distinctive managerial feature of American industrial capitalism. It was especially appropriate for conglomerates and diversified firms, but it became a fashionable organizational form in the 1950s and other enterprises implemented it as well. Neil Fligstein has claimed, however, that the introduction of the M-form was not only a matter of finding a more appropriate organization, but was also the outcome of competition between professional groups for the control of the respective enterprise. A third reason for its introduction was the more complicated organizational demands of combining national and international markets in big business.

Thus, the parallel introduction of marketing and the M-form in European business was not accidental; the two innovations offered groups of reform-minded managers in a company a golden opportunity to form alliances. These groups typically desired changes laden with American practices and attitudes, and indeed it is hard to imagine that an internal reorganization of a firm, which after all entails a redistribution of managerial authority, could be value neutral.[120] As Bruce Kogut has shown, British firms were the European forerunners in applying the parallel innovations. During the 1960s the percentage of British enterprises with the M-form jumped from 20 to 80. Its spread in France and West Germany was similar, from 10 to 50 per cent between 1967 and 1977. But the development then stagnated; in the later 1980s the percentage of M-form companies in these two countries did not exceed 60, 20 points below the British level. There are few data about the diffusion of the M-form in other European countries. Six of seven Swiss firms included among the world's 200 largest manufacturing enterprises in 1972 had adopted the M-form; the same applied to four of seven Italian companies, and five of seven Swedish firms. From case studies we know additionally that many firms of much smaller size also introduced the M-form. According to Whittington and Mayer, the trend towards divisionalization and decentralization was found in all types of firms, regardless of the structure of ownership and size (above a certain threshold, of course).

A couple of examples illustrate the depth of change introduced by the innovations just described. The Norwegian company *Norsk Hydro* was founded at the beginning of the twentieth century to produce fertilizer and magnesium by electrolytic technology using the country's abundant and cheap electrical power. During the 1950s *Norsk Hydro* expanded operations tremendously. Its top management recognized the need for organizational restructuring and looked to American for advice. In 1962 a commission of directors visited a number of chemical companies in the United States and evaluated their structures. After several months of such visits, one member of the commission wrote to his colleagues in Norway: "We believe we now largely know how we shall suggest how the future of our company should be set up."[121] The suggestion was to divisionalize. The first division was created in 1964. To test the new structure's viability, a well-defined but rather small part of the company, magnesium production, was chosen for this first step. In the same year *Norsk Hydro* decided to take part in the search for oil on the Norwegian shelf. Having no maritime experience, it bought two shipbuilding firms, *Bergens Mekaniske Verksteder* and *Akers Mekaniske Verkstad*. The purchases both diversified the company's activities and doubled its workforce from 9,500 to 20,800. In 1965 Norsk Hydro implemented the M-form throughout its entire operations. In this example divisionalization was not introduced all at once but over a period, during which a redistribution of managerial power and operations took place.

The official introduction of the M-form in company organization did not always reflect the real structure of decision-making. Research on M-form companies in France, Germany, and the UK has shown that paper and practice did not always match. Sometimes an M-form reorganization conceded little decision-making authority to the divisions themselves, contradicting the whole concept. Whatever the case, formal introduction of product-based divisionalization signified a first victory for those managers, usually younger, who were less preoccupied with physical output. But it did not mean the rejection of the traditionalists or centralists. As often with major internal changes in large enterprise, it took time before a new system worked and received full consent. Big business entails bureaucracy, and bureaucrats have their own means to ignore, delay, or sabotage unwanted innovations. At *Norsk Hydro* it took several years before divisionalization worked as intended. Between 1964 and 1973 various groups of managers battled for control. Finally, the centralist-minded group was restricted to supervision, legal aid, and so forth; thereafter most decision-making took place within the divisions. *Norsk Hydro*'s experience is much more representative for the introduction of the M-form than the total change from one day to the next. Of course, a few firms, such as the German chemical giant *Bayer*, did shift radically from a centralistic organization to a divisional one at one go. And others went even further, not only divisionalizing, but also outsourcing central company services. For example, *Mannesmann*, the German pipe producer, transferred its market research and advertising services to an independent company in 1972. Such important changes were clearly not decided in a single moment, but were products of a tug of war over a considerable time.

The spread of the M-form reinforced other Americanizing features in the operations of European enterprises. It entailed, for example, the adoption of a new style of process control, or management accounting. Here, too, American companies were first to implement this idea. Control was no longer a post hoc evaluation conducted by middle management but an operational instrument by which the company's top management continuously monitored divisional performance in order to take corrective action if necessary. A new executive position was even created for the purpose: the controller (comptroller) or chief financial officer (CFO). For German companies the change was so significant that the English terms "controlling" and "controller" were retained for the new meaning. The M-form also brought the breakthrough for management consulting firms in Europe, for all known divisionalizations were carried out with the help of a consultancy (see ch. 3). The US-based McKinsey & Company, which focussed on advising top management, was particularly active in this area, assisting among others the German chemical companies BASF and Bayer, the Swedish gas company AGA, and the Norwegian pharmaceutical firm Nyegaard & Co. (today Nycomed) in the 1970s and early 1980s. The Swedish electrotechnical giant ASEA, from 1988 merged with the Swiss Brown Boveri & Cie. into the multinational ABB, divisionalized as early as 1962 with the help of the American Stanford Research Institute. As more and more enterprises adopted the M-form, non-American consultancies also became involved in the reorganizing process. *Norsk Hydro,* for example, was advised by a Norwegian firm called *Industrikonsulent,* a consultancy with no direct American links. The case shows how American ideas, consulting and the M-form of organization became internalized into European business life.

The M-form is of course just one example of enterprise governance. We know more about it than other organizational innovations for the simple reason that it is easily detected. It is usually shown in company organization charts. But the M-form was only one of several organizational instruments transferred from the United States to Europe in the 1950s.

A dramatic example of the value of American methods of organization and planning is the Tignes dam in the French Alps.[122] Its construction in the late 1940s and early 1950s was a project of national prestige, a symbol of French post-war modernization. The dam was the highest one in Europe and created the largest of all French reservoirs. Much was at stake, technologically but politically. The construction company that received the contract was a well-established one that had studied the possibilities at Tignes before 1939, but it had no experience in the construction of such large and difficult dams. When the project ran into deep trouble, it was entrusted to the young French engineer Paul Montagné, who had worked on similar sites in the United States. Montagné continued to use the American heavy machinery of his predecessor, but he used it in an Americanized way. He reorganized work processes and extended the working week to six and a half days. He raised productivity by bringing in stronger lighting that improved visibility and increased security. He abandoned railway track in favour of roads that could accommodate the large US dump trucks. Montagné summed up in retrospect: "Since we used American-made equipment almost entirely, we had to use American methods of work."[123] He also improved the received technology and as a result saved 40 kg of cement per ton concrete. In 1953 the Tignes dam came into a double use, as a reservoir and as an object of study in construction management. Tignes provided the French construction industry with a technological superiority in the building of high-mountain dams that was envied throughout Europe. It represented both the successful transfer of American technology and organizational procedures and their enhancement by indigenous entrepreneurs. Similar learning processes in other projects in the French construction industry have been documented with respect to superhighways, the Channel tunnel, public works, and oil exploration.[124]

MARKETING RESEARCH

Marketing research is a logical consequence of the marketing re-definition of the enterprise presented earlier. The marketing concept puts customer demand in the forefront, so research into that demand is an essential part of a successful firm's management. Since the marketing concept of the firm was first and most thoroughly developed in the United States, it is natural that marketing research also first emerged there. In 1955 Lyndon Brown, one of America's experts in this field, stated: "Marketing and distribution research is a peculiar American institution. It developed first in this country as a result of the intense pressure created by our economic growth."[125] His claim is largely but also misleading. There had been indigenous activities in marketing research in Europe before 1945, and several of those involved had been forced to emigrate to the United States, where they significantly influenced the development of American marketing research, especially motivation research. Among prominent names are Ernest Dichter and Paul Lazarsfeld from Austria and George Katona from Hungary.

The earliest European institution for marketing research was established in Germany. In 1925/27 Wilhelm Vershofen founded the *Institut für Wirtschaftsbeobachtung der deutschen Fertigware* in Nürnberg. In 1934, he and Ludwig Erhard (the later West German economics minister and chancellor) remodelled it into the *Gesellschaft für Konsumforschung* (Society for Consumer Research or GfK). During the interwar years there were also several such institutions in the UK. Before 1945 there was at least one enterprise for marketing research in Sweden (1932), France (1939), the Netherlands (1940), and Switzerland (1941). Yet these European initiatives were minor compared with those in the United States.

American marketing research companies, such as the American Institute of Public Opinion (AIPO) that conducted the Gallup polls, were more advanced than their European counterparts not only in size and organization but also in the application of technology. Even before the Second World War punch card systems, counting machines and sorters were used and exported to Europe, in most cases made by International Business Machines (IBM). This technology not only expressed the lead held by the American office-machine industry, but also the state of the art the United States had achieved in statistical, demographical, and mathematical methods. Especially relevant for business management was Operations Research (OR), which was developed in the United States and UK during the war to improve military decision-making. After the US mathematician George Bernard Dantzig developed the simplex method, an algorithm for expressing planning problems in linear programming, in the late 1940s, OR began to be applied to industrial management. The goal of OR is to determine a company's optimal allocation of resources that will achieve the most profitable output. This is achieved by using mathematical models that take into account relevant business variables such as buying power, demographical data, sales of own and of competing products, rates of interest, size of consumer credits, and all in a given region. In 1959 representatives of European institutions discussed this technique positively and considered it very important; however, they could not envisage its immediate application in Europe for the simple reason that the necessary computers were too expensive. In due time OR came to be widely applied in large European companies, but the combination of scientific methods and office machine technology that OR embodied constituted a substantial advantage for the United States during much of the post-war boom period. Later the French especially excelled in OR, and even claimed to be ahead of American analysts. In our context it is not so important to establish whether this was true or not, but to note that America remained the reference point for French OR practice.

        The American leadership in marketing research in these years was also the result of the innovative application of new statistical and polling methods. One of the most important was the *consumer panel*. This is a poll that asks the same group of persons the same questions at regular intervals and is thus able to measure the dynamic of answers over time. Nowadays more than one-third of all investment in market research goes into such panel studies. The method was developed by Arthur Charles Nielsen in 1933, and first applied in the drug and food sector. The British company, *Attwood Statistics*, started the first European consumer panel, the *Attwood Random Panel*, in 1945. Other European companies, such as the French *Stafco* and the German *GfK,* followed from the mid-1950s. At about the same time Nielsen's company, ACNielsen, brought its panel methods to Europe; it soon established branches in many countries and in 2004 is by far the world's largest firm in the supplying of market information.

        In the late 1940s an additional approach to gathering information about consumers and customers developed in the United States: motivational research. Initially developed by the Austrian émigré Ernest Dichter, motivational research is founded on the thesis that consumer behaviour in modern industrial societies is related not only to income but also to non-material attitudes and preferences. Dichter achieved prominence with pioneering studies of why people bought Chrysler Motor's Plymouth car and Procter & Gamble's Ivory soap as opposed to other brands, including those manufactured by the same companies. The challenge for Dichter and associates in the prosperous America of the 1950s was to find ways to sell more and new products even to satiated consumers. The central problem for European marketing, however, was not the overfed, but the unwilling customer. A considerable number of Europeans resisted the purchase of mass-produced goods, considering them to be a denial of individuality. Motivational research helped European business overcome such reluctance. By identifying obstacles to consumption and suggesting remedies, it paved the way for mass consumption and even revised notions of consumer individuality. "In short, through Motivation Research consumption came to (be) seen primarily as an area for the active construction of selfhood."[126]

The European reception of these American innovations in marketing research varied in timing and extent. As in the case of economic institutional change, West Germany and Austria were initially in a special situation because of the Allied military occupation. To obtain information about public opinion in its zones of occupation the United States established an *Opinion Survey Section* in Germany and the *United States Information Agency* in Austria. Both organizations employed mainly indigenous personnel, who were sent to America to learn their jobs. In Austria the American occupation authorities encouraged Siegfried Becker, who had become the director of the US agency in that country to found the *Österreichische Gallup-Institut* (Austrian Gallup Institute) in 1949. With similar encouragement several indigenous German organizations for the study of public opinion emerged early: the Emnid institute in Bielefeld in 1946, the Institute for Opinion Research in Allensbach and Infratest in Munich, both in 1947. The first two, however, for many years restricted their activity to polling public opinion and represent a long-standing European practice of separating opinion polling from commercial market research.

From the early 1950s American marketing research companies began direct engagement in Europe. ACNielsen established subsidiaries in Belgium, France, West Germany, Ireland, the Netherlands, Sweden, Switzerland, and the UK. Nowland & Company opened bureaus in Brussels, Paris, and Düsseldorf. McCann-Erickson, J. Walter Thompson, and Young and Rubicam set up offices in several European countries. Ernest Dichter's *Institute for Motivational Research*, founded in 1946, founded a franchised *Dichter-Institute* in Zurich as early as 1948; between 1962 and 1971 it spread also to Rome, London, Barcelona, and Frankfurt. Related firms built up networks of cooperation based on American principles and methods. By 1959 the Gallup Organization commanded a network comprehending the whole of western Europe, except Portugal and Spain; the New York-based International Research Associates (now INRA group) had affiliates in all but Portugal. Some American market researchers even moved themselves; Elizabeth Nelson, for example, moved to London and a co-founded Taylor Nelson (now TNS), the world's fourth largest market information group in 2004.

Despite this diffusion of market research companies throughout Europe, the bulk of the demand for their services came from American subsidiaries or American-based companies trying to penetrate European markets.

"A characteristic phenomenon is the fact that companies with American capital interests rank prominently among the users of market research organisations. Through their American origin, these companies are familiar with the application of analytical methods for opening up new markets. Moreover, they are instructed accordingly by their parent companies."[127]

American firms were more advanced in methods, machinery, technologies, capital, organization, trained personnel, foreign direct investment, and foreign cooperation. The American market was larger, and market research was more accepted there than in Europe.

Usually European common structures are built on top of national ones. In the case of marketing and opinion research it was the reverse. In 1947 Alfred Max, director of *L'Institut Français d'Opinion Publique*, invited a few persons to discuss the idea of forming a European discussion forum in the field. The intended founding session in Prague in the spring of 1948 was prevented by the coup d'état in Czechoslovakia, so the creation of the *European Society for Opinion Survey and Market Research* (*ESOMAR*) by 29 representatives from seven countries occurred in Amsterdam in September 1948. ESOMAR established itself as the most important organization in its field first in Europe, and from the 1980s in the world. ESOMAR originally intended to concentrate on market research in its European context. The French founding member, Hélène Riffault, was very explicit about this intention. ESOMAR was conceived as a forum for individuals—not organizations—with the purpose of promoting a distinctly European character of marketing research and thereby strengthening the legitimacy of a largely new and little known profession.

> "We felt a great need to meet researchers form other countries and exchange experiences and ideas… We felt that we should have some form of formal organisation. WAPOR [World Association of Public Opinion Researchers] had already been set up, but that was mostly public opinion research, not market research and had an American perspective. We wanted to show potential clients in Europe that we were a new profession which they needed, a profession with advanced technologies, discipline and ethical rules."[128]

Riffault's words expressed a vision rather than a reality. Even a decade later the number of firms engaged in market research in Europe remained limited. In 1956 there were only fifty-four in all: two each in Finland, Italy and Norway; three in both Denmark and Switzerland; four each in Belgium and the Netherlands; five in Sweden; eight both in France and West Germany; and thirteen in the UK. These enterprises had organized themselves in national pressure groups in only a few countries: the UK (founded in 1947), Germany (1949), France (1950 and 1955), and in Italy (1954).[129]

During the build-up of marketing research in Europe the American model was so preeminent that close imitation was the general rule.

> "The organizations founded in Europe after the Second World War were more after the American pattern, even accepting the American practice of connecting market research with public opinion research. At bottom, this practice was alien to the concept of trade research as it had prevailed on the European continent, which had regarded the two fields as different subjects."[130]

The contrast between the European and the American approach to market research was especially evident in the area of psychologically oriented research. Two schools of thought competed for supremacy during the 1950s: a "mathematical mechanistic" one, which trusted only in quantification, and a "subjective psychological" one, which maintained that human behaviour cannot be quantified. In the United States both schools coexisted without difficulty, complementing one another. In Europe, by contrast, practitioners argued energetically about which version was the "correct one". The "correct one" was the one using verifiably scientific methods. The quarrel was not only methodological; it was existential. For the most profound deficit of European market research, exceeding all issues of methodology, company size, and so forth, was its very legitimacy. If it was to survive in the European economy, marketing research had to secure business recognition that the services it offered were soundly based, and therefore worth buying. Given the initial scepticism of European business, the quarrel about marketing research methodology was fought with no holds barred. For example, Hans F. Kropff, who championed the mathematical approach, accused the Swiss representative of the psychological approach, F. M. Feller, of being a charlatan, since Feller's results could not be corroborated statistically. Such accusations were potentially devastating for the individual and debilitating for the entire field. The episode reflected the widespread preconceptions marketing research—as well as advertising—had to contend with in Europe.

In the United States, by contrast, the field's legitimacy had long been established. Researchers tallied opinions and carried out market research without specific qualms concerning its scientific merit. In one of the first handbooks in market research, published in 1937, Lyndon Brown addressed the problem of "the scientific method". But before raising potentially thorny issues such as objectivity and rationality, he quoted passages from several works on scientific methodology that effectively dismissed the whole problem: "Hard work, plus common sense, with no talk about it", and "...I can see nothing original or distinctive". Brown then summed up: "It is impossible to define scientific method categorically, because there are many different scientific methods."[131] Similarly, in 1950 William Fox wrote in his book with the revealing title *How to Use Market Research for Profit*:

> "From time to time, one hears people talk about market research as a 'science'. The charitable view is that English is being used carelessly. Market research is no more a science than chalk is cheese. It is at most an art, and a useful art, but that is all."[132]

As other American practitioners, Fox did not bother about the "scientific" quality of market research as long as its results made money in an honourable way.

And yet this was the crux of the matter for Europeans: was market research honourable work? For many, especially on the Continent, it was highly suspect. Such persons believed in the adage 'Good products sell themselves!', and this conviction instilled disbelief and mistrust in marketing in general. In their view only inefficient or superfluous goods needed promotion. Such attitudes were intensified, especially in Germany, by the social protest movements in the late 1960s and 1970s. The 1968ers excoriated the materialistic society of modern capitalism and urged the rejection of what they called "consumption terror", the compulsion to consume material goods. In the following decade the burgeoning ecologist movement and associated Green parties ecologists promoted the renunciation of consumption as the new public virtue. In both cases, even many of those who did not have a renunciatory lifestyle agreed with this criticism in principle. In short, Europeans tended to have difficulty accepting the untroubled American acceptance of material consumption. The widely felt moral ambiguity of increased consumption delayed the social acceptance of marketing research as a legitimate business activity. Market research could be said to spy on persons' secret consumption wishes. Did it not aim at ferreting out incipient demands that could be exploited by producers?

European market researchers worked in several ways to win legitimacy for their profession. One was to locate the field in or close to traditionally respectable institutions. Universities, for example, could give "a promise of lending scientific legitimacy to a profession that still lamented a lack of confidence on the part of both business and the public at large."[133] Many market researchers lectured part-time at universities. The universities considered such employment to be an honour and therefore paid it extremely badly, but market researchers never forgot to advertise their university position on visiting cards or the front page of their books. Other ways were to establish industry-wide codes of standards and ethics (usually taken from the United States) and to raise the educational standard of practitioners by hiring persons with academic training in the area. Yet all this took time. In 1959 the European Productivity Agency still maintained: "Decisions based on intuition can in no way be justified today,"[134] indicating that dubious scientific quality of market research was still a major concern. Some prominent authorities in the field, such as Ludwig Erhard, held the view:

> "The basic question for all researchers in our field is whether his interest is focussed only on what is to be calculated or whether he can see the human being behind it, and does not shy away from the fact that character and behaviour of men are not accountable."[135]

However, the question of market research's legitimacy in Europe could not be put away until the profession had acquired the same degree of acceptance as in the United States. This was by and large achieved by the end of the post-war boom. Thus, the British marketing expert Max Adler could write in 1970:

> "Motivational research is now an accepted technique to discover the real answers to the question - Why? Conventional market research is statistic-based. Motivational research is not, but the fact does not detract from its usefulness as background information."[136]

This usefulness of market research can be briefly demonstrated by the case of mass-produced food in Italy. Since the sales of such foods failed to meet expectations of the food industry, distributors asked themselves why? Market research provided some answers. In 1963 Max Gloor from Nestlé pointed out American and European housewives allocated their time differently. Americans spent 1.5 hours a day cooking meals, while Europeans used 3 hours. Behind the different allocation of time lay a different conception of the housewifely role. Continental housewives thought that cooking expressed their affection for their family. Freshly prepared, home-made food was thus considered superior to prepacked, pre-fabricated, or processed food. A 1957 survey showed that, in contrast to the United States where 92.4 per cent of all housewives preferred brand-name products, Italian women showed little interest in them. The Italian market research company, Misura, found out that Italian women perceived prepacked food often as tasteless, false, artificial, and even poisonous. In Italy as elsewhere women carried out more than two-thirds of consumers' purchases. Thus, as long as Italian women resisted mass-produced goods, the change from a traditional to a modern society was blocked. Market research suggested that the cause of the rejection was psychological. Cooking, washing, and home-making defined the role of the traditional Italian housewife, the *massaia*. The *massaia* acted as the centre of the family; she received her psychological rewards from the affective bond which made her family gravitate towards her. And the *massaia*'s home-made cooking was a key expression of the solidity of these bonds. Consequently, the consumption of prepacked food was perceived as a threat to the adherence of the family, or as the Italian market-research consultant Gabriele Calvi expressed in his study in 1961:

> "The woman discovers that the use of mass produced foods in a domestic setting takes away a large part of her duties and deprives her of one of her most proved weapons in securing her government over the hearts of her family….The woman consequently finds herself in a defensive position, in which natural foods become an ideal to protect, and mass produced foods a threat that has to be fought off."[137]

Italian producers, retailers, and even politicians took this resistance seriously, for it represented an important barrier to the country's modernization. Without the consumption of mass-produced goods prosperity and social integration were threatened. Not only researchers but also politicians and managers discussed remedies, suggesting mainly advertising. Finally, it was the strong and steady economic growth of the 1960s that changed the traditional attitudes. Economic growth led to a demand in labour, including women, and more demand for labour meant the possibility of additional income to the *massaia*. With more money but less time, Italian women slowly accepted mass-produced food.

By the end of the post-war boom marketing research was expanding faster in Europe than in the USA; and a large part of this expansion was due to American FDI. But this growth was not merely a one-way transfer, it also expressed an intensive cross-fertilization across the Atlantic. In 2004 ACNielsen is still by far the largest marketing information company in the world, but European ones are now among the top ten of this industry, too. Nonetheless substantial differences remain. The United States still spends twice as much for market research as Europe, and Japanese spending for such services is less than a quarter of the American.

ADVERTISING

Until the 1950s advertising in Europe, except in the UK, laboured under an even greater lack of social acceptance than marketing research. A widely held perception was that advertising's main purpose was to disguise the lack of quality of the goods it promoted. Thus, it was intrinsically a morally dubious activity. Werner Sombart, a leading German economist at the beginning of the twentieth century, described advertising as "lepra-like rash"; his colleague Gustav Schmoller considered it a "dishonest art"; and the contemporary German comedian Otto Reuter popularized this disdain in mocking verse:

> "Radam, climbim, and trumpet call,
> advertisements gigantic, not small,
> the company name five foot square,
> if that won't help, then nothing to be fair."

In left-wing circles advertising's reputation was if anything even lower. In Marxist theory distribution was a mere annex to the central issue of production. Advertising was thus socioeconomically parasitic because it did not contribute directly to the process of producing goods. Lastly, independent of its ethical quality, the practice of advertising was not construed to be a part of business management. Advertising was an art form, designed and executed by creative artists. The now

famous posters by Toulouse-Lautrec and contemporaries confirmed this attitude.
Since real artists are not trained but born, advertising could be neither learned nor
criticized by non-artists such as business managers.

The potential consequences of a negative attitude towards both market
research and advertising for an industry's competitiveness were seen in chapter
two's presentation of the American and European film industries. In spite of its
admittedly lower artistic quality, the American film industry triumphed over its
European rivals. The tools of victory were sophisticated market research coupled
with deliberate and massive advertising. American film-makers first produced what
film-goers wanted and then told them where and when to find it.

In 1945 the differences between American and European advertising were
considerable. Perhaps the primary one was attitudinal: American advertising
experts had a nonchalant matter-of-factness about their activity and did not
scrutinize it for social legitimacy as did their European colleagues. Second,
American advertisers used much more sophisticated methods. They readily adopted
the methods of modern social sciences. Thus the pioneering insights of George
Katona's study of consumers, Psychological Analysis of Economic Behaviour,
published in 1951, were quickly put into US advertising practice, but it took about
ten years to transfer these new views to Europe. It was normal for Americans to
pursue advertising academically and to justify decisions rationally. This was not the
general rule in Europe where advertising personnel could not give scientifically
founded reasons for doing this or that and relied on (irrational) inspiration. In the
United States, by contrast, it was not the advertisers who behaved irrationally, but
the consumers. The concept of the irrational consumer has been long advocated and
practiced in the United States and is now generally acknowledged throughout the
world. A third long-standing difference was the sheer omnipresence of advertising in
the United States. As late as the mid-1960s, the German observer Klaus Hallig
could write:

> "Advertising in the United States possesses a size that justifies it being seen as an
> integrating part of life in the USA. It accompanies the daily life of the average citizen to
> an extent perceived by Europeans with astonishment..."[138]

Fourth, American advertising was for many years organized on a much
larger scale than in Europe. Full-service advertising agencies were common in the
United States but infrequent in Europe; there the bulk of advertising was carried out
by very small firms, which in most cases did little else than place the advertisements
they received from firms in relevant newspapers.

Given these differences, the emergence of full-service advertising agencies
in Europe during the 1950s represented a major Americanization of the industry.[139]
Such agencies offered clients a comprehensive service from market research to
organization and realization of advertising campaigns, including the evaluation of
the results. These services simply could not be realized by the traditional small
firms, many of them one-man shows. The influx began in the 1920s when American
agencies such as Walter J. Thompson or Erwin Wasey had founded branch offices in
Europe. After 1945 they reinvested and were joined by McCann-Erickson, BBD&O
(Batten, Barton, Durstine & Osborne), Ted Bates, Young & Rubicam, Foote, and

Cone & Belding to name the best known ones. Their entry into the European market forced indigenous European firms to adjust the size and form of their organizations as well as the range and quality of products in the direction of the American model. The experience of European employees in American-owned agencies also contributed to the transfer of American methods and attitudes. The co-operative, teamwork style of working that prevailed in US agencies strongly formed their employees. And this influence lasted a long after employees had left the US agency.

Indeed the American model of advertising company was taken over by the European industry also without contest. In 1959 Hubert Strauf, one of the old hands of German advertising, explained this attitude:

> "In the United States, where the fast development of the free-market economy with its huge industrial mass production triggered the battle for markets long before, a form of organizing modern advertising was developed, which is keyed to such demands. That is where the cradle of the modern advertising agency stands."[140]

The psychological priority of the American advertising agency was reinforced by its economic success. As in the case of management consulting, the most important clients in the beginning were American firms operating in Europe: Reader's Digest, Douglas Aircraft, or Bristol-Myers. But soon indigenous European companies recognized the value of the comprehensive service offered by the American-style agencies. Some of the old advertisement companies tried to compete by expanding to the size of the agencies, but only a few were successful. Hanns Brose, the owner of a German agency, attributed this defeat to a traditional "working method of practical action," which narrowed perspective in two ways: on the one hand, by short-term contracts, and on the other, by product-based communication with the purchaser, or consumer. Instead, the American-style advertising agencies tried to construct long-term relationships with their clients lasting for years or even decades. To achieve this, communication was directed not only towards the consumer but also, and with at least as much intensity, towards the ordering company.

Once established, the indigenous European advertising agencies undertook to become visible to potential clients. They founded national interest associations such as *Federazione Italiana della Pubblicità* or the *Gesellschaft Werbe-Agenturen*. In some cases an established organization could be used; thus the French *Office de Contrôle des Annonces* became the *Fédération Française de la Publicité*. Membership in such an association amounted to a seal of quality, for only agencies that met the established quality rules were admitted. These standards reinforced the Americanization, for they were largely the same as those of the American Association of Advertizing Agencies (AAAA). The most important were: (1) full service agency, (2) exclusion of competition between clients, and (3) independence from other companies. The introduction of the agency form of enterprise into European advertising transformed the industry and represents one of the most rapid and profound examples of the Americanization of the European economy. The trend towards a full-service advertising agency was not only based on its superior organization and the esteem for the American model. Most of all it reflected a fundamental change in the European economy in the direction of American conditions. Mass consumption began to appear in force in Europe in the 1950s, and mass consumption requires mass production. Mass production in turn requires corresponding structures of sale and, as a corollary, of advertising. In all these the United States was precursor, model, and catalyst.

Not only forms and habits were taken over but style as well. American style, or what was perceived to be American style, became fashionable during the post-war boom. Finland can serve as an example here. In 1951 a Finnish producer of biscuits and confectionery introduced chewing gum under the trade mark of "Jenkki" (meaning Yankee) and soon became market leader. Another example is Paulig, a Finnish coffee firm. It started American-style advertising in 1950, creating a beautiful and smiling "Paula girl", who became a national celebrity. The campaign, together with the model herself, was taken over from the United States. Since the campaign was a great success, it ran for several years. Witty and humorous advertising campaigns, such as the famous ones the New York agency Doyle Dane Bernbach started for Avis and for Volkswagen, attracted attention and formed the style of the branch for a decade.

Reactions to the influx of American style varied. For example, the use of the English language in advertisements boosted sales in Italy but hurt them in France. Some national markets, such as the Scandinavian or the German-speaking ones, resembled each other and could be worked with the same slogans and images. But generally any advertising campaign covering several countries of Europe had to adjust to individual national taste. These adjustments were often minor but nonetheless essential. Apart from these national differences, though, the trend in advertising went in the same direction all over Europe: towards the American model.

Still, the inexorable Americanization did not proceed without reservation. Johannes Schmiedchen, a German old hand in the industry, doubted in 1953 that the "dollaricans" could equal the qualities of their German colleagues. His attitude was totally unfounded. But, as in many other sectors of industry, managers who felt economic pressure by superior American competition, reacted not always rationally. A certain hesitation can partly be attributed to differences in the actual economic environment. The post-war boom in Europe was a seller's market in which little sales effort was necessary. The central economic problem even in the consumer goods sector was to increase production rather than sales. At the Second Congress for Sale and Marketing in 1964, the German shirt producer Walter Seidensticker summed up: "We were all too much rooted in production and the building-up of new factories to use the chance (to introduce new sales methods - H.G.S.) offering itself in good time."[141]

In 1960 the degree of Americanization as measured by spending on advertisement per inhabitant divided Europe into three categories. The benchmark was the American figure of 64 US dollars, which was predictably considerably higher than anywhere in Europe. The highest spending in Europe clustered around 20 dollars; this group included Switzerland 28, UK and Sweden 24, Germany 21, Denmark 19, and Norway 18. In the middle group spending averaged 10 dollars: Belgium 12, Austria 11, the Netherlands 11, France 8, and Finland 7. The last group consisted of Portugal and Italy, which spent 4 and 3 dollars respectively. Ten years later in 1970 Germany clearly headed the Europeans, spending 65 dollars compared with 21 in Great Britain and only 17 in France. The US benchmark had meanwhile risen to 90.[142]

CONCLUSION: EUROPEAN ENTERPRISE RESHAPED

The Americanization of European economic life on the microeconomic level—how enterprises manage themselves and their markets—proceeded unevenly during the post-war economic boom. During the periods of the Marshall Plan and the Productivity Mission Americans and American-trained Europeans tried actively to transfer the American model of management education to Europe with the intention of modernizing European business practices. But except for INSEAD and one or two others, the success was quite modest. It took another decade for modern management training to displace the traditional forms to any extent. In this process of re-orientation we find large variations between the different countries, the German-speaking ones being the most unaffected. A few sectors, though, became thoroughly and unanimously Americanized, e.g. the profession of chemical engineering was based on American principles, experience, and curricula. Furthermore, a significant number of individual managers took over American principles, after having been taught by American advisers in special courses for working managers. The content of these courses was ultimately based on the basic American conviction that competition will guarantee the best results for both producers and consumers, that to become more competitive a commercialization of relations within enterprises and within society in general would be beneficial, and that the economy should play generally a larger in daily life..

Americanization of the formal internal organization of European enterprises, however, proceeded quickly and substantially. As they grew in size, nearly all European large or diversified firms introduced the American multidivisional organization, or M-form, which in theory created several sub-enterprises (divisions) within a single mega-enterprise (the original firm). The adoption, moreover, was typically advised by an American business consultancy, which supervised the introduction. Very often a system of constant financial control, or management accounting, was also introduced. Marketing was another central concept of American business that Europeans began to adopt in the 1960s but did not fully digest until some time later. The marketing idea substantially reorients the focus of business activity away from production to the consumer. A company's establishment of a department of marketing did not necessarily represent the implied fundamental change of thinking, just as the introduction of the M-form in some firms was an appearance on paper rather than in reality. However, such major changes represent a struggle for power between old and new groups of managers, and we must see their implementation as a cumulative process. The new managers received their ideas and thrust from the superior American model. Often the introduction was not the end but the beginning of a change of the power balance.

The effects of the various internal reorganizations and implementations were similar to those of management education: they promoted competition, not only with other firms but within the enterprise between divisions and units of production. Consequently, they commercialized the internal structure of the firm, and they established new, deliberate bonds and relationships while uprooting the traditional ones, all of which made Americanization so fruitful.

Mass distribution entailed the use of several new managerial instruments such as marketing research and advertising. Both were known in Europe before the 1950s, but the amount practiced was small and the methods, compared with American ones, infantile. Marketing research and opinion polling were slowly accepted, in part as imported American companies, but the two activities were long held separate, unlike in the United States, and especially commercial market research had to struggle hard to establish its legitimacy in many countries. The general European response to advertising was similar mixed. Advertising came to be recognized as a necessary part of the modern economy, but it retained a suspect aura and was not an accepted or appreciated part of daily life for most Europeans as it was for most Americans.

All these takeovers represented steps towards commercialisation and the European acceptance of a deeper influence of economic issues in daily life. In the 1950s many Europeans perceived mass-produced goods as levelling and directed against individualism. The perception reflected the traditional approach towards distribution as the allocation of goods rather than the promotion of sales. Europeans who were used to only a small variety of goods inside their shops could not imagine that there could be many more varieties, and all of them mass-produced and thus comparatively cheap. The reality of the limited markets in European countries, compared with the large single American market, played a role as well. But as national European markets became more integrated and the consumers' purchasing power increased as well, the American idea that mass production fosters individualism because it enables the single person to buy more variety began to take root in Europe, too.

During the 1950s much American machinery, technology, and expertise were taken over in Europe and applied on both the micro- and macroeconomic level. Still, in many cases the transfers– always selective and adapted—lacked a deep understanding and internalization of the basic principles—the un-reflected habit—which would generate and stabilize a transformation. Perhaps this lack was grounded in the difference between the two worlds: on the American side an abundance of everything, on the European side a shortage of much. In sum, the basic problem in the cultural and institutional transfer in these years was that the United States offered solutions for a situation which was not yet at hand in Europe.

The discrepancy lessened substantially during the 1960s. As the economic gap between the United States and western Europe narrowed, American solutions and behaviour became more appropriate for Europeans. The European economy of shortages in the 1950s was a sellers' market with limited need for new ways to increase sales: demand exceeded supply, and goods sold as quickly as they were produced. By the 1960s economic growth had generated a steadily enlarging mass consumer market with a more stable balance between supply and demand. The incipient buyers' market made European business more receptive to the American sales-enhancing practices of market research, advertising, and market-oriented management education. In short, during the 1950s the Americans offered Americanization—with mixed results. During the 1960s Europeans demanded Americanization—with much more success. In the Americanization of the European economy the 1950s should be understood as a preparatory phase that paved the way for the transformation of the 1960s and beyond. The respective changes began in the late 1950s and extended into the early 1970s. In case of a periodization of Americanization during the post-war boom, then, we should speak of the "long 1960s" rather than of "long 1950s".[143]

As said before, there was little incentive to learn from the United States during the 1970s, but since the second half of the 1980s another wave of Americanization emerged. It questioned the role of the state, not only in the economy but additionally in other fields which were traditionally considered as such parts where the state had to guarantee basic standards of human existence, such as utilities, education, health care, and the like. At the same time the role of finances within the economic sector was re-defined as well as the relation between the (financial able) individual versus traditional groups. All these changes, to be taken up in the next part of the book, were related to the IT-revolution and globalization.

PART 3

AMERICANIZATION'S THIRD WAVE
FROM THE 1980s

CHAPTER 5

ECONOMIC SLOWDOWN AND THE AMERICAN MODEL

"Until the end of the 1980s we Americans had the feeling of having lost touch with modern industry. Now we know, of course, since the beginning of the 1990s it is just the other way round. America shows itself as very innovative."[144]

John Kornblum, US diplomat, 2002

By the end of the post-war boom the influence of the American economic model in Europe had waned considerably. Growth and prosperity increased self-confidence in a European way dominated by the social-political priorities of the welfare state. Yet within a decade of so the United States was once again a central society of reference for European politicians and businessmen. What lay behind this reversal of influence? The answer is connected to economic and political weaknesses that began to surface in the late 1960s and early 1970s. An emerging trend with far-reaching consequences was the slowdown, and even decline, in manufacturing, which has been the engine of economic growth in most countries since the start of industrialization. Beginning with the UK in 1965, however, the engine began to sputter. After three decades of sustained industrial expansion at record levels, economic growth suddenly slowed. A de-industrialization began to occur in all developed economies, first relatively, later absolutely. The slowdown was exacerbated by the oil-price shocks of 1973/74 and 1979/80 that each increased the price of oil threefold. The slump reduced the tax revenues that states needed to carry out promised social programmes and stopped the expansion of the job market that had kept unemployment low most everywhere. The new situation challenged the prevailing recipes of economic policy-makers. The Keynesian "magic square", which defined the aims of economic policy during the 1950s and 1960s (no inflation, economic growth, balanced foreign exchange, full employment) was known to be contradictory in itself, but it held despite this. However, from the early 1970s Keynesian policy was overwhelmed by a hitherto unknown economic situation: inflationary price increases coupled with stagnating output and increasing unemployment. "Stagflation", as it came to be called, was not foreseen by economic theory and thus could not be adequately explained. Yet without explanation stagflation could not be effectively countered. The stagflationary years compelled economic and political leaders in Europe and the US to reconsider the policies of the post-war boom. At first many governments simply muddled through, waiting for the return of better times. Yet as prices, unemployment, and government budgetary deficits continued to rise while output stagnated or even declined, policy-makers opened ears and minds to the teachings of the Chicago school. Two of the most distinguished representatives of this group of economists at the University of Chicago, Milton Friedman and Friedrich August von Hayek, published major studies on supply-side economics and monetarism already in the 1950s and 1960s, but their views were given little attention at that time. In the 1970s neglect was replaced by adulation. Hayek and Friedman were awarded the Nobel Prize in Economics in 1974 and 1976 respectively. Both were cited for achievements in monetary theory, economic fluctuations, and the complexity of stabilization policy. Both, moreover, rejected Keynesian-style macroeconomic management, criticizing the state's role in economic life in general and strongly opposing welfare-state economics in particular. In their view, such policies not only obstructed economic growth, but also undermined personal liberty. For Hayek and Friedman only a capitalist economic order based on private property and a free, competitive market could bring about prosperity and freedom for all individuals. Any other order was a Road to Serfdom, as insisted by Hayek in a 1946 book. Conservative politicians found in the libertarian, or neo-liberal, economics of the Chicago school support for their dissatisfaction with or rejection of the economic and social policies of the post-war welfare state. Beginning with Margaret Thatcher's victory in the United Kingdom in 1979 and Ronald Reagan's election to the presidency of the United States in 1980, conservative parties won power in several countries in the 1980s. Convinced that state intervention in the economy and state-ownership had caused stagflation and its ills, Thatcher and Reagan embarked on radical reversals of inherited economic and social policies. Their policy mixes—Thatcherism and Reaganomics—set out to rebuild their countries' economic and political standing in the world. Reagan's campaign pledge of 1980 promised the restoration of "the great, confident roar of American progress and growth and optimism".[145] His administration also devoted much energy and large resources to regaining American military predominance in the world after the defeats and humiliations of the Nixon and Carter administrations. Reagan's claim that his supply-side economic policies with their sweeping tax cuts brought the return of economic growth in the mid-1980s can be disputed, but the so-called Reagan Revolution did reinvent core features of the American capitalist model: privately owned production guided by the competitive forces of a free market. Thatcherism followed the same lines with similar results, but because the UK had a substantial state sector to dismantle; privatization played a much bigger role there than in the US. In West Germany the conservative government of Chancellor Helmut Kohl did not immediately adopt such libertarian policies on assuming office in 1982, but it expressed support for them in principle and in due time put some aspects in practice. Other conservative governments in Europe adopted parallel positions.

Social democratic parties and governments, however, could not so readily embrace the new policies, for their vision of society was closely linked to the social and economic management principles of welfare-state economics. To give up those principles would mean also giving up the social democratic vision. Yet increasingly they had to concede that the welfare state could not be expanded further; its costs were outrunning the economic capacity. Even preserving the status quo of welfare provisioning became increasingly untenable; policies of holding the line increased state indebtedness and hindered the resolution of new economic problems. By reducing the workforce in manufacturing de-industrialization also sapped the vitality of industrial trade unions, which were staunch supports of the welfare state. The resurgence of the American model of market capitalism under President Reagan received a fillip by the failure of two rival models in 1989/90. The bursting of the Japanese stockmarket and real-estate bubble in 1990 severely weakened the attraction of a once dynamic competitor that represented a different version of industrial capitalism. Even more important, of course, was the collapse of the Soviet Union and its allies in eastern Europe. It not only ended the international rivalries of the Cold War and redrew the political map of Europe, but also eliminated the alternative socio-economic model of real existing socialism, a centrally planned economy and society. Some commentators, especially American, quickly and self-assuredly concluded that these events confirmed that liberal democracy and the free market were inherently superior forms of political and social organization.

Yet it would be wrong to think that renewed attraction of the American model was based only on the decline of competitors and otherwise unearned by its own achievements. In fact, the United States became once again the world's prime power in technology, especially the new technologies of personal computing and gene manipulation, and international finance as well as finding itself the world's sole military superpower. Supporters of the American model attributed the resurgence to the return to basics: that is, the libertarian economics of the Chicago school as embodied in the Reagan Revolution. According to this group, economic growth could be lastingly stimulated only by lowering the state quota of GNP; in their view, the state inevitably undermined the private initiative of the free market, which was the sole true source of economic dynamism.

The message was unambiguous: If Europe wanted to catch up with the United States, it would have to follow the recipe of the American model. It would have to reduce the state quota, which in many countries amounted to more than one-half of the gross national product. It would also have to reduce the role of the state in organizing and regulating the conditions of production and distribution. In other words, to catch up with America, European countries would have to privatize and deregulate. Adoption of the recipe was not an easy matter except for dogmatic Thatcherites, for it embodied a direct challenge of many long-standing practices of European political economy that had widespread public support, including the post-war welfare state. If, in the end, most countries came to implement at least partial versions of the neo-liberal economic programme, it was not due to a deliberate US mission to Americanize Europe as in the 1950s, but was the result of accumulated economic pressures generated by the globalization of trade and finance and by changes in demographic structures that upheaved the relationship between government income and government spending.

DEREGULATION TO INCREASE COMPETITION

Regulation and deregulation are politically as well as economically determined strategies regarding the control of economic activities. Regulation has historically been used when markets did not supply the necessary goods and services in the needed quantity and quality – or when specific socio-economic groups had acquired enough political power to change law in a direction that promoted their interests. Deregulation occurred when regulation failed, or when the balance of political power changed. Economic "failure" was seldom clearly indicated in either option; the choice taken was largely influenced by habit, discourse, and political-economic constellation.

The shift in economics discourse from regulation-friendly Keynesianism to the neo-liberal economics of the Chicago school established economic criteria as the determinant of regulatory policy. In 1970 Alfred Kahn published his landmark study, *The Economics of Regulation*, in which he claimed that regulation of public utilities reduced wealth and impeded economic growth. Faced with the perplexing challenge of stagflation, many American politicians, Republican and Democrat alike, began to see deregulation as a means of stimulating economic growth. The first case of substantial deregulation occurred in 1978 when President Jimmy Carter signed into law the Airline Deregulation Act that removed government economic control of the passenger airlines. Prior to the act the Civil Aeronautic Board (CAB), a federal authority established in 1938, had regulated fares, routes, and schedules with the express obligation of ensuring a reasonable rate of return for the companies. Henceforth, the airlines themselves could set prices and services of domestic flights according to market competition. Supporters of the legislation, among them Alfred Kahn as chairman of the subsequently dismantled CAB, argued that deregulation, or market competition, would serve the interests of passengers as well as stimulate economic growth. And events seemed to bear out the claims. The average price of fares fell, while the number of passengers and passenger-miles increased. The competitive business climate, however, was not so beneficial for many individual airlines. Several venerable carriers such as Eastern, TWA (Trans World Airlines), and Pan American World Airways ("the world's most experienced airline") did not adjust well to the new situation and ultimately went bankrupt. But it was naturally the positive side of airline deregulation—the cheaper fares and increased traffic— that both American and European proponents of deregulation pointed to.

The transfer of deregulation to Europe was a complex process that often went hand in hand with privatization. Nonetheless, because theoretically each can be carried out independently, we look first at deregulation and then at privatization. Both processes are still under way, so a final evaluation cannot yet be undertaken. We must also limit the sketch of trends to a few areas—electrical utilities, railways, and telecommunications. The experience of deregulation in other areas such as water supply, air transport, banking, and so forth follows basically the pattern described there. Public utilities whose services were tied to lines or pipes have traditionally been seen as *natural monopolies*. Water or gas supplies and the associated delivery pipelines were usually owned by the same company, which thus bundled generation, transport, distribution, and marketing under its control. The company's operations were based on a state concession to supply a defined area. In return for the service monopoly, the company had to accept to serve all customers in the area and to submit its calculation of prices to governmental control. Especially during economically difficult periods, such as the 1930s, state control was extensively applied to reduce prices for consumers even though it meant that many private utilities ran into financial difficulties. Still, the principle of natural monopolies was unquestioned until the 1980s. Impressed by the initially positive effects of deregulation in the United States, the EU leadership already in the 1980s urged member countries to deregulate the energy sector as a means of reducing disparities in living conditions and economic activity and of promoting economic integration in the Union by stimulating cross-country investment. At first only a few countries, among them non-EU Norway, took up the suggestion. But within the Commission the advocates of deregulation grew in strength and insistence. On 19 January 1997 the Commission decreed the deregulation of energy throughout the Union: electrical power utilities were required to separate generation, transport, local distribution, and market into separate entities with independent accounts. To promote competition, existing power grids were to become accessible to multiple suppliers. The decree also stipulated the minimum market percentage that must be governed by competition and not subject to "natural monopoly": 23 per cent immediately; 28 per cent by 2000; and 33 per cent by 2003. Competition was defined to mean that a customer could choose an alternative supplier from outside a monopoly area. Such a choice would entail a fee to the owner of the transmission line, but it would also permit customers to contract rock-bottom prices or to support suppliers of "green energy".

In all countries the deregulation was implemented gradually. At first only very large customers could choose their supplier; from 2000 private households also had this option in most countries. The Scandinavian countries were particularly quick to reorganize their energy sectors along the new lines and established a common spot market for electricity, the Nordic Power Exchange or *Nord Pool*, in 1998. Other countries were not so eager. The EU leadership sent France, Portugal, and Italy several reminders to deregulate, and in 2001 the countries still lagged behind decree's timetable. France, for example, agreed to deregulate only under condition of an escape clause, the so-called *service public-clause*: should a deregulation measure endanger the common good, it can be abandoned.

Before deregulation the size and structure of the energy sectors in individual countries varied considerably. In 1998 the three largest countries—France Germany and the UK—accounted for nearly 60 per cent of all electricity generated in Western Europe, while the ten countries at lower end of scale (Austria, Belgium, Denmark, Finland, Greece, Ireland, Iceland, The Netherlands, Portugal, and Switzerland) together produced less than Germany alone. An open energy market, therefore, would consist of very unequal competitors: a few heavyweights and many lightweights. The internal organization of the sector ranged from national monopoly suppliers in France (EdF) and Italy (ENEL) to the conglomeration of local and regional power authorities in Norway. Other countries were characterized by a mixture of a few large and very many small firms. Deregulation set in motion a steady stream of mergers, acquisitions, and takeovers. The consolidation movement did not stop at national borders. France's EdF bought a large regional supplier in Germany, giving it a turnover double that of its nearest European competitor, Italy's ENEL. The largest Swedish electricity company, state-owned *Vattenfall*, invested in enterprises round the Baltic Sea, especially in Germany and Poland, and was in 2004 the biggest supplier in Sweden, the third largest in Germany, and the fifth largest in Europe overall. The third and fourth largest firms in Europe were the German companies *e-on* and *RWE*. All other power suppliers taken together accounted for less than half of the turnover of the smallest of the big five. Thus, even though it is still incomplete, deregulation to date has oligopolized European energy supplies to an unforeseen extent. And an oligopolistic market in which a small number of firms dominate sales is not well suited to bringing the benefits of competition to consumers.

As mentioned above, France has been a very reluctant supporter of deregulation from the start. A central reason is the important role of Electricité de France (EdF) in the French economy. EdF is not simply an enterprise owned by the state; it is perceived by Government, management, and employees as an integral part of the French state and therefore as a tool of the state's economic policy. For example, in response to the oil crises of the 1970s the French cabinet directed EdF to invest heavily in nuclear energy, an investment that is the largest in Europe. Some critical commentators have suggested an additional reason for France's hesitation in deregulating electricity supplies: that EdF could not cope with real, open competition. They point out that despite EdF's size advantage, its competitiveness is potentially weakened by overstaffing and the civil-servant mentality of its employees. This may well be the case. All utilities companies that lost their monopolies under deregulation have sooner or later been forced by the cost-cutting pressure of competition to dismiss large chunks of their workforce. Yet when EdF's management attempted in 2003 to improve its competitive position by cutting staff, the public protests by employees received sufficient governmental support that the proposal was withdrawn. Deregulation has also provoked unintended changes in technology and investment patterns. Up to 1995 electricity utilities ordered almost exclusively conventional power stations fired by fossil fuels. Since then the demand for combined cycle gas turbines power plants (CCGT) has rocketed. Worldwide orders of such gas-powered stations rose from 13 per cent of all new power-plant deliveries in 1995 to 49 per cent in 2000, and a further rise to 66 per cent was predicted for 2004.[146] CCGT-technology has many advantages: it combines electric power and steam generation. Its efficiency, the ratio of energy input to work output, is much higher than in other fossil-powered stations. CCGT entities can be built in small sizes, enabling them to be placed near towns or inside industrial parks where there was a demand for steam as well as electricity. The technology is environmentally friendly, practically smokeless, and the amount of carbon dioxide emitted is 40-50 per cent less than that of coal- or lignite-fired power plants. CCGT stations can also be constructed in very short time, between 18 and 24 months, whereas the construction of conventional fossil power stations typically takes five years and hydroelectric stations between ten and twenty. Another great advantage of CCGT stations is their short-term availability. While nuclear power stations need days, and coal- and oil-fired stations need hours to reach full capacity, a CCGT unit required merely minutes. Only hydroelectric generation is quicker (instantaneous). Lastly, CCGT stations are much cheaper to construct than all others: construction costs are less than half those of a coal-fired power station of the same capacity and roughly one-fifth of the sum needed to build a hydroelectric facility. In view of the fact that the technology of electricity generation by combined cycle gas turbines with all its seeming advantages was operational first in the 1990s, one might wonder about a causal link with deregulation. Was it just by chance that these two developments happened at the same time? And, if CCGT generating units had such seemingly overwhelming advantages, why were there any new orders for traditional generating technology? The answer to this last question is that CCGT is a short-term technology. The units can work effectively for only a few years; their longevity is related mainly to how often generation is started up and closed down. In contrast, coal-fired stations last between thirty and fifty years, hydroelectric stations fifty to a hundred. On the basis of lifetime operational costs, the single kWh generated by CCGT is quite expensive. But the technology's economics are very much in keeping with the short-term necessities of the spot market trading in electricity that deregulation promotes; they are quite inappropriate for long-term investment.

A great structural problem in power supply is swings in demand. To provide the same amount twenty-four hours a day is easy and cheap. The ability to cope with variations in demand differs according to generating technology. Nuclear power generation is the least capable: its output is constant. Coal- and oil-fired stations can increase and decrease output to handle moderate swings, but short-term peak demands are best met by quick-responding gas-turbine or water-driven generators. In a deregulated market the differences have noticeable economic consequences, for inflexible suppliers will be outcompeted by rivals with more adaptable sources, who can reap substantial rewards. One day's activity at Nord Pool's spot market illustrates this. On 14 July 1998 the price of electricity was lowest between three and four o'clock at night (31.40 SEK/MWh) and highest between 11 and 12 o'clock in the morning (83.06 SEK/MWh), an increase of 265 per cent! At the same time, the swings varied according to location. Between 6.00 and 17.00 Stockholm and Oslo had identical prices, but at 01.00 electricity in Oslo was 36 per cent more expensive than in Stockholm (51.44 to 37.85 SEK/MWh).[147] These variations represent an average day in the summer; they are wider on winter days, not only in Scandinavia but in the whole of Europe. The example shows clearly that a provider that is able to concentrate sales on times of peak demand could earn much money. The capability of CCGT to cope with swings and peak demand explains their popularity with companies that own power distribution and must now compete in an open market. Before deregulation, such a short-term approach emphasizing quick and maximum returns was alien to public utilities in both Europe and the US. Before deregulation, of course, monopoly utilities earned a lot of money. However, they could not earn too much because if they did the monitoring state authorities would step in to lower prices. Thus, instead of paying out earnings to the full, public utility companies reinvested a substantial portion in technology. All large technical systems need so-called *redundancies* in order to operate continuously and reliably at full capacity. These redundancies guarantee output in times of repairs, maintenance, accidents and so on; they represent a system's security margin. In electrical utilities redundancies comprehend not only the actual generation of electricity but the entire network. Transmission lines, substations, intake cables, monitoring meters, and most importantly on-the-spot trained personnel to fix things that go wrong. In this area the allowable response time to a problem is often extremely short. Quick service by a taxi-driver is measured in quarters of an hour. Fire brigades must respond within minutes to be effective. In the generation and distribution of electric power, however, technical help must arrive instantaneously; there are often only seconds available to prevent a glitch from becoming a catastrophe. In such situations it is useless to call in a technician from home; an appropriate specialist needs to be always available on-site.

And that presence as well as other redundancies that guarantee security cost money. The more security is provided, the more money is needed; in the end owners and managers have to find the optimal balance between technical security and commercial necessity. Deregulation changed long-standing definitions of this core relationship. The optimal balance under monopoly conditions was not the same as under competitive market conditions. Deregulation forced all utilities companies to think and act in competitive terms. To improve market position ambitious companies bought up local and foreign rivals. They also undertook to reduce costs by increasing productivity and reducing workforces. Another cost-cutting measure was to reduce redundancies. This is easily done and inconsequential during normal operations. The system is simply more exposed to risk; the customer is unaffected. If something does go wrong, however, the likelihood of a tangible impact on users is very great.

Before deregulation, substantial interruptions in electricity supply, or blackouts, were almost unknown in large parts of Europe; many Europeans, including the author of this book, have never experienced one. They were astonished, therefore, to learn of massive blackouts along the US east coast and in California in 2001 and appalled when similar power outages occurred again in 2003. But they were shocked when blackouts also hit large parts of Europe the same year. In late August 2003 large parts of London missed electricity for several hours; a month later the same thing happened to some four million persons in Copenhagen and southern Sweden. A few days after the blackout in Scandinavia, the electricity supply collapsed throughout the whole of Italy as well as in parts of neighbouring Switzerland. The country came to a standstill: airports had to close; trains stopped on the track; even car traffic broke down when traffic lights ceased to function. Fortunately, the blackout started on a Saturday night, so it had little effect of the country's industrial production.

The cause of the blackouts was not insufficient power generation but inadequate transmission facilities. In North America as in Europe all power grids are interconnected to protect against possible failures. Technical reasons require that supply and demand are always balanced within a very small time-gap. Any significant move on one side has to be adjusted immediately on the other side, a task that needs close monitoring by trained personnel. The slightest maladjustment can send a domino effect of disruption throughout the grid network. If the required adjustment does not happen, pre-defined parts of the grid disconnect automatically in order to prevent destruction. Thus, if demand slumps, so does generation. If a transmission line breaks, other lines have to take the charge additionally. If this is not possible, both supply and demand currents are automatically blocked in order to save the grid from physical damage. When the supply line disconnects, power stations have to close down. A recoupling of the demand line after a few minutes of downtime would mean that demand would be much larger than supply, an imbalance that results in yet another automatic disconnection. Supply and demand transmission, therefore, have to be reconstructed stepwise, which is why the reestablishment of electricity distribution after a significant blackout needs hours, sometimes days. The collapse of electric power always causes big economic problems; not only are tons of frozen goods wasted, but many production lines must stop. No official accounts of the cost of the blackouts of 2003 exist, but the losses were surely enormous. For example, the power outage in Detroit in August 2003 forced the shutdown of 53 of the 154 car plants in the region; it took three days to get them all working again.

How fragile some transmission grids have become is shown by the blackout in Italy in September 2003. The start was modest: Accidents cut off two major power lines (380 kV), one in France, and one in Switzerland, which caused another Swiss line (220 kV) to shut down because of overload. Though these were significant incidents, quantitatively the lines carried a small fraction of the total Italian consumption. Italy lost no more than 6000 MW, the equivalent of three to five large power stations. But the excess demand caused automatic disconnections that rolled through the Italian grid without interruption. The grid administrators lost control within four decisive seconds! What happened to the oversupply on the Swiss and French side? Demand was instantly increased by starting the huge pumps connected to water storage basins in the two states and in Germany, and supply was turned down. The example underscores that the security of power transmission systems depends on technical redundancies and the on-site presence of trained specialists. Moreover, both are needed simultaneously; one can not replace the other.

Although the Italian blackout was unpredicted, its scenario was not unimagined. A few economists had predicted that deregulation would lead to underinvestment in transmission. These critics argued that if power generation firms were forced to make their own grids accessible to third parties, the incentive to invest in the grids would fall, because the companies would effectively be aiding competitors. Alternatively, firms that owned only the line networks would tend to exploit their monopoly position in transmission to pay out high dividends rather than to plough back earnings into the network. Meran and Schwarze argue that a grid company "as a merchandizing surplus maximizer would trade less electricity than a grid owner that owns generation."[148] Because of a grid company's monopoly position, the effects of underinvestment in equipment and technology can be disguised for a number of years. The disconnection of supply, transmission, and distribution encouraged by deregulation thus promoted short-term economic thinking in the electricity sector. Available data on investment in the sector seem to show that the critics were right. In the United States, for example, investment in power lines has fallen by two-thirds since the start of deregulation, causing Bill Richardson, a former US secretary of energy, to describe America as a "superpower with a third-world grid."[149] Also in Germany deregulation has been marked by a similar drop in grid investment.[150]

The difficulty of deregulating of electricity utilities stems from the nature of the product: electricity can not be stored in great amounts; it has also become vital to the economy, the environment, and modern lifestyles. These qualities make the sector a frequent source of political contention. In 2000 the sitting Norwegian government fell over the issue of when, where, and whether to construct a single gas-driven power station. When the German government tried to build up the supply of renewable energy by forcing the country's electrical utilities to buy wind- and solar-generated energy at higher prices than they could sell it to consumers, the firms threatened to reduce their output and import electricity. But the imported power would inevitably come from France or Poland; it was therefore generated by either nuclear- or coal-based stations. Neither source was acceptable to the environmentalist minister of energy, so the initial plans were curtailed.

Power supplies can in principle be regulated either by market or by statute; a mix is usually unworkable. By opting for deregulation, Europe's political leadership has adopted the American model of market orientation, trusting that competition will work in the best interests of all, consumers and producers. However, up to 2003 the fall in electricity prices that proponents of deregulation foresaw had not materialized. Neither has the hoped for growth of small enterprises in the energy sector occurred. Rather the opposite has taken place: with few exceptions the market has become oligopolistic. Furthermore, the security of supply has deteriorated greatly. The higher prices that were earlier paid to the state-sanctioned monopolies represented an insurance premium providing for substantial protective redundancies in technology as well as in personnel. It is too early for a conclusive evaluation of the effects of the deregulation in electrical utilities, but it seems likely that many Europeans would prefer security of supply over lower prices.

Deregulation of the telecommunications sector was based on the same combination of political-economic reasons used in breaking up electrical utilities and the CAB: natural monopolies and strict governmental controls led to artificially high prices for consumers and inhibited economic growth, especially of small- and medium-sized business. Once again, as with electricity and airlines, deregulation started in the United States. In 1982 the Reagan administration ordered the breakup of the giant American Telephone and Telegraph Company (AT&T), which as the parent company of the Bell System had dominated American telephone service since 1900. AT&T did not exercise a complete monopoly, but the few other existing telephone companies did not constitute real competition. Before deregulation AT&T was a colossus: in 1970 it was by far the largest American company with assets totalling 53 billion dollars; its closest rival at the time, Standard Oil of New Jersey, was worth a modest 19 billion dollars.[151] AT&T had an outstanding international reputation for its technological excellence and reliability of its services and products; it also devoted considerable resources to pure and applied research in telecommunications: its Bell Laboratories were world-famous. Yet the company's overwhelming presence made it an obvious target for those dissatisfied with telephone bills and services; "Bell-bashing" had a long tradition in American society.

The breakup of AT&T was designed to bring the benefits of price competition directly to consumers. AT&T continued to exist as an integrated telecommunications services and equipment company, but it could no longer provide direct telephone access to consumers. All local exchange services, the so-called last mile, were to be provided by independent suppliers. The predicted effects, however, were not realized. Although competitive pricing between alternative providers did emerge, it turned out that most private telephone customers did not bother with choosing between different local and long-distance carriers with their different rates. According to The Fall of the Bell System by Peter Temin and Louis Galambos, private persons as well as small- and medium-sized enterprises (SME) found the process of choosing providers too complicated; the alternative rate schedules, and even the companies themselves, often changed frequently. In contrast, big firms were able to reduce telephone costs by systematically taking advantage of rates competition, or even by obtaining services tailored to their needs. In general, the deregulation did make telecommunications a competitive market, resulting in lower rates that were perceived to be more in accordance with the actual cost of operation. But it was above all the rates of long-distance telephoning that declined; local rates actually rose in a number of areas. It is in the nature of things that private persons place mostly local calls, while telephone use of companies, according to size and specialization, has a higher proportion of long-distance calls. So it could be argued that before deregulation, large firms in fact subsidised the telephone use of private persons and SME by paying higher prices for its usage profile. From this perspective the deregulation of telecommunications in the US has benefited corporate customers more than individual consumers.

In 2002, twenty years after the initial deregulation of AT&T, Eric Benhamou, chairman of Palm Inc. and member of the US President's Information Technology Advisory Committee, noted with regret that "we had blind faith in competition."[152] In his view, competition in the telecommunications sector had backfired: it had forced down prices to a level that discouraged investment while the sector's rapidly changing technology demanded more investment, not less. This underinvestment had resulted in a lack of broadband access, a new core technology in the burgeoning IT industry. While there was a sufficient long-distance network of glass fibre cable, the gap in the "last mile" was widespread. American conditions compared unfavourably with Benhamou's experience of the situation in France, where the telecom market was much less deregulated, and a single company, France Telecom, was the chief provider. According to Benhamou, France Telecom's performance surpassed that of American suppliers in three key areas: it was quicker to provide service; its personnel was better trained; and the connections never failed. In Europe, before deregulation, telecommunication services were provided by the respective national postal authority (PTT), and each activity, mail and telecommunication, subsidized the other at different times. Because of this linkage with the state, deregulation of the telecommunication sector in Europe was a complex process. In the United States telecommunication was just another commercial service provided by private enterprise. In almost all European countries, by contrast, control of telecommunication was understood as a part of national sovereignty and a tool of national economic policy. The respective government decided its PTT's general goals concerning employment, revenue, or technological development, which might actually differ from sector-specific goals in telecommunication. To deregulate telecommunication European governments had to transform the entire PTT sector. The implications of deregulation were thus far-reaching. To carry out the policy required a changed understanding of the economic role of the state, from being a steersman to being a night watchman—a crucial step towards the American model of market capitalism.

The legal-administrative status of PTT employees was a large problem. They were usually civil servants with special rights regarding security of employment and pensioning. One way to facilitate reorganization was to legally separate postal and telecommunication services, as the UK has done as early as 1969. The progressive widening of EU's authority also pushed the transformation by weakening independent national control over the PTT sector. In the 1980s the EU Commission first suggested, then decreed, basic lines for the deregulation of PTT in the Union. Within this framework, member countries formulated individual national laws specifying the actual terms of deregulation. This legislation began to be put in place in the 1990s, but the deregulation of telecommunication in the Union was still not complete in 2004. The results so far have been similar to those in the US. Overall rates came down and demand increased; and long-distance calls particularly became cheaper while local calls became relatively more expensive. In most countries customers can chose their service provider, often even on a call-by-call basis, but very few actually do so. Large firms typically negotiate special deals. In contrast to the American experience, in most European countries the traditional telecom provider has remained dominant, often with a market share close to 90 per cent, which is larger than AT&T ever had. Technological development has received a boost, though its potential advantages and risks were understood by few people.

The spectacular success of mobile phones in Europe shows that the promised benefits of deregulation can sometimes be realized. In contrast to cable-based telecommunication, mobile telephony started deregulated. In this new and rapidly expanding field competition abounds, with several large providers in most countries. The technological gains for the European economy have been considerable. Throughout the twentieth century American companies had a consistent technological superiority in telecommunications. This is no longer true; since roughly 2000 the European telecom industry has largely eliminated the technological gap. Significantly, the world's largest producer of mobile phones in 2004, Nokia, is a European company. Railways are the third area in our sketch of deregulation. As in the case of telecommunication, the United States and Europe had substantially different starting points. Whereas American railway policy has generally minimized government controls, European railway policies have historically been emphatically state-interventionist. On the Continent railways not only transported goods and passengers, they were also a central element in military strategy. From the late 1940s, with a few small exceptions, they were also everywhere directly owned by the state. Railway employees thus were state employees. In some countries the railways even carried out functions not directly related to transport, such as policing. Because of these semi-state tasks European railways tended to be economically inefficient and inflexible. Yet their kind of organization and management worked well enough as long as railways were the principal means of transport.

But after 1945 the use of cars and trucks to transport people and goods became ever more widespread. Motor vehicles were more flexible, more individual, and, since their owners did not have to pay for either the use or the construction of the road network, their transport was cheaper than the railways'. The railways coped badly with these competitors. Even as highways became increasingly congested, they had only modest success in offering a convincingly alternative mass transport; railway agents had difficulty adopting a passenger-friendly service attitude after decades of being figures of authority. By the 1980s the economic situation for most railways was very bad indeed: rolling stock had become outdated, track networks outworn, and the burden of debt enormous. In 1993 Europe's largest railway, *Deutsche Bahn* (DB), declared an accumulated debt of 41 billion dollars. It was clear that European railways had to undergo a profound transformation to avoid a total collapse. The dominant international political-economic opinion at the time considered that deregulation would restore the railways' competitiveness. From 1990 the EU Commission accepted the viewpoint and formulated several framework laws regarding the deregulation of railway policy and the promotion of competition in the railway sector.[153]

In Germany the Kohl government designed a deregulatory package for the country's state railway, the Deutsche Bahn, which was implemented stepwise between 1994 and 1999. It created a state monitoring body for technical standards and security and divided the old DB into separate stock companies, one each for long-distance, and local traffic, cargo, track, and railway stations. All these companies were placed under the roof of one holding company. All shares were owned by the state, but future privatization was not excluded. DB's debts and pension liabilities were assumed by the state, which also paid DB an additional four billion dollars between 1994 and 2002 to cover earlier liabilities such as compensation for environmental damages and the like. Under the new arrangements the existing track network can also be used by other approved railway operators, and in 2004 more than 200 private companies, mainly in local traffic, did so. In addition, a few big firms, such as the chemical giant BASF, have started to operate their own cargo trains. All users of the network are required to pay track fees based on the cost of construction and maintenance.

In Sweden many features of railway deregulation were similar to German measures, for example the takeover of debt by the state and a separate agency for operational security, but the matter of the track network was handled differently. When *Statens Järnväger* (the state railways, SJ) was deregulated in 1998, the transport company that succeeded them had no organizational connection to the track. Even before the official deregulation private railway companies serving local traffic had started to use the rail lines as well special cargo carriers, such as the "paper-trains". SJ continues to have preferential treatment on the network, so-called "grandfather rights", which are based on convention rather than legal rights. However, as of 2004 the Swedish government has preserved state ownership of the track system, which gives it an instrument to use in the campaign to shift traffic from road to rail. Consequently, track usage remains heavily subsidized; in 2001 the subsidy amounted to nearly 85 per cent of the real cost. Thus, the Swedish state has not entirely pulled out of the country's railways but has continued to use parts of the system to promote political-economic policies: to reduce road transport, to serve persons without cars, to improve or preserve economic infrastructure, and so on. This middle position—between American-style total privatization and the European tradition of state ownership—has met widespread approval in the Swedish society. In Italy *Ferrovie dello Stato* (state railway, FS) was changed from a state agency into a stock company in 1992, but deregulation and divisionalization did not take place until 1998. The FS's debts were partly taken over by the central government in 1996, and extremely favourable conditions for local transport, including state subsidies, made it possible for FS to reduce its remaining debts from 46,500 to 450 billion lire within two years! Maintenance and management of rail network rest in the hands of the *Divisione Infrastruttura*, which is paid for track usage. FS is required to maintain a wide offering in passenger transport, and is thus not free to close or change services as could a private company. And, in principle, private competitors have right of access to rail track. In spite of these changes, however, FS operations are still very bureaucratic and inefficient.[154] Obtaining information about connections and buying the according tickets can be quite time consuming! Deregulating Italian railway has so far not achieved the hoped for increases in efficiency and economic competitiveness.

The British railway system is the oldest in the world, and it was the last to be nationalized in Europe (1947). Like its counterparts in other countries, British Railways (British Rail from the 1960s) steadily lost ground to road traffic for both cargo and passengers. Modernizing railway operations was hampered by a history of company fragmentation, a series of bad management decisions, the cumbersome bureaucracy of government control agencies, and continuing political disagreement about transport policy in general. Deregulation and privatization were proposed as a way out of the quagmire during the Thatcher years, but the Railway Act implementing the policy came first in 1993 under the conservative government of John Major. The terms of the breakup were more extreme and complicated than elsewhere. British Rail (BR) was divested of its operational activities. These operations were divisionalized according to the familiar formula, but in addition, in order to instil competition, each division was further divided into several firms. No less than 25 regionalized operators emerged, each with its own subsidy. In accordance with the business logic of private companies, they each optimized timetables according to their regional needs. As a result passengers needing the services of more than one company encountered annoying difficulties coordinating travel times, and the number of persons travelling by rail dropped further. After 1994 system's tracks, tunnels, and stations were owned and operated by a group of companies known as Railtrack. As a privately owned and listed company, Railtrack's purpose of existence was to turn a profit, and it formulated pricing policy and investment activity accordingly. Because of the heavy competition for goods transport, the track-usage fee for freight-trains was kept extremely low, and those for passenger-trains high, in compensation. Train operators were thus forced to raise fares, which in turn drove down passenger numbers. Complaints about the inadequacy of Railtrack's services peaked after several fatal train accidents in 1999 and 2000; and in late 2002 Railtrack was taken over by a non-profit organisation, Network Rail. So far, the outcome of deregulation (and privatization) of the British railway system has been little short of disaster. Competition in the sector has brought few benefits to society as a whole. Connecting travel has become difficult; the frequency of passenger trains has declined, and standards of cleanliness and safety have deteriorated. Fares and rates have gone up, and traffic has gone down.

While the companies paid dividends to shareholders, the state (and thereby society) granted subsidies to the companies.

Deregulation of the French national railway *SNCF* did not begin until 1997. Several of the changes implemented were the now familiar ones. The French state assumed 70 per cent SNCF's debt and redefined SNCF as an independent enterprise offering the transport of passengers and goods by rail. Other issues differed from the cases presented earlier. SNCF is no longer directly run by the government but it is still owned by the state and still regarded as an instrument of national economic policy. In 1997 the government demanded that SNCF contribute to employment policy by increasing its workforce; and in return for the creation of 20,000 new jobs SNCF was awarded 20 billion francs later that year. The deregulation legislation placed the management of the country's track network under a separate company, Réseau Ferré de France (RFF), while maintenance and construction of track stayed with SNCF. The emergence of competitive railway services, though, was hindered by RFF's non-disclosure of track-usage fees for several years. It would appear then that the French government did not really want to subject SNCF to competition and therefore executed the deregulatory steps ordered by the EU in a way that upheld traditional practices.

In sum, the results of deregulation of European railways are mixed. One could argue that with such a slow moving system as the railway – the construction of a major new track can take up to twenty years – there is still hope for a more positive outcome. But the reform's first aim of reviving the railway as an effective alternative to road transport has yet to be reached. Indeed, up to 2004 the organizational efforts and investment costs of monitoring and developing the new structures were in many cases higher than before deregulation. The second goal—relieving the financial burden on the state—has also fallen short of expectations in many cases. The burden has been reduced but not to the extent hoped. The third aim—the injection of competition in railway operations—was generally not fulfilled. Moreover, where real competition did emerge, as in Britain, its effect was the opposite of that intended. Since the mid 1980s the US economy has grown faster than the European on average and generated more jobs. It seemed clear that Europe was losing its competitive edge compared with America and, until 1990, with Japan as well. Understandably, European political and economic leaders looked to the United States for solutions, as they had done a generation earlier. Seeing that the American economy was less regulated and more open to market competition, they concluded that the European economic position would improve if American structures were put in place. Thus, they became convinced that deregulation would be revive the sluggish European economy. At the same time a number of public utility monopolies had become so expensive to uphold that a change was unavoidable. In the case of national railways deficits were so huge that substantial change was urgent. In that context it was thus natural for leaders to choose the policy prescription that dominated the political-economic discourse of the time, namely, deregulation.

In 2004 many cases of deregulation were still under way, so that any general evaluation must be incomplete. However, the experience of more than a decade is enough to yield some reasoned conclusions. In a few sectors deregulation has definitely produced a positive outcome: in air traffic, banking, and telecommunication European enterprises are nowadays more competitive than in the 1980s. In some other areas the consequences of deregulations have been mixed. Water supply, sewage, and railways belong to this group. In some cases service has improved and prices have even come down; in other cases service has deteriorated and costs (prices plus subsidies) have increased. The difference in results seems to have been a function of the terms of deregulation. Radical breakup to maximize competition, such as was applied in the case of British Rail, would appear to be more destructive than creative. The third group consists of those sectors in which deregulation has so far failed to achieve its goals, namely better services, lower prices, and a competitive structure that would guarantee both in the future. To this group belong the electric utilities, and there are indications that gas utilities are heading in the same direction. In electric utility sector competition has been undermined by a wave of concentration and the development of an oligopolistic market. At the same time underinvestment in transmission facilities has weakened the security of supply. The result has been a rash of blackouts, and experts in the field predict that they will become commonplace. Electricity prices, which initially had come down, went up again, after it became clear that private consumers and small- and medium-sized enterprises are reluctant to follow price differentials and change providers accordingly. In all cases deregulation has strengthened private industry at the expense of politically controlled administration. In some cases it has brought about an enrichment of investors at the expense of the community. This has happened especially in those cases where private utilities paid dividends to shareholders while delaying technically necessary investment to an extent that threatened the system's existence. Because government for political and economic reasons cannot allow utilities to collapse, they have to rescue the endangered companies with the taxpayers' money, as in the cases of the London Underground and the British company Railtrack.

PRIVATIZATION TO PROMOTE GROWTH

In Europe both past and present the State's role in the economy has frequently extended beyond regulation to full, or partial, ownership of entrepreneurial enterprises. In twentieth-century Europe the development of state-owned enterprise was pushed forward by the socialist movement—both the social democratic and the communist variant—and welfare-state economics. Many Europeans perceived state ownership to be socially more just than private enterprise, because profits would end up in the government budget, to be used for the benefit of all. State-owned firms can be considered more responsive to the people's interest— or the national interest—because they are subject to control by an elected government and its public administration. And not a few Europeans agreed with Lenin and others that private big business was a promoter and exploiter of war and should therefore be put under the control of the peace loving people. State ownership in the European economy thus tended to increase in step with democratization; both nationalized industry and the suffrage increased after the First

World War and, in a different combination, after the Second World War. The development of the welfare state also enlarged the state's quota in the economy, since most of the welfare services were owned or regulated by the state. For these reasons most Europeans long regarded state ownership in general as a good economic institution. Indeed, state authority per se tends to evoke popular consent in most European countries; a diffuse attitude that 'the state is good' or 'administration knows better than I do' is uncommon. Yet if most Europeans have been largely content with state ownership, why did their leaders start the massive programmes of privatization programmes that have been under way since the late 1980s? The general answers are to be found in the economic and political upheavals of the 1970s and 1980s in both the United States and Europe that were sketched in the chapter's introduction. Public affairs commentators and politicians began to perceive that the services of private firms were often much cheaper than those of publicly owned companies, in public transport up to forty per cent. Second, public ownership had become a growing financial burden on government budgets; the sale of publicly owned services could be seen as a means both to reduce indebtedness and to obtain an injection of income in the public purse. Third, a changing climate of opinion on business affairs interested the masses in the stockmarket. Until the 1980s few ordinary people were interested in shares; they invested in houses, cars, and other consumer goods. As these appetites were saturated, shares became more and more an attractive investment. Such persons welcomed the flotation of such seemingly blue-chip companies as public utilities. For instance, the initial offering of British Telecom in 1984 was over-subscribed tenfold.

These pragmatic reasons in favour of privatization were supplemented by economic theory. The Chicago school economists had, as mentioned earlier, long asserted the general superiority of private enterprise, and these assertions were developed into formal arguments.[155] There are basically two different approaches, the political and the contractual. The political approach denies the will of politicians to keep state-owned firms competitive. Politicians want to be re-elected, and with goal in mind they press for the overstaffing of state-owned firms. In return, this large and over-staffed state sector, anxious to keep its privileged employment, self-consciously supports government parties. The alternative contractual approach does not deny the good intentions of politicians but maintains that in state-owned firms—in contrast to private ones—managers are not adequately paid and, furthermore, are not penalized for making bad decisions. It does not matter that one can find historical evidence for or against both approaches; what matters is that since the 1990s many European decision makers both in and outside government have become convinced that state ownership in principle hobbles competitiveness, and that therefore it is to be avoided or at least reduced—if politically possible.

Some examples of privatization occurred during the 1960s and 1970s. For instance, the state-owned share in the Volkswagen company was reduced in 1960 in an attempt to strengthen the popular roots of capitalist thinking in German society. To achieve a wide distribution among the public, share purchases were limited to a few per person. But many buyers sold their three or four shares quickly, and the goal of establishing a shareholding people was not achieved. Similar initiatives in other countries were equally disappointing.

The Conservative Thatcher Government in the UK was the first in Europe to put privatization in the forefront of its economic agenda. It saw the rebuilding of a privately owned market economy as the cure-all for the country's economic ailments. Immediately after taking office in 1979 it sold off several reasonably competitive companies: British Aerospace, Britoil and Cable & Wireless. After re-election in 1983 it offered 50 per cent of the monopolist British Telecom (BT) to the public in 1984. In this case Thatcher's move met resistance. Whereas the sales in 1979 had affected few other than company employees, in the case of BT a major public utility was at stake. There was a considerable outcry, and BT's engineers even went on strike against the proposed sale, but the protests were to no avail. In 1991 and 1993 the remaining state shares in BT were privatized. Although BT's staff was reduced by half, the company's service record improved, and the price of BT shares rose 150 per cent in the decade after the initial public offering. In short, it was a success story excess for the dismissed employees. By the end of the Conservative Party's third parliament in 1992 nearly all state-owned corporations had been privatized. (An exception was the nuclear power stations, which nobody wanted to buy; they had to stay with the state). The British economy also resumed growth during these years, and the recovery increased support for privatization policy, which became almost a British export item. Emboldened by its past successes the Conservative government in 1997 proposed to privatize the London Underground, the world's oldest and the country's most important public-transport network. Tony Blair's Labour government rejected that plan, but replaced it by a quasi-privatization, a public private partnership (PPP), that was put in place in 2003.

Other countries privatized much less and much later. When Belgium's Christian Democratic Prime Minister Wilfried Martens tried to initiate the privatization of several state-owned enterprises, including the national airline Sabena, in the mid 1980s, he was thwarted by vigorous protests from the country's labour unions. In 1992 the terms of the Treaty of Maastricht required the Belgian government to undertake a massive reduction of the public debt in order that the country could join the proposed common European currency. Faced with this and other urgent financial needs the parliament approved a special authorization of privatization in 1995. The then prime minister, Jean-Luc Dehane, used this authorization to decree privatisation amid massive protest by the employees affected. In the case of Sabena, privatization proved to be disastrous, though not entirely of its own making. When the airline's shares were placed on the market, Swissair purchased 49 per cent of the flotation and later took a credit of 87 million dollars from Sabena. But when world air traffic collapsed after the attack on New York's World Trade Center on 11 September 2001, Swissair defaulted; Sabena was not able to raise the missing capital and the airline went bankrupt. Late privatization was not the only reason for the unfortunate outcome, but the growing economic difficulties that all national airlines encountered from the 1990s indicates a negative connection between state ownership and competitiveness.

The most extensive programme of privatization in Europe took place in Italy, where the extent of state-ownership, as well as the related problems, was huge. In 1993 the losses of IRI, the main state holding company, amounted to the equivalent of 30 billion euros. That equalled the GNP of countries such as Hungary or Peru! Under such circumstances, IRI and other state-owned companies were no longer sustainable. In addition to the financial pressure came the political pressure. The Italian government wanted to internationalize its economic system, to enlarge the stock market, to stimulate competition, and to widen economic ownership. Privatization was seen as the best means to do so. Between 1992 and 1999 sales of state-owned enterprises raised no less than 90 billion euros, the equivalent of 12 per cent of GNP in 1992. The numbers would seem to show that Italian privatization was a big economic success. However, a closer look reveals structural deficiencies.

To a large extent privatization in Italy was carried out through initial private offerings (IPO). Traditionally, Italian tycoons had set up what was called a "cascade" of holding firms: a chain of holding companies in which the each holding company owned or controlled a decisive voting bloc in its neighbour company in the chain. This structure, for instance, enabled the Agnelli family to control Fiat: although the Agnellis owned only ten per cent of company's shares outright, they disposed over nearly forty per cent of the votes.[156] By means of such Chinese-box cascades the country's established entrepreneurial families acquired control over many of the privatized enterprises. Thus, the Agnelli family succeeded in directing Telecom Italia, the huge former state monopoly, with a personal investment of only 220 million euros, a tiny 0.6 per cent of the company's total shares.[157] Italy's economic elite also extended its economic control beyond its direct investments by using interlocking directorates. They were widely applied and represented a formidable instrument to direct enterprises without actually investing capital in them.

Privatization in Italy had two primacy goals: to inject competition into the national economy and to relieve the state of economic burdens. The latter goal was largely achieved. But competition could not be raised significantly as long as the old structures, not of ownership but of control, prevailed. Some steps to change this have been taken in recent years. For instance, in order to exclude imbalanced decision-making the government approved legislation to strengthen the rights of minority shareholders in 1998. This *Legge Draghi* was named after an official of the Ministry of Treasury, *Mario Draghi*, an MIT-trained economist. Nonetheless, by cascades and networking a handful of rich Italian family firms can still control large parts of the Italian economy and reduce competition. Italian privatisation was a success financially, but rather a failure in promoting a free-market economy.

In many countries, major cases of privatization occasioned a public debate that aired the pros and cons of policy's principles. The debate over the proposed sale of the Norwegian state oil company, Statoil, is a good example. Statoil was established by the Norwegian government in 1972 after the discovery of oil and gas under the Norwegian Sea. Its mandate was to promote Norwegian national interest in the development of the resources. Statoil quickly became the largest operator on the Norwegian continental shelf and by 2000 was by far the largest enterprise in the country. It was a major supplier of natural gas to the European market and one of the world's biggest sellers of crude oil. It had also built up substantial international activities with over a third of its workforce employed outside Norway. In 2000 a proposal by the Labour government at the time to partially privatize Statoil provoked a vigorous exchange between the young oil and energy minister, Olav

Akselsen, and the Labour Party veteran Finn Lied, who had been minister of industry at the time of Statoil's founding, Akselsen, arguing for privatization, emphasized the financial benefits of privatization and the company's need to operate without national policy constraints: 1) Statoil had had no state privileges since the 1980s; 2) Statoil's dividend to its owner, the state, was negligible compared with the royalties paid for pumping oil, royalties that all the oil companies regardless of ownership; 3) Statoil's competitors had merged and the company needed to be able to meet the new challengers from a strong position; 4) in 2000 less than 50 per cent of Statoil's activities were situated in Norway; 5) new owners are best even for Norwegian firms connected to the networks of Statoil; and 6) to sell would mean to double the dividend.[158] Lied, who had coined the programmatic slogan "sustainable energy development", rejected all points: 1) Statoil had always had full freedom of decision making; 2) if the aim of privatization was to share know-how and risk, Norwegian oil-policy had proven its success over the previous 30 years; 3) it was not true that only private ownership stimulates an enterprise growth—Statoil itself contradicted such a view; 4) it was not possible to be "a bit private"; 5) to connect the fate of an enterprise to the stock exchange defeats long-term policy; 6) there was much more oil to be pumped from Norwegian territory—Statoil's future did not depend on international engagement. What is important here is not the rightness or wrongness of one or the other contention, but rather that the debate itself was a sign of the Americanization of political-economic discourse in a European country. It is clear that some issues were not very much to the point, yet they might have been politically helpful in persuading others. It is also noteworthy that Akselsen, the proponent of privatization, did not maintain that state ownership was inferior to private ownership in principle. This contention was raised by Lied – and rejected. Lied's remarks also reflected the traditional European scepticism of a capitalist economy driven by the stock market. In the end, though, Lied's defensive position was overrun. On 18 June 2001 American banks floated Statoil's initial public offering (IPO); the Norwegian state has remained the company's largest shareholder.

In a number of cases European governments were eager to sell their companies and to increase competition, but wanted to keep a certain control at the same time. Thus, in such cases as the British airport operator *BAA*, the Spanish oil giant *Repsol*, or the French car maker *Renault*, the government concerned kept a so-called golden share, which carried a decisive voting power. In May 2003, however, the European Court of Justice ruled that such golden shares were illegal. Once again it was an institution of the European Union that pushed forward certain general principles of political-economic reform. And because the EU was founded on liberal economic principles, the direction of reform was toward American-style market forces and away from European-style administration. The Americanizing implications of privatization can also be seen in the terminology of the stock market. Until the stock-market boom of the late 1990s the common expression of European business for selling a company's start-up shares at the stock market would have been "flotation", but it has now largely been replaced by the American term "initial public offering", or IPO. And its use is not restricted to business publications such as The Economist or The Financial Times.

Although privatization has been carried out unevenly throughout Europe, no country has excluded itself completely from the trend. And few areas of state activity have been excluded from the policy in principle. One such area is national defence, but the state monopoly of force in internal affairs has been breeched in a number of ways.

This development has potentially far-reaching implications for democratic societies. Quite apart from representing a potential threat to the state itself, private organizations authorized to exercise armed force, even if specifically under government control, can undermine society's trust in the neutrality and authority of state institutions. In the United States private security services such as Pinkertons and Burns have a long history of supplying private customers, especially large department stores and banks, with specific protection. With the emergence of shopping malls and similar constructions that blur the distinction between private and public space, the relationship of private security services to the official representatives of public order, the police, has also grown fuzzy. A generation ago, private security companies politically had a bad smell in European society, possibly because of historical associations with the paramilitary organizations of the interwar period. A general attitude was that such companies acquired and exercised police power in a questionable way beyond the usual public control. For reasons that are not entirely clear, this critical attitude has dissipated, and the provision of protection services has burgeoned. In 2002 there were 7850 private security companies operating in the UK alone, and they employed 162 thousand persons. In 1989 the Swedish security firm, Securitas, which dated from 1934, determined to expand internationally and in 2004 it offered services in 19 countries. In 1999/2000 it acquired the venerable American companies Pinkerton and Burns International, becoming thereby the largest provider of private security in the world.

Privatization has also been urged as the solution to growing difficulties in state education. The guru of privatization, Milton Friedman, has long advocated that the state get out of education, even primary education, and in an interview in 2003 expressed satisfaction that there had been some progress in this direction in the United States.[159] In Europe the debate has been almost exclusively limited to the question of private versus state higher education. It is a debate that is coloured by a considerable degree of misconception and misinformation. The widespread European perception is that institutions of higher education in the United States are overwhelmingly outstanding in quality and mainly privately owned; in this perception the excellence of education and research is deemed to stem from the mode of financing: student fees, private donations, and commissioned research funds. Such views are both misleading and downright wrong. Not all American colleges and universities are world leaders; and although many of the most famous (and excellent) are privately owned (Harvard, Stanford, Yale, Columbia, Chicago, or Princeton), there are also state universities of similarly world-leading calibre (California-Berkeley, UCLA, Michigan, Wisconsin, North Carolina, or Texas). But in contrast to British and Continental universities, all American institutions of higher education—including those owned by the state—are managed with a high degree of autonomy and flexibility with many features of an ordinary business enterprise. The state bureaucracy and politicians usually have little to do with the operations, including the long-range planning, of state-run universities; these affairs are handled by the university president, deans of faculty, and the various internal decision-making councils and boards. State universities also routinely supplement state financial grants by accumulating endowments based on individual private donations and actively pursued "capital campaigns". Private institutions, on the other hand, frequently receive considerable public monies to support specific research or pedagogical projects. The notionally high tuition fees of many private universities are also somewhat misleading, for many students—especially postgraduates—are awarded scholarships that considerably reduce the personal costs. Autonomy, financial self-responsibility, and competition are the distinguishing hallmark of American institutions of higher education. And the differences between private and state institutions are much less clear than in Europe.

There are two features that most European universities and institutions of higher education have in common: 1. they are owned, funded, and controlled by the state; and 2. their degrees have fairly equal standing both in society and among employers. The Grandes Écoles in France and "Oxbridge" in England constitute, to be sure, a sort of premier league, but otherwise the differences in prestige between universities are considered pretty negligible. After European universities were opened to mass education in the late 1960s, many of them became unwieldy large with more than 50,000 students, and the quality of both teaching and research deteriorated. In the Anglo-Saxon system a university could in principle control the balance between the numbers of students and staff, whereas on the Continent ministers simply ruled that the universities should accept more students regardless of other conditions.

The end of the sustained economic growth of the post-war boom worsened the situation, for university financing could not keep pace with ever increasing numbers of students and the universities' to expand and modernize facilities. These difficulties and the inability to solve within the traditional structures prompted many would-be reformers to look to the American model. A selective look at the model produced quick conclusions: American universities are world leaders in research in almost areas of real importance from economics and business management to computing, engineering, biochemistry, and medicine. American universities are predominantly privately owned, not state-owned. The scientific and scholarly excellence of American universities, therefore, is founded on private ownership. On the basis of this logic, educational reformers in many European countries insisted that the privatization would solve the problem of the universities. The attraction of the American model, thus interpreted, was especially strong in management and technical education because these were the fields in which American schools were perceived to have unique competence.

One of the first European universities to apply the recipe of privatization was Chalmers, the Technical University of Göteborg, Sweden, which was wholly privatized in 1994. It had started as a private establishment in 1829 on the basis of a donation by William Chalmers, one of the directors of the Swedish East Indian Company. On 1 July 1937 it had been taken over by the Swedish state, and on the same day in 1994 it became once again a private institution with a new endowment. Official statements claim that the transformation was a clear success. Staff, however, concede privately that the university's economic situation is not good.[160] Yet, financial betterment was the very goal of privatization! The situation at *Danmarks Tekniske Universitetet* (DTU) in Copenhagen is similar. DTU was reorganized as a private foundation in 2001. One half of the initial capital endowment of 3.5 milliard Danish crowns was an outright gift, the other half was a loan. Not long after its establishment, the new institution's rector, Lars Pallesen, admitted that he doubted that he could convince any bank to grant DTU a loan, meaning thereby that it was not really a viable business undertaking. Europe has had private business schools for some time. Several of these were mentioned in chapter five in connection with the introduction of American business management. In recent years additional private institutions for management training leading to an MBA degree based entirely on American curricula have been established. An example is the ESCP-EAP European School of Management; in 2004 it had campuses in Paris, Oxford, Madrid, and Berlin. The school emphasizes that its degrees are accredited by EQUIS and AACSB, American standards that insure the quality of management studies. As with other Americanized (or American) institutions of this type, the ESCP-EAP programmes and teaching staff are ranked according to specific criteria, in this case the Financial Times listing. This scheme assesses quality solely on the basis of publications in 40 business journals. No other journals or scholarly products, such as this very book, carry any weight in the ranking. Such explicit and narrowly defined ranking practices have previously been unknown in European higher education.

Another recent trend promoting Americanization in European higher education could be called educational FDI. A number of US universities have set up branches in Europe, teaching an American curriculum in English with a mainly American staff. Especially Germany has become an attractive market for these branch schools because of the country's lack of native providers of MBA studies. The Krannert Graduate School of Management from Purdue University runs the German International School of Management and Administration in Hanover; Duke University's Fuqua School of Business has constructed a subsidiary in Frankfurt, and Northwestern University on in Koblenz. Germany is, of course, not the only market. The Graduate Business School of the University of Chicago has opened a satellite campus in Barcelona and the absence of management education in the former socialist countries of east-central has led to much activity there. In the Czech Republic, however, British universities have taken the lead. In 2002 only four of fifteen business schools in the country were subsidiaries of American institutions, the rest were British.[161] The development of educational FTI has also produced contention the World Trade Organization (WTO). American and Japanese representatives have argued that European policies on the financing of higher education disadvantage the new foundations. The favouring of state-owned universities and schools, according to these arguments, constitutes unfair competition because it violates WTO principles that all service-providers should have equal access to all markets. Yet few Europeans have ever imagined education to be a market! The core idea of European higher education has always been to impart cultural and scientific knowledge, not to train students according to the economic utility of marketplace. Ironically, while American MBA training was establishing an ever stronger presence in Europe, many of its characteristics were being increasingly attacked in the United States itself. In a 1996 book, *The collapse of the American management mystique*, the American business expert Robert R. Locke claimed that the competitiveness of the American economy was in fact being undermined by the platitudinous cult of the MBA. He was not alone in his views. A 2002 poll of 28 leading professors of American management schools on the most important books in their field revealed that there was no major new contribution to management education since 1973. In commenting on the poll, Lucy Kellaway, a prominent columnist in the Financial Times, concluded:

"The reason for this is that the truths about management and organisations are not deep. They are pretty obvious and unchanging. What is true about people, organisations, motivation and leadership 60 years ago is still pretty much true now."[162]

Why then did so many Europeans seem to be eager to adopt the American approach to business? There are two reasons: The American economy thrived in the 1990s, and Europeans naturally wanted to take part in that growth. Management education was generally perceived as one of the reasons for American prosperity and therefore an area that Europeans needed to learn from. The second reason is a truly European one. Europe had failed to construct a common managerial qualification equivalent to the MBA. The growing mobility of persons and the growing economic integration, however, demanded common standards. For instance, a French investor in Austria had little idea what the degree "Diplom-Kaufmann", awarded to graduates of business colleges in that country, meant in terms of managerial qualifications. Such business needs were a partial basis for subsequent EU directives that promoted Americanization in the Union's higher education sector. The Bologna Process, which was initiated in 2000/2001, entailed that European universities reorganize their basic degree curricula to liken the BA and MA degrees that characterize American (and British) universities. An additional justification for the standardization was that it would enable European students to pursue degree courses anywhere in the Union. Once again, the efforts of the EU leadership to promote European integration works in favour of an Americanization of the Union, since there is no single European model to deflect the seductive attractions of the American model.

The structure of student fees has been a fundamental division between American and European higher education that has widened since the educational revolution of the welfare state. In principle, tuition in higher education in Europe is free; in American education it is not, and at private universities the notional cost of tuition can be high indeed. The intractable difficulties of university financing have recently begun to undermine the welfare-state principle of free tuition. In January 2004 Tony Blair's Labour government secured legislation that would permit British institutions of higher education to charge tuition fees of up to 3,000 pounds per year. The public and parliamentary outcry was considerable. Opposition to the perceived injection of capitalist economics into state-owned higher education generated the largest internal protest of Labour MPs against a Labour Government since the Second World War![163] The protesters brought forward several reasons against the reform: 1) The state should pay for higher education because it is a necessity for the nation's economy and for society as a whole; 2) Differential levels of fees would separate students according to income – and via scholarships – according to intelligence, which was socially and politically undesirable; 3) The equality of the degrees across institutions would be undermined, which would destroy the central social principle of equal access. Although the opposition was defeated—narrowly, its position reflects widely held opinions on the Continent, where in 2004 similar suggestions on university financing were aired, so far without result.

The collapse of centralized state socialism in eastern Europe brought about, of course, the most comprehensive programmes of privatization. The first such transformation took place in the eastern provinces of Germany that had constituted the German Democratic Republic until 3 October 1990. As elsewhere in Eastern Europe, the country's industrial plant and infrastructure were utterly run down. Therefore the German Government, which inherited the GDR's state property by default, had to decide whether to rebuild individual industrial enterprises before selling them, or to privatize straight away. The conservative government of Chancellor Kohl, which was already pushing for privatization in western Germany, opted for the latter course. The policy carried a high price. First, potential sales income was forfeited because the dilapidation of the firms was so advanced that ownership was transferred for the nominal sum of a single Deutschmark. Second, a number of sales were effected only because the government granted respective buyers hundreds of millions of Deutschmarks in subsidy.[164] And still most of the former state enterprises in eastern Germany did not survive. Privatization was a huge failure, economically and socially. In spite of an annual transfer of some four per cent of Germany's GNP into these regions, the unemployment rate rose to about 20 per cent of the eastern German workforce in the following decade. However, the economic costs of the alternative policy—reconstruction before privatization— would probably have been even higher, though the social costs might have been reduced.

The other former socialist states also wanted to privatize their economies, in part because state-owned enterprise was the very symbol of the discarded socialism. However, unlike the former GDR, they did not have an economically strong successor that could shoulder the bills. Ten years after socialism's collapse only seven of twenty countries in Eastern Europe had regained 1990 GNP levels. There was no alternative to privatization; the questions were simply how and when to privatize. The 'when' was simple: as soon as the respective political constellation allowed; often there was massive protest against privatization, for all employees feared that it would cost them their job. The question of 'how' was even more complicated. Besides restitution of expropriated property to former owners, there were three different ways to proceed: sale to the highest bidder; sales by voucher, and sales to insiders. Restitution no where played an important role; it was limited to small firms and farms. The three models named had different advantages and disadvantages: 1) Sales on the open market were efficient, but slow. The companies concerned received capital and know-how, and the government received money, but the method was widely considered socially unjust because few other than foreigners were in a position to the enterprises on offer. 2) Sales by voucher entailed the distribution of vouchers the country's population, who could exchange them for company shares of their own choice. The demand for particular shares determined the "price", which was defined in terms of vouchers. This kind of privatization was quick and equitable, but it did not inject new capital or know-how into the respective firms, and the state got no money. 3) Sales to insiders meant sale to the companies' former managers. Its advantage was speed, but it was neither just, nor efficient; nor did it raise new capital or bring in new expertise.

Hungary, as well as a couple of other countries, opted for sales.[165] The process of economic reform had started earlier there than in other states of Eastern Europe, and the communists were also relatively weak. Additionally, the state had high debts in foreign exchange that pre-dated 1990. Betting on its historically close relationship with Central Europe, above all with Austria, the Hungarian government hoped to attract enough FDI to kick-start the economy and reduce foreign indebtedness. Judged in terms of economic growth and levels of employment, Hungarian privatization was a success.

Most of the countries, however, chose privatization by voucher- or insider-sales.[166] The policy of the Czech Republic, which distributed vouchers between 1992 and 1995, was at first praised by the World Bank:

> "The Czech Republic's mass privatization program has been the most successful to date. ...The Czech experience illustrates how a well designed voucher privatization program can overcome many problems. It can depoliticize restructuring, stimulate development of capital markets, and quickly create new stakeholders with an interest reform."[167]

But Czechia's economy stagnated after 1995, and the World Bank revised its evaluation in 1998. What had gone wrong? The Czech people had not invested their vouchers directly in enterprises but had avoided risk and opted for industrial funds, which in return changed the vouchers into shares. Yet this very rational investment behaviour backfired under the conditions of the transition period. The funds were set up by managers from the old order who had no interest in a real change. Consequently the funds did not try to maximize profit but rather avoided pushing for change that would have set aside the old structures of economic authority. Dubious and even illegal transactions also occurred, which enriched some individuals but impoverished the enterprises concerned. Despite a promising beginning, Czech privatization failed to reach its goals of a competitive and expanding economy.

Russia is the prime example of insider privatization. During General Secretary Gorbachew's policy of perestroika, or restructuring (1986-1991), leading company employees assumed control of their respective enterprises, and it was thought to be politically impossible to remove them. The consequences were similar those in Czechia. Since the insiders were more interested in preserving their own employment and inherited structures of decision making, capitalist-oriented industrial management did not emerge. In 1995/96 the Russian government contracted large loans at Western banks, secured with profitable firms in the energy sector. The credits were not repaid, and the enterprises were sold. Abetted by manipulation and shady dealing, a small oligarchy of insiders wound up in control of the country's most attractive industrial assets. In short, the privatization of the Russian economy was a spectacular failure.

Correlating the amount and type of privatization with economic performance between 1990 and 2001 shows that the amount was much more important than the type. The differences in type show fairly little correlation with performance, although there was a slight, positive bias towards "sales". In other words, western economic counsel could provide little guidance for the former socialist countries in their transition period; politics mattered much more.[168]

In one respect this last result of privatization in Eastern Europe is in line with results in Western Europe. The fairly clean division between the economic and the political sphere, which at one time existed with regulated and state-owned public utilities and key services, has become blurred. The United States has proceeded further down the road that other countries and therefore provides the model. It is very likely that this trend will go on. If so, private firms will increasingly take over tasks that traditional political theory has always attached to the sovereign state.[169] Another negative result is the possibility of a kind of economic hostage taking such as exemplified in the British firm Railtrack. Railtrack paid dividends to its investors at the expense of technically necessary investment. When the foreseeable crisis surfaced, the government bailed out the company with high subsidies at taxpayers' expense. Although the same thing happened in United States with respect to parts of the power-grid, privatization policy was not questioned in either country.

Of course, the balance of privatization is not entirely negative. For a variety of reasons—economic, political, military, and incidental—European states had engaged themselves in sectors which did not inherently have to be under political control and direction, for instance railways and telecommunication. In such areas privatization made political-economic sense and has generally worked well.

In areas directly affecting citizens' health and welfare, however, privatization has not eliminated the need for regulation, either by the state or by another authority accountable to the public. For instance, the monitoring of hospital standards used to be part of the public health system. Common standards of training and administration meant that deviations in practice were seldom significant. Privatisation necessitated establishing a new watchdog authority to insure that firms did not undercut standards of quality for the sake of increasing profits.. Both policies, privatization and deregulation, were initiated to enhance competition and flexibility, but at times they worked at cross purposes. In principle, there is no solution to these contradictions; they can only be minimized by optimal design and practice. Deregulation and privatization has rendered economic policy an even more complicated task than ever.

TECHNOLOGICAL CHANGE

During Americanization's third wave the most significant technology transfer was not in nuclear or space technology but in computing, or information technology (IT). In the 1940s, this was by no means predictable. The first 'computer', a calculation machine that can be programmed, was constructed in Germany during the war, and after 1945 the work of Alan Turing and associates put computer science in the UK in the lead. From the 1950s onwards, however, no country could match American resources in the field. To the 1970s much direction and funding came from the armed forces, not from the free market. Still, established American companies in business equipment, above all IBM, developed computing divisions that dominated the market, which consisted of selling and servicing large mainframe computer systems to institutional customers such as big business, universities, and government. France tried to catch up; its government heavily subsidized the country's leading computer company, Bull. But according to Albert Broder a mixture of too much and too little state intervention, combined with the limited home base of the French market, prevented Bull from becoming a major world player in information technology.[170] In 2004 Bull had fewer than 10,000 employees; in comparison, IBM had 319,000. Similar attempts by Italy's Olivetti, Germany's Nixdorf, Sweden's ASEA, and several other European contenders also failed.. What distinguished American IT firms?

To start with, both sides of the US market—supply and demand—were by far the largest in the world for many years; up to the 1970s 80 per cent of world production in IT came out of the United States. American demand in world terms was only little less. The computer industry in Japan and the Far East became a considerable world factor first in the 1980s. However, it was software, not hardware, that was the key to the IT revolution of the 1980s. And this side of computing was long neglected by the industry's leaders, who were fixated on machines. One of the biggest mistakes IBM's management ever made was to hand over software development for a new type of machines, nicknamed personal computers or PCs, to a young software company in Redmond, Washington by the name of Microsoft. At the time IBM considered PCs insufficiently promising to invest much of its own resources in product development. Indeed, most major developments in personal computing occurred away from the traditional powerhouses of corporate America in new companies located in the less structured business environment of the west coast, in the Seattle region and, especially, in California's Santa Clara county, subsequently world famous as Silicon Valley.

The American IT start-ups of the 1970s-80s—Microsoft, Apple Computer, Sun Microsystems, Cisco Systems, etc.—had several common features: their founders were young and enthusiastic; they did not separate work from private life in a traditional way; initially they suffered from a lack of funds; they were very flexible; they networked heavily; they lived in a cluster with proximate communication; and they combined a long-term vision with a short-term personal commitment to their actual working place. After Silicon Valley had become an icon of the new techno-economy, European countries tried to imitate it, but all failed. Silicon Valley's success derived not only geographical proximity and inventiveness, but also from a flexible, yet intensive, work ethos and a deliberate pursuit of high-risk business activity. The risk seeking also included persons outside the companies' workforce, who provided venture capital for the projects. Such attitudes and investors were largely missing in Europe. Supplying high-risk venture capital was widely considered to be an acceptable investment strategy in the United States; in Europe it tended to be regarded as speculation. The connotation was positive in the first case and negative in the second. Differences in the taxation of investment—capital gains as well as capital losses—probably also affected investment behaviour, but tax-law in itself reflects social and political attitudes. In addition to being relatively starved for venture capital, start-up IT companies in Europe tended to be quickly absorbed by established enterprises. Europe has few examples of successful start-up companies in information technology. One is Finnish Nokia, which entered the IT sector after being squeezed out of its original product area, pulp and paper. Germany's SAP, started by former IBM employees and specializing in business software, is another. Otherwise Europe's computer industry has stayed in the hands of established firms, such as Siemens from Germany, Philips from The Netherlands, Olivetti from Italy, and Schneider from France. Yet despite this engagement by long-standing leaders of European industry, IT and PCs in Europe are heavily Americanized: expressions, habits, and structures were all taken over from the United States.

The same observation applies to the Internet, an essentially American innovation. In 1973 the U.S. Defence Advanced Research Projects Agency initiated a research program to investigate technologies that could interlink communication networks. The idea was to construct a decentralized network that would be able to survive a nuclear attack by the Soviet Union. Initially, the network was reserved for military use but after a few years universities were also connected to what was then called ARPAnet. As it was part of a US federal research program, the network became an integral part of the American infrastructure for digital communication.

In its early years, though, this infrastructure was neither accessible to the general public, easy to use, or flexible. Exchangeable information was largely limited to alphanumeric text, and the main activity was sending and receiving electronic mail. To overcome the limitation, Tim Berners-Lee, who at the time worked at the European nuclear research centre CERN, invented in 1989 *Hyper Text Mark-up Language*, better known by its abbreviation HTML. It is a coding procedure rendering documents of all types (text, numbers, and graphics) compatible across languages and computer systems. HTML made possible the development of the Internet information service known as the *World-Wide Web*, or www. And a few years later, in 1993, the final breakthrough to the mass internet usage of today's IT world came with the invention of the graphical WWW-browser "Mosaic" by Marc Andreessen of the National Center for Supercomputer Applications (NCSA) at the state-run University of Illinois-Urbana. Thus, as with computers so with the internet, the combination of state-funded research and investment (partly for military purposes) and civilian venture capital laid the foundation for American dominance of the Internet. This dominance expressed itself not only in the access to the Internet, which was long more wide-spread in the US than anywhere else, but to also in the standards and solutions to general networking problems. Thus, the basic rules of the Internet are of American design, as are its characteristic activities. Americans were the first to sell books, music, clothes, stock market shares, and other items on large scale via the Internet, and consequently American standards defined the proceedings concerning issues such as security, billing, ownership, legal matters and so on. Virtual market places need a technical infrastructure, a platform. These platforms were developed first in the United States and define both technology and protocol, what to do, when and how. Examples are *e-bay*, the platforms for auctions, or *Yet2.com* for the transfer of technology. Language researchers have established the link between the choice of words and the modes of thinking. The importation of so many IT-related words from the United States marks a noticeable Americanization of cultural communication. A short evaluation on this linguistic phenomenon on France and Germany by the economists Robert Locke and Kathrin Schöne sums up the situation:

> "It is remarkable how quickly and completely Frenchman and Germans involved with entrepreneurship and entrepreneurial education took to these American expressions. If Americanization means the adoption of American expressions and words into the language of this French and German business community, then the two countries in the high tech entrepreneurial era have been Americanized."[171]

The development and spread of personal computing and the emergence of mass usage of the Internet has made IT more and more an American domain, and more and more an involuntary instrument of Americanization. The US lead in the 1970s has been increased. The United States has constantly invested more in this sector than European countries (and Japan), both absolutely and relatively:

IT investment as percentage of *gross investment in equipment*

	1980	1990	2000
France	5.4	7.8	12.8
Germany	11.5	13.9	16.7
Italy	12.2	14.2	15.5
Japan	6.9	8.7	16.4
UK	4.5	9.4	14.7
United States	13.5	21.9	28.0

Source: Handelsblatt, March 8, 2003

Information technology has revolutionized people's communication. Historically, the revolution started with the telephone, which over time made written letters unfashionable, with a use restricted to exceptional and official occasions. Telephone use in Europe also changed during the 1970s and 1980s. It was no longer reserved for the exchange of short messages and concise information, but an instrument for conversation and chatting; and its availability was also expanded and it became a normal part of a household's furnishings. All these features had been long been a part of American society. Computer-based information technology took this revolution in communication another giant step forward. IT quickly made both the written letter and the telephone obsolete for many transactions. Modes of internal communication have also been greatly changed by the use of electronic mail. From 2000 General Electric reduced the transaction costs of company business by carrying out the bulk of its communications online. Electronic mail also increases the transparency of communications while reducing transaction costs. European businesses have been much slower to adopt e-mail as normal company practice. An explanation for this delay in applying modern communication technology has been suggested by Peter Hall and David Soskice, who maintain that Europe tends to innovate in increments, whereas the United States is readier to embrace to radical innovation.[172] Therefore, radical innovations have a better chance of implementation in the United States than in Europe. If this is true, it explains two facts: 1) the American origin of many transformational innovations; 2) the European capacity to absorb American ideas and values and adapt and refine them.

Since the 1990s all industry and services connected to a substantial amount of data processing, such as telecommunication, computing, or banking, have expanded more rapidly than other sectors. Collectively they were labelled the "new industry" or "new economy", and its centre, symbolically and to a considerable extent in fact, was America's Silicon Valley. Yet the American technological lead in IT in the 1990s was never totally unchallenged, as American industrial might had been in the 1950s. In one of the most dynamic corners of the new economy, mobile telephony, the products and standards were to a large extent set in Scandinavian Europe. Not only were several of important enterprises in mobile telephony located there—Eriksson in Sweden and world leader Nokia in Finland—but also the region contained buoyant consumer demand, open markets, and—very significantly— cooperation between competing providers and state administrations. This cooperation enabled the establishment of technical standards that were compatible over the whole of Europe, so that the same mobile phone (cellular phone in the US) could be used in all European countries. This Nordic and then European cooperation was founded on the traditional understanding of how competitors could conduct business matters for the benefit of all— producers and consumers. It had nothing to do with the new policy trends of privatization and deregulation, it had a long heritage in practice. In the United States, by contrast, the development of mobile telephony was slowed considerably by the fragmentation of producers and suppliers, which meant that standardization did not emerge for some time; the consequent geographic limitations of mobile phones made them much less attractive consumer items than in Europe. In other areas of e-commerce, the gap between Europeans and Americans was not as large as often imagined. GE's pioneering role in implementing online internal communication has been noted, but European companies also began to adopt the medium in business operations. For instance in March 2000, BASF, the world's largest chemical firm, started to purchase its supplies by internet-auction. Seven firms took part in that initial auction regarding the purchase of 2000 tons methanol. BASF ended up with an offer that was ten per cent lower than the going market price. The example confirms that the application of IT could reduce costs and that firms which took up e-commerce early could obtain competitive advantages in their industry. But the Internet could also be used to build European-American industrial cooperation. In 2000 the European firms BASF, Bayer, and Ticona joined forces with American competitors DuPont and Dow to establish a World-Wide-Web site, Omnexus, for international trading in plastics. On the world's stock exchanges in the 1990s shares of new-economy companies were traded up to very high prices by a bullish market. Especially in the United States, enormous amounts of venture capital poured into start-up companies, especially internet-related firms that acquired the collective epithet "dotcom" after the American WWW-suffix for commercial company. When the dotcom bubble burst in 2001, both the American and the world economies went into a long backslide. Billions of assets on paper vanished. At the same time a good amount of the American lead in IT melted away. By the time the high-tech sector began to recover in late 2003, the IT start-ups that had been based more on marketing than on tangible services and products had been shaken out. According to the New York Times, the surviving companies had been able to show actual results as opposed to promises.[173] Although the newspaper did not put it this way, such an enterprise resembles the traditional profile of European business. John Cassidy, the author of Dot Con. summed up:

> "...the internet boom and bust was about America-how it works and what it thought of itself in that short interregnum between the end of the Cold War and September 2001."[174]

Biotechnology, particularly DNA-based applications, has been another dynamic area of the high-tech economy since the 1980s. Its products, however, have not met the easy adoption that IT innovations have received. Europeans, especially, have so far been very resistant to the use of gene-manipulated foodstuffs, a major commercial activity of biotechnological companies. The rejection is not limited to consumer behaviour; it is expressed in trade policy. The EU Commission has prohibited the importation of specific gene-manipulated foods such as maize and soybeans. The interdiction has caused friction between the Atlantic trading partners, for the American government has naturally insisted that the Union's market be opened to the new products. EU spokesmen grounded the Union's policy in the prevailing lack of knowledge about the possible repercussions of gene manipulation on other plants and animals, including human beings. They pointed to cases of unforeseen and disastrous consequences of the use of pharmaceutical products, particularly the drug *Thalodomide*. The Thalodomide containing sleeping pill "*Contergan*" (alias, "Softenon", alias Noctosediv, and other 65 trade-names) showed exceptionally few side-effects in trials, was put on European markets in 1957. After being linked conclusively to massive malformation in about 5,000 embryos, the pill was taken off the market in November 1961. How could the tragedy happen? Before being approved for public use, Thalodomide had passed all the prescribed tests, including tests on pregnant rats. It had been ingested probably a million times or more by adults and children without causing any harm. For a long time physicians simply could not believe that the 'harmless sleeping pill' was responsible for the horrible malformations they were seeing. Exactly how the malformations were caused has still not been established. It has been discovered that the active substance is enantiomorph (a substance with two identical constructions except for a "left" and a "right" version), something which was not known in 1957, and that only one of the two enantiomeres causes a reaction in human embryos. Rat embryos do not react to either version.

To cut the story short, in 1957 science evidently did not the means to discover all potential damage in a new drug. The Contergan-shock had a contradictory effect regarding American and European attitudes towards the products of modern science and biotechnology. On the one hand, it led to the US Food and Drug Administration adopting very stringent standards for the approval of new pharmaceutical products, and since the United States is the world's largest market for medicinal drugs, pharmaceutical companies everywhere have been forced to adopt the American standards.[175] On the other hand, the affair persuaded many

Europeans to be extremely conservative in accepting new products and practices developed by a science and technology they could little understand. This attitude was later reinforced several times. The accidental release of substantial quantities of the extremely toxic gas dioxin from a chemical plant in Seveso, Italy in 1976 was a big blow to public confidence in modern technology, and the nuclear disaster at Chernobyl in 1986 undermined it even further. Such events have supported the emergence of vigorous environmentalist political movements in many European countries that additionally promote sceptical attitudes towards biotechnology in general and gene-manipulated foods in specific. In this field it would appear that Europe has clearly rejected Americanization. It is an attitude that many Americans have difficulty understanding. As William Steere, CEO of Pfizer, a leading American pharmaceutical company, maintained in 1999:

"Europe seems to be entering a period of the Dark Ages, where witchcraft and sorcery are prevailing.   There's a definite anti-science attitude in Europe that is not as pronounced in the United States."[176]

CONCLUSION: A CURE FOR EUROPE'S ECONOMIC ILLS?

Since the end of the 1980s American proceedings, habits, and solutions of problems were again sought after in Europe. This time there was no productivity or other mission initiated by the United States; the new wave of Americanisation rested entirely on demand by Europeans. America had indeed become attractive again; and like in the 1950s, American supremacy did not rest on one factor only. In the fields of the economy, politics, military power, financial strength and economic theory parallel trends enhanced America's weight in the world at the same time. Since the 1980s United States' growth-rates lay constantly up to 50 per cent higher than European ones. It remained the most powerful state in the world after the collapse of the Soviet Union, in fact the only one which could intervene with military or other means of power at any place of the globe. It became the centre of the IT-industry and the new economy. While all other industrialized countries had large problems with unemployment, the United States created jobs. Most of these new jobs, in the IT-business or in finances or in households, where clean and environmentally friendly. All this created the impression that the United States was not just temporarily in better shape, but that it enjoyed structural advantages on several levels. The US-administration was much less involved in the country's economy, a fact which economists suggested to be the major reason for America's economic success in general and in the new economy particularly. This was in line with economic theory which emphasized the macroeconomic effects by the supply-side; an approach for which the Chicago school was used as a symbol. Thus, the American model offered Europeans, who suffered heavily from de-industrialization and from an over-burdened welfare-state, a positive aim. At the same time America suggested even the means to reach this aim by applying theoretically backed economic policy, namely deregulation, privatization and a help for IT-related industry. With the promise of so many positive items – the creation of new jobs (all of them nice, clean and environmentally friendly), the reduction of the burden of administration, the promise of new income for the state through privatization-gains, that is with the vision to solve all major problems at once - which administration and which people would not have opted for American solutions?

The necessity for changes was first sensed in the UK, which, during a long period of slow growth, had significantly fallen back within Europe. The conservative Thatcher Government started with privatization in the early 1980s, and, twice re-elected, sold out what could be sold. While the privatization of enterprises such as Cable & Wireless caused no problems, the sale of public utilities did. Resistance of the employed had to be overcome, and the branch of industry had to be deregulated first. Otherwise a monopoly would have been privatized, which would have resembled to a license for to print money. Thus privatization and deregulation were related to each other.

In many cases privatization was a great success, not only in the UK. Airlines (e.g. Lufthansa) or car-production (e.g. Renault) became more competitive. Other cases were more difficult. Globalization, decentralization, new technologies (such as nuclear power, use of toxic intermediates) and differentiation of values had enlarged exposure to crime and violation to an extent the police could no longer meet. The gap was bridged by private security. However, the privatization of security may in the long run undermine the state monopoly on authorized power, and in the end even the consent of the governed. From a traditional point of view the privatization of secondary education, which took place above all in management- and technical education, can be questioned. On the other hand, the traditional state-financed systems were worn out, too expensive, and could no longer provide the necessary quality. The solution of the problem lay in the right mix of the Continental and the American systems. However, the precondition for to find this right mix was not at hand, since Europeans applied a highly selective perception of the American system of higher education.

The most comprehensive privatizations took place in the former socialist countries, of course. All the three models of privatization, sale, distribution of vouchers and sale to insiders, have been used by the various countries. None had the desired result, all turned out to be problematic in one way or another, though sale to insider had the most negative results. Not so much ownership but the execution of control became the most important problem. It seems that the transition period from socialism to capitalism was not finished by privatization, but will go on until the problems of management and control are tackled.

Like privatization, deregulation became important and comprehensive in Europe since the 1990s. Its results were mixed. Some cases, such as telecommunication, were very positive. Others, such as railways, were questioned.

Generally deregulation and privatization caused problems in all countries. With power supply all signs tend into the direction of a general and major failure. Deregulation failed to promote competition, because the reaction of the industry was a massive wave concentration. At the same time the policy caused a severe reduction in the security of supply, because all firms have to cut back their so called redundancies, which represent the buffer in case of emergency. Alone in 2003 the costs related to the break-down of electric supply in several countries may have surpassed by far any savings from reduced rates. For the general public this kind of deregulation will become even more expensive in future. The policy is not stopped and reversed, but extended to other fields, such as the supply of gas, and to other countries such as France.

A stop or reversal of policy on a regional or national scale was no longer possible, since EU-rules required deregulation and competition. In autumn 2003 the EU-Commission ordered EdF to pay back one billion Euros of state-subsidies. At the same time the EU-Commission suggested new rules for hostile takeovers, which tore down legal barriers of defence. These are two examples for a general trend: in the EU it was the administration in Brussels which became the prime motor for European deregulation and privatization in order to promote competition. This was very much in line with American basic values of competition and commercialisation. Even a trend towards individualization can be claimed, since with deregulation organizations and private persons can chose their supplier and sometimes the type of quality, for instance "green" energy, generated from renewable sources.

One of the major points of attraction of America was its success in IT. Because of the overwhelming competitiveness in the fields of computers, software or the internet, American standards, habits and processes were taken over, including the respective language. Though several European countries, above all France, tried to catch up, it was neither possible to create a counter-weight to the massive orders by the American armed forces, which laid the foundation to the US-supremacy in this field. Nor was it possible to create centres of creativity such as Silicon Valley. In the application of IT-technology Europe was not so much behind, and in some sectors (mobile-phones, broad-band access) even ahead of the United States. However, the dynamic of Silicon Valley was related to an American environment, extremely flexible and risk-taking, including an easy access to venture capital. This could not be imitated.

While American solutions have been taken over in the fields of privatization, deregulation, and in the IT-industry, they met strict resistance in bio-technology. The UK represented again a special case. While it was a fore-runner in deregulation and privatization, and thus in these fields only ahead of the flock of European countries, it behaved differently in the latter case of bio-technology. There it counted into the American camp of risk-takers.

The general changes on the macroeconomic level were matched or even promoted by changes on the microeconomic one. American solutions of financing enterprise were taken over parallel to new definition of safety and risk and of the relationship between the common and the individual.

CHAPTER 6

COMPANIES AND CONSUMERS

"In order to be Europeans the Germans have to change and so they did.
This change has a price: to become American."[177]

Professor Harold James, Princeton, 2002

The deregulation and privatization of Americanization's third wave helped to push forward an ever-strengthening globalization of the world economy. The growing amount of direct economic activities by European transnational or multinational enterprises (MNEs) on other continents, especially evident from the 1990s, has tended to dilute their original national character or association. This process opened a gap: what would replace the original business culture of such newly globalized enterprises? The mixture of national, European, and American business cultures revealed rather a lack of definition than a deliberate direction. American MNEs by and large did not have similar problems of corporate national identity. Consumers, governments, and, not least, the firms themselves understood American MNEs straight forwardly as American companies. The European situation was more complex. Some MNEs of European origin called themselves "European firms" (e.g. Bayer); others (e.g. Daimler Chrysler or AXA) stressed their multinational character. This lack of an identifiable corporate culture that all those who dealt with the company both internally as employees at all levels and externally as customers or clients (including government representatives) made many European firms vulnerable to the take-over and adaptation of "foreign" corporate-cultural practices that were neither always necessary nor beneficial. A recent example of this contention is the attempted transfer of the American corporate-cultural practice of "diversity management".

Diversity management emerged in the United States in the early 1990s. The policy is designed to guarantee that all groups of an enterprise's employees shall have equal rights of employment and opportunities of promotion. It emerged as a response to US legislation to promote affirmative action and to outlaw discrimination in the workplace: firms convicted of "unjust" hiring or promotion (unjust with respect to gender, race, religion, and so on) were subject to heavy fines. But whereas anti-discriminatory policies are re-active—activated in cases of real or perceived discrimination—diversity management is an active managerial tool that purports to prevent discrimination. To this end diversity management encourages company employees to organize around a specific group identity—ethnicity, race, sexual orientation, and the like—to represent that group's interests in the workforce, especially in matters of promotion. The attraction of diversity management is based on two assumptions: 1) There is reasonable hope that employees who can express themselves in a way of their own choice will be better and more effective workers; 2) an enterprise that implements such a policy will have a formidable case against

163

accusations of unjust promotion in a court of law. Diversity management is particularly found in large corporations and in publicly owned establishments. In 2003 the Ford Motor Company proudly announced that it had no less than eleven "Employee Resource Groups".[178] And diversity management is prominently presented on the website of the U.S. Coast Guard. In contrast, European practices in personnel management have underlined the common ground of being employed by the same firm. Additionally, the cultural and racial diversity of company workforces was considerably less in Europe than in the US. However, the support given by the European Court of Justice to policies of affirmative action convinced several firms, such as Royal Dutch Shell and Siemens, to adopt the instrumentation of diversity management. Yet when their policies are examined closely, they turn out to be largely programmes for the promotion of women. The point here is not to evaluate the justification or necessity of diversity management in Europe but to underscore that the specific American managerial policies were taken over even though the preconditions and content of the policy were quite different.

The entry of the very American practice of diversity management into European corporate life is but a small example of the deep-going Americanization of the European systems of corporate finance and the changing position of stakeholders' and shareholders' interests in determining managerial goals that has characterized European big business from the 1990s. American standards of economic risk and safety, for instance in accounting or arbitration and generally in the sphere of business and civil law, have also been increasingly exported to European economic life. Especially this last issue reflects the American trend towards a comprehensive individualization and commercialization of society: whether the issue was salaries, sports, consumer credit, or pensions, collective solutions based on common interests gave way to individual solutions.

CHANGING PATTERNS IN FINANCING ENTERPRISE: FROM BANK CREDITS TO MARKET CAPITALIZATION

Until recently Continental small and medium-sized investors emphasized long-term security and stability. They bought state bonds, real estate, or deposited their money with dedicated savings banks. Buying shares of enterprises was considered the preserve of rich "capitalists", and investment funds were largely unknown. Traditionally, Continental Europeans perceived commercial banks as the servants of manufacturing industry, agriculture, and trade. They were a necessary instrument for the national economy but of secondary importance to the individual. Thus, the inherent economic dynamism of the financial sector was barely understood by many. The Anglo-Saxon attitude tended to put banking institutions in the forefront; the American economic historian Charles Kindleberger mocked this in asserting that new settlements in the American West always started with three institutional buildings: the pub, the church, and the bank.[179]

The financial needs of modern industry were largely met by two types of banking institutions: the specialized bank and the universal bank. The specialized banks, also merchant banks, tended to concentrate on companies heavily engaged in international trade. Universal banks were joint-stock commercial and investment banks that took deposits as well as providing commercial services and long-term loans. Especially in Germany the universal banks focused their engagement on specific industrial sectors and often became house banks for individual enterprises. In most cases the house bank became a major shareholder with representatives on the company's board of directors. Over time a stable relationship of mutual trust usually emerged between the partners. In his influential comparative studies of economic backwardness Alexander Gerschenkron has suggested that house banks were a necessity for late industrializers. Subsequent research on industrial innovation, however, has shown that both specialized and universal banks have served well in the promotion of industrialization.[180] But the universal bank has tended to risk less, to be less aggressive and hence less innovative. Because universal banks not only granted – or refused – loans, but also often supervised the enterprise in one way or another, their inherent cautiousness inculcated a tendency to risk-aversion among industrial managers. As a result universal banks tended to have more difficulties adjusting to internationalization than specialized banks.[181] A number of Continental universal banks have acknowledged this; when Deutsche Bank, Germany's largest universal bank, took over the British-American investment company Morgan Grenfell in 1989, it justified the move by pointing out that international banking "thinks" Anglo-Saxon; thus anyone who wants to succeed in international banking has to follow accordingly.[182]

During the 1980s and 1990s, the combined effect of the growing international engagement of large American banks such as Citibank (now Citigroup Inc.) and the emergence of a free capital market across country borders following the Single European Act (1986) and the Economic and Monetary Union (1999) made the Anglo-Saxon type of finance became more and more important for European business. Increasingly Continental European companies shifted financing bank credits to equity, i.e. the stock market. The long-term rise in share prices (briefly halted by a sharp downturn in 1987-8) made it easier for firms to cover financial requirements on the stock exchange than by bank loans. Thus, the American style of financing industry by equity became standard European business practice as well, and ties to house banks loosened. In 1998 the Financial Times quoted an investment banker on the development: "To put it crudely, Europe's financial markets are Americanising."[183] The following table documents this trend in the two decades between the early 1980s and 2000.

Equity market capitalization as percentage of GDP, 1980s–2000

	Early 1980s	1990	2000
Italy	5.2	15.7	66.1
France	6.2	33.6	100.6
Germany	10.6	26.8	61.6
UK	43.3	98.5	179.0

Source: Colli (2003), pp. 14, 25; Fédération Internationale des Bourses des Valeurs (FIBV), Statistical Yearbooks.

Italy is a good example of how the structures of both business financing and private assets have changed. Italy represents a third type of industrialization with heavy state involvement.[184] The country industrialized late and never developed a fully adequate banking system. In order to prevent widespread bankruptcy and to stimulate economic growth the state took over many companies. Alongside the state was a small handful of extremely rich and influential families who owned and directed substantial chunks of the country's economy: among them Agnelli (Fiat), de Benedetti (Olivetti), Ferruzzi (Ferruzzi – agri-business), Berlusconi (media), and Pirelli (Pirelli – rubber). In the early 1990s 151 family groups controlled 4,000 enterprises with half a million employees. Under these conditions privatization unleashed a huge jump in share prices on the country's main stock exchange in Milan: from an index number 134 in 1982 to 257 in 1990, best performance in Western countries.[185] The structure of corporate liabilities as well as private investment thus changed markedly.

The financing of corporate and private capital in Italy, 1977–1996 (in per cent)

	1977	*1987*	*1996*
A) Corporate liabilities			
Credits	75.2	39.1	45.4
Equity	16.5	57.6	52.8
Bonds	8.3	3.3	1.8
B) Private assets			
Bank deposits	84.3	49.4	37.9
Bonds	14.9	38.8	38.3
Stocks	0.8	11.8	23.8

Source: Colli (2003), p. 15

The table's main message is that business financing and private investment in Italy underwent a dramatic shift in only two decades: from credits and savings to stocks and bonds. The change reduced the role of banks in the economic life of both companies and individuals and increased the role of the stock market. A similar pattern can be found in many European countries in the last three decades. Yet in many countries the shift of influence from banks to stock market has been less dramatic in reality than it appears on paper. In all countries the increased engagement of individuals in the stock market has occurred largely through impersonal investment funds rather than through personal contact with a broker. And except in the UK, Scandinavia, and the Netherlands, most investment funds are directed by the established banks; hence the effective power of banks in individual, household economies has diminished little.

Both established firms and newly founded companies began to use the stock exchange as a primary source of capital. Several large European enterprises, such as Germany's Daimler-Benz, even paid the high costs necessary to be listed on the New York Stock Exchange (NYSE), the worlds largest, in order to attract American investors. In the two decades before the crash of 2000 enormous sums were raised on all the world's exchanges. European equity capitalization was increasing fast during these years, but it was still a long way behind American. Michael Hartnett, a senior international economist at Merrill Lynch, commented on the development:

> "Europe is developing an international equity culture. It has some way to go, as German financial assets per capita were only US$ 44,000 at the end of 1999, compared to US$ 127,000 in the US. In fact, our research shows Europe and Japanese holdings of equities as a proportion of financial assets are at similar levels to those of the US 10 years ago."[186]

The burgeoning trend was abruptly broken by the collapse of the bull market at the beginning of the twenty-first century. Very quickly the value of shares fell generally by 50 per cent, and the fall put a stop, at least temporarily, to this mode of financing European enterprise. New firms have been especially hard hit. During the years 2001 to 2003 the amount of initial public offerings (IPOs) plummeted in Europe. Flotations also declined sharply in the United States, too, but much less than in Europe.

Initial public offerings, 1998-2003 (1000 billion US$)

Year	US	%	EU	%	Rest	%	Total
1998	40	47	25	29	20	24	80
1999	78	54	46	32	20	14	144
2000	76	41	63	35	43	24	182
2001	38	51	17	23	19	26	74
2002	25	49	6	12	20	39	51
2003	19	42	3	7	23	51	45

Source: Financial Times, February 19, 2004

European companies had become enthusiastic supporters of IPOs as a financial tool and in 2000 they raised nearly as much capital as their American counterparts. But their practice changed quickly following the bursting of the 1990s bubble, and they again preferred conventional means of financing, such as bonds, credits, etc. In 2002 and 2003 not a single significant IPO was launched in Germany. Moreover, European firms suddenly became aware that the cost of a flotation in Europe was about 50 per cent lower than American costs.[187] Both the American model of equity financing and the American capital market thus lost favour in the European business community. IPOs were the subject of speculation in financial papers, but few made it to the stock market. It can be doubted, though, that this represents a permanent roll-back of Americanization in European business finance. More plausibly, it demonstrates the coexistence of new and old patterns. Which one, if either, will achieve dominance depends on world economic developments in the next decade.

The traditional European, credit-based method of business financing has also shown weaknesses, particularly connected to the costs of bad loans and the ensuing possibility of bank failures. New international rules on banking have emerged to counter these weaknesses. In 1988, after many years of negotiations, the world's major economies concluded an international agreement, effective from 1992, that defined the ratio of a bank's own capital to the amount of credit to be loaned. It was called the Basel Agreement (subsequently Basel I) after the Swiss city that is the seat of the Bank for International Settlements, an institution created after the First World War to facilitate international capital movements. The purpose of the standardization was to eliminate national disadvantages that might arise from varying national legislation on bank capitalization in an increasingly globalized financial market. The agreement's provisions were quickly perceived as inadequate, and negotiations on a new agreement started in 1996. Basel II was signed in 2004 and will be in force from 2006. It comprehends three changes: 1) The ratio between a bank's own capital and its outstanding loans is to be raised in order to increase bank security. 2) The bank's control of a creditor's financial operations is to occur continuously rather than after the end of set periods, akin to the continuous control of the manufacturing process referred to in chapter four. 3) Banks are obliged to provide much more public information about internal operations in order to enable the market to assess their exposure to risk. From the European perspective the points two and three represent a "shift of paradigm".[188] The last point is especially contentious, since it will not really be "the market" that will judge the risk position of a given bank, but rather the four North American rating agencies, approved by the Securities and Exchanges Commission (SEC) of the US Federal Government, which have established offices all over the world: Moody's Investors Service, Inc.; Fitch, Inc.; Standard & Poor's; and Dominion Bond Rating Service Limited.[189] Not surprisingly, American banks played a decisive role in the negotiations behind Basel II. Although the agreement will not officially be in force before 2006, European banks have tried to apply the rules as soon as possible. This compliance has meant that already from 2002 new loans have been granted only under the terms Basel II.

The new procedures have upset many European firms. In traditional Continental banking practice, part of a company's security for loans consisted of intangibles: trust, reputation, and long-standing, even personal, relationships. Basel II broke with this by demanding tangible, accountable collateral. Applicants for credit had to submit first-class securities; otherwise the credit's cost increased, or its size was reduced. Although most bank loans were indeed scrutinized before Basel II, the new agreement compelled all borrowers to disclose full details of their financial standing. Creditworthiness had to be evaluated by an independent credit rating agency, and this credit rating determined the interest rate of the loans granted. These rates could differ substantially; in autumn 2002 the so-called *spread* between companies rated "AA" (very sound) or "BBB" (not very good) amounted to 270 basic points (2.70 per cent). Under such conditions firms that really needed financial support had difficulties obtaining it not only on the equity market but from the banks, too. Stated broadly, the European tradition of establishing creditworthiness was ultimately grounded on trust: the American one was based on numbers. Trust is a subjective, variable quality, whereas figures are uniformly accountable and controllable by all. The Basel II agreement represented the triumph of Anglo-Saxon banking practices and a transformation of Continental attitudes in business finance.

The significance of Basel II is demonstrated by the example of financing of small and medium-sized enterprise (SME), the backbone of the European economy. From Norway to Italy SMEs relied on credit from their respective (house) bank. They had neither the time nor the means to compare prices and conditions of several banks at regular intervals, but trusted in the services of their house banks. The (house) bank trusted the firm in return and accompanied it through good and bad times. Such trust was the core value of house banking. In a way house banking acted like insurance. Credits might have been a bit more expensive, but the difference could be understood as the premium for not being dropped in times of crisis. This core relationship of mutual trust between bank and client was undermined by Basel II. It was also undermined by the gradual demise of the local bank branch and increasing instability of bank personnel.

The extent of the changes can be seen in Germany, one of the strongholds of house banking. Small and medium-sized enterprises in the country have complained since 2001 that their credit needs were not being met satisfactorily by the banks, and in 2003 they were polled about their banking connections.[190] There were numerous complaints. Many firms claimed that their bank's behaviour had become erratic; they could not understand why loan conditions were being changed. They complained that banks arbitrarily reduced the value of they securities offered, reductions that increased the cost of credit received. SMEs also complained that bank personnel changed every three years, noting that the fluctuation impeded the establishment of trusting relationships. Lastly, they asserted that the quality of financial advice given by banks had deteriorated. The latter two changes were interrelated. As noted in chapter four, house banks had often functioned as a kind of business consultant to long-standing clients. The quality of this consulting inevitably suffered from the continual changing of bank personnel; clerks and credit managers required considerable time to acquire full knowledge about the financial situation of clients and local economic conditions. By Anglo-Saxon standards most European countries in the 1990s were "overbanked", that is there were more bank branches per inhabitant than found in the United States. Increasing competition in the financial sector during this decade forced many European banks to close branches and dismiss employees. Overall banks became more competitive, but the cost was the loss of close, even intimate, relations with customers; fewer personnel had to serve more clients. The German poll just mentioned showed a clear, directly negative relationship between the regional, national, or international orientation of a given bank and the mark it received from SMEs. The Deutsche Bank, the country's most internationally oriented financial institution, received the mark "insufficient"; small and middle-sized businesses asserted that it "had said good-bye" to them. The regionally organized savings banks received the best grades, but even their services were not considered "good", only "satisfactory". After 2000 neither the traditional American nor the traditional Continental ways of financing enterprise worked properly any more. The collapse of share prices blocked the growth of equity capitalization, yet the universal banks were unable to recover their position of the early 1980s. In trying to become more competitive by specialization they reduced their ability to function as house banks. The financing of European enterprise shifted slowly but surely from a trust-based to a market-based relationship.

As often, language is an indicator of a way of thinking, and the introduction of new words an indicator of innovation. In early modern times, the Western world was dominated by Italian banks. Consequently, innovations such as a "giro" or "agio" were taken over as financial instruments and as business terminology. In the nineteenth century the pioneering role of French bankers in the development of joint-stock investment banks brought such expressions "tranche" and "escompte-bank" into wide use. Similarly, the dominant role of American financial culture in the last three decades has inserted many English expressions into Continental banking, such as "rating", "timing", "spread", "swaps", and "working capital". Theoretically, all these terms could have been translated into other languages, but as in the case of "giro" they were not.

The measurement of good and bad, or large and small, also changed in line with the new financial orientation. Up to the post-war boom Europeans widely understood a good firm, or a large one, terms of size of output, sales, or workforce. Such an understanding represented a stakeholder's view of business. A stakeholder is any person or groups of persons with a vested interest (a stake) in the operations, performance, and behaviour of a company. From this point of view companies are responsible not just to their owners but also to their employees and to the community at large. This communitarian approach to business is very Continental, and has never had widespread support in the United States or even in the UK. Nonetheless, turnover has long been accepted as a world standard of company greatness. The American business magazine Fortune based its famous lists of the 500 largest firms on turnover for many years.

In the 1990s a new standard of business greatness took over: market capitalization. The standard first gained hold in American business circles and its acceptance reflected the spread of the American model of equity financing of business. The shift might seem inconsequential, but the consequences are in fact enormous. Workforce and turnover are tangible economic values; market capitalization, however, is the total market value of a company's outstanding shares if sold on a given day at the price quoted on the stock exchanges where they are listed. The standard is based on the assumption that such a total sell-out would never be practiced, for if it were, the market price would fall inevitably to almost zero. Yet this theoretical value became extremely important for the financing of enterprises, because it suggested the opening price of new shares when new equity was needed. Market capitalization thus mirrored future expectations, including the potential effects of speculation. Persons outside the financial world could hardly understand this kind of measurement, which implied, for instance, that in 2000 the value of the Finnish telecommunications firm, Nokia, exceeded that of all Belgian companies listed on Brussels' stock exchange. Though "common sense" laughed at the incongruity of such a measurement of economic, stock investors embraced it, and it channelled billions of dollars into equity on the world's stock exchanges. In both the United States and Europe market capitalization became the basis of investor and managerial decision-making. For example, when the two Swiss pharmaceutical giants *Ciba* and *Sandoz* merged in 1996 to form *Novartis*, the question was who would own Novartis, or in other words, how were the two constituent companies to be valued? In an earlier age the relative size of turnover or workforce would have been decisive; in 1996 the standard of valuation chosen was market capitalization. It ruled 55:45 in favour of Sandoz, the much smaller firm as measured by workforce, turnover, number of patents, etc. Those taking the decision believed in the incorruptible dictates of the market and its ability to foresee the future. However, not everyone was persuaded by the Smithian logic. A business observer of the leading Swiss daily, Neue Zürcher Zeitung, commented critically:

> "When we consider certain trends at American stock exchanges, for instance rising rates of software-firms, which still have to prove not only their ability, but their right to exist, a deep uneasiness emerges about the functions of a ruler and a referee, which stock exchanges received. …But what disturbs us even more is the supremacy of economic issues. All steps are accepted as long as they lead to a better competitiveness."[191]

With privatization and the diffusion of stock market mentality in European business came another aspect of American (and British) corporate practice that had been rarely seen earlier: the hostile takeover. The structures of Continental business—house banks, networks of family ownership, interlocking directorates, consensual and communitarian culture—mediated against the practice of one company acquiring control of another against the will of its owners or directors. In Italy, for instance, Mediobanca, an investment bank in Milan, had such a wide network of personal relationships and information that it effectively controlled corporate deals in the country. Without its consent, hostile takeovers were nearly impossible. In other Continental countries attempts of hostile takeovers were also largely unsuccessful, even when well prepared, and potentially positive for both parties. For instance, the bid by de Benedetti/Olivetti to takeover the Belgian Société Générale in 1998 was repelled by the combined support of Belgian banks, government, and trade unions.

The appearance of hostile takeover battles in Germany is a particularly significant example of Americanization of European corporate culture because the country was long considered impregnable against uninvited foreign purchase of firms. Foreigners could buy German enterprises, to be sure, but only with the consent of the firm and its house bank. As Heinrich von Pierer, Siemens's CEO, explained to the Financial Times in 2000:

> "We are an engineering company: we know how to build ourselves from the inside. We do not need to make overprized acquisitions that prove difficult to integrate." … "And hostile takeovers are the worst thing you can do. These are moves that make no sense." He added: ""You may call me a social romantic, but I do not believe financial markets should play such a strong role."[192]

The attempt by the Italian Pirelli group (tires and rubber products) to acquire control of its German competitor Continental in the mid-1990s demonstrated the Pierer's attitude was not an isolated one. The opposition of the German corporate world to the move was so widespread that Continental's house bank, the Deutsche Bank, was compelled to renounce its alleged approval of the deal and intervene in favour of Continental. The "misunderstanding"—Pirelli claimed to have secured the bank's support of its takeover bid—indicated cracks in the fortress of Rhenish Capitalism.

The breach of the walls came shortly thereafter. In late 1999 the British telecommunications firm *Vodafone Airtouch* launched a hostile bid to takeover German *Mannesmann*. The latter was a venerable German engineering company, established in 1890, that had pioneered the production of seamless steel tubing and in the 1960s had branched into machine building. Mannesmann widened its diversification in the 1990s to include mobile telecommunications. It quickly became the second largest mobile service provider in Germany, after Deutsche Telekom. And in 1998-9 Mannesmann also acquired provider companies in Austria, Italy, and Britain (Orange), thus becoming Europe's third-largest mobile service provider. It was this aggressive expansion into telecommunications that attracted the attention of rival Vodafone. At the time Vodafone's attack on Mannesmann represented the world's biggest-ever hostile takeover bid, and the battle for shareholder support was heated. In the end the British company won out in spite of the demands by Mannesmann directors and employees and the regional government of Rhineland-Westphalia that the company's banks should oppose the sale. Vodafone retained Mannesmann's mobile telephone and internet services, which represented twenty per cent of the employees and forty per cent of turnover, and sold all other divisions in bits and pieces. The hostile takeover and dismantlement of Mannesmann, which had been one of Germany's largest enterprises, was a dramatic indication that the traditional corporate culture of cooperation and consensus no longer protected against American-style aggressive business practices. When Bayer, one of the age-old giants of the German (and world) chemical industry, hived off its industrial chemicals division in 2002 in order to concentrate on what was called "Health Care", the only reason given by its CEO was that financial markets expected a higher performance than the concern as a whole could meet. Thus the traditional firm had to go.[193] Such flouting of company traditions and stakeholders' interests in favour of market expectations represents a clear Americanization of German corporate behaviour. The implication of Bayer's move was that companies were no longer tied to a mission of enterprise, such as to provide quality goods; instead they should pursue only the core capitalistic goal: to make money. Of course, Europeans, as well as Americans, have always known that making money was central to any business activity, but the bluntness by which money-making was from the 1990s proposed as the only and exclusive goal was new.

A final change in the structure of European business financing in recent years is the spread of the American practice of leasing. Hiring rather than purchasing equipment or buildings enables an enterprise to avoid committing its own capital to the acquisition of fixed, non-productive assets. Leasing developed as a significant business practice in the United States during the 1920s and after 1945 became especially prominent in the transportation sector; nowadays it is also widely used in computing. In Europe leasing was not unknown but was insignificant for many years. The largest Belgian leasing company, S. A. Locabel, established in 1961, explained this lack by the existence of alternative, better-known financial instruments and a psychologically based reluctance to rely on goods owned by others.[194] Since the 1980s, however, the high entry costs and rapid obsolescence of modern technology has helped make leasing one of the fastest growing services in Europe. Leasing is especially used to supply airplanes, trucks, office space, and office equipment. Around 2000 leasing (the English word was also taken over) accounted for about fifteen per cent of all European investment – a tremendous growth from nearly zero two decades earlier.

RE-DEFINING SHAREHOLDERS: FROM THE RICH TO THE MASSES

The role of the stock exchange in European society changed profoundly during the 1990s. Suddenly all manner of people became interested in it. Whereas the exchange's activities were almost never mentioned on the radio and television news before the 1990s, since then they are a prominent part of information programmes. The reason is that ordinary Europeans, like Americans earlier, had started to invest in publicly traded stock, whereas up to the 1990s the buying of corporate shares had been largely the preserve of the rich. The entry of the masses into stock buying had two main causes: First, many people had built up a financial surplus in their household economy. After acquiring houses, cars, and the like, they were looking for other placements than ordinary savings accounts. Second, the future adequacy of state pension schemes was under question because of population ageing in most European countries was simultaneously raising the payout and decreasing the intake of the schemes. The implied threat to the standard of living of future pensioners generated a demand for private, stock-based pension funds, an investment instrument that had been widely used for many years in the United States.

Traditionally, people on the Continent have made little use of pension funds, especially after the experience of fund bankruptcies during the Great Depression. But in the last two decades pension funds gained prominence throughout Europe as companies have established private pension schemes for employees. While in some countries, such as Italy, the schemes' capital has remained in the hands of the sponsoring firm, in others legislation requires that the pension contributions must be paid into a separate fund. In addition to the company-based pension funds, there have also emerged numerous autonomous investment funds that serve the savings interests of private individuals. Most investment funds have a defined relation to risk that determine their investment strategies. Pension funds have typically emphasized long-term security. Hence they concentrate their holdings in so-called blue-chip stock from a country's largest and most reliable companies, which typically dominated the respective national share index. This preference for blue chips inherently favoured big business, which thus can re-finance itself on better terms than small companies. Such investment behaviour is not related to the overall performance of firms but to the relative performance of only the largest firms. Therefore, a stock market dominated by investment funds cannot be claimed to be the most economically efficient in the allocation of financial capital. Furthermore, risk-minimizing funds invest almost exclusively in very secure shares, that is, in enterprises that receive the highest credit standing from the rating agencies. If a fund holds stock in a company whose credit rating falls below a preset level (e.g. "BB"), the fund has to sell those shares. This action protected the liquidity and performance of the respective fund. Because a sell-out by investment funds inevitably causes the affected company's share price to plummet, managers do everything possible to receive and to maintain a good rating. In this way rating agencies, and even individual stockmarket analysts employed by banks to advice clients, became extremely powerful. Their effect was especially evident during the investment boom of the late 1990s, when they were able, by uttering a few words, to create or to destroy billions of dollars of equity. This influence had existed earlier, of course, but then the evaluation had focused on the real economic behaviour of the companies involved. In the 1990s many analysts, following the move to market capitalization as the standard of a company's worth, shifted their focus to stock's performance on exchange. Thus, the economic source was no longer analysed but rather the evaluation of the source. Since a firm is analysed before its stock is bought, this means that the institutional analysers in reality analysed the market analysers. The inherent uncoupling of investment decision-making from tangible economic performance made the financial markets much more volatile than before. And the volatility forced both fund and company managers to consider short-term advantages much more seriously than before, for short-term instability could immediately undermine the economic future of all parties involved: investors, pension funds, and listed companies. Short-termism used to be one of the reproaches European managers aimed at their American counterparts. The Americanization of European business financing in the 1990s confronted them with the same constraints.By 2000 pension funds had become fairly widespread in France, The Netherlands, Sweden, and Switzerland, but even in these countries the sums involved were far smaller than in the United States. In Germany, Europe's largest national economy, investment funds still played a minor role. In 2002 the country's savings amounted to 3,660 billion euros, of which only 425 billion, roughly 12 per cent, belonged to funds. At the same time national capital markets become more interrelated than ever before, as shown by the increasing correlation between share price indices on national stock exchanges:

Interrelation of stock market indices, 1975-2001

per cent correlation	in 1975-1998	in 1990-2001
USA-France	43	65
USA-Germany	38	58
USA-Italy	23	47
USA-UK	58	71
UK-France	42	75
UK-Germany	40	66
UK-Italy	33	63
Germany-France	44	78
Germany-Italy	34	61
France-Italy	50	69

Source: ZEW news, January/February 2003, p. 3.[195]

The strong and increasing correlation of share prices between the major European countries is a logical consequence of the integrationist policies of the European Community. However, the most striking aspect of data is the jump of about 20 percentage points in correlation between share prices on the American and European markets. This shows that no country, not even the US, can control capital markets by national policy alone. The significance of this globalization of stock exchange can not be fully grasped through abstract figures, but it can be illustrated by examples. During the last two decades the German company *Degussa* has become a leading world enterprise in the production of fine chemicals. On its way it merged with several other German chemical companies such as *Hüls, Röhm, Th. Goldschmidt*, etc. In the course of these mergers, the company's management deliberated over the name of the new firm. The Th. Goldschmidt company was older, but the board of directors chose the name Degussa because the capital markets were more familiar with it than with any of the others. According to Degussa's CEO, Utz-Hellmuth Felcht, other considerations such as ease of pronunciation, memorability, or longevity played no role in the choice of name: the sole reason was capital-market recognition.[196]

The upsurge in public involvement in the stock market contributed to a reorientation of corporate managerial goals that would have far-reaching implications. In 1986 the American professor of business Alfred Rappaport published a book with the programmatic title *Creating Shareholder Value: the New Standard for Business Performance*. Rappaport redefined the relationship between the enterprise and its setting. Simply put, the message of *Shareholder Value* was that companies conduct activities in the interest of their shareholders (i.e. owners and not their stakeholders (i.e. employees, community, etc.). According to this view, even customers' interests were subordinated to the goal of maximizing shareholder value. The radicality of this focus was intensified by the understanding that it referred to share price and not, for example, company profits or dividends. The ultimate aim of managerial policy was the achievement of a high market value on the stock exchange.

The policy of shareholder value was swept forward by lucky timing; its introduction coincided with a period of sustained rise in share prices and governmental support for the libertarian economics of the Chicago School. At the same time the policy responded to practical economic interests of the American public. Many Americans, wealthy and less well-to-do, had contributed to pension funds to provide for their old age, and a large proportion of the capital of the funds was invested in ordinary shares. Shareholder value was therefore an issue that tapped strong roots in American society.

In Europe, however, shareholder value was resisted for some time; in part because shares played a lesser role in personal savings, in part because lack of practical experience in the stock market meant that few Europeans understood the nature of corporate finance. The Swiss are probably better informed about finances than other Europeans, given the country's strong activity in international financial services. But even in Switzerland a public opinion survey in 1993 revealed an impressive ignorance of the sector. Fifty-three per cent of those polled believed that corporate profits after deduction of all costs and taxes amounted generally to 25 per cent of business turnover. The reality was three per cent. There is nothing to indicate that a comparable poll a decade later would have more accurate perceptions. For persons with such a faulty perspective of corporate financing the concept of shareholder value represented an unreasonable demand.

Many companies and CEOs followed the mantra of shareholder value from the late 1980s, but none more successfully than the General Electric Company under Jack Welch. As chief executive officer of General Electric from 1981 to 2002 Welch transformed it from an electrical products giant into a global multi-business concentrating on services. His policies doubled GE's revenues and profits between 1993 and 1999, but even more importantly they increased the share price of company stock five-fold, far ahead of the mere doubling of the benchmark Dow Jones Industrial Average.[197] Welch's vigorous commitment to maximizing the price of company stock earned him the nickname "Mr. Shareholder Value". His managerial achievements gained much adulation in the business press. The Financial Times in London designated GE the "World's Most Respected Company" for five years running from 1999 to 2003. New York's Fortune magazine called General Electric "America's Most Admired Company" for four consecutive years from 1999. Yet Welch's legacy was not without blemish. When he published his memoirs in 2001, the Financial Times' reviewer, Michael Bonsignore, a retired chairman and CEO of Honeywell, commented on star executive's views of management with some astonishment:

> "I was struck, for example, by how little reference is made to customers and what GE's initiatives are doing for them. Community responsibility, another ingredient for long-term vitality of any company, gets surprisingly little mention beyond the benefits from taxes paid by GE. Diversity receives only a few paragraphs, even though the great majority of GE managers are white and male. Jeff Immelt, Jack's successor as chairman and chief executive has a wonderful opportunity to bring these aspects of GE up to world-class standards."[198]

The last sentence was a thinly disguised rebuke of Welch's vision, of course, but it was also a rejection of shareholder value as managerial priority. Welch's counterpart in Europe, Heinrich von Pierer, Siemen's chairman of the board (equivalent to CEO), avoided using the term shareholder value and preferred to talk of achieving a "meaningful balance between capital and labour."

Whether or not they used the actual term, nearly all European big business followed the managerial precepts of shareholder value from the second half of the 1990s. Like GE, they focused on improving share prices on the equity market and divested themselves of those parts of their firms that did not show attractive returns on investment. Like GE, which moved from electrical products to insurance and health care, some even acquired new firms in product areas totally unrelated to their original core business—when these had the "right" figures. Like GE's Jack Welch, European chief executives became driven by figures. Their business strategies were no longer geared to providing quality services or products, but were guided by balance-sheet numbers. In many ways this was a logical extension of lessons learned from American management practices in the 1960s and 1970s. At that time European businesses Americanized company strategy by putting customer demand at the centre of operations instead of production. A company's head of marketing became the most powerful person after its CEO, and its strategic decisions were governed by external forces. The concept of shareholder value recast managerial perspective once again. The focus on customer satisfaction was replaced by a concentration on position in the capital market. And inside the enterprise the head of the finance division supplanted the marketing director as most influential manager after the chief executive.

The move away from customers towards capital markets made firms much more flexible. In theory they no longer needed roots in the marketplace or product identity. Defining business performance by shareholder value freed companies from such traditional concerns. Taken to its logical extreme, shareholder value meant that an enterprise became defined simply as a hierarchically organized group of persons with the intention to make money by legal means. In practice, though, the concept applied only to joint-stock companies. How radical the consequences of pursuing shareholder value could be for individual enterprises can be illustrated by a few cases. In 1996 Jean-Marie Messier took over the helm of ailing *Compagnie Générale des Eaux*, a 150-year-old water and waste-treatment utility in France, and set about transforming it beyond recognition. Changing the firm's stodgy name to the sprightly Vivendi, Messier built up an international media division alongside the core environmental-services division. Rapid acquisitions in both Europe and North America turned Vivendi into the world's second biggest provider of entertainment, and for several years the company's share price considerably outperformed France's CAC-40 index in spite of doubts about the viability of the company's incongruous products. Two other examples of the spin-offs, mergers, splits, and fusions that came with the focus on shareholder value come from the chemicals sector. In 1994 the newly appointed Harvard-educated boss of Germany's sprawling chemical giant Hoechst, Jürgen Dormann, set in motion a massive restructuring programme following the precepts of American-style shareholder capitalism. The first non-chemist ever to head the company, Dormann decided that Hoechst needed to move from commodity chemicals to "life sciences" (pharmaceuticals, agrichemicals, biotechnology, and the like). Much of the traditional chemicals production was shifted to a subsidiary, Hoechst Celanese Corporation, which was then demerged in 1999 to become independent Celanese AG. In return, drug companies in France and America were acquired. Hoechst's transformation was capped in 1998-9 by its merger with the French pharmaceutical company *Rhône-Poulenc* to form a new company called *Aventis*, with head offices in Strasbourg. In 2004 Aventis was in its turn taken over by the Paris-based *Sanofi* in a hostile takeover bid. Similarly following the logic of stock market performance, the two venerable Swiss-based chemical/pharmaceutical giants, Ciba-Geigy and Sandoz, concluded one of the world's largest corporate mergers in 1996 to form a new company called *Novartis*. Both these mergers contradicted traditional management notions. Long-established corporate identities were demolished, and billions of investment in market communication and promotion of product-customer loyalty were thus wasted. Hoechst, Geigy, and Sandoz had been internationally recognizable brand names for over a century; how many ordinary people have heard of Sanofi or Novartis?

Redefining business performance in terms of return on capital also prompted investors to react differently. As long as a company's performance was defined according to output or sales, share prices rose when new hirings were announced because it signalled to investors that demand for company products was buoyant. In the 1990s business climate, however, share prices rose when a company reduced its workforce! Investors' reactions were based on a reinterpretation of workforce as a potential financial burden (high wages, pension obligations, etc.) rather than as an asset. Reducing that burden would logically enhance the company's rate of return on equity.

Although most European chief executives adjusted strategy to accommodate the profitability demands of shareholder value, few joined Vivendi's Messier or Hoechst's Dormann in enthusing over its precepts. In the early 1990s Ulrich Hartmann, CEO of the German electrical utility *Veba*, implemented a new strategy based on systematic cost management and divestment of non-core products in part as a reaction to market speculation that the company was a prime target for a hostile takeover because its equity was priced lower than the total value of its constituent parts. Hartman removed this discrepancy by dismissing 10,000 employees and selling off businesses amounting to five billion DM. The actions made him a star in business magazines and capital markets. But when asked in 1996 if he was proud of being the first to reshape a German concern according to the principles of shareholder value, he answered: "No, on the contrary. I think the way the discussion proceeds in Germany at the moment is terrible."[199] He also said he had dropped the expression shareholder value in favour of "value-oriented firm policy."

A thorough critique of the concept shareholder value was published by the Swedish Institute of Management (IFL) in 2001. It argued that the concept was short-sighted and understood the realities of the workshop floor in a negative way.[200] Another widespread criticism was that emphasizing shareholder value encouraged chief executives to use shady means to bolster share prices of their companies. In doing so they could not only make their own job more secure, but at the same time realize greater personal gains from the stock options they possessed. Awarding managers and employees shares or stock options is a time-honoured instrument to stimulate commitment and loyalty in the given firm, because their personal payoff is thereby linked to the firm's business performance. However, they really only function in that way when the corporate cultural climate is predisposed towards long-term employment. Moreover, the value of stock options is intrinsically volatile, so executives being partly paid in stock options may be tempted to focus on their company's short-term performance at the expense of long-term strategy in order to maximize the value of their options. The findings of a recent study of executive behaviour by the US National Bureau of Economic Research show that this is indeed a real possibility. The study relates the fraud scandals of Enron, WorldCom, and Global Crossing directly to the use of stock options as a part of executive salaries.[201]

European managerial scepticism regarding shareholder value policy was evident in the official communications of many companies. Such enterprises—as we have seen, Germany's Siemens was one—paid rather lip-service to the concept but did not really follow it. Yet the fact that even sceptical executives felt they had to make a bow to stock-market-determined performance shows how pervasive the concept was in the 1990s: it was not possible to ignore it. Nonetheless, the sceptics were proved right. When the almost decade-long bull market collapsed in spring 2000, the golden bubble of shareholder value burst in Europe and elsewhere. In the following two years share prices fell internationally by at least 50 per cent; indeed, the value of many dotcom companies crashed through the floor. Still, although shareholder value has lost its audience, it has left enduring traces on business management and the structure of European enterprise. At the very least it has resulted in company accounts becoming more open to public examination than a generation ago, for the public has become potential investors in corporate equity and informed investment decisions are in the best interests of all parties. More importantly, running businesses according to shareholder value undermined the relationship between the enterprise and its stakeholders, a relationship that had traditionally been strong in European economic life. We have seen that Siemen's Pierer and Honeywell's Bonsignore emphasize the central role of stakeholders' support for long-term viability of enterprises, and it appears that many European companies are trying to rebuild once-held trust among their employees and local community.

This may not be easy because the single-minded concentration of financial figures also expressed itself in what most Europeans perceived as American managerial greed. In American big business, top managers, especially chief executives, have typically received very high salaries, much higher than European counterparts. Around 1990 Chrysler Motor's CEO, Lee Iacocca, earned annually almost fifteen times more than Germany's Daimler-Benz's boss, Edzard Reuter: 17.5 million dollars compared with 1.2 million.[202] Yet Daimler-Benz was larger than Chrysler and took over the American company only a few years later. This was not an isolated case. In 1990 Stephen Wolf, the head of United Airlines, earned 1,272 times more than a starting flight attendant in his company. In Europe a spread of more than 100 times was considered shameless. But shame with regards to an enormous salary was not a relevant response in the American business community: on the contrary, the higher the pay, the higher the value of the given person, and the higher his or her self-esteem.

During the 1990s boom top executives became a scarce commodity, and qualified persons could command much higher pay than before on both sides of the Atlantic. Although European executive salaries remained much lower than in the US, three factors caused a narrowing of the gap: 1) Multinational takeovers (FDI). Chrysler and Daimler-Benz are again a prime example. The merger of two car companies resulted in internal salary disparities that obviously could not continue. Since it was impossible to lower the salaries of the new company's American executives to much extent, the pay of the executives on the German side had to be raised. 2) High demand for globalized information technology (IT). The combination of high demand for services, relative shortage of qualified personnel, and commonality of linguistic and technical background generated a mobile labour market that tended to reduce salary differentials between Europe and the US. 3) Payment in stock options. The wide use of stock options to top up basic salaries potentially gave managers of dynamic European companies a means of approaching American pay levels.

The inclusion of stock options in managerial pay was yet another sign of the Americanization of business financing in 1990s Europe. Both in the US and in Europe the instrument was first used and most widespread in the IT-sector with its many start-up companies whose worth initially was usually more potential than real. The awarding of stock options to managers (and even to employees) was a means to compensate for modest beginning salaries and to stimulate work-dedication. Indeed, it soon became a precondition for the hiring of key specialists in the sector. In more traditional sectors the distribution of stock options to company personnel was usually tied to specific performance conditions. The Hoechst chemical conglomerate, for instance, introduced stock options for its top managers in 1997, but they were transactionable only if the company's share price had risen by at least 25 per cent, and they could not be executed before a period of two years had elapsed. Many Europeans, especially young IT specialists, became very enthusiastic about receiving options as a supplementary salary; their potential value often exceeded the ordinary pay. Many overlooked the considerable risk involved. The stock market collapse of 2000-2001 rendered most options worthless over night, and their European holders were stunned and dismayed. Even financial newspapers, which should have been more informed about the risks of stock market instruments, showed concern, though irony often was evident. For instance, the Norwegian business daily *Dagens Næringsliv* (the Norwegian equivalent of the *Financial Times*) shed crocodile tears in describing the sudden impoverishment of the young chief executives of start-up IT companies whose now "verdiløse gulrøtter" (worthless carrots) used to make them run faster.[203]

After the market meltdown stock options were no longer a compelling topic, but executive salaries still were. Every country had an example or two of exorbitant salaries, pensions, or golden parachutes that created public discussion, sometimes even in parliament. But when the paycheck of Richard Grasso, head of New York Stock Exchange (NYSE), became known in 2003, there was a cry outrage in both the United States and Europe. In the previous two years millions of dollars worth of equity had disappeared at the NYSE, and although the exchange was organized as a non-profit organization, Grasso's contract as its director entitled him to 188 million dollars that year (salary, bonus, pension all included), of which he had refused 48 million. By contrast, the average chief executive salary of the 30 largest companies listed on the Frankfurt stock exchange was 1.5 million euros (ca two million US dollars), and the highest (Daimler-Chrysler) was just under five million euros (ca six million US dollars). Germany's Jürgen Schrempp, Daimler-Chrysler's CEO and a member of NYSE's supervisory board, resigned in protest. After months of acrimonious public discussion, Grasso was forced to resign, despite the backing of influential friends, such as New York's former mayor Rudy Giuliani. Too much greed was unacceptable even in the United States, though there remains a significant difference between American and European definitions of 'too much'.

RISK-TAKING AS AN ECONOMIC VIRTUE

Traditionally, American and European business have had fundamentally different attitudes towards risk and risk-taking. Americans associated risk with opportunity and gain, Europeans with potential failure, even disaster. The different associations had repercussions for entrepreneurial behaviour. Business bankruptcy in the United States tended to be understand as the failure of the given business idea not the person, as long as there was no fraud involved. The same entrepreneur's next business idea could be brilliantly successful, and talented bankrupts could usually secure backing for later projects. By contrast, a European businessman who had gone bankrupt was branded a personal failure. He (or she) would have considerable difficulties starting up again because banks and suppliers would be extremely reluctant to provide credits to a sometime failure. The greater consequences of failure meant that many potential European entrepreneurs hesitated to start businesses if the perceived risks were high. Similar differences existed in the attitudes towards business financing. America's lead in mobilizing information technology has been due in part to the greater availability of venture capital. Providing venture or risk capital carries a positive connotation in American business culture, where such risk-taking in untried companies tends to be regarded as shaky speculation in Europe.

The European preference to avoid financial risk-taking is anchored in legislation on corporate accountancy. The legislation typically allows companies to build up hidden reserves of capital that can be used to redeem bank loans, to maintain dividend levels, or drawn on generally in times of slack business. The corporation's owners, the shareholders, often were never informed of these reserves; sometimes even the board of directors did not know their full size. By contrast, American rules on corporate accounting express openness to risk-taking. Financial reserves must be declared so that shareholders have full information about the company's real value and thus about the extent of risk their investment involves. The differences in attitude and legislation have created some difficulties for the internationalization of equity markets. For example, when several large European corporations, such as financial conglomerate AXA and the financial providers Swiss Re and ING, applied for listing on the NYSE, the Exchange demanded that their balance sheets be drawn up according to the American standards, the Generally Agreed Accounting Proceedings or US-GAAP.

Although experts in international business finance were aware of the differences between European and American accounting practices, many underestimated how much the results could deviate. In the case of the Dutch banking and insurance company ING the gap was enormous. According to Dutch accounting procedures, ING made a profit of 4.5 billion euros in 2002, whereas according to US-GAAP it had suffered a loss of 9.6 Billions![204] Regarding shareholder equity the gap reversed direction: US-GAAP declared an equity of 25 billion Euros, Dutch accounting rules only 18.2 billion. Clearly, such wide differences in national accounting rules made it quite hazardous to invest internationally without additional special knowledge. All parties agreed that the differences should be eliminated but opinions differed as to which set of accounting practices should be adopted. The problem was not new. An international committee based in London had been negotiating a set of international accounting standards since the 1970s. In 2000-2001 it released its final version of the code, which was adopted by the London Stock Exchange and recommended by the European Commission. But the globalization of capital markets in the 1990s had been in fact largely an Americanization of international finance, and many American stock market experts claimed that the US accounting standards were better. Some Europeans shared this view. For instance, Manfred Gentz, board member of Daimler-Chrysler, insisted on the superiority of US-GAAP on the grounds that American stock exchanges were more strictly controlled than European ones. Others regarded an Americanization of accounting as leading to a catastrophic changing of European corporate culture. Thus, Hans-Heinrich Otte of the German accounting firm BDO Deutsche Warentreuhand, complained:

> "By taking over American rule, you destroy culture!" And "The Americans look down
> on us as some kind of developing country. They see only their quarterly profits; while
> with us hidden reserves and creditor protection receive larger attention."[205]

Otte's reaction was perhaps exaggerated, but his linking of standards and cultural attitudes is broadly correct. Moreover, country-specific standards can affect business competition in the respective domestic markets. The operations of indigenous companies are naturally geared to the required technical or accounting standards, which can give them a competitive advantage over foreign businesses, whose unfamiliarity in theory and in practice can entail costly investments.

The American-European tug of war over accounting standards took an unexpected turn at the beginning of the twenty-first century. On 2 December 2001 after ten months of escalating financial difficulties and plummeting share prices the Houston-based energy giant Enron, a product of the privatization and deregulations of the American energy provisioning that had become one of the US's largest companies in barely 15 years, filed for bankruptcy. It quickly transpired that the company's astounding expansion and high-flying stock market position had been achieved by dubious means. Its high turnover and profits was the product of "creative bookkeeping", a euphemism for illegal accounting procedures. The bankruptcy was all the more shocking because Enron's fraudulent accounts had been vetted and approved by auditors from Arthur Andersen of New York, one of the world's five largest and best regarded accounting firms. Enron's demise unleashed an avalanche of sordid revelations. Many other firms, nearly all of them connected with Arthur Andersen, were uncovered to have cheated, too. Shortly after Enron's collapse, the telecoms giant WorldCom (now MCI) also admitted to illegal bookkeeping and declared bankruptcy, the largest failure in American history. The trials that followed the scams were a damning indictment of the American corporate culture. The key banking institutions involved, Merrill Lynch and Citibank, were assessed substantial fines. For its role in covering the fraud the two companies' auditor, Arthur Andersen, was banned from auditing American companies and the firm was liquidated in August 2002.

The Enron-WorldCom scandals clearly undermined the argument that American corporate accounting was superior to other standards, but the advocates of

US-GAAP pressed their case again after US Congress passed the Sarbanes-Oxley Act, which laid down strict disclosure rules. However, only a year later, in November 2003, massive business fraud was uncovered by the FBI. This time foreign-exchange traders had cheated not only customers but their own institutions, among them some of the first names in international banking—J.P. Morgan Chase, Société Générale, UBS, and Dresdner Kleinwort Benson. Once again international acceptance of American accounting standards was stalled. The tougher accounting standards required by the Sarbanes-Oxley Act made a US listing safer for potential investors but at the same time most costly for the corporations. Adecca, the Swiss-based world leader in supplying short-term labour, received a bill of 100 million euros for the auditing and legal costs of its NYSE listing in 2003.[206] That amounted to a quarter of its net earnings that year. Such enormous costs clearly reduced the attractiveness of a listing at the NYSE. Even the Wall Street Journal conceded that they might lead to a de-listing of European companies on the Exchange.

But the export of other aspects of American business and civil law regarding the economic risks of consumers and producers continued. From a European point of view American legislation on compensation is both erratic and strange. Europeans have difficulty comprehending the legal logic behind the chain of reversals in convictions and fines that frequently occur in American compensation lawsuits.[207] They have no trouble, however, accepting the obligation to pay compensation if a company's product turns out to be damaging or dangerous. Thus, after the health danger of asbestos became incontestable, the Swiss-Swedish engineering concern *ABB* paid huge amounts to customers of its American subsidiary Combustion Engines, which had used the dangerous substance in many of its products. The payments nearly broke ABB's neck, but the company did not contest its obligation to compensate. On the other hand, European notions of risk-compensation are still characterized by a common-sense regard for personal responsibility. This is illustrated by the outcome of recent lawsuits against tobacco companies in Germany and Norway. Instead of awarding compensation to the smokers who had raised the suits as has happened in the United States, the courts cleared the companies of responsibility on the grounds, simply put, that everybody knows that smoking is a health hazard and that nobody is compelled to smoke.

European resistance to American business law derives not only from a different understanding of risk and responsibility, but also from a rejection of the underlying commercialism of legal practice in the United States. Whereas European lawyers are typically paid a set fee for services rendered, American corporate or civil-law lawyers often are paid by commission. If they win their case, they can claim a percentage of the settlement, in exceptional cases up to 50 per cent. American lawyers are also allowed to approach potential clients and offer their service by public advertisement. Both aspects contribute to making American civil-law practices much more aggressive than European. The American class action lawsuit is an expression of these different legal environments. Such lawsuits, in which one or more persons raise grievances on behalf of all potential claimants, have become a powerful instrument of consumer activism in the US. To date, they are largely unknown in Europe, but European companies that do business in the United States are subject to class action regarding these activities. There have also been attempts by European plaintiffs to launch class action suits against European companies and institutions in American courts of law. The latest of these was initiated in a New York court in April 2003 by a Hamburg group of social benefit recipients against the City of Hamburg.[208] To date it is uncertain whether the American court will hear the suit; doing so would signal an important inroad of Americanization in European attitudes of risk and responsibility as well as in civil-law practices.

THE CONSUMER AS INDIVIDUAL

A commonplace observation is that Americans and Europeans have different attitudes about the place of the individual in society. The difference is often expressed as the atomized individual versus communal or group solidarity. A thought-provoking version of this contention can be found in the comparative study of public opinion published by the American-based National Bureau for Economic Research in April 2001 under the title *Inequality and Happiness: Are Europeans and Americans different?*[209] It documented that Americans, even the poor, were generally happier than Europeans. The existence of strong social inequalities made the polled Europeans unhappy; to the Americans it was largely a matter of indifference. The reason was that Europeans considered the structures of inequality to be long-lasting and impenetrable, whereas Americans regarded them as temporary and porous. The Americans believed it possible to rise from dishwasher to millionaire; Europeans did not. Both were wrong. The move is indeed possible, but it is also highly exceptional. Remarkably, the different perceptions were not caused by real differences in societal experience. Both intergenerational and career social mobility were quite similar in the countries surveyed. The different perceptions of nearly the same reality rested on different attitudes towards individual risk and reward within society.

There are nonetheless many signs that Europeans have begun to adopt an American-style emphasis on personal distinctiveness and individual separateness in daily lifestyles. The development of economic prosperity characterized by mass production and mass consumption from the 1950s stimulated the spread of consumer individualism in Europe as earlier in the United States. Increasingly, Europeans expressed their individualism by small material distinctions: the type of car, the kind of food, the sort of holiday journey, and so on. It was no longer enough simply to have a car or holiday.

The present-day epitome of consumer individualism in mass society is perhaps socially defined residential location. At first glance this is an old phenomenon, represented by villa districts and up-scale avenues. Nowadays it takes the form of gated communities. Gated communities are settlements that are set off from their surrounding town by a fence or wall and accessible only through gates. They were known in the Middle Ages, but largely disappeared with the demise of feudal society.[210] From the late eighteenth century urban space in Europe (and North America) became in principle open to all; only Beijing continued to maintain a "forbidden city" for the Chinese Emperor into the twentieth century.

In the last quarter of a century gated communities, separated by walls, boom chains, even barbed wire, and watched by private security guards electronic surveillance, have reemerged as a yet another expression of consumer individualism in today's mass society. They are particularly found in areas of new or rapid expansion, and laid out deliberately by developers to provide home-buyers with an immediate sense of both community and special, individual identity plus a sort of additional security the general public could not enjoy. In the United States gated communities are particularly concentrated in the West and in the South; in 2002 they contained about seven million households.[211] Exclusiveness and security are the reasons given by those who felt attracted by gated communities. Since the 1980s Europe has also seen the establishment of gated communities. They first appeared on the Mediterranean coast in Spain and France as second-home settlements for vacationers and retirees. Subsequently, they have been constructed—on a smaller areal scale—in a number of major cities: Madrid, Lisbon, Milan, Rome, Vienna, and London. Modern gated communities are a sociological paradox. On the one hand, they seem to move away from the modern socio-political principles of individual equality and open society by promoting segregation and social control. On the other hand, their residents can be said to have used their consumer resources to assert an individual lifestyle choice rather than be engulfed by an anonymous process of modernization with its uncertainties and insecurities.

Consumer individualism and commercialization can also be seen in the changing role and organization of sports in European society; and as so often American developments have set the pattern. From its emergence in the mid-nineteenth century sports activity typically took place in a collective environment, the club or association. This was particularly true of team sports, of course, but it also applied to individual activities. Cyclists, runners, or gymnasts trained and performed in groups; and these often had meeting and training quarters as well as distinctive dress that gave group identity. Participation in club-based sports peaked during the 1950s and 1960s. Since then sports participation has become increasingly individualized and moved into the fitness studio. In place of the traditional group-focussed activity at a specific time and place, the fitness studio offered the advantages of flexible training according to individual needs and possibilities; customers could come and go at any time. This approach to sporting exercise first developed in a big way in the United States in the 1980s and was introduced to Europe in the following decade. In 2000 11 per cent of Americans were members of a fitness club; in Europe the proportions were much lower with the highest participation found in the UK, Switzerland, and Germany.[212] Besides promoting individualization, fitness studios have also changed the contents of sports activity. Instead of training for a particular sport or athletic discipline, the fitness studio focuses on physical fitness as a healthy lifestyle, and it often sells health services and products as well as entertainment. In short, sports activity in the fitness studio has become a commercial, consumer product.

Similar trends can be found in team-sport associations. They could not be logically individualized, but they have become commercialized on both sides of the Atlantic. For many years most sports teams were associations of amateur participants, who paid the costs of club activities by membership fees. Club assets were owned collectively by members and profits were excluded. With few exceptions, the team's members came from the local community or area. In Europe this local rooting of sports teams continued to dominant even in the early years of professionalism. Well into the 1950s European footballers (soccer players) often turned down offers of higher salaries to remain with their original home club.

Professional team sports first emerged in the United States at the beginning of the twentieth century. Until the 1950s, though, baseball was the only one that could be described as a sports business with a large following, and the size of its income-generating audience was essentially limited to the capacity of the stadium. The development of television in the 1950s revolutionized the business of sports, first in the US then in Europe. Telecasting sports matches eliminated restrictions on audience size, which in turn unleashed the economic potential of mass advertising for television companies, team owners, and players alike. Team sports became big business. Ownership of a sports team was a business investment, and players were capital assets that were bought and sold. American football, basketball, and ice hockey joined baseball as big-time professional sports; individual competitions like golf and tennis soon fallowed. From the 1980s player trade unions had developed in many sports, and players acquired the right to freely offer services to the highest bidder. Ties of allegiance between teams, players, and local community increasingly disappeared: not only did players shift teams, but also teams shifted cities to take advantage of changing business conditions. Perhaps the epitome of unabashed sports commercialization came in 1999 when the billionaire Robert McNair bought a team license from the American National Football League (NFL) for the then record sum of 700 million dollars. McNair's purchase was strictly a business decision. His to-be-established football team had no name, no logo, no audience, and no players; they still had to be acquired. [213]

Parallel developments in Europe have been largely limited to football or soccer. Football clubs have reorganized themselves as joint-stock companies and used the capital raised to build up assets; that is to buy players and modernize their stadiums. By 2001 forty European clubs had gone public, though only Manchester United had been able to maintain the price of its initial offering. Football matches had become glitzy show business, dominated by media attention to star players like David Beckham. Accordingly, television rights replaced ticket sales as the main source of team revenue. The monies thus generated were enormous. In 2003 the management agency Roland Berger valued these rights for France, Germany, Italy, Spain, and the UK at about 3.6 billion euros, of which England's Premier League received the largest share.[214]

Income from Football TV Rights (in million euros)

	Season 2001/2002	*Season 2002/2003*
England, Premier League	720	735
Italy, Serie A	461	422
France, Ligue 1	379	366
Germany, Bundesliga	278	290
Spain, Prima Division	295	214

Source: Die Zeit, July 31, 2003

In both the United States and Europe team sports had become a commercial product available to the individual consumer according to taste. Yet although sports commercialization occurred first and most strongly in the US, its development in Europe was not a true Americanization effect but rather the consequence of the business logic of modern media.

One example of consumer individualism that can legitimately be called an Americanization is the modern fast food restaurant, especially epitomized by McDonald's. The McDonald's Restaurants opened in Illinois in 1955 and, using franchising, expanded rapidly throughout the United States and Canada. The company went public in 1965 and introduced its trademark "Big Mac" product in 1968. In the 1970s McDonald's moved into Germany, the UK, and other European countries as well as Japan. In 2003 McDonald's was the world's largest fast food supplier, feeding 46 million persons daily in 30,000 restaurants located all over the globe. Each of the larger European countries—Germany, the UK, even France—had over a thousand McDonald's restaurants. As an icon of Americanization McDonald's became the equal of Coco-Cola. In his book *The McDonaldization of Society* the American sociologist George Ritzer claimed that the restaurant chain had overwhelmed Europe, and he even compared it to a cultural Chernobyl:

> "...McDonaldization, as a form of Americanization, does represent something unique and more threatening than all of its predecessors that were seen as imperilling Europe. McDonaldization does have at least to be more than a second culture; to be a kind of cultural Chernobyl. On of the things that makes McDonaldization unique is that it brings together in one package a threat to both European business and cultural practices. Previous manifestations of the American menace have tended to represent one or the other, but not both."[215]

What made McDonald's so attractive for Europeans? A combination of characteristics that add up to a profile of the American business practices: 1) The speed of service by which food was served. 2) Low Prices. 3) Self service. 4) Good quality of products. 5) Customers were taken seriously, even though they may spend relatively little. 6) Though food was served and eaten quickly, McDonald's was physically a real restaurant with seating, tables, and restrooms. Traditional European fast food suppliers—for example the sausage stand—offered their products for immediate consumption while standing and had no the facilities for customers. 7) Catering to the interests of young people, who in Europe were not so used to eat in a restaurant. Thus, eating out at McDonald's could be associated with an enhancement of social prestige among youngsters. In other words, McDonald's had found a lucrative niche. Its activities had a profound impact on patterns of consumption and behaviour, although the expression "cultural Chernobyl" is clearly exaggerated.

A second icon of Americanization's consumer individualism that Ritzer attacked was the plastic credit card:

> "The credit card is also the premier symbol of an American life-style that much of the rest of the world is rushing to emulate. While there is much to recommend such a lifestyle there is another side to it that is largely ignored. That other side is the rampant expansion of the consumer culture and its attendant problems – consumerism and indebtedness, fraud, invasion of privacy, rationalization and dehumanization, and homogenization stemming from increasing Americanization."[216]

Personal cards entitling the holder to prearranged credit for the purchase of goods and services emerged in the United States in the 1950s. Two types became available, the house credit card, issued by major department stores and retail chains such as petrol stations, and valid only there, and the general credit card, valid wherever stores, restaurants, etc. cooperated with the card's issuing financial institution. Although it may seem to be an impersonal financial instrument, the credit card in fact imparts to its bearer a social identity. Paying for goods or services with cash is essentially an anonymous transaction. Using a credit card, however, represents an individualization of the consumer. It identifies the purchaser by name, by signature, and increasingly by photograph.

The first general credit cards, Diners Club and American Express, catered to the needs of well-to-do travellers; they were mainly accepted in payment by airlines, major hotels, and up-scale stores. Potential cardholders had to document an above-average annual income, and although the amount of credit allowed in any single transaction was unlimited, with few exceptions it had to be repaid within three weeks of the monthly billing. Despite these restrictions, the concept was sufficiently successful that within a few years, the major American commercial banks took it up and two rival general credit cards—Bankamericard (later Visa) and MasterCard—were launched. These cards were issued on more relaxed conditions—essentially to most bank customers in good standing—and quickly became accepted by a wide range of businesses at all price levels. In short, for individual consumers they could function as a substitute for in-pocket cash as well as extending immediate purchasing power by proving revolving credit. In practice the use of credit cards in general merchandising grew slowly until the 1980s. In 1984 58 per cent of American consumer expenditures were paid by personal bank check, 36 per cent by cash, and only 6 per cent by credit card.[217] Eight years later check payments still dominated, but payments by card had overtaken cash (22 and 20 per cent respectively). By 1997 the proportion of American private consumption paid by plastic had increased still further to 34 per cent, amounting to 453 billion dollars. Since the mid-1990s a number of larger retailers like Sears have negotiated agreements that allow them to combine their original house credit cards with one of the general credit cards. Sears' management has reported that income from its co-branded credit card "has been a major source of company profits..."[218] American general credit cards have become iconic and effectively monopolize the instrument throughout the world, although the actual issuing banks and terms vary from country to country. In 2002 1.8 billion credit cards were in circulation world wide. Sixty per cent were associated with Visa International and 33 per cent with MasterCard; American Express and JBC (Japan) each issued three per cent, and the more exclusive Diners Club accounted for less than one per cent.[219]The two most widespread American general credit cards—Visa and MasterCard—are not issued by the eponymous parent organizations but by participating banks, so when they expand operations into Europe in the 1960s they had to accommodate the practices of European banks. In 1968 MasterCard concluded a joint venture with EuroCard (later Europay), a European association of major national banks like Barclays, Deutsche Bank, Credit Suisse, and Bank of Ireland that had developed a bank card to complement its existing common chequing system, Eurocheque, EuroCard was a direct debit card; purchases on the card were charged automatically and immediately to the cardholder's bank account. Because it did not grant consumers credit, the debit card was cheaper and simpler for all participants—cardholder, issuing bank, and participating businesses. In the early 1970s Visa concluded a similar agreement with European banks. The alliances between European banks and credit card companies were beneficial to both sides in different ways. The American-based credit card companies secured European market recognition while the banks controlled expansion of credit instruments. MasterCard and Visa functioned as credit cards only under specific conditions; unlike in North America, plastic money in Europe functioned overwhelmingly by direct debiting. At the end of the twentieth century the UK was the only European country where a substantial proportion of payment cards (30 percent) were full-fledged credit cards. Nonetheless, the American card brand names have displaced all others in time. In 2003 MasterCard had the largest market share with 50 per cent, followed by Visa with 42 per cent, American Express 7, and Diners Club 1.[220]

Co-branding of credit/debit cards was also imported into Europe around 2000. Although the most frequent partners in co-branding are businesses like Lufthansa, SAS, or Norwegian Automobile Association, non-commercial institutions such as the World Wildlife Fund (WWF) and universities have also negotiated special versions of MasterCard, Visa, or even Diners Club that bear the institutional logo. In return for promoting the card's use, the co-branding partner receives a small commission related to the size of purchases. The holder of a co-branded card is entitled to the same financial services as regular cardholders and enjoys the additional advantage of expressing a particular personal commitment or identity. Co-branding is thus a perfect example of the commercialized consumer as individual.

Yet despite surface appearances the omnipresence of MasterCard and Visa in Europe does not signify unambiguous Americanization. To be sure, many western Europeans nowadays purchase goods and services using a plastic card rather than cash. But the cards are issued by the financial institutions of individual European countries according to the terms and procedures appropriate to each. And European banks have primarily adopted the low-risk, low-cost model of direct debit payment card rather than the American-style credit card with its higher risks and costs. So far plastic money in Europe has not created an explosion of credit-based consumption; it is limited by the cardholder's bank balance and simply makes purchasing more convenient by eliminating the need to carry cash.

CONCLUSION: THE TRIUMPH OF FINANCES

The rejuvenated free-market capitalism that was swept over Europe by Americanization's third wave promoted a mentality of commercialization that substantially altered the attitudes and behaviour of both companies and consumers. The most fundamental change concerned the method of business financing. Following the American model that dominated the global economy, European enterprises increasingly shifted from their long-standing reliance on bank credits to the stock market to obtain operational and investment capital. The shift undermined the traditionally close cooperation between banks and industry that had been a central feature of business financing in many countries. These relationships were further weakened by international agreements (Basel I and Basel II) that imposed largely American rules for the credit rating of the world's banks and their clients. An importance consequence of the weakening of bank-industry ties was that the traditional obligation of house banks to defend their industrial clients in time of business adversity was overturned. Enterprises could no longer depend on a stable bank relation and became structurally more exposed to economic risk from various quarters. They were thus vulnerable to hostile takeovers even in economies that had traditionally been protected by all-powerful universal banks, as Germany's Mannesmann learned to its regret.

The shift from bank credits to equity capitalization subjected the accounts of European enterprise to the fluctuations of the stock market. From the 1980s the inherent instability of stock exchanges was increased by the entry of institutional and commercial investment funds. Funds generally set a premium on short-term gain rather than on long-term performance. Hence, they react quickly to changes in share prices and stock ratings and their buying and selling in large blocks of shares greatly enhanced the volatility of international capital markets. Investment funds contributed to a democratization of shareholding. Instead of being an activity for the rich and the few, investing in corporate stock became accessible to persons of modest means. This in turn stimulated the redefinition of business performance from an emphasis on promoting the well-being of a company's stakeholders to a concentration on the economic interests of its owners, that is its shareholders. Shareholder value as a general business strategy was first practiced by American companies such as General Electric, but in the late 1990s it also was applied in European business by the likes of France's Jean-Marie Messier and Germany's Jürgen Dormann. In both the United States and Europe the emphasis on shareholder value, together with deregulation and privatization, redrew the structures of European enterprise. In the name of increasing return on capital assets and thereby increasing share price on the stock market, a number of venerable and renown corporate names were swallowed up by mergers and takeovers, while still other companies completely redefined their business activities. Even though many European executives never fully embraced shareholder value and support for it weakened after the stock market crash of 2000, the concept injected a potent dose of American-style free-market capitalism into European corporate culture.

Shareholder value is predicated on the commercialization and individualization of social relationships. During the last decades of the twentieth century these processes became more and more evident in European consumer behaviour. The displacement group-based athletic activity by individual-based physical fitness training is one indicator, the predominance of spectator professional sports matches over amateur contests another. But although these two phenomena are most widespread in the United States, they developed in Europe by their own social logic and thus do not signify Americanization. The Americanizing dimension of other changes in European consumer individualism, however, is clearer. McDonald's, MasterCard, and Visa were all introduced to Europe by American parent companies. Yet closer examination of how they function there shows that they have been edited, adapted, Europeanized. Plastic money in Europe is still largely governed by traditional low-risk financial mentalities and thus tied to tangible bank account balances rather than giving American-style access to consumer credit. Even the McDonald's chain, because it is constructed as a series of individual franchises, exhibits alongside the internationally standard Big Mac and company colours noticeable national distinctiveness.

CHAPTER 7

INDUSTRIAL RELATIONS AS A BARRIER TO AMERICANIZATION

European reception of the American model of free-market industrial capitalism has always been an uneven process with variations over time and from country to country. The ups and downs of Americanization are due to many reasons, but an underlying structural cause was suggested already in a small book published in 1906 by the German economist Werner Sombart. Bearing the programmatic title "Why is the no socialism in the United States?", it raises a profound question and points out the central issue of industrial relations in economic life.[221] Up to now this book has not dealt much with work in the European economy—the relations between employees and employers—as a subject of Americanization. Work is of course a potentially very broad topic; here we will concentrate on worker participation in company management because it touches the core of industrial relations, namely the control of economic power in the enterprise. As we shall see, there have been and still are deep-seated differences between European and American perceptions and implementations of worker participation. And these differences constitute a persistent barrier to the Americanization of European economic life.

Worker participation is an umbrella expression covering several related issues and definitions.[222] In Europe the concept has been a central part of sociopolitical debate since the early nineteenth century, and all political movements from Left to Right have formulated opinions and, when possible, implemented appropriate policies. For all but the Far Right (e.g. fascist parties) worker participation belonged to the struggle for industrial democracy and the empowerment of the workers' movement. This anchoring in collective political goals meant that worker participation went beyond workers' campaign for material betterment such as higher wages or shorter working hours. In the UK and especially in the US the concept's ideological content was much weaker, even absent, which enabled it to be interpreted as a means to increase the economic position of individual workers. From this context we can separate the theory and practice of worker participation into three pairs of issues that find the United States, and to a certain extent Great Britain, and Europe on opposite sides.

1) focus on the individual and personal betterment (US) versus focus on the collectivity and social equity (Europe).[223]

2) concentration on material goals or money (US) versus concentration on immaterial goals or power (Europe).

3) use by management to improve the firm's performance (US) versus use by society to instil specific social and political values and practices in the management of companies (Europe).[224]

WORKER PARTICIPATION IN EUROPE AND THE UNITED STATES TO 1945

        In most countries the attitude of the trade unions to worker participation was determined by tradition and experience. British and American unions were constructed from the inside of enterprise; their basic unit was a group within a certain plant, the shop stewards in the case of the UK. In contrast, on the Continent trade unions often formed first outside the actual workplace as a local organization or club and had to force their entry into the plant. Consequently, in the two Anglo-Saxon countries the basic trade union strength was located in the individual enterprise, whereas in Continental Europe it rested with the central organisation. Similar differences developed with respect to the role of politics and ideology in union activities. Trade unions in the US and UK emphasized pragmatic economic concerns over theoretical issues. In the US this materialist orientation has been so strong that the trade union movement has refrained from making binding ties with any political party. In the UK the trade union movement undertook to build up the Labour Party in 1900 and kept it an instrument of its economic interests for almost a century. On the Continent, by contrast, trade union movements tended to be dominated by political parties, usually socialist ones, which dominance enhanced the strength of theoretical and ideological considerations in union activities. Versions of the Continental concept of industrial democracy were enunciated in Great Britain from the 1890s by groups of intellectuals whose anti-capitalist critique, concern for social justice, and theory-based argumentation contributed to moving Britain's Labour Party in the direction of the European approach to worker participation. Guild Socialism condemned the wage slavery of capitalism and advocated a decentralized workers' control of industrial production. The more famous Fabian Society, whose goal was "the reconstruction of society in accordance with the highest moral principles",[225] pushed for the nationalization of the means of production as the key to expanding democratic citizenship to include social rights on an equal footing with political rights such as suffrage. Similar ideas were propagated in the United States by the League for Industrial Democracy (LID). Founded by social radicals such as Jack London and Upton Sinclair in 1905, its declared purpose was "to educating Americans about the need to extend democracy to every aspect of our society."[226] But whereas Fabians and Guild Socialists came to exercise considerable influence on the thinking and policies of British trade unions and Labour Party, the LID faded almost without a trace.

        The first example of worker participation as practice would seem to be a works council established by George Cadbury in his chocolate plant in Birmingham (Bournville after 1878) sometime between 1860 and 1870. At first the council was only a vehicle for workers' complaints; in due course, though, it was able to influence factory administration as well. Both the works council and Cadbury's managers were careful not to oppose the rights of trade unions to represent workers' interests. In fact the council was set up with the recognition of the respective unions and its terms of reference included the „stipulation that trade union rules and customs should not be contravened by such councils without the written consent of the union concerned."[227] Such accommodation of trade union interests no doubt contributed much to the effectiveness of the Cadbury works council. Cadbury's initiative remained an exception in British industry for many years, but similar exceptions were found in other countries. In Germany's manufacturing industry in 1891 there existed at least five workers' committees, which could express their views to management though without a direct influence on decision-making. Heinrich Freese, owner of a Berlin company that produced Venetian blinds, took the concept a step further in developing what he called a *constitutional firm*, that is his enterprise had a constitution that gave the works council the right to delegate workers' representatives to the board of directors.

The First World War gave rise to an enormous demand for labour that strengthened the economic and political position of the workers' movement throughout Europe. In the UK the shop steward movement had acquired special strength during the war years; for a few years it even threatened to turn into a rival for the regular trade unions. This challenge to their existence by parts of their own movement caused the British unions to tread carefully regarding any demands for an alternative basis of workers' representation such as an institutionalized worker participation. Similarly, proposals to establish some form of worker participation were blocked in Belgium, Denmark, and Norway, despite support by governmental committees. In Germany and Austria, however, socialist-inspired revolutions brought in worker participation as national standards. In 1920 the German social democratic government passed legislation requiring all large industrial enterprises to set up works councils, which had the right not only to be informed about certain issues, but also to co-determine with management the hiring and firing of factory workers. Austria's government, also dominated by the country's Social Democratic Party, enacted similar laws. In both countries the decision was taken under heavy political pressure from radicals in the workers' movements, including the Bolsheviks in Soviet Russia. The German and Austrian works councils were understood as a form of immaterial and collective worker participation that promoted industrial democracy.

During the 1920s worker participation was a topic of controversy in the United States as well. The *American Plan*, an initiative by company owners, envisaged a form of worker participation by means of informal workers' committees. However, since the Plan limited these rights of representation to company unions, the independent trade union movement predictively opposed it bitterly, and it "collapsed" under the "organising drive by industrial unions in the 1930s."[228] The trade union movement's strenuous rejection of the American Plan underscored its fundamental approach to industrial relations "that collective bargaining is the preferred channel for worker representation and participation at the workplace. The American system of collective bargaining is based on the concept that a duly certified union is to serve as the exclusive representative of workers."[229] The concentration on organized group interests obviated demands from the American trade union movement for worker participation and industrial democracy.

During the same years on the Continent institutions of worker participation not only lost support, they were even partly reversed. Class cooperation rather than class conflict came to be the preferred principle for industrial relations. Under the pretext of removing the corrosive social effects of class conflict, fascist and right-wing regimes tried to banish industrial conflicts by suppressing workers' movements and by preaching the national economic solidarity of employees and employers. Fascist Italy led the way with its *Carta del Lavoro* in 1927. In Germany after 1933 the National Socialist regime redefined the duties of the existing works councils and incorporated them in the *Deutsche Arbeitsfront* (DAF), which charged with creating industrial peace by promoting the mutual understanding of workers and managers. Similar organizations, *sindicatos verticales*, were introduced in Spain by Franco's government. The fascist regimes did not deny the existence of labour disputes but insisted that they were to be resolved by authority from above, if necessary by the use of force.

Elsewhere in 1930s Europe the influence of trade unions was actually strengthened with the official approval of employers' representatives and government. The most important of these national agreements for industrial peace and worker-owner cooperation took place in Norway (1935), Switzerland (1937), and Sweden (1938).[230] The agreements profoundly changed the climate of industrial relations in these countries and set the stage for the development of full-fledged worker participation. It can even be plausibly argued that the hard-handed implementation of industrial cooperation in the fascist countries paradoxically prepared the ground for later acceptance there of the concept and institutions of worker participation.

WORKS COUNCILS AND CO-DETERMINATIION IN EUROPE AFTER 1945

The Second World War, like the First, generally strengthened the workers' movements throughout Europe and in the United States. But growth in organizational power did not change the negative opinion of the two American trade union associations—the craft-based AFL and industry-based CIO (merged as AFL-CIO from 1952)—towards worker participation, and business owners largely shared this attitude. In 1951 a large conference on "Creating an Industrial Civilisation" was held in [where?] with high-ranking participation from labour, capital, politics, and science.[231] The task was to work out the future direction of American society. The pathetic discussion in the section on *"Participation by the Labour Forces"* revealed the participants' lack of interest. Theoretical ideas and ideological issues were absent; the concepts of social equity and industrial democracy were not mentioned. The discussion was purely anecdotal. One industrialist told the audience that "his company had the regular procedure by which the local manager talks with small groups of employees from time to time in an effort to give them a better view of the whole operation and to generate their pride and enthusiasm about the whole as well as their specific part."[232] Afterwards it was pointed out that such talk sessions were feasible only in small enterprises. Although it was perhaps understandable that no one referred to the experiences of other countries regarding worker participation, the conference's inadequate treatment of the topic brought out clearly how differently Americans—politicians, owners, managers, and trade union leaders—thought about society than Europeans.

From the same conviction of American superiority that underlay the programmes of economic assistance in the reconstruction of the European economy after 1945, American business and political leaders tried to persuade Europeans to adopt the American model of industrial relations. The US Productivity Mission sponsored the travel of European workers' and employers' representatives to the United States for the purpose of showing them the advantages of American-style industrial relations. The initiative failed utterly, even in West Germany and Austria, which were directly influenced by American occupational forces. In these two countries the works councils established in the early 1920s had been abolished by the Nazis. As part of its democratization programme the Allied Control Council reestablished them. Subsequently, their number and remit were extended by national legislation: Germany in 1952, 1972/76, and 2001; Austria in 1974. The post-war works councils established worker participation based on direct and general election of workforce representatives. Their terms of reference were inspired by the political idea of industrial democracy and expressed the non-material goal of collective social equity in the workplace. Other European countries enacted similar legislation to include worker participation in industrial relations. The Netherlands, Belgium, Switzerland, and the Scandinavian countries instituted works councils of varying scope and competence. Generally, maintaining an excellent relationship between the trade unions and the works councils, as characterized the arrangements at Cadbury's, was a crucial prerequisite for the effective and beneficial functioning of these institutions. And everywhere works councils signalled a workplace atmosphere of cooperation rather than conflict. In Germany the 1952 legislation entrenched the requirement of a "trustful cooperation" (*vertrauensvolle Zusammenarbeit*) on the part of both owners and workers' representatives. But such a trustful cooperation can not be dictated; it depends on a corresponding attitude in the general public that cooperation between capital and labour benefits society at large. Without this trust in cooperation, works councils lose their purpose of existence.

Elsewhere in Europe support for worker participation either petered out after the immediate post-war years, or it did not appear until much later. In order to counteract the influence of spontaneously established revolutionary workers' committees, the French government enacted a law setting up enterprise committees in the late 1940s, but it quickly became a dead letter. Similarly, Italy's 1948 constitution formally allowed the establishment of works councils, yet for many decades they were found only in the two large state-owned enterprises ENI and ENEL. Works councils were not permitted in Spain until after the death of General Franco in 1975. When they were finally introduced in 1980, they were organized along the German model of dual worker participation with representatives by the workforce as a whole and by the trade unions.

The globalization of business activity and decision-making that became increasingly evident from the 1970s persuaded European trade unionists that to strive for transnational works councils. The first attempt to set up a recognised, international, enterprise-wide works council occurred in the Dutch chemical firm of Akzo in 1975. But it failed even though the trade union effort was internationally coordinated and combined strike pressure and negotiations.[233] Later efforts that enlisted governmental support were more successful. The works councils set up in state-owned enterprises by the French socialist government in the 1980s included an international representation. This direction was pushed forward in 1994 by a Council Directive of the European Union that stipulated the establishment of a European Works Council (EWC) in all businesses employing at least 1000 persons within the European Community and with 150 workers in two Member States. The EWC confirms the traditional European approach to worker participation with its politically motivated focus on collective and non-material issues. Both American and Japanese transnational firms attempted unsuccessfully to stop the directive. The EWC's results since its enforcement in 1999 have been mixed. In 1996 the Dutch employer S. M. Dekker expected that his positive national experience with works councils would also apply to the EWC: "As managing director of the *Algemene Werkgevers Vereninging* (AWVN), one of the most prominent employer's organisations, I can vouch for the beneficial influence that works councils have had on the labour relations of Dutch companies."[234] An evaluation by German economist in 2003 was more cautious:

> "Whether works councils support or hinder the development of firms is an open question. The results from empirical studies are mixed. Establishments with works councils have a higher degree of flexibility and higher productivity, but also higher wages and a lower degree of profitability. The impact on innovation and investment, as well as on employment, is ambiguous. Works councils support on-the-job training and most internal reorganisation measures."[235]

In general one can conclude the effect of works councils varies according to the overall business goal of the company. If owners and managers are devoted exclusively to maximizing profits, works councils are of little help. Shareholder value does not go together well with works councils. If, however, the company's aim is to advance its own fortunes while paying attention to the economic interests of its stakeholders, works councils can contribute to its realization. But there must be a reasonable agreement between company environment and societal environment. To function effectively, works councils need a social environment that stresses cooperation and accommodation rather than competition and conflict. For this reason works councils are more appropriate in the welfare-state economies of Europe than in the free-market competitive capitalism of the United States. What is good for Europe needs not be good for America—and vice versa.

Works councils were not the only form of organized cooperation between employers and employees that emerged after the Second World War. In the late 1940s Belgium introduced trade *union delegations*, Sweden and Norway *production committees*, and Denmark cooperation committees. common to these institutions was that they had rights of information and consultation about managerial decisions and were based on trade union representation. Their implementation was also voluntary, after agreement between employers and employees, and it is a mark of the strength of the workers' movement in these countries that such committees came into being in nearly all sizeable firms. The scope of cooperation was steadily enlarged from individual workplace to company at large and finally in the 1970s to corporate board of directors. The drive behind this development came from a general belief in cooperation, from the strength of the labour movement, and from the political commitment to social justice as well as the empowerment of workers and their organisations.

In West Germany worker codetermination on corporate boards of supervision (*Mitbestimmung*) was achieved in 1952 only after much heated controversy. The Social Democratic Party and the trade unions were for it, the Christian Democratic Union and the employers' association against. In its fight against codetermination, German business was aided by individual American employers' associations as well as by the (US) National Association of Manufacturers (NAM). These oppositional groups ran a vigorous advertising campaign denouncing the proposals in numerous German newspapers shortly before the bill on codetermination in the mining industry was passed. The NAM saw plant-level codetermination as an obstacle to the continued development of a free market economy in Germany, as a step towards socialism and the creation of monopolies that would block an effective reform of the German economy, that is its Americanization. Both American employers' associations and the US government advocated modelling industrial relations according to an approach called *"human relations"*. The core idea of human relations was to adapt conditions in the workplace to fit workers' personal requirements, that is to "humanize" work. In contrast, the German approach to industrial relations, whether seen from the workers' or the employers' standpoint, focussed on the sharing of power. Both approaches intended to avoid shop floor unrest and trade union militancy.

Once the West German legislation on works councils and codetermination came into effect on 1 January 1952, the alternative approach of human relations that had been urged so strongly was soon forgotten. Already in 1953 the German expert on management issues Ludwig Kroeber-Kenneth affirmed: "The enthusiasm with which the seemingly attractive game of human relations was taken up has now totally dispersed".[236] The once so dreaded codetermination came to be not only accepted but even esteemed as an important contributor to the productivity of the West German economy. This form of worker participation brought no specific material advantages to either workers or owners; its support derived from political considerations. Nowadays there are few complaints about the institution. Indicative of its widespread acceptance is that the French-German pharmaceutical merger, Aventis, headquartered in Strasbourg, voluntarily introduced the German law of codetermination as well as German-style works councils.

Codetermination was taken up by other European governments, political parties, employers' associations, and trade union movements in the 1970s. In 1977 Ireland installed worker-directors in all state-owned firms as an instrument to promote social justice and industrial democracy. Three years earlier the British Labour Government had published an overview of "Worker Participation and Collective Bargaining in Europe" as part of a national debate on industrial democracy. The report commented approvingly on applying the German system of codetermination to all publicly listed British enterprises.[237] Even the hitherto reluctant Trade Union Congress (TUC) came around. Hem C. Jain reported in 1980: "The British TUC has strongly advocated the adoption of a worker participation system similar to the codetermination model in West Germany, asking that 50 percent of the directors be appointed by the unions."[238] This last proviso—trade union control—proved to be the crux. Everywhere the proper functioning of worker participation institutions depended on a strong trade union presence in the workforce. The TUC's standpoint was relentless: "Whenever the term 'worker participation' is used...it must be taken as to mean 'trade unionist participation."[239]

Industrial relations in United States were also affected by the general trend towards left-wing politics during the 1970s. Many company managers conceded that the perceived alienation of American workers was due to the inability to influence the conditions of their workplace. The notion of worker participation gained popularity as a solution for many economic ailments including to "help society with today's inflation."[240] In practice, however, the suggested remedies were re-worked versions of the human relations approach of the 1950s: *quality working life programmes* (QWL), *"Quality Circles", "Employee Involvement", "Labour-Management Participation Teams",* and the like. Although the AFL-CIO acknowledged the "laudable objectives" of the initiatives, it observed that they shared the misguided perspective of the ill-fated American Plan: "QWL advocates ... ignored the conflict side of the employment relationship and stressed only the need for and value of cooperation."[241] A survey of American trade union opinion at the time confirmed the negative appraisal, which could only be reversed by anchoring "proper union involvement" in the programmes:

> "(1) workers and/or employers may see these processes as substitute for, rather than as supplements to, the collective bargaining process and established grievance procedures; (2) workers may begin to question the need for a union if they see employers listening to and solving their problems through QWL or other direct worker participation processes; (3) union leaders may become too closely identified with management or get co-opted into managerial decisions, lose touch with their members, or experience heightened internal political instability or conflict; and (4) informal participation processes may turn out to be simply another short-lived strategy for employers to gain greater control over and effort from workers without providing them with any real power to influence important decisions within the firm."[242]

In other words, while in Europe workers' movements and employers' associations collaborated to extend institutions of codetermination and worker participation to more and more businesses, in the United States the development of some form of industrial democracy based on immaterial ends through collective processes stalled. American employers were unwilling to concede any substantial degree of economic power to workers' representatives. And American trade unions mistrusted not only the employers but their own constituents too much to get seriously involved in worker participation. In fact, the unions stopped some experiments on worker participation because they felt they were loosing influence over the workforce.

WORKER PARTICIPATION AS MANAGEMENT TOOL

Worker participation can take the form of sharing decision-making power or of sharing the results of company performance; in most cases it was one or the other, seldom was it both. Sharing the results of company performance is called material worker participation, and it appears that American companies have pioneered and pushed forward this form. "Since the war (1945 - H.G.S.) there has been a phenomenal growth in all types of employee financial participation in the USA."[243] In the mid-1970s American businesses carried out 90,000 cash-based profit-sharing schemes, 137,000 special tax-benefit schemes, and an unknown number of stock bonus schemes. The bonus schemes typically ran for five years and were financed by contributions from both employees and employers. They tended to be administered by company management and often invested in its own stock, so their investment activity served to shore up the price of company shares as well as providing an economic benefit to employees. Since in most cases the bonus was withdrawn if the person left the company, the schemes also were a means to uphold the stability and loyalty of the workforce. At the executive level stock options and similar incentive plans were particularly widely used; they were found in 90 per cent of American companies with annual sales over 100 million dollars.

In Europe material worker participation has never attained similar popularity, and even where found it is not meant to strengthen employees' ties to their company. For example, the bonus scheme proposed by Swedish trade unions in the 1970s was intended to overcome capitalism! The scheme's funds were to be managed by the trade unions, not by company owners as in the US, and were to be invested in such a way that the social democratic unions would buy out Swedish capitalists. After much bitter controversy, the funds were finally set up in 1984. However, a change in the Swedish government and a general change of socioeconomic climate prevented the funds from developing as anticipated, and they were dissolved in 1992, their capital going into the enterprises' R&D funds. A similar project with the aim of re-distributing wealth and economic power was also aired in Denmark, but it never matured for much the same reason as mentioned in the Swedish case. In France, by contrast, material worker participation was government policy already in the 1950s, and on paper coverage was extensive. It was officially started as a voluntary measure in 1955. General de Gaulle's government reaffirmed the policy in 1967 and made it compulsory for all firms with had more than 100 employees and earnings over five per cent after deductions and taxes. The French government's motivation was political rather than economic. Material worker participation was seen as way to reduce social conflicts between capital and labour in French society; it was not primarily intended either to enrich individual workers or to improve labour relations at individual firms. In fact, given the modest size of many French businesses the requirement did not apply to very many companies. Based on the findings of later parliamentary investigations, the Sudreau Committee in 1975 and the Delouvrier Committee in 1978, the legislation was adjusted with the result that material worker participation became more widespread in France than anywhere else in Europe.

There are surely many reasons—historical, economic, sociological, political, and ideological—why material worker participation has not become as widely established in Europe as in the United States, but they are not easy to confirm definitely. Certainly the action programmes of European trade unions have seldom included the instrument as a major priority. And European entrepreneurs have not been strong supporters either. The statement of the Confederation of British Industry (CBI) in 1978 illustrated owners' lukewarm opinion of material worker participation: "Thus financial participation, the CBI believes, could be useful in some circumstances, but it should not be regarded as a substitute for proper pay and conditions, nor as a major factor in the improvement of industrial performance."[244]

The European advocates of worker participation intended it to give the workforce a voice—for some even a codeterminating role—in the decision-making of companies. It was not meant to be a managerial tool to co-opt workers' representatives into the owners' viewpoint. Yet this was the general American interpretation that found its first expression in the American Plan of the 1920s. This initiative failed, as we know, but in the 1990s American business owners finally succeeded in establishing worker participation as a management tool on a broad scale. This latest organization of employee involvement has been called *high performance working places* and is focussed on by white-collar workers in the middle levels of company hierarchy. After overcoming its historic reservation regarding worker participation, the AFL-CIO decided to cooperate; its Department of Corporate Affairs even described the venture as a *"Center for Workplace Democracy"*. This flattering designation was not shared by all: one union leader suggested an alternative term, *"adversary participation"*. Nonetheless, this approach, which allows employees to participate in the design of the workplace, the organization of the work process, and a variety of other specifically work-related issues has been widely installed in American companies.

Lastly, opinions regarding the effects of worker participation on business productivity have remained mixed with European and American commentators predictably coming down on different sides. The respective literature on American firms is contradictory, which hardly indicates strong endorsement. In contrast, a comprehensive study on "Employee Direct Participation in Organisational Change" (EPOC) sponsored by the European Commission in 1997 revealed widespread belief in the benefits of worker participation: "All forms of direct participation were considered to have a strong impact on economic performance - in the case of quality nine out of ten respondents reported a strong impact."[245] Company managers overwhelmingly regarded worker participation as "very useful". In short, while Europeans held up the positive effects of worker participation, Americans doubted them. Both sides are probably right for their respective countries.

CONCLUSION: A EUROPEAN BULWARK AGAINST AMERICANIZATION?

The ideology and practice of industrial relations in Europe and in the United States have differed considerably over the last hundred years. A telling expression of these differences is the institution of worker participation. Worker participation has developed to be sure on both side of the Atlantic but in separate ways. It has always been stronger in European economies where it with their collective, cooperative approach to business. More specifically, it emerged from the workers' and trade union movements and secured the political support of social democratic parties. In the post-war years the strength of these social and political forces pushed through institutions of worker participation as an integral part of the European welfare state. All these elements were consistently weaker in the United States. There worker participation was considered by representatives of both labour and capital as a tool of management rather than of the workers. Predictably, then, American trade unions regarded worker participation with caution or even hostility. Given these differences, any Americanization of industrial relations in Europe was strongly resisted as shown by the rejection of the American human relations approach. For many years European-style industrial relations constituted a barrier against the easy transfer of American economic and social practices to Europe in general.

The political and economic changes of the 1980s and 1990s have weakened this barrier. Even before the 1989 collapse of communist Europe heightened disillusionment with high-flown rhetoric of social justice and collective rights, these ideas had come under strong attack from the libertarian economics and politics of Reaganism and Thatcherism. The welfare state, the core idea of the social vision launched by Europe's labour movement and its middle-class sympathizers, seemingly reached its practical, financial limits by the 1990s, and its survival in any form required cost-cutting. Future provisioning of welfare services has grown increasingly dependent on the proceeds of investment funds, thereby weakening the financial and ideological linkage to the work environment. And this environment has also been changed substantially by the growing obsolescence of the Fordist approach to industrial work with its large-scale regimentation and the decline of industrial employment generally. As a result the tightly knit workers' milieus that once fed the collectivist vision of the European trade union movements and their political allies, the social democratic parties, have steadily dissipated, a development of potentially far-reaching consequences for European society and economy.

These and other changes that are being pushed by the seemingly inexorable logic of globalization put the European approach to industrial relations with its core institutions of worker participation and codetermination under increasing economic, social, and ideological pressure. But it is unlikely to fade away easily and quietly. Indeed, the compulsory introduction of European Works Councils by the European Union in 1999 may have injected new life into it. Although the spirit of loyalty to one's firm that long characterized the work relationship in Europe at all levels and was a key factor in the functioning of worker participation has undoubtedly weakened, but it remains much stronger still than in the American economy. Many European executives still invoke a special firm ethos that exists beyond financial and personal considerations. In 2002 the Belgian top-manager André Leysen confirmed this in insisting that enterprises have "a soul, which has rights of its own..."[246] How long such an ideal, almost romantic vision of industrial relations can stave off the effects of commercialization, financial accountability, short-termism, and shareholder value is a big question mark for the future of the American model of free market capitalism in Europe.

CONCLUSION

In the course of the twentieth century European society and economy became increasingly like American society and economy. This Americanization was not a smooth, continuous process; it was a jerky, time-lagged development characterized by surges and pauses. In essence it represented the takeover—selective, adaptive, and voluntary—of basic American organizational forms, procedures, attitudes, and values by European producers, consumers, and political and economic decision-makers. The transfer was incited and encouraged by various channels of communication: newspapers and trade journals; business and recreational tourism, study tours, and lectures; exhibitions, radio and television; physical example and personal behaviour. The simple model of cultural-institutional transfer suggested in the introduction—namely, sender, carrying medium and receiver—seldom applied, for in most cases the identity of the components can not be clearly established. Only in the decade or so immediately following the Second World War was there a deliberate attempt by American political and economic leaders to spread their country's institutions to Europe. Before and after this brief period of official activism the United States was not directly involved in the Americanization of Europe; it was simply the society of reference. Thus, the transfer model can only be used if a passive agent is acceptable as a possible "sender". Such vagueness is not necessarily inappropriate, for passive diffusion and unreflected accommodation were indeed characteristic of the Americanization process. Already in 1964 the American author McCreary observed that an Americanization of Europe was taking place in part without deliberate reflection on either side.[247]

The extent of Americanization varies considerably within Europe, and some authors have claimed that this or that country has become more Americanized than others.[248] Such contentions suppose a thorough comparison of various issues constituting Americanization, but in fact the required research is still lacking, and such a ranking is largely guesswork. However, on the evidence presented in this book I propose two general statements: Economically more advanced countries tend to be deeper affected by Americanization than less developed ones; and smaller countries seem to be more Americanized than larger ones. In northwestern Europe the two features often went together. American influence there was also enhanced by a greater frequency of travel, general cultural accessibility and liberalism. The UK represents a special case; it was after all the cradle of modern industrialization. In addition to sharing a cultural-linguistic heritage with the United States, the UK had long nurtured a set of economic values and institutions that had much in common with those of the US. Thus British economic development was in many cases less susceptible to Americanization; up to the 1960s it frequently came up with its own, parallel solutions. Indeed, in the first half of the twentieth century the Continent could have learned much from the UK as well as from the US, as it had done in the nineteenth century. But after 1945 the potential attractiveness of the British model was overwhelmed by the enormous economic vitality of the American model. British standoffishness to Americanization faded from the 1960s, and under the Thatcher government the UK even became a standard-bearer for such American-style policies as deregulation and privatization.

WAVES OF AMERICANIZATION

The Americanization of Europe varied not only in space but also in time. Phases of intense transfer alternated with periods of little or no exchange. The oscillations can be likened to waves: swells building up to a crest, then receding, to swell and crest again later. Other authors have also observed these waves and have suggested schemes of periodization.[249] Here I propose my own, which encompasses three waves.

The first wave of Americanization occurred in the interwar years. It had been building up slowly from the beginning of the century, but the crest did not appear until the rationalization movement in the 1920s. Compared with the later waves, this first one was shallow and soon retreated. The world economic crisis paralyzed international transfers of all kinds, and the American model itself was in deep crisis in the 1930s. The Second World War transformed this situation dramatically: on the one side an exhausted Europe dominated by devastation, on the other a rejuvenated United States as the world's supreme economic and political power.

The second wave of Americanization paralleled the long post-war economic boom from roughly 1950 to the early 1970s. The American occupation policies began to generate swells soon after the war's end, and the implementation of the European Recovery Programme (ERP, or the Marshall Plan) from 1948 signalled the beginning of a long and substantial crest. At first this wave of Americanization had a strong directive colouring, generated by the ERP's activity, the US Productivity Mission, the American-dominated Organization for European Economic Cooperation (OEEC), and similar official and semi-official exchanges. European resistance to these American teaching efforts during the early 1950s was not small, and a number of Americans involved in the initiatives returned home disappointed over the unwillingness of Europeans to transfer American institutions and values readily and extensively. But few like to be compelled, even when it is for their own good; to be lasting cultural transfers must occur by consent. The sluggishness of European response to Americanization in the early 1950s reflected the gap between the European and American economies at the time. For instance, European mail-order houses would have liked to receive orders by telephone as in the United States; however, the infrastructure was simply not at hand. As the European economies became more buoyant from the second half of the 1950s, voluntary Americanization accelerated and continued strongly for a good decade. The crest broke and began to recede from the end of the 1960s and the early 1970s, depending on the branch of industry concerned. Americanization dwindled away because Europeans had caught up with, or even overtaken, their former teachers. Contributing to the ebb were the oil-price shocks of the 1970s as well as American economic and political difficulties connected with the war in Vietnam. European eyes turned from the US to Japan, whose electronic and car industries (especially

Toyota Motors) had gained worldwide attention with their just-in-time (JIT) manufacturing and lean production methods, radical revisions of Ford's assembly-line mass production that substantially reduced labour costs, inventory, and space requirements.

By the second half of the 1980s a third wave of Americanization had swelled up. As previously it was not derived from superior economic performance alone, but from a general show of strength, in economic policy and growth, finances, technology, and military and political issues. From the mid-1980s to 2000 the American economy grew about 50 per cent faster than the West European. The dotcom sector and bio-technologies boomed, as did financial services. In the 1990s the United States became the world's single superpower. Europeans were generally uneasy about this last development but enticed to emulate all other issues. Several countries tried to set up their own "Silicon Valleys", using public monies to compensate for the lack of venture capital that sustained such initiatives in the US. Economic slowdown and shifting population structures encouraged cutbacks in the welfare state in many European countries, and embellished the attractiveness of market-liberal economic policies of privatization and deregulation associated with the American model of capitalism. At the end of the millennium the crest of this third wave of Americanization rode high. But since 2000 the seduction of Americanization has paled a bit. First the dotcom bubble burst, and in 2003 the Bush administration launched the second gulf war against Iraq, and the international value of the US dollar slumped in the wake of huge governmental budget deficits. At the moment, in mid 2004, it is not clear whether the third wave of Americanization will peter out or revive itself.

This third wave differs from the previous two in that it has run parallel to, and been reinforced by, the globalization of the world economy. Globalization is not Americanization. For instance, the spread of the Japanese-style management in the last two decades of the twentieth century represents the former, but not the latter. Still, because American solutions have by and large dominated the world economy since the 1980s, globalization has often resembled Americanization. And, to be sure, the basic principles behind globalization are those associated with Americanization: more competition, commercialization, primacy of the economy, and individualization. Other aspects of globalization, such as the declining role of national governments, are also compatible with the typical American perception of government. But not all. The growing role of international institutions, such as the World Trade Organization (WTO), the UN, and others, for example, fit uncomfortably into the American system.

The three waves identified were not equal in height and strength. The impact of the first wave was limited to a few specific sectors of the productive economy. The second and third waves, however, have transformed production, distribution, and behaviour in almost all areas of society and economy. One might say that the second wave carried out the rough work, while the third wave has extended the features and polished them. The third wave has by no means played itself out and will doubtless figure as the most profound phase of the Americanization of European society.

THE ROOTS OF AMERICANIZATION REVISITED

In the introduction I linked Americanization to the takeover of clusters of cultural values, codes of behaviour, and organizational preferences that characterize the typical American way of life. These were: (1) a strong and positive role of the economy and its requirements in society and daily life; (2) a deep trust in the benefits of competition and the market place; (3) an acceptance of increasing commercialization of social relationships; (4) the primacy of individuality for all members of society and their activities; and (5) a preference for social bonds based on achievement and choice rather than on tradition and ascription. Now is the time to evaluate these clusters and their explanatory usefulness in the history of the Americanization of Europe.

THE PRIMACY OF THE ECONOMY

Americans and Europeans both accept the importance of economic reasoning—profit and loss—in society, but their opinions have frequently differed a good deal regarding whether economic reasoning should take precedence over other values such as cultural ideals or political goals. Great American presidents reflected on their countrymen's materialistic penchant. Woodrow Wilson remarked: "It is only once in a generation that a people can be lifted above material things", while Franklin D. Roosevelt maintained that people do "tire quickly of ideas"[250] Perhaps they toyed with the idea that the American people would be more governable if it were more idealistic. But whereas Americans take the universality of the economy's primacy for granted, Europeans do not and hold up this difference of opinion as a defining characteristic of the two cultures. The British author Cal McCrystal condensed the issue in one sentence: "Economic adventure is often seen as the key to American materialism, as money is sought with steadfastness and passion, and the only generally accepted standard of excellence is property."[251]

The contrast between the American and the European approach showed itself clearly during the first wave of Americanization in the development of the film industry in Europe and the United States. The European approach to film-making was founded on bourgeois artistic concepts taken from stage theatre and opera. Though films should entertain, their main purpose was popular edification. This pedagogical intention was also shared European socialists and communists such as Bert Brecht and Sergeij Eisenstein. The American film-makers, exemplified by Metro-Goldwyn-Mayer, reversed the order on economic grounds: edification was perhaps commendable, but entertainment came first. Following the primacy of economic reasoning enabled Hollywood to achieve and maintain a worldwide dominance in the film industry.

The insistence on the priority of economics in political and social affairs made considerable inroads in Europe during the second wave of Americanization. One of the first areas to be affected was central banking. By tradition European central banks were politically controlled instruments of economic policy. Their role was to finance governmental operations as well as to promote and protect the well-being of country's economy. The American tradition placed the central bank outside governmental control. The central bank's chief role was to protect the integrity of the country's banking system and to control monetary policy in a way that promoted stable prosperity. To achieve these goals the governors of the central bank had to be independent of political directives; in the American view a central-bank policy based on "non-political" economic reasoning was better for the country than politically motivated intervention. At the heart of the difference was the placement of trust: Europeans trusted in the politics of their elected government; Americans trusted in the truths of economic reasoning. During its post-war occupation of Germany and Austria the United States achieved the reconstruction of the central banks there along American lines. Although both central banks were acknowledged successes, it took decades before other European countries freed their central banks from political intervention. The third wave of Americanization finally swept in the American model in the 1990s. The venerable Bank of England has set policy independently since 1997, and the European Central Bank, established in 1998 in Frankfurt to control monetary policy in the euro area, was constructed as an American-style central bank, independent of national governments.

The obvious need for economic reconstruction in post-1945 Europe tended to accentuate the priority of economy in many countries. West Germany especially took up this American orientation, for it helped the society and individuals to avoid confronting with their political past. In the 1950s the activities of the US Productivity Mission and the efforts to establish American management education in Europe deliberately promoted recognition of the primacy of economism. The rising standard of living and consequent changes in lifestyle brought about by the long post-war boom worked into the same direction. European attitudes became less idealistic and more materialistic. Commercial advertising of goods and services gradually permeated everyday life and invited to increased consumption. Market research became a socially accepted activity that was seen as serving the interests of consumers as well as producers. The development of self-service retailing marked perhaps the deepest penetration of economic reasoning in European daily life of the second wave of Americanization. Self-service eliminated the personal relationship in sales; whereas over-the-counter retailing depended on human interaction, self-service excluded this as far as possible. And the reason for the change was economic: self-service was not necessarily better than over-the-counter service, but it was definitely cheaper.

From the 1990s advances in information technology (IT) have further intensified the impact of economism on individuals. The development of the single-user microcomputer, the personal computer or PC, and the Internet has blurred the boundaries between workplace and private sphere; they are no longer necessarily separated. Before the IT revolution, work in a company's sales department was very different from selling one's private car; the two activities were carried out at different times and at different places. Today's e-commerce has eliminated the distinction. IT enables a person to work at home at hours determined by oneself. The freedom of choice and individual flexibility implied in such outsourcing fit easily into the American value-system. But IT-related working routines have also become common in many European countries in recent years and has brought the American primacy of the economy directly into individuals' homes.

A country's welfare provisioning reflects the society's view of the relationship between politics and economics. The welfare state in Europe has been a symbol of the dominance of political goals over economic forces; its absence in the United States has attested that country's adherence to economism. For many years there was little change in this contrast. But since the 1980s the third wave of Americanization with its combination of economic and technological change and ideological rethinking has washed hard against the foundations of the European welfare state. Initially, the problem was simply a growing imbalance between state revenues and welfare outlays, which led many governments to cut costs by reducing levels of support. Increasingly, however, European cost-cutters began to follow the lead of neoliberal American Reaganites and British Thatcherites to put in question the fundamental reasoning behind the welfare state and to assert the primacy of the economy over politics. According to the neoliberals, private and unregulated enterprise performed better in principle than enterprise organized and/or owned by the state or cooperatives because the first followed the neutral dictates of the market economy, whereas the second was liable to distortion by self-interested politics. By the mid-1990s almost all European governments began to follow the neoliberal argumentation to one degree or another, setting in train substantial programmes of privatization and deregulation. Industrial plants, railways, airlines, telecommunication, postal services, and a number of other utilities were the first to be returned to the private sector. Since the turn of the millennium state-owned social institutions—kindergartens, elementary and secondary schools, and universities— have also been included in the agenda of the privatizers. The consequences of a widespread privatization here are potentially enormous, for state ownership and direction of these institutions have been a central element in the process of state- and nation-building in modern Europe, and a fundament of social cohesion. Despite these developments, the welfare-state principle of politics over economics still has considerable vitality in Europe, but the third wave of Americanization has clearly removed many areas of European life from the realm of social and political agreement and placed them under the mandate of the market.

Privatization and deregulation also embody the primacy of economism in terms of managerial leadership. Community-owned utilities customarily had a monopoly on services in their region. Theoretically, the monopoly rent could be handed back to the customers through low prices, but in many cases this was not done. Instead, the managers, typically engineers, invested in technology to keep their facilities up-to-date and reliable. The maintenance of a modern, robust technical plant reduced stress and accidents but also resulted in surplus capacity and personnel. The manager-engineers defended these decisions as technologically necessary; and both owners and consumers believed them for many years. Increasingly, however, economists claimed—correctly—that utility systems have an economic optimum as well as a technical-functional optimum. Running utilities according to the economic optimum required less technological modernization and fewer redundancies; it resulted in a cheaper operation, and the savings could be passed on to the consumer. The privatization and deregulation of public utilities has entailed a transfer of public trust from the engineer, who emphasized security, to the economist, who emphasized low prices. It is not by chance that today's utility companies are headed more often by economists than by technicians and engineers.

The most profound transformation of relationship between politics and economics occurred without doubt in the former socialist countries of Eastern Europe after 1989. However, without to do justice to this revolutionary economization, a total upheaval of all aspects of life, would take another book.

COMPETITION AS CURE-ALL

Cooperation and regulation have traditionally been prominent features in the organization of economic life in Europe. Competition was not excluded from the European economy, but it tended to be specifically regulated by the state or semi-public institutions, such as guilds, whereas in the United States competition was limited only by informal institutions and general legislation. In the course of the nineteenth century the British became strong adherents of a laissez-faire economy governed by competitive markets, but Continental Europeans remained sceptical, viewing competition as an important, but not all-important, factor of national economic policy. The American dogma that unfettered competition would naturally provide the best results for all befitted the economic opportunities of an open country with a moving frontier. In Europe, by contrast, economic opportunities were constrained by geography and density of settlement. As a result, implicit and explicit social contracts emerged, which laid down what defined groups could and could not do. Regulation of competition and economic behaviour in general thus became common in Europe for the purpose of safeguarding the interests of specific groups in society. Regulation took many forms. One of the most notorious was the cartel agreement by which companies colluded to control prices, and thereby profits, by restricting competition. The development of such business practices at the end of the nineteenth century called forth dramatically different governmental responses in Europe and in the United States. American politicians quickly conducted a vociferous campaign to outlaw cartels (trusts) as incompatible with a competitive market economy, whereas European governments tended not to prosecute and even defended cartels so long as the arrangements could be shown to serve the public interest. Especially during the troubled interwar period, the economies of Continental Europe and the UK became heavily cartelized. There was little sign of an Americanization of attitudes at that time. Indeed, the most radical and comprehensive expression of the tradition of economic regulation in modern capitalist Europe was the state corporatism implemented by the various interwar fascist regimes.

After 1945 the United States intervened actively in Europe against the regulatory tradition. American-sponsored aid programmes and agencies (e.g. ERP, OEEC, and GATT) required participating countries to open up to foreign competition and promoted international free trade. The Productivity Mission and American management education extolled the virtues of economic competition, although it is unclear how deep the message penetrated. Still, there is one clear indicator of a transfer of the American competitive principle: decartelization.

Although European governments, including the British, remained convinced of the necessity and even the desirability of cartels after 1945, the United States exported its strict anti-cartel policy to Europe, both directly in its zones of occupation in Germany and Austria, and indirectly through opinion-building efforts. By the late 1950s the anti-cartel campaign had acquired wide support in many countries. Thus the 1957 Treaty of Rome establishing the European Economic Community explicitly prohibited cartel agreements and similar concerted practices that restricted competition. Although several decades went by before similar prohibitions were incorporated in the national legislation of all individual states, the Treaty marked the breakthrough of an Americanization of competition policy in Europe. Competition came to be recognized as the superior operating principle of a modern industrial economy. But the traditional cooperative approach has not been entirely scrapped, and advocacy of the competitive principle in Europe remains temperate.

The primacy of competition compelled European enterprise to change its business practices and structures of authority and decision-making. Up to the second half of the 1950s enterprises focussed entirely on the production of goods. There was such a hunger for, and shortage of, goods that production could not meet demand. Distribution resembled more an allocation than sales. As long as competition was more on the input side (personnel, supply of raw materials, energy, access to new technology, financing) than on sales, European industry saw little reason to learn from American methods of distribution. This attitude was bound to change, of course, when the sellers' market faded. The arrival of American advertising agencies heralded the transition to competition; market research was the next step. Together they provided businesses with knowledge about potential customers and products that would improve market position. However, such agencies could only offer a helping hand. To compete successfully and long-term in a free market economy, business structures had to be reorganized and redefined. The introduction of the American management concept of marketing, which placed competition at the centre of the enterprise, represented a revolution in the boardroom: managers in production and in sales exchanged positions regarding influence, decision-making, and authority in the enterprise. The former lightweights on the board of directors became the heavyweights and vice versa. At the same time, often even parallel, many companies changed their internal form of organization and introduced product-defined divisions. The divisions had their own accounting system, and through their results they competed within the same enterprise for financial resources, power, management personnel, and growth. In these ways the principle of competition became thoroughly rooted outside and inside European enterprise from the 1960s.

However, despite these institutional and attitudinal transfers European business could never really catch up. American business generated further ideas and instruments in support of an aggressive competition. The latest innovation to stimulate internal competition within the enterprise as of 2004 is stock-tracking. Tracking stocks distinguished between the performance of different divisions within one firm, relating their performance directly to the capital market, and thus enhancing competition. European firms cannot follow before a change in their legal systems. Whether it will take place or not, American enterprise seemed to be always one step in front, when not the means but the principle of competition is considered.

In European perception (surely exaggerated!), America is driven by a competitive market. The core of market activities are carried out at the stock exchange. The stock exchange, above all the world's largest the "NYSE" (New York Stock Exchange, often referred to only by the abbreviation, because everybody is supposed to know it), is the symbol of the market and represents it as a social institution. The contribution of the NYSE to Americanization can be seen and heard in daily news reporting on radio and television. Some twenty years ago European news programmes consisted of political and social news, accident reports, and the weather forecast; reporting on business was infrequent and virtually no financial information was given. Since the 1980s, however, all news broadcasts report the latest share prices on the world's major stock exchanges, often by direct, on-site interview. The value of this reporting is largely symbolic: the information too general and limited for large investors and irrelevant for small ones. But the symbolic value is great, the news of the market's gains and losses communicates a central message to listeners: 'your life is bound to the market and its underlying principles, namely competition'.

The deregulation and privatization that swept over Europe in the third wave of Americanization represented another injection of the competitive principle. Banking and other financial services were deregulated and opened up for competition. Public utility companies lost their monopoly position and had to compete in a free market. The intensification of the competitive principle also made possible a business practice that had hitherto largely been limited to American capitalism, namely the hostile takeover. But this extreme expression of competition was long resisted in many countries. In the mid-1990s the attempt by the Italian tire company Pirelli to acquire control over its German competitor Continental was scuttled by the German commercial banks, an action that gave rise to the epithet "Germany Inc." implying that the country was a closed shop. Yet a few years later, in 2000, Germany's Mannesmann, a steel-tube manufacturer cum fast-growing communications group, succumbed to a hostile takeover by Britain's Vodafone AirTouch, the first such takeover of significance in Germany and at the time the world's largest by far.[252] At the same time hostile takeovers also emerged in Italy: for example, the acquisition by Olivetti of an unwilling Telecom Italia in 1999. Even France, where large-scale mergers and acquisitions used to be arranged by the state, has experienced hostile takeovers. In 1999 the government stood aside as the oil company Total devoured its nearest rival, Elf Aquitaine. And in spring 2004 the French pharmaceutical firm Sanofi-Synthélabo successfully launched a hostile bid for its larger French-German rival Aventis (previously Rhône-Poulenc and Hoechst). Here, too, the French financial-markets authority did not block the bid, but when Strasbourg-based Aventis approached the Swiss group Novartis and American Johnson & Johnson about being a white knight against the predator, the Paris government made clear that it wanted a French only solution. By 2004, however, such protection of national champions has become the exception. More typical of the current climate of opinion is the recently agreed merger of two venerable and proud national carriers, KLM and Air France. Free market competition has largely replaced state-regulated protectionism.

This said, the conviction that competition is the natural and superior way to organize economic activities seems to be widely held only among decision-makers in industry and politics. A majority of the European electorate remains sceptical and does not want to exchange the welfare-state economy with its emphasis on equity and security for a market economy governed solely by the competitive principle. To be sure, Europeans understand that competition is a necessary driving force of the modern industrial economy, but they are still deeply divided about its desirability and morality.

COMMERCIALIZATION

Commercialization is a mindset that interprets all relationships in society in commercial, financial terms of 'cash equivalents'. It signifies a shift in how a society's values are defined: individuals and activities are no longer valued for non-material reasons—friendship, kinship, custom, or culture—but are rather defined primarily according to paid relationships. On the personal level, commercialization loosens the rigidities of traditional social hierarchies and promotes in principle a social order in which individuals are defined by their acquired skills and merit as well as the ability to consume rather than by circumstances of birth. On a societal level, depending on the thoroughness and consistency of application, it can result in a predominantly materialist society that is incapable of idealistic relationships and reasoning.

Commercialization permeates many of the elements of Americanization related in earlier chapters. In the first wave it was spread especially by scientific management and the rationalization movement. Rationalization's single-minded focus on raising productivity by discovering and imposing the single most efficient way of carrying out an activity injected a strong dose of commercialization into the organization of work and the workplace. This connection did not go unnoticed; it was revealed and deplored by many European observers, a criticism immortalized in such films as Charlie Chaplin's "Modern Times" and René Clair's "A nous la liberté". Mass production, of course, provided a groundwork for a greater importance of material values, but it was the introduction of mass distribution in the second wave of Americanization of the 1950s and 1960s that tangibly promoted commercialization in European society. In order to function properly, mass distribution had to be organized more rationally than previous systems of distribution, or sales. Mass distribution required a constant, comprehensive bookkeeping of all activities, not just of financial transactions but of the daily movement of all employees. In principle, it limited consumption to specific, discrete amounts, the prepackaged size, and thereby tended to exclude customers who wished to purchase less than this defined amount. Mass distribution reduced the personal relationship between seller and buyer to a minimum. Personalized treatment of customers became the preserve of exclusive shops selling exclusive goods at premium prices.

American foreign direct investment directly transferred commercialized attitudes to Europe by introducing the use of external management consulting agencies. Until then, European companies used traditional contacts—banks or tax counsellors—as a source of management advice; such people had personal knowledge of the companies concerned, of course, but few of them had explicit training in modern business administration and most gave the advice without charge, as friends of the firm. By contrast, the Americans sought advice from persons who were in principle strangers to the company in question, but who were professionally qualified in management techniques. The outside consultants conducted their studies and offered their advice for an agreed fee; the contracting company thereby bought the services and its handling of the recommendations was uninfluenced by personal ties to the advisers. Gradually, larger European firms also adopted this procedure, for they perceived that the commercialized system of the management consultancy provided more informed and effective advice. Similarly, the development of agencies for market research and advertising reduced the personal, non-material dimension of business in favour of commercialized relationships.

The transfers of the third wave of Americanization were especially laden with commercialization. The most potent bearer of the dogma, privatization, has appeared earlier. Here it is important to underline that privatization is more than the mere sale of government-owned industries and services to private investors. It implies, and frequently results in, the monetarization of decision-making and relationships. This implication is particularly evident in the moves to privatize public utilities, health and welfare services, and schools. Such services are a central part of the European welfare state's core concept of social citizenship and their maintenance is an essential part of "European originality" according to the European Commission in 2001.[383] To date the commercialization of public services is largely limited to public utilities (water, electricity, etc.), but proposals to extend privatization and its implications to health and education continue, and continue to provoke controversy and rejection.

The increased commercialization of European life in the 1990s has also begun to affect the national identity of European private enterprise. Until then most enterprises, even emphatically transnational firms, were associated with a specific national identity, usually the country where the firm had been originally established. Nowadays, however, such associations—often based on little more than sentiment and convenience—are losing their holding power. Strictly commercial reasoning, e.g. taxation, can convince a company to move its headquarters from one country to the next, thus shifting a potentially long-standing national identity. For example, one of Norway's most venerable industrial enterprises, the engineering and shipbuilding group, Kværner, moved its headquarters to London in 1996 after purchasing the British construction firm Trafalgar House. A few years later, the country's industrial flagship for almost a century, the Norwegian energy-metallurgical-chemical conglomerate, Norsk Hydro, threatened to follow Kværner's example and take its operational centre to London. And in 2003 the well-known Italian tire company, Pirelli, moved its legal seat to Luxemburg as part of its expansion into energy and telecom cables. The weakening and even severing of national ties in European business is further illustrated by a German example. In the early 1990s the German federal government pressed West German chemical companies to take over and rebuild the dilapidated chemical plants in the reunited provinces of eastern Germany. Commercial reasons for the action were weak, but the companies' national loyalty was sufficient to convince them to participate. In 2004 managers of the companies concerned could not imagine taking such a step; the world market in the sector, they argue, would no longer allow such deviations from strict commercial decision-making. However that may be, it seems clear that the commitments of large European enterprise to a particular national base can no longer be taken for granted. The weight of economism and commercialization in business decisions has risen to a level that overwhelms non-material reasoning.

Managerial thinking has not been the sole cause of this shift; it is also the result of the commercialization of investor relationships. For decades most European firms could count on a certain stability—social and national—in the composition of their shareholders. This stability, or shareholder loyalty, tended to downplay an absolute priority of a profit-loss mentality in the conduct of the enterprise. In the 1990s, however, non-personal investment funds have become very influential in the world's stockmarkets. And such funds have by definition a limited loyalty to the companies whose stocks they purchase, for the funds' purpose of existence is turning a maximum profit. They buy and sell according to strict commercial evaluation of a company's stockmarket performance. The logical consequence of this commercialization of shareholders has been the commercialization of enterprise operations.

These changes have also promoted an Americanization of corporate accounting practices. Continental accounting standards allowed companies a substantial leeway in storing hidden reserves to cope with potential bad times. This practice was particularly advantageous for company managers, who could thereby show steadier growth, and for company banks, which could more easily justify the loans provided. The American accounting standard, by contrast, did not permit hiding reserves and therefore showed a company's real value more accurately. It also stipulated a quarterly financial report in addition to the annual reports required in Europe. The American approach in principle provided investors more accurate information, and as investor relations became more and more important to European firms in the 1990s, it was transferred to European practice.

INDIVIDUALIZATION

Both Americans and Europeans value individualism highly, but each side also claims that it is more individualistic than the other. The resolution of this seeming paradox is that individualism is defined differently: using their respective points of view, both sides are right.

Americans tend to define individualism in terms of personal choice of the components of a high standard of living. Thus, the American marketing analyst George Katona characterized the burgeoning "post-conformist consumer society" of the 1960s as an historic opportunity for the masses to actively construct a selfhood. Mass consumption enabled people to develop different tastes and preferences and thereby to express their individuality more profoundly than before. This vision was widely held in the United States after the Second World War. In his famous 1960 "non-communist manifesto", *The Stages of Economic Growth*, the American economic historian Walt W. Rostow foresaw as the final stage of economic development an "age of mass consumption" that would emancipate people from material wants and enable them to develop an individuality founded on non-material interests; in this phase humankind could even escape boredom. Typical European opinion, by contrast, disagreed with Katona's and Rostow's vision and defined individualism as contradictory to mass production and mass consumption. Real individuality cannot be bought, even not by the acquisition of products of symbolic value. Mass consumer society was in this view levelling and stupefying rather than emancipating and uplifting. For Europeans individuality was a non-material quality that came largely from upbringing and the inbred cultivation of personal character.

The long post-war boom brought a hitherto unknown prosperity to Europe and with it the inroad of the American vision. For many Europeans self-service retailing was the first taste of consumption-related individuality. Service shops provided guidance and guaranteed quality but limited choice in both kind and quantity. Self-service shops enlarged the variety of items on offer three to ten times, and the choice was up to the individual customer. Even salt could be purchased in different varieties according to individual preference. Mail order retailing was another opportunity to unfold individuality. In on-site retailing the active mover of proceedings has traditionally been the offering side. The potential customer enters a given shop and inquires about what is on offer. The setting of the activity—the physical and administrative arrangements, the examination of the products—is determined by the shopowner. All this is different with mail ordering. Here sovereignty rests with the customer. The "shop" comes to the customer's home as a kind of petitioner. The customer need not dress up and go out but can make and submit ordering decisions while eating or clothed in underwear. (S)he, the individual, controls the operation.

The IT revolution of Americanization's third wave further reinforced the trend of individualization. Internet browsing, chat rooms, and many more IT-related innovations offer possibilities to spend one's time in an ever more individual way. Deregulation has expanded the range of consumer choice: for example, one can elect to buy cheap, or clean, electrical energy. Some of the newly available choices are completely open, others are not. Downsizing the welfare state has necessitated the making of choices concerning health care, pensions, and so on. But while the individual is nominally free to exercise preference, it is a fallacious freedom because the maintenance of original welfare-state coverage is not one of the alternatives.

CHOICE VERSUS ASCRIPTION

The introduction included a suggestion that Americanization could have a fifth characteristic: the exchange of traditionally ascribed bonds and activities for those of one's own choosing. There was some evidence for suggestion: for instance, the use of prepared or processed food instead of home-made cooking, or customer abandonment of the corner grocery in favour of distant supermarkets. These are, to be sure, behaviours initiated in the United States and commonly considered typically American. However, many other aspects of the decline of ascriptive behaviour, such as dwindling participation in churches and religious associations, trade unions, political parties, and so on, did not originate in the United States. They and similar departures from traditional behaviour are more properly interpreted as part of the generalized process of modernization rather than a sign of Americanization.

Other issues—for example, the spread of the English language—may at first glance also be popularly perceived as Americanization. That English was the language of choice for such transnational corporations as the European aircraft builder, *Airbus*, or the electro-technical group *ABB* (created in 1988 by the merger of Swedish *ASEA* and the Swiss *BBC*) was logical given the linguistic mixture of the owners. But that English would become the official language of both external and internal communication in the classic French firms *Total* (oil), *Vivendi* (public utilities, music), *Air Liquide* (technical gas), or *Renault* (cars), and the venerable German electro-technical giant *Siemens* is more remarkable. However, the choice of English alone is not sufficient to indicate Americanization; English is, after all, the official language of a number of other countries that are significant players in the world economy. The spread of English as a lingua franca is rather a sign of economic globalization. Though globalization has been heavily pushed by the American economy, it is a distinctive process. Globalization could have occurred under Japanese leadership, for example, and the primary common language of the international economy would still most likely be English.

THE AMERICANIZATION OF THE WORLD?

Europe, of course, was not the only continent subjected to Americanization in the past century. The process can be seen almost everywhere. Unfortunately, there is no research on this topic concerning Africa, the Near East, India, or China, but some studies on Americanization in Japan and Latin America do exist.[254]

Japan has long puzzled the West because since the Meiji Restoration in 1868 it has successfully reorganized its economy and administration according to Western standards without simultaneously introducing substantial changes in the country's basic value system of cooperation, group-rules, and obedience. The unique bifurcation of the transfer process in this case was produced the justification behind the Westernization: the changes were undertaken not for personal gain and advancement but for the promotion of Japan's national interest. The official slogan was *fukoju kyohei* ("rich country - strong army") not: 'rich people…'! The social cohesion thus implied lasted until roughly 1990. Since the bursting of the speculative bubble at that time the famous life-long employment (which actually existed only for male workers, and those only in large firms amounting to no more than about 15 per cent of the Japanese work force) can no longer be relied on, and unemployment officially became a topic of concern. In 2004 a newspaper report estimated that five per cent of school children were truants; a behaviour largely unknown earlier. These are just two indicators that Japanese society has indeed begun to take on characteristics of contemporary Western society.

During the American military occupation of 1945–1952 Japan was subjected to a good deal of Americanizing influence. US administrators dissolved the large family-owned conglomerates (*zaibatsu*), interdicted cartels, and even introduced a new style of writing based on less complicated characters. Especially during the Korean War Japanese industry received considerable economic aid from the United States, so that the difference between Japan and Germany with regard to American economic transfers was not large. In fact, Japanese industry was more prepared than its German counterpart to learn from the United States and was more eager to take over American technology, proceedings, and organization. Japanese researchers have subsequently claimed that Japan as a result became more Americanized during the 1950s and 1960s than Germany. Their assertion is grounded, though, in an interpretation of Americanization that separates values, behaviour, and self-perception from organizational forms and technology. It should be clear by now that I do not accept such a separation, but Japanese colleagues continue to respond to the insistence that Americanization must mean changes in both value systems and technology and organization with resistance and disbelief.[255] According to the definition used here, the Americanization of Japanese economic life did not really begin before the 1990s.

Since the proclamation of the Monroe doctrine in 1823, the United States has regarded Latin America as its own backyard. However, neither the people nor the governments there have had much liking for the tutelage exercised by their northern big brother. This resentment coupled with a different linguistic and religious culture built a solid wall against Americanization in spite of heavy direct investment by US companies. But during the Second World War the situation became more fluid. The United States dedicated many of its economic resources to the production of armaments and was interested in obtaining additional supplies. Latin America was cut off from European suppliers and was therefore susceptible to an assisted development of indigenous industry. Official US economic missions visited several countries in South America and assisted industrialization there. For instance, Brazil's ambitious industrial project of the Volta Redonda steel mill, which more than doubled the country's output of ingots and rolled steel and created a model residential community for its workers, was constructed between 1941 and 1946 with the aid of the Morris Cooke Mission and the Export-Import Bank of Washington. After the war, American preferences and new American economic missions pursued a liberalizing agenda akin to that advanced in Europe: free trade and a reduction of state intervention in the economy. In the immediate post-war years there was considerable American FDI, but this ebbed, according to Rui Guilherme Granziera, when the Marshall Plan channelled most American investment into Europe. In the end, the assistance described left little trace of Americanization; the wartime missions involved un-American state intervention, and the liberalizing admonitions of the early post-war missions were ignored. Nelson Rockefeller's 1946 foundation to promote Latin American development, International Basis Economy Corp., surely diffused some degree of

Americanization, but there is insufficient information about it at the present time to offer any firm conclusions.

This very brief comparative foray confirms that the most important barriers to Americanization are innate differences in economic and social culture. Similarities in culture facilitate transfer; while dissimilarities inhibit it. This observation explains to a considerable degree why the impact of American values and institutions was stronger in Europe than elsewhere. But Europe also set limits to what it would willingly absorb.

LIMITS AND BARRIERS TO AMERICANIZATION

If asked whether they wanted more Americanization, most Europeans nowadays would probably answer no. This should not be surprising. Recall the first sentence of this book's introduction: In it Hubert Verne, sometime chief of staff and spokesman for President François Mitterrand and French minister of foreign affairs between 1997 and 2002, characterized American dominance as a threat to his country's intellectual integrity. Present-day European opinion objects both to the term's implication of foreign takeover and, more importantly, to its core values. Contemporary Europeans generally do not want a more comprehensive economism of society, a further extension of the principle of competition, or a more pervasive commercialization of daily life. Such views are expressed not only by leftist trade unionists, anti-globalizes, greens, and social democrats, but also by moderates and conservatives. Thus, John Gray, who had advised the Thatcher government and supported its Americanizing programme in the 1980s, urged the rejection of neoliberal ideas in 2001 because they "have exhausted their relevance", and he protested American attempts to impose its model on the rest of the world.[256] A few years earlier the prominent Swiss top-management trainer, Gottlieb Guntern, suggested: "A long-term strategy is needed that emancipates Europe from the slavish aping of American management ideas."[257] At a symposium on capital markets and corporate governance, organized by the German stock marketing institute (*Deutsches Aktieninstitut*) in 2002—that is, after the collapse of the Texas-based energy giant Enron and the subsequent revelation of systematic accounting fraud—all experts opposed the adoption of American standards of corporate accounting and supported the retention of existing European practices.[258] The most comprehensive critical attack on Americanization came from the renown Swiss conservative daily, *Neue Zürcher Zeitung*:

> "But what is even more important is the primacy of the economy. Each step is justified if it enlarges the power of competition. By the aims of a better market position (measured by market share), security of a 'critical size' (I do not know a sound definition of that concept), ...all steps become legitimized, even though the consequences may be harmful for people, especially the employees."[259]

Yet, aside from such jeremiads and perorations, are there signs of a tangible resistance to Americanization in contemporary Europe?

In spite of the considerable Americanization described in earlier chapters, Europe has maintained its distinctiveness in many ways. In the 1960s, American tire producers could not imagine Europeans to pay up to fifty per cent more for a new product, the radial tire that promised a bit more safety and comfort than the conventional tire. But Europeans have generally preferred safety and stability in economic matters, even at the cost of foregoing opportunity. All attempts to construct a market for venture capital in Europe have so far failed. In the United States venture capital has a positive connotation as risk-taking investment that can generate both economic growth and personal riches. Part of the argument in favour of privatization and deregulation has been that they establish conditions for the beneficial operation of venture capital. In Europe venture capital has tended to be negatively perceived as largely non-constructive speculation. In Greece, for example, privatization and deregulation destabilized the country's financial markets. Investors became more speculative and enticed by the prospect of short-term gains, while long-term investment declined. The publicly quoted joint-stock company lies at the centre of American model of industrial capitalism. European capitalism has been and still is less fixed on the stock market; large parts of its economy are still dominated the family firm. Family-owned companies tend to operate according to a long-term perspective of growth and prosperity, emphasizing stability and avoiding large fluctuations. Such a business orientation does not necessarily result in lower economic performance. A recent comparison of family-owned and joint-stock companies in the United States and in France revealed that the earnings of family-owned firms outperformed those of publicly traded corporations in both countries![260] The inherent economic superiority of the American model is also questioned by research showing that a major contributor to European economic success in the 1970s and after 2000 has been the un-American practice of close cooperation between capital and labour.[261]

In short, what is good for America is not always good for Europe. The cogency of the economic reasons for and against Americanization has fluctuated over time, as has the perception of the changes involved. When the power of definition rested with the United States, as was the case especially during the 1950s, 1960s, and 1990s, there was a tendency for Europe to take over more than it could truly absorb. But Americanization is neither good nor bad in itself. In many cases adapted American ideas and practices improved the European economy, while in others they weakened it. The second result has particularly occurred when American principles stood too far from European norms, for example, when American commercialization conflicted with European justice (that is, what Europeans defined as "just"), or when the American principle of competition won over the European principle of cooperation.

THE LESSONS OF HISTORY?

For Europeans the main reason to Americanize was to catch up to American productivity and prosperity. In 1950 this argument was very compelling, and in 2004 it is still attractive. However, productivity and prosperity are not the exclusive prerogative of the American model. Europeans have shown that they can be increased by using European principles as well as by American ones, by cooperation as well as by competition. Moreover, to apply new principles effectively one has to understand them fully. American principles are entrenched in the American life, whereas Europeans have first to learn them. This results in a time lag that can never be completely eliminated. Our survey has provided many examples of Europeans learning a few lessons, only to discover that Americans had already moved on to the next step. European Americanization thus frequently missed the goal of catching up to the leader. Yet as long as the American model continues to consistently outperform alternative models of economic organization, Americanization will persist. But transfer of economic institutions should also consider their non-economic suitability, their social or cultural acceptance. Therefore, Europeans are well advised to remember their areas of strength and advantage, and to start from there when implementing Americanizing practices.

In chapter seven we saw that many American management practices, such as shareholder value, alienated the European workforce. Does it matter? Yes, because it is the workforce, not the shareholder, that creates a company's tangible value, its productive output. According to the managing director of the German branch of TCW (Trust Company of the West, one of the largest of its kind in the world), Horst Wildemann, roughly eighty per cent of an enterprise's aims are achieved by human resource management and less than twenty per cent through management by numbers.[262] Innovative, quality products and services can best be obtained from a workforce that is loyal to its company XYZ and even proud to be employed there. For instance, after the Second World War many West German employees developed a special loyalty to "their" respective firm, where they tended to spend their entire working life. The relationship was underlined not only by non-aggressive trade unions, but also by cooperative works councils, which sometimes even convinced their colleagues to accept cutbacks in order to bolster the firm's economic position. Rhenish Capitalism, as the system of cooperative capitalism came to be called, was characterized by a close cooperation between industrial management, banks, political authorities, and the workforce. Between 1950 and 1990 it was the epitome of West German economic strength, but the third wave of Americanization in the 1990s diluted Rhenish Capitalism considerably. One result is that the proportion of German workers who declared a positive relationship in their company has nowadays fallen below the proportion of such attitudes among American workers.[263] While American workers perceived the advantages of the concept of shareholder value, German workers saw only the disadvantages. What boosted productivity in America undermined it in Europe.

The introduction of the same innovation into different societies can thus produce different results. Higher education and public health are sectors where this outcome could clearly happen. In both areas the American model is strongly characterized by private provisioning, that is, the burden of paying for the services falls in principle on the private resources of the recipient, in these cases the student or the sick. On the surface, and especially in the eyes of the model's European advocates, this principle of private financing has produced the world's best universities and its most advanced medical treatment. Hence it is very tempting to believe that a transfer of the American model in these sectors would solve all of the weaknesses that beset higher education and public health care throughout Europe.

But that would be a mistake. On the one hand, private provisioning of education and health care conflicts profoundly with the European principle of social citizenship; on the other hand, the reality of American practice is much more complex than popular conceptions of the model would allow.

These examples underscore once again the lesson of this history of the transfer of American institutions to European society. The principles and practices of one society or culture cannot be successfully transferred to another without adjustment or voluntary accession. Successful and lasting transfer entails a psychological and cultural embodiment, and involves more than a technical and organizational adjustment. I close with a last word from two business gurus of the Harvard Business School, Coimbatore Prahalad and Venkat Ramaswamy: in their 2004 book, *The Future of Competition. Co-Creating Unique Value with Customers,* they propose the "new idea" that the offering side (the seller and producer) should cooperate with its customers for the benefit of both.[264] European enterprise has done so for decades. How ironic that the principle of cooperation might some day be re-imported from the United States as an "American" business strategy? Perhaps European economic and political decision-makers should remember a bit more in what Europeans used to be good at and not be so easily swept away by the American wave.

Notes to introduction

[1] Quoted by Ignatius, D. (2002). What bothers Europe, American power isn't the problem, just how it's used, in: *International Herald Tribune*, Friday February 2nd.

[2] The book *Culture Matters. How Values Shape Human Progress* was edited by Samuel P. Huntingdon and Lawrence E. Harrison in 2000. It comprehends contributions on to what extent cultural values affect the economy. The contributors include besides the editors 20 others distinguished authors, such as Robert B. Edgerton, Davis Landes, and Seymour Martin Lipset.

[3] Zeitlin (2000). p. 2.

[4] E.g. Wagnleitner (1999) or Flanzbaum (1999).

[5] E.g. Whitley (1999).

[6] E.g. in the series "Our National Problems" Royal Dixon wrote on "Americanisation" already in 1916, and Edward Bok`s reminiscent thoughts were printed in the 11th edition in 1921.

[7] Brittain (1974). p. 119.

[8] Kuisel (1993).

[9] Ibid, p. 4.

[10] Viz. Schröter (1996). p. 260f.

[11] Nolan (1994).

[12] Kipping & Bjarnar (1998).

[13] Viz. Kipping and Bjarnar, who used this model in their introduction.

[14] Schröter (1997).

[15] Jarausch & Siegrist (1997); Schröter (1997).

[16] Schröter (1997). p. 154f.

[17] There is little besides Fink (1995).

[18] Locke (1996).

[19] *The Economist*, April 29th, 2000, p. 13.

[20] Full titles in the list of literature.

[21] McGlade (2000). p. 53.

[22] Schröter (1994). p. 484f; idem (1996) p. 142.

[23] Ritzer (1998).

[24] Gillingham (2002).

[25] Klein (2001).

[26] Some of these characteristics are reflected elsewhere, see: Handlin (1949); Lundén (1988); Pförtner (1999).

[27] Investment Company Institute, Federal Reserve, quoted by: *Die Zeit*, No. 41, October 5, 2000.

[28] North (1997). p. IV.

[29] Ibid., p. II; see: North (1990).

[30] Citation from Zeitlin (2000). p. 8.

[31] Chandler (1990).

[32] Chandler & Amatori & Hikino eds. (1997).

[33] Fear (1997); Schröter (1997).

[34] See: Moen & Schröter (1998). p. 7.

[35] Harris (1993). p. 178.

[36] Lederer & Burdick (1959).

[37] Dahrendorf (1963). p. 220.

[38] Ibid., p. 224.

[39] Jarausch & Siegrist (1995). p. 1.

Notes to chapter 1

[40] Quote from: Fischer (2002). p. 61.
[41] Schwarzenbach (1917). Annual Reports of AGUT.
[42] Wilkins (1974).
[43] Feldman (1989).
[44] Taylor (1911). p 7.
[45] König (1990).
[46] See also in the following: Kipping (1999). p. 195.
[47] Kogut & Parkinson (1992). p. 184.
[48] Erker (1996 a), Erker (1996 b).
[49] Shearer (1997).
[50] Ibid. p. 588, fn. 50.
[51] Quoted after Pfoertner (2001). p. 74.
[52] Djelic (1998). p. 49 (see also in the following).
[53] Siegfried (1927). p. 168f.
[54] Bakker (2003). p.107.
[55] Braun (2002). p. 180.
[56] Variety, June 24, 1921 (quoted after Braun (2002). p. 182).
[57] Arcolakis (2003).
[58] Hachtmann (1996). pp. 39, 44.
[59] Enström (1927). p. 1.
[60] Quoted after Wilkins (1974). p. 68.
[61] Schröter (1992).
[62] Schröter (1987). p. 503 (Schiedam had a share of 0.6% and Holliday a share of 0.9% of the world market in 1938, p. 510).

Notes to chapter 2

[63] Niebuhr (1952).
[64] Hampden-Turner & Trompenaars (1993). p. 19f.
[65] The 'communist party line' was the ideological line of argument defined by the party, not an economic instrument. (Quotation: Djelic (1998). p. 78).
[66] JWT: J. Walter Thompson's advertising agency - citation from: Hultquist (2003). p. 498.
[67] Bossuat (1992).
[68] Djelic (1998). p. 79.
[69] In million dollars: 1948/52: 13.750 (100 per cent), 1948/49: 5.953 (43 per cent of the total), 1949/50: 3.523 (26 per cent), 1950/51: 2.377 (17 per cent), 1951/52: 1.356 (10 per cent).
[70] Barjot (2002 a).
[71] Quoted from the British Public Record office by Boel (2000). p. 248.
[72] Puig & Alvaro (2003). p. 36.
[73] Cited after Kipping (2000).
[74] Up to now there is only one comprehensive evaluation on the reports of the persons concerned, provided by Guigeno on the 4500 Frenchmen who visited the USA (Guigeno (2002)).
[75] Quoted after Wend (2002). p. 133; Segreto (2002); Bloemen & Griffith (2002).
[76] Hara (2002). p. 180.
[77] Pentzlin (1952). p. 16.
[78] Cited after Herrigel (2000). p. 359.
[79] Willet (1989). p. 8.
[80] Herrigel (2000). p. 376.
[81] Cited after Kipping (1998). p. 55.

Notes to chapter 3

[82] McCreary (1964). p. VIII.
[83] Dunning (1998). There are no similar evaluations; I presume the British case can be generalized.
[84] Dunning (1998). p. 78.
[85] Dunning (1998). p. 88.
[86] Pells (1997).
[87] McCrary (1964); Puig & Alvaro (2003).
[88] McCreary (1964). pp. 185 and 88.
[89] McCreary (1964). p. 164f.
[90] McCreary (1964). p. 163.
[91] Kipping (1999). p. 125.
[92] Schröter (1996 b).
[93] Quoted from: Andersen (1933). p. 81.
[94] Berghahn (1986); Berghan (1994).
[95] France in 1986, Norway in 1988, Denmark, the Netherlands and Spain in 1989, Italy in 1990, Greece and Ireland in 1991, Finland in 1992, and Belgium in 1993.
[96] Citation from Nordhoff's letter dated July 13th, 1954 (cited after Wellhöner (1996), p. 105); see also: Kleinschmidt (2004).
[97] Nordhoff called it the "suck-exhaust-production" ("Ansaug-Auspuff-Produktion", Nelson. (1968). p. 135).
[98] Bigazzi (2000).
[99] Tolliday (2000). p. 117.
[100] Ferretti (1999). p. 284ff.
[101] Kipping (2000); Ranieri (2002).
[102] Kipping (2000). p. 233. On the steel industry see also Mioche (2002); Ranieri (2000).
[103] Schröter (2004).
[104] Röper (1955). p. 42.
[105] Nieschlag (1962). p. 499.
[106] Gloor (1963). p. 104.
[107] Quoted from: Henksmeier (1962).
[108] Both quotations: Eklöh (1958). p. 17.
[109] In 1972 the number of supermarkets per million inhabitants was in Denmark: 65, Belgium: 62, UK: 58, Switzerland: 55, The Netherlands: 47, Germany: 46, France: 40, Italy: 11 (Lescent-Giles (2002)).
[110] Eklöh & Eklöh (1958). p. 142.
[111] Ibid, p. 141.
[112] Quoted from McCreary, p. 87.

Notes to chapter 4

[113] See on management education the contributions of: Amdam, Bjarnar, Byrkjeflot, Chessel, Engwall, Gemelli, Gourvish, Gunnarson, Kipping, Locke, Norstrøm, Sogner, Tiratsoo, Zagmani and others.
[114] Gemelli (1997).
[115] Karlsen (2002).
[116] Gemelli (1998).
[117] Locke & Schöne (2004), pp. 103ff.
[118] Without author (1958). p. 19.
[119] Hallig (1965). p. 64.
[120] See the opposite view in: Kogut (2000). p. 32.
[121] Letter of Prydz to Francis, dated March 5th, 1963 in Hydro's archive, cited after Rönning (1997). p. 50.
[122] Varaschin (2002).
[123] Quoted from: Varaschin (2002). p. 205.
[124] Bonnaud (2002).

[125] Brown (1937). p. 14.
[126] Arvidsson (2000). p. 293.
[127] Kapferer (1956). p. 68.
[128] Cited after Downham (1998). p. 16f.
[129] Kapferer (1956). p. 85f, 175ff.
[130] Kapferer (1956). p. 59.
[131] Brown, p. 74.
[132] Fox (1950). p. 316 (Fox was Director of Market Research Remington Rand Inc.).
[133] Arvidson, p.282.
[134] EPA, *Market Research in Europe*, p. 26.
[135] Erhard, L., lecture at the annual conference of the Verband Deutscher Marktforscher in Köln, October 24th, 1968 (cited after Kapferer, p. 81f.).
[136] Adler (1971). p. VIIf.
[137] Cited after Arvidsson.
[138] Hallig (1965). p. 3.
[139] Schröter (1998).
[140] Emphasis as in the text (Strauf (1959)).
[141] Seidensticker (1964). p. 114.
[142] Schröter, (1998). p. 29; calculated from: Segereto (2002 a). table 2, p. 89.
[143] Abelshauser (1987).

Notes to chapter 5

[144] John Kornblum served as US ambassador in Germany, to NATO and at several international diplomatic conferences on economic questions. Comment by John Kornblum at a conference on culture and enterprise in: Pohl (2002). p. 51.
[145] http://www.whitehouse.gov/history/presidents/rr40.html. Accessed 15 May 2004.
[146] Jopp (2000). p. 40.
[147] Nandrup (1998). p. 26.
[148] Meran, G. & Schwarze, R. (2004). p. 95.
[149] Financial Times, August 18, 2003.
[150] Die Zeit, September 18, 2003.
[151] Temin & Galambos (1987). p. 10.
[152] Interview in the *International Herald Tribune*, November 9, 2001.
[153] Hensher & Button (2001).
[154] An example: in summer 2003 it took me more than one hour at the central station in Florence to get information on how to travel from a remote station near Lucca to Zurich. In order to buy the ticket, I had to queue a second time.
[155] Schnitzer (2003).
[156] Amatori (2003). p. 17.
[157] Colli (2003). p. 34.
[158] VG (a Norwegian newspaper), June 16, 2000.
[159] Kane (2002).
[160] Oksholen (2003).
[161] Locke & Schöne (2004). p. 198.
[162] Kellaway, Financial Times, April 4, 2002.
[163] Mustad (2004).
[164] Fischer (1996).
[165] The others were Bulgaria, Estonia, Latvia, Moldavia, Poland, and Slovakia.
[166] Countries which opted for voucher-privatization were Bosnia-Herzegovina, Czech Republic, Lithuania and Russia, while Albania, Belarus (White Russia), Croatia, Macedonia, Romania, Slovenia, and the Ukraine sold to insiders.
[167] World Bank (1996). p. 56.
[168] Schnitzer (2003).
[169] Andersen (2000).

[170] Broder (2000).
[171] Locke & Schöne (2004). p. 188.
[172] Hall & Soskice (2001). p. 38f.
[173] Lohr, New York Times, October 26, 2003.
[174] Cassity (2002). p. 6.
[175] Bartmann (2003), pp. 222-225.
[176] Cited from: The Financial Times, November 8, 1999.

Notes to chapter 6

[177] James (2002), p. 48 (verbatim).
[178] These were: Ford employee African-Ancestry Network, Ford Asian Indian Association, Ford Chinese Association, Ford Finance Network, Ford Gay, Lesbian or Bisexual Employees, Ford Hispanic Network Group, Professional Woman's Network Group, Women in Finance, Ford Parenting Network, Ford Interfaith Network, Middle Eastern Community Ford Motor Company (http://www.mycareer.ford.com/ontheteam.asp, May 13, 2003).
[179] Kindleberger (1996), p. 182.
[180] Black & Moersch (1998), p. 170ff.
[181] Steinherr (1989), p. 188.
[182] „They have to become more Anglo-American if they want to make it. " John Furth, head of the New York office of Roland Berger & Partners, a major consultant agency, commenting the attempts to become major financial players on international markets by Central European banks (Financial Times, June 6, 2000).
[183] Financial Times, December 18, 1998.
[184] The corresponding theory has been worked out by Alexander Gerschenkron (1952).
[185] Amatori (2003).
[186] Schwarz (2000), p. 16.
[187] Frankfurter Allgemeine Zeitung, October 10, 2003.
[188] Deutsche Bundesbank, Basel II – Die neue Baseler Eigenkapitalvereinbarung (http://www .bundesbank.de/bank/bank_basel.php, April, 25, 2004).
[189] Fitch was accuired in 1997 by the newly founded French firm Famalac. Dominion Bond Rating Service Limited is a Canadian enterprise, founded in 1974.
[190] Frankfurter Allgemeine Zeitung, November 19, 2003. The evaluation distinguished between Sparkassen (savings-banks), Genossenschaftsbanken (cooperative banks), and the four largest banks Hypo-Vereinsbank, Dresdner Bank, Commerzbank and Deutsche Bank.
[191] Kern, F., Neue Zürcher Zeitung, March 26, 1996.
[192] Financial Times, November 27, 2000.
[193] Address of CEO Werner Wenning to the share holders (Aktionärsbrief 3, 2003, p. 3).
[194] Historie du leasing, http://www. dungnet.com/locabel2000/FRlea_his.htm, printed September 9, 2003.
[195] Reading aid: a change of 1 per cent in the US lead to a change of 0.43 / 0.65 per cent in France.
[196] Conversation with Prof. Utz-Hellmuth Felcht on enterprise history in Frankfurt, February 25, 2003.
[197] The Economist, 16 June 1999.
[198] M. Bonsignore, in: Financial Times, October 13, 2001. It is open for speculation to what extent the critique was related to the tough negotiations between the two CEOs during their negotiations of a proposed a merger of the two companies.
[199] Interview with Ulrich Hartmann in: Die Zeit, September 6, 1996.
[200] Ullenhag (2002), p. 19.
[201] Hall & Murphy (2003).
[202] Hampdon-Turner & Trompenaars (1993); c. around 1990 - the year was not given.
[203] Dagens Naeringsliv, October 9, 2000.
[204] Wall Street Journal, March 18, 2003.
[205] Frankfurter Allgemeine Zeitung, November 26, 1996.
[206] The Wall Street Journal, June 2, 2004.
[207] This refers for instance to the famous law-suits on smoking in California, 1998-2001.

[208] Hinz & Kunzt, No. 120, April 2003.

[209] Alesia, R & di Tella, R. & MacCulloch, R. (2001).

[210] We know of St Cloud's Montretout enclave in Paris 1832 and Llewellyn Park in New Jersey 1854.

[211] USA today, December 15, 2002.

[212] The figure for Germany was 5.3 percent. Denmark was the least enthusiastic country and reached only 2.4 per cent. (Frankfurter Allgemeine Zeitung, November 15, 2000).

[213] Die Welt, October 9, 1999.

[214] In 2000 the UK-TV Channel BSkyB paid 1.54 Billion Euros for the English TV football rights during the season 2002/2003 (The Business, May 18, 2003). General figures from: Die Zeit, July 31, 2003.

[215] Ritzer (1998), p. 74.

[216] Ritzer (1995), p. XV.

[217] Evans & Schmalensee (1999) p. 26.

[218] Ibid., p. 35.

[219] Die Zeit, September 18, 2003.

[220] Frankfurter Allgemeine Zeitung, March 25, 2004.

Notes to chapter 7

[221] Sombart (1906).

[222] Bolle de Bal (1989). pp. 11-25. See: Jain (1980); Knudsen (1995); Thorsrud (1984).

[223] I distinguish between industrial democracy and worker participation. Worker participation is focussed on the economic part and especially on that of the respective enterprise. In contrast, industrial democracy has broad political and social objectives. I share Jain's views: "It seeks to eliminate or restrict the rights of the dominant industrial hierarchy and calls for the expansion of employee rights. It also aims at exerting political pressures on governments, making them more responsive to employee and union views for redesigning the total economy toward more socially oriented goals." (Jain (1980). p. 4).

[224] I want to underline, that again I argue with trends, there are many single cases to be found, which stood against the majority Europe seems to vary even more. British ideas were quite often near to the American counterpart. Antagonist approaches to industrial relations, traditionally upheld in e.g. Italy or France, seem to correspond with American ideas, too. However, Europe and America contrasted sharply in the ideological concept of the role of capital in society. Most Europeans were concerned about the ideas of *social justice*. Policy should balance labour and capital in the 'right' way. Of course, there existed different concepts for this social justice, e.g. social ideas fostered by the Catholic Church (catholic dominated regions), feelings of a traditional equality of human beings (especially in Northern Europe), or a human approach to fairness (UK). At the same time, countries with a traditionally strong and well educated social democratic party focussed on the aspect of *power* (for instance Germany). Things become even more complicated when the manifold overlapping are taken into account. Sweden's Social Democrats were very much concerned with power, Italian workers were strongly influenced by communist ideas and considerable parts of German workers felt trust in the Catholic Church. However, we concentrate on common general traces in Europe.

[225] The Oxford Companion to British History, ed. John Cannon (2002), 361.

[226] Originally Intercollegiate Socialist Society, renamed in 1921 (http://www.publiceye.org/research/Group_Watch/Entries-82.htm, p. 3, printed out on June 6, 2002).

[227] Cadbury's Publication Department Bournville Works, (1921) *A Works Council in Being*, p. 3, Bournville.

[228] Kochan & Katz & Mower (1984). p. 3. In his foreword the President of the Industrial Union Department of the AFL-CIO Howard D. Samuel acknowledged the book and its content formally.

[229] Ibid.

[230] The Norwegian agreement was only on information and participation, the Swiss and Swedish ones intended a certain industrial peace. In Switzerland the watchmakers signed a contract with the employers on May15, 1937, while the machine-building and metal-workers followed on July 19, 1937. The Contract of Saltsjöbaden, near Stockholm, in 1938 was even wider, it included all industrial workers.

[231] Staley (1952).

[232] Staley (1952). p. 179.

[233] Carley (2001); Schröter (1997).

[234] Dekker (1997). p. 1.
[235] Hübler, (2003). p. 397.
[236] Kroeber-Keneth (1953). p. 218.
[237] Her Majesty's Stationary Office (1974). p. 141.
[238] Jain (1980). p. 36.
[239] Wood et al. (1974). p.13.
[240] Stokes (1978). p. 5.
[241] Kochan & Katz & Mower (1984). p. 5.
[242] Ibid., p. 8.
[243] Reilly (1978). p. 33.
[244] Reilly (1978). p. 29.
[245] European Foundation for the Improvement of Living and Working Conditions (1997). p. 1.
[246] André Leysen (2000). Fare-well words to CEO Manfred Schneider, in: Bayer Aktionärsbrief, No 1, 2002, p. 39.

Notes to conclusion

[247] McCreary (1964). p. VIII.
[248] Heinonen & Pantzar (2002). p. 55.
[249] For instance, Dominique Barjot wrote about a first period from 1870 to 1945, during which Americanization took place first in an uncertain way while it later accelerated, and another phase from 1945 to 2000 (Barjot 2002 a, p. 8-12). Zeitlin suggested a period, defined by "the transnational standard of productive efficiency", from "the late nineteenth century to the end of the 1960s, and once again perhaps in the 1990s" (Zeitlin, 2000, p. 1). Kipping and Tiratsoo spoke about the boom-phase (2002, p. 12). The most precise suggestion was given by Kudo, Kipping and Schröter (2003, p. 5-11). Concentrating on Germany and Japan, the authors claimed the following four periods: 1. end of the nineteenth and beginning of the twentieth century, 2. the interwar period, 3. immediately after the Second World War, and 4. during the 1950s and 1960s.
[250] Quote after McCrystal, C., Financial Times, February 21st, 2004.
[251] Ibid.
[252] Its value (all in thousand billion $) was 172.2, while Pfizer vs. Warner-Lambert in 1999 amounted to 111.8. Sanofi vs. Aventis stood in January 2004 at 68.7, and TotalFina vs. Elf amounted to 63.1 in 1999.
[253] Communications of the Commission: Leistungen der Daseinsvorsorge in Europa (2001/C 17704), January 19, 2001.
[254] On Japan: Barjot (2002 b); Kudo & Kipping & Schröter (2004), on Latin America: Granzierra (1998).
[255] At a Japanese-German conference in March 2000 the German participants, especially Hilger and Kleinschmidt, applied the key-word Americanization very reluctantly, because they considered the relations to values. The majority of the Japanese participants had no qualms with the notion, since they understood it as the construction of more superficial similarities. Both sides had right from their point of view.
[256] Interview of John Gray in: Süddeutsche Zeitung, February 13th, 2001.
[257] Interview of Gottlieb Guntern in: Die Zeit, February 21st, 1997.
[258] Die Welt, December 11th, 2002.
[259] „Was aber noch mehr berührt, ist der Primat des Wirtschaftlichen. Jeder Schritt wird gerechtfertigt, wenn er nur die Konkurrenzfähigkeit erhöht. Mit den Zielen der Erreichung einer besseren Position im Markt (gemessen am Marktanteil), der Sicherung der ‚kritischen Größe' (für die ich keine wirklich fundierte Definition kenne), ... werden alle Schritte legitimiert, mögen ihre Folgen auch für viel Menschen, insbesondere die Mitarbeiter, schmerzlich sein." (NZZ, March 26, 1996).
[260] Die Welt, January 20th, 2004.
[261] The Holland Herald praised the cooperative approach of the Dutch (No. 37, October 2000, p 15); Andrea Colli (2003) related the Italian upswing during the 1990s to a substantial extent to a new cooperative approach between labour and capital.
[262] "..., dass die Erreichung der Unternehmensziele etwa zu 80 Prozent von der Menschenführung und zu nicht einmal zwanzig Prozent vom Management der Zahlen abhängig ist." (Wildemann, H., FAZ, May 5th, 2003).

[263] A recent poll showed 30 per cent of American workers explained them to be engaged with their job, in contrast to 15 per cent in Germany. In the latter country the same amount had without open declaration opted out (Die Welt, January 20th, 2004).
[264] Prahalad & Ramaswamy (2004).

LITERATURE

Abelshauser, W., (1987). *Die Langen Fünfziger Jahre. Wirtschaft und Gesellschaft der Bundesrepublik Deutschland 1949-1966*, Düsseldorf: Schwann

Adler, M. K. ed. (1971). *Leading cases in market research*, London: Business Books

Albert, M. (1991). *Capitalisme contre Capitalisme*, Paris: Seuil

Alesia, R & di Tella, R. & MacCulloch, R. (2001). Inequality and happiness: are Europeans and Americans different? *NBER Working Paper* April 2001

Allgemeiner Deutscher Gewerkschaftsbund (1926). *Amerikareise deutscher Gewerkschaftsführer*, Berlin

Amatori, F. (2000). Between state and the market: Italy, the futile search for a third way, in: Toninelli, P. A. ed., The rise and the fall of state-owned enterprise in the western world, Cambridge: Cambridge University Press

Amatori, F. & Colli, A. & Crepas, N. eds. (1999). *Deindustrialization and reindustrialization in 20th century Europe*, Milan: Franco Angeli

Ambrosius, G. & Hubbard, W. H. (1989). *A social and economic history of the twentieth century*, Cambridge, Mass.: Harvard University Press

Ambrosius, G. (2001). Institutioneller Wettbewerb im europäischen Integrationsprozeß seit dem 19. Jahrhundert, in: *Geschichte und Gesellschaft*, vol. 27, 4, pp. 545-575

Ambrosius, G. (2001). *Staat und Wirtschaftsordnung: eine Einführung in Theorie und Geschichte*, Stuttgart: Steiner

Amdam, R.-P. (1998). Management education in Norway, 1945-1970s: the role of intermediate organisations, in: in: Schröter, H. G. & Moen, E. eds., Une américanisation des entreprises? *Entreprise et Histoire* No. 19, pp. 35-46

Amdam, R. P. & Bjarnar, O. (1998). The regional dissemination of American productivity models in Norway in the 1950s and 1960s, in: Bjarnar & Kipping eds., The Americanisation of European business, pp. 91-112, London: Routledge

Amdam, R.-P. & Norström, C. J. (1994). Business administration in Norway, in: Engwall, L. & Gunnarson, E. eds., *Management studies in an academic context*, pp. 66-83, Uppsala: Uppsala university press

Amdam, R.-P. & Sogner, K. (2002). The diffusion of American organisational models to Norwegian Industries 1945-1970, in: Kipping & Tiratsoo eds. *Americanisation in 20th century europe*, vol. 2, pp. 193-206, Lille: Université Charles de Gaulle

Andersen, K. (1933). Die Aufsicht über Trusts und Kartelle in Norwegen, in: *Kartell-Rundschau*, pp. 77 – 83

Andersen N. A. (2000). Public market – political firms, in: *Acta Sociologica*, vol. 43, No. 1, pp 43-62

Arcolakis, M. (2003). The Greece film industry in the 1930s: representations of the economic structure on the screen, in: Dritsas, M. & Gourvish, T. eds. (forthcoming)

Arvidsson, A., (2000). The discovery of subjectivity: motivation research in Italy 1958-1968, in: Passerini, L. ed., *Across the Atlantic. Cultural exchanges between Europe and the United States*, pp. 279-294, Brussels: Peter Lang

Atkinson, R. & Flint J (2003). Fortress UK? Gated communities, the spatial revolt of the elites and time-space trajectories of segregation, *manuscript*, Department of Urban Studies, University of Glasgow

Baade, F. (1957). Weltmacht Verbraucher, in: Zentralverband Deutscher Konsumgenossenschaften (ed.), *Wirtschaft für den Verbraucher*, pp. 16-19, Hamburg: Zentralverband Deutscher Konsumgenossenschaften

Bakker, G. (2003). Building knowledge about the consumer: The emergence of market research in the motion picture industry, in: *BH*, vol. 45, No 1, pp. 101-127

Bakker, G. (2003). Entertainment industrialized: the emergence of the international film industry, 1890-1940, in: *Enterprise & Society*, vol. 4, no. 4, pp. 579-586

Bakker, G. (2001). Selling French films in foreign markets: the international strategy of a medium-sized French film company, 1919-1938, *EUI Working paper*, 3, 2001, Florence: European University Institute

Baklanoff, E. N. (1978). *L'américanisation de l'Europe occidentale au XXe siècle. Mythes et réalités*, Paris: Presse de l'université de Paris Sorbonne

Baklanoff, E. N. (1978). *The economic transformation of Spain and Portugal*. N. York: Praeger Publishers

Barjot, D. ed. (2002 b). *Catching up with America: Productivity missions and the diffusion of American economic and technological influence after the Second World War,* Paris: Presse de l'université de Paris Sorbonne

Barjot, D. ed. (2002 b). Catching up with America: the story of Productivity Missions in the French public works industry after the Second World War, in: Barjot, D. ed., *Catching up with America,* pp. 359-384, Paris: Presse de l'université de Paris Sorbonne

Barjot, D. (2002 a). Introduction, in: Barjot & Lescent-Gilles & Ferriere le Vayer eds., *L' américanisation en europe au XXe Siecle: Economie, Culture, Politique,* volume 1, pp. 7-37, Lille: Université Charles de Gaulle

Barjot, D. (2002 c). Introduction générale, in: Barjot, D. ed., *L'américanisation de l'europe occidentale au XXe siècle. Mythes et réalités,* pp. 7-33, Paris: Presses de l'université de Paris Sorbonne

Barjot, D. (1998). Le seconde découverte de l'amérique, in: Schröter, H. G. & Moen, E. eds., Une américanisation des entreprises? *Entreprise et Histoire* No. 19, 1998, pp. 99-108

Barjot, D. & Lescent-Giles, I. & de Ferrière le Vayer, M. eds. (2002 a). *Américanisation en europe au XXe siècle: économie, culture, politique,* vol. 1, Lille: Centre de Recherche sur l'Histoire de l'Europe du Nord-Ouest, Université Charles de Gaulle

Barjot, D. & Réveillard, C. eds. (2000 c). *L'américanisation de l'europe occidentale au XXe siècle. Mythes et réalités,* Paris: Presse de l'université de Paris Sorbonne

Battilossi, S. & Cassis, Y. eds. (2002). *European banks and the American challenge: competition and co-operation in international banking under Bretton Woods,* New York: Oxford University Press

Beck, U. (2003). *Global America?: the cultural consequences of globalization,* Liverpool: Liverpool Univ. Press, 2003

Berghahn, V. (1986). *The Americanisation of West German Industry, 1945 - 1973,* New York: Berg

Berghahn, V. (1996). Deutschland im "American Century", 1942-1992. Einige Argumente zur Amerikanisierungsfrage, in: Frese, M. & Prinz, M. eds., *Politische Zäsuren und gesellschaftlicher Wandel im 20. Jahrhundert. Regionale und vergleichende Perspektiven,* pp. 789-800, Paderborn: Ferdinand Schöningh

Berghahn, V. (1984). Deutschland, Amerika und die Weltwirtschaft, 1933-1960; in: *Neue Politische Literatur,* vol. 1984, pp. 335ff

Berghahn, V. (1991). Technology and the export of industrial culture: Problems of the German-American relationship 1900-1960, in: Mathias, P. & Davis, J. A. eds., *Innovation and technology in Europe: From the eighteenth century to the present day,* pp. 142 – 161, Cambridge/Mass: Cambridge University Press

Berghahn, V. (1994). West German reconstruction and American industrial culture, 1945-1960, in: Pommerin, R. ed., *The American impact on postwar Germany,* 65-81, Oxford: Oxford University Press

Berghahn, V. & Friedrich P. J. (1993). *Otto A. Friedrich,* Frankfurt: Campus

Berland, N. & Boynes, T. & Zimnovitch, H. (2002). The influence of the USA on the development of standard costing and budgeting in the UK and France, in: Kipping & Tiratsoo eds. *Americanisation in 20th Century Europe,* vol. 2, pp. 129-144, Lille: Université Charles de Gaulle

Berndt, C. (1998). *Corporate Germany at the crossroads?: Americanization, competitiveness and place dependence,* Cambridge: ESRC Centre for Business Research, University of Cambridge

Bertrams, K. (2002). From Exchange programmes to the legitimisation of university-based management education: the case of Belgium, 1920-1970, in: Kipping & Tiratsoo eds. *Americanisation in 20th Century Europe,* vol. 2, pp. 225-242, Lille: Université Charles de Gaulle

Bigazzi, D. (2000). *Mass-production or 'organized craftsmanship'? The Post-War Italian automobile industry,* in: Zeitlin & Herrigel eds., *Americanisation and its limits,* pp. 269-297, Oxford: Oxford University Press

Bijker, W. E. & Hughes T. P. & Pinch, P. T. eds. (1984). *The social construction of technical systems. New directions in the sociology and history of technology,* Cambridge: Cambridge University Press

Bjarnar, O. & Kipping, M. (1998). The Marshall Plan and the transfer of US management models to Europe: an introductory framework, in: Bjarnar & Kipping eds., *The Americanisation of european business,* pp. 1-17, London: Routledge

Black, S. W. & Moersch, M. (1998). Financial structure, investment and economic growth in OECD countries, in: Black, S. W. & Moresch, M. eds., *Competition and convergence in financial markets. The German and Anglo-American models,* pp. 157-180, Amsterdam: Elsevier

Blaich, F. (1984). *Amerikanische Firmen in Deutschland 1890-1914,* Stuttgart: Steiner

Blakely, E. J. & Snyder, M. G. (1997). *Fortress America: Gated communities in the United States*, Washington: Brookings Institution

Bloemen, E. & Griffith, R.T. (2002). *Resisting revolution in the Netherlands*, in: Barjot, D. ed. *Catching up with America*, pp. 113-121, Paris: Presse de l'université de Paris Sorbonne

Boel, B. (1998 a). "Americanization": uses and misuses of a concept, in: Szaló, M. ed., *On European identity: nationalism, culture & history*, pp. 217-235, Brno: Masaryk University

Boel, B. (1998 b). The European Productivity Agency: a faithful prophet of the American model? In: Kipping & Bjarnar eds., *The Americanisation of European business*, pp. 37-54, London: Routledge

Boel, B. (2000). The United States and the Postwar European Productivity Drive, in: Passerini, L. ed., *Across the Atlantic. Cultural Exchanges between Europe and the United States*, pp. 241-254, Brussels: Peter Lang

Boje, P. (1997). *Ledere, ledelse og organisation 1870-1972*

Boje, P. (1997). *Ledere, ledelse og organisation. Dansk industry iefter 1970*

Bolle de Bal, M. (1989). Participation: Its contradictions, paradoxes, and promises, in: Lammers, C. J. & Szell, G. eds., *International handbook of participation in organizations*, pp. 11-25, Oxford University Press, Oxford.

Böllhoff, D. (2002). The new regulatory regime - the institutional design of telecommunications regulation at the national level, in Heritier, A. (ed.), *Common goods: Reinventing European and international governance*, Lanham, M. D: Rowman and Littlefield Publishers, pp. 227-257

Bonin, H. (2001). The regulation of French banking and stock exchange markets (19th-20th centuries): state interests and common interest, from total liberalism to state interventionism? In: *Regulierung auf globalen Finanzmärkten zwischen Risikoschutz und Wettbewerbssicherung*, pp. 20-36, Frankfurt: Knapp

Bonnaud, L. (2002). Infrastructure finance since the Second World War: an American model or a dead end? In: Barjot & Lescent-Gilles & Ferriere le Vayer eds., *L'Americanisation en Europe au XXe Siecle: Economie, Culture, Politique*, vol. 1, pp. 263-280, Lille: Université Charles de Gaulle

Booth, A. (2002). British retail banks, 1955-1970: a case of an 'Americanisation'? in: Kipping & Tiratsoo eds. *Americanisation in 20th Century Europe*, vol. 2, pp. 309-324, Lille: Université Charles de Gaulle

Bossuat, G. (1992). *L'aide américaine et la construction européenne 1944-1954*, Paris: Ministère de l'Économie et des Finances, Comité pour l'Histoire Économique et Financière de la France

Bossuat, G. (2002). Les Etats-Unis et le bon gouvernement économique de la France au temps des aides, in Barjot & Lescent-Giles & de Ferrière le Vayer eds. *Américanisation en Europe au XXe Siècle: Économie, Culture, Politique*, pp. 113-136, Lille: Université Charles de Gaulle

Braun, H.-J. (2002). "Hollywood and nothing else?" The Americanisation of the American film industry in the Weimar Republic, in: Kipping & Tiratsoo eds., *Americanisation in 20th Century Europe*, pp. 176-191, vol. 2, Lille: Université Charles de Gaulle

Broder, A. (2000). Manque de moyens, absence de logique politique ou espace économique restreint? La politique de l'informatique en France: 1960-1993, in: Hau & Kiesewetter eds., *Chemins vers l'an 2000*, pp. 117-172, Zurich: Peter Lang

Brown, L. B. (1937). *Marketing and distribution research*, New York: The Ronald Press Company

Bryn, S. (1992). *Norske Amerika-bilete: om amerikanisering av norsk kultur*, Oslo : Norske Samlaget

Bossuat, G. (2002). Les États-Unies et le bon gouvernement économique de la France, in: Barjot & Lescent-Giles & de Ferrière le Vayer eds., *Américanisation en Europe au XXe Siècle: Économie, Culture, Politique*, pp. 113-136, vol. 1, Lille: Université Charles de Gaulle

Buck, T. (2004). The "Americanization" of international corporate governance in business history: some propositions for executive stock options in modern Germany, in: McDonald, F: & Mayer, M. & Buck T. eds., The process of internationalization: strategic, cultural and policy perspectives, Basingstoke: Palgrave/Macmillan

Buck, T. & Tull, M. (2000). Anglo-American contributions to Japanese and German corporate governance after World War Two, in: *Business History*, vol. 42, No. 2, pp. 119-140

Bud, R. & Gummet, P. eds. (1999). *Cold War, hot science, applied research in Britain's defence laboratories, 1945-1990*, London: Harwood

Byrkjeflot (2001). The Americanisation of Swedish and Norwegian management in: Kipping & Tiratsoo eds. *Americanisation in 20th Century Europe*, vol. 2, pp. 111-128, Lille: Université Charles de Gaulle

Byrkjeflot, H. (1998). Engineers in Germany and the United States. A discussion of the origins of diversity in management systems, in: Schröter, H. G. & Moen, E. eds., Une américanisation des entreprises? *Entreprise et Histoire* No. 19, 1998, pp. 47-74

Cailluet, L. (1998). Selective adaptation of American management models: the long-term relationship of Pechiney with the United States, in: Bjarnar & Kipping eds., The Americanisation of European business, pp. 190-207, London: Routledge

Carreras, A. et. al. (2000). The rise and decline of Spanish state-owned firms, in: Toninelli, P. A. ed. *The rise and fall of state-owned enterprise in the Western world,* pp. 208-236, Cambridge: Cambridge University Press

Cassidy, J. (2002). Dot Con: the greatest story ever sold, New York: Harper Collins

Cassis, Y. (1997). *Big business: the European experience in the twentieth century,* Oxford: Oxford University Press

Cassis, Y. (2002). La city de Londres face à l'américanisation, in: Barjot, D. (ed.), *L'américanisation de l'Europe occidentale au XXe siècle. Mythes et réalités,* pp. 139-154, Paris: Presses de l'université de Paris Sorbonne

Cassis, Y. (1995). *The evolution of financial institutions and market in twentieth-century Europe,* Aldershot: Scolar Press

Cassis, Y. & Couzet, F. & Gourvish, T. eds. (1995). *Management and business in Britain and France : the age of the corporate economy,* Oxford: Clarendon Press

Ceaser, J. W. (1997). *Reconstructing America : the symbol of America in modern thought,* New Haven: Yale University Press

Chelini, M.-P. (2002). American influence on price stabilisation and currency fluctuations in Post-War France (1945-1958), in: Barjot & Lescent-Giles & de Ferrière le Vayer eds., *Américanisation en Europe au XXe Siècle: Économie, Culture, Politique,* pp. 137-150, vol. 1, Lille: Université Charles de Gaulle

Chandler A. D. Jr. (2001). *Inventing the electronic century: the epic story of the consumer electronics and computer industrie*s, New York: Free Press

Chandler, Alfred D. Jr. (1990). *Scale and Scope, The dynamics of industrial capitalism,* Cambridge: Cambridge University Press

Chandler, A. D. Jr. & Amatori, F. & Hikino, T. eds. (1997). *Big business and the wealth of nations,* Cambridge: Cambridge University Press

Chandler, A. D. Jr. & Hikino, T. (1997). The large industrial enterprise and the dynamics of modern economic growth, in: Chandler & Amatori & Hikino eds., *Big business and the wealth of nations,* pp. 24-57, Cambridge: Cambridge University Press

Chandler, A. D. & Hikino, T. & Nordenflycht, A. (2001). Inventing the electronic century: the epic story of the consumer electronics and computer industries, New York: Free Press

Chauveau, S. (2002). Antibiotiques, screening, management et marketing: une américanisation de l'industrie pharmaceutique française? in: Barjot, D. (ed.), *L'américanisation de l'europe occidentale au XXe siècle. Mythes et réalités,* pp. 195-206, Paris: Presses de l'université de Paris Sorbonne

Chessel, M.-E. (2002). American influences on the reform of French management education in the late 1960s: the case of the FNEGE (Fondation Nationale pour l'Enseignement de la Gestion des Entreprises), in: Barjot & Lescent-Giles & de Ferrière le Vayer eds., *Américanisation en Europe au XXe Siècle: Économie, Culture, Politique,* pp. 247-262, vol. 1, Lille: Université Charles de Gaulle

Chew, D. H. (1998). *Discussing the revolution in corporate finance,* Malden: Blackwell Publishers

Colli, A. (2003). Finance, governance and convergence: the Italian pattern during the 20th century, manuscript, Milan: Università Bocconi

Colley, R. H. (1948). How straight can we shoot in long-range sales forecasting? in: *Sales Management,* July 1st, 1948, pp. 94-100

Coopey, R. & Porter, D. (2002). Did Bradford have anything to learn from Chicago? American influences on mail order retailing in Britain, in: Kipping & Tiratsoo eds., *Americanisation in 20th Century Europe,* vol. 2, pp. 277-289, Lille: Université Charles de Gaulle

Costioglia, F. (1989). The "Americanization" of Europe in the 1920s, in: Feldman, G. D. et al. eds., *Beiträge zu Inflation und Wiederaufbau in Deutschland und Europa 1914-1924,* pp. 181-209, Berlin: Colloquium Verlag

Crouzet, F. (2002). Conclusion, in: Barjot, D. ed., *Catching up with America,* pp. 359-384, Paris: Presse de l'université de Paris Sorbonne

Crouzet, F. (2002). Quelques conclusions, in: Barjot & Lescent-Giles & de Ferrière le Vayer eds., *Américanisation en Europe au XXe Siècle: Économie, Culture, Politique*, pp. 427-438, vol. 1, Lille: Université Charles de Gaulle

Dahrendorf, R. (1963). *Die angewandte Aufklärung, Gesellschaft und Soziologie in Amerika*, Frankfurt: Fischer

Dauchelle, S. (2002). La place des Etats-Unis dans la reconstruction d'une industrie française d'armement (1955-1958), in: Barjot, D. (ed.), *L'américanisation de l'Europe occidentale au XXe siècle. Mythes et réalités*, pp. 155-172, Paris: Presses de l'université de Paris Sorbonne

Daviet, J.-P. (2002). Productivity missions and their influence of the modernisation of the French wool industry, in: Barjot, D. ed., *Catching up with America*, pp. 385-394, Paris: Presse de l'université de Paris Sorbonne

Dekker, M. S. (1997). Preface, in: Verbung, L. G., *The European works council in the Netherlands*, pp. 1-3, The Hague: Kluwer

Dezalay, I. (1990). The big bang and the law: the internationalization and restructuring of the legal field, in: Featherstone, M. ed. *Global culture: Nationalism, globalization and modernity*, London: Sage

Djankov, S. & Murreil, P. (2002). Enterprise restructuring in transition: A quantitative survey, *Journal of Economic Literature* 40, 739-792.

Djelic, M.-L. (1998). *Exporting the American model. The Post-war transformation of European business*, Oxford: Oxford University Press

ten Doesschate, J.F. (1934). Frivillige kjedeforretninger i Amerika og Holland, in: *Norges Grossisttidende* 8, 156-158 and 9, 185-187

Dore, R. (2000). *Stock market capitalism - welfare capitalism. Japan and Germany versus the Anglo-Saxons*, Oxford: Oxford University Press

Dosi, G. & Giannetti, R. & Toninelli P. A. (1992). eds. *Technology and enterprise in a historical perspective*, Oxford: Oxford University Press

Downham, J. (1998). *ESOMAR, a continuing record of success*, Amsterdam: ESOMAR

Dritsas, M. (2004). Greek business development and the diffusion of national and European patterns, in: Dritsas, M. & Gourvish, T. eds. Forthcoming

Drucker, P. (1946). *The concept of the corporation*, New York: New American Library

Dreyfus, F.-G. (2002). Les Etats-Unis et l'américanisation de l'Europe, in: Barjot, D. (ed.), *L'américanisation de l'europe occidentale au XXe siècle. Mythes et réalités*, pp. 89-94, Paris: Presses de l'université de Paris Sorbonne

Dunning, J. (1998). US-owned manufacturing affiliates and the transfer of managerial technique: the British case, in: Kipping Bjarnar eds., *The Americanisation of European business*, pp. 74-90, London: Routledge

Edelmann, H. (2003). *Heinz Nordhoff und Volkswagen: ein deutscher Unternehmer im amerikanischen Jahrhundert*, Göttingen: Vandenhoeck & Ruprecht

Eklöh, H. (1958). Der Siegeszug der Selbstbedienung, in: Stiftung "Im Grüene" ed., *Schriftenreihe der Stiftung "Im Grüene"*, Neure Aspekte der Selbstbedienung, pp. 9-19, vol. 8, Rüschlikon

Eklöh, H. sen. & Eklöh, H. jun. (1958). Ein heißes Eisen: Selbstbedienung bei Frischfleisch, in: *Dynamik im Handel*, pp. 140-144

Elixmann, D. & Kulenkampff, G. & Schimmel U. & Schwab, R. (2001). Internationaler Vergleich der TK-Märkte in ausgewählten Ländern - ein Liberalisierungs-, Wettbewerbs- und Wachstumsindex, *WIK Diskussionsbeitrag* No. 216, Bad Honnef, February.

Ellwood, D. W. (1998). The limits of Americanisation and the emergence of an alternative model: the Marshall Plan in the Emilia-Romagna, in: Bjarnar & Kipping eds., The Americanisation of European Business, pp. 149-168, London: Routledge

Ellwood, D. W. (1992). *Rebuilding Europe. Western Europe, America and Postwar reconstruction*, London: Longman

Enström, A. F. (1927). Amerikanisering, in: *Teknisk Ukeblad*, vol. 74, June 17

Engwall, L. (1998). The making of Viking leaders: perspectives on Nordic management education, in: Engwall & Zagmani eds. *Management education in historical perspective*, pp. 66-82, Manchester: Manchester University Press

Engwall, L. & Zagmani, V. eds. (1998). *Management education in historical perspective*, Manchester: Manchester University Press

Engwall, L. & Zagmani, V. (1998). Introduction, in: Engwall & Zagmani eds., *Management education in historical perspective*, pp. 1-18, Manchester: Manchester University Press

Erker, P. (1997). "Amerikanisierung" der westdeutschen Wirtschaft? Stand und Perspektiven der Forschung, in: Jarausch, K. & Siegrist, H. eds., *Amerikanisierung und Sowjetisierung in Deutschland 1945-1970*, pp. 137-146, Frankfurt/M: Campus

Erker, P. (2000). The long shadow of Americanization: the German rubber industry and the radial tyre revolution, in: Zeitlin & Herrigel eds. *Americanization and its Limits*, pp. 298-315, Oxford: Oxford University Press

Erker, P. (1996a). Das Bedaux-System. Neue Aspekte historischer Rationalisierungsforschung, in: *Zeitschrift für Unternehmensgeschichte*, vol. 41, pp. 139-158

Erker, P. & Lorentz B. (2003). *Chemie und Politik. Die Geschichte der chemischen Werke Hüls*, München: C.H. Beck

Erker, P. (1996 b). *Wachsen im Wettbewerb. Eine Zeitgeschichte der Continental Aktiengesellschaft (1971-1996) anlässlich des 125jährigen Firmenjubiläums*, Econ Verlag: Düsseldorf.

Ermarth, M. ed. (1993). *America and the shaping of German society, 1945-1955*, Providence, R.I.: Berg

Esposito, C. (1994). *America's feeble weapon. Funding the Marshall-Plan in France and Italy 1948-1950*, Westport: Greenwood Press

European Foundation for the Improvement of Living and Working Conditions, ed. (1997). New forms of work organisation. *Can Europe release its potential? - Results of a survey of direct employee participation in Europe*, Dublin: European Foundation for the Improvement of Living and Working Conditions

Evans, D. S. & Schmalensee, R. (1999). *Paying with plastic. The digital revolution in buying and borrowing*, Cambridge: MIT Press

Fear, J. R. (1997). Constructing big business: The cultural concept of the firm, in: Chandler, A. D. Jr., & Amatori, F. & Hikino, T., *Big business and the wealth of nations*, pp. 546-574, Cambridge: Cambridge University Press

Fauri, R. (1999). Between government and market: "Scientific management" in Italy in the interwar years, in Amatori, F. & Colli, A. & Crepas, N. eds. *Deindustrialization and reindustrialization in 20th century Europe*, pp. 99-115, Milan: Franco Angeli

Featherstone, M. ed. (1990). *Global culture: Nationalism, globalization and modernity*, London: Sage

Feinstein, C. H. & Temin, P. & Toniolo, G. (1997). *The European economy between the wars*, Oxford: Oxford University Press

Feldenkirchen, W. (2002). The Americanization of the German electrical industry after 1945: Siemens as a case study, in: Kudo & Kipping & Schröter eds., *German and Japanese Business in the Boom Years*, pp. 116-137, London: Routledge

Feldenkirchen, W. (2002). Productivity missions and the German electrical industry, in: Barjot, D. ed., *Catching up with America*, pp. 285-300, Paris: Presse de l'université de Paris Sorbonne

Feldman, G., (1989). Foreign penetration of German enterprises after the First World War: the problem of "Überfremdung", in: Teichova, A. & Lévy-Leboyer, M. & Nussbaum, H. eds., *Historical studies in international corporate business*, pp. 87-110, Cambridge: Cambridge University Press

Ferretti, R. (1999). Industrial reconversion, the local community and the "network of enterprise". The case of Bologna after World War Two, in Amatori, F. & Colli, A. & Crepas, N. eds. *Deindustrialization and reindustrialization in 20th century Europe*, pp. 284-297, Milan: Franco Angeli

Fink, H. (1995). *Amerikanisierung in der deutschen Wirtschaft: Sprache, Handel, Güter und Dienstleistungen*, Frankfurt/M: Peter Lang

Fischer, W. (2002). American influence on German manufacturing before World War I: The case of the Ludwig Loewe Company, in: Barjot & Lescent-Giles & de Ferrière le Vayer eds., *Américanisation en Europe au XXe Siècle: Économie, Culture, Politique*, vol. 1, pp 59-69, Lille: Université Charles de Gaulle

Fischer, W., et al. ed. (1996). *The impossible challenge*, Berlin: Akademie Verlag

Flanzbaum, H. (1999). *The Americanisation of the holocaust*, Baltimore: John Hopkins University Press

Fleming, D. & Thörnqvist C. (2003). Nordic management-labour relations and internationalization – converging and diverging tendencies, in: idem eds. *Nordic management-labour relations and internationalization*, pp. 9-22, Copenhagen: Nordic Council of Ministers

Fligstein, N. (1990). *The transformation of corporate control*, Cambridge, Mass: Harvard University Press

Fox, Willard M. (1950). *How to Use Market Research for Profit*, New York: Prentice-Hall

Fridenson, P. (1987). En tournament taylorienne de la société caise (1904-1918), in: *Annales* 42, pp. 1031-1060

Fridenson, P. (1993). L'industrie automobile francaise et le plan Marshall, in: Girault, R. & Lévy-Leboyer, M. eds., *Le plan Marshall et le relèvement économique de l'europe*, Paris

Galli, G. & Pelkmans, J. eds. (2000). *Regulatory reform and competitiveness in Europe*, Cheltenham: Edward Elgar

Garcia-Ruiz, J. L. (2002). Barreiros Diesel and the Chrysler Corporation, 1963-1969, a troubled Americanisation, in: Kipping & Tiratsoo eds. *Americanisation in 20th Century Europe*, vol. 2, pp. 375-388, Lille: Université Charles de Gaulle

Geiger, T. (2002). American hegemony and the adoption of income statistics in Western Europe after 1945, in: Barjot & Lescent-Giles & de Ferrière le Vayer eds., *Américanisation en Europe au XXe Siècle: Économie, Culture, Politique*. vol. 1, pp. 151-167, Lille: Université Charles de Gaulle

Geiger, T. (2002). The British state, the British defence industry and the influence of American technology in the 1950s, in: Barjot, D. ed., *Catching up with America*, pp. 157-170, Paris: Presse de l'université de Paris Sorbonne

Gemelli, G. (1997). European management education between American influence and national traditions (1950s-1970s), in: Olsson, U. ed., *Business and European integration since 1800. Regional, national, and international perspectives*, pp. 100-128, Gothenburg: Graphic Systems

Gemelli, G. (1998). The 'enclosure' effect: innovation without standardization in Italian postwar education, in: Engwall & Zagmani eds., *Management education in historical perspective*, pp. 127-144, Manchester: Manchester University Press

Gemelli, G. ed. (1998). *The Ford-Foundation and Europe (1950s-1970s)*, Brussels: European Interuniversity Press

Gemelli, G. (2001). *American foundations and large-scale research: construction and transfer of knowledge* Bologna: Clueb

Gemzell, C.-A. (1989-1993). *Om politikens förvetenskapligande och vetenskapens politisering. Kring velfärdsstatens uppkomst i England*, vols. I-III, Copenhagen: Institut for samtidshistorie

Gerschenkron, A. (1952). Economic backwardness in historical perspective, in: Hoselitz, B. F. ed., *The progress of underdeveloped areas*, pp. 3-29, Chicago

Gillingham, J. (2002). Background to Marshall-Plan technical assistance: Productivism as American ideology, in: Barjot, D. ed. (2000). *Catching up with America*, pp. 53-66, Paris: Presse de l'université de Paris Sorbonne

Girault, R. & Lévy-Leboyer, M. eds. (1993). *Le plan Marshall et le relèvement économique de l'europe*, Paris

Glimstedt, H., (1998). Americanistaion and the 'Swedish model' of industrial relations: the introduction of the MTM system at Volvo in the postwar period, in: Bjarnar & Kipping eds., *The Americanisation of European Business*, pp. 113-148, London: Routledge

Glimstedt, H. (2000). Creative cross-fertilization and uneven Americanization of Swedish industry: Sources of innovation in Post-War motor vehicles and electrical manufacturing, in: Zeitlin & Herrigel *Americanisation and its Limits*, pp. 180-208, Oxford: Oxford University Press

Glimstedt, H. (1993). *Mellan teknik och samhälle. Stat, marknad och produktion i svensk bilindustri 1930-1960*, Gothenburg: Graphic Systems

Gloor, M. et al. ed. (1963). *Neuzeitliche Distributionsformen*, Paul Haupt: Bern

Godelier, E. (2002). American influence on a large steel firm: how Usinor learnt and adapted US methods in France, in: Barjot, D. ed., *Catching up with America*, pp. 277-284, Paris: Presse de l'université de Paris Sorbonne

Godley, A. & Church, R. eds. (2003). *The emergence of modern marketing*, London: Cass

Godson, R. (1976). *American Labour and European Politics*, New York: Crane

Gourvish, T. (2002). Americanisation, cultural transfers in the economic sphere: a comment, in: Kipping & Tiratsoo eds. *Americanisation in 20th Century Europe*, vol. 2, pp. 405-408, Lille: Université Charles de Gaulle

Gourvish, T. & Tiratsoo, N. eds. (1998). *Missionaries and managers. American influences on European management education, 1945-1960*, Manchester & New York: Manchester University Press

Granovetter, M. (1992). Economic action and social structure: The problem of embeddedness, in: Granovetter, M. & Swedberg, R. eds., *The sociology of economic life*, pp. 53-83, Boulder: Westview Press

Granziera, R. G. (1998). Engagements of war and economic planning in Brazil, 1942-1955, in: Schröter, H. G. & Moen, E. eds., *Une américanisation des entreprises? Entreprise et Histoire* No. 19, 1998, pp. 75-84 de Grazia, V. (1998). Changing consumption regimes in Europe, 1930-1970. Comparative perspective on the distribution problem, in: Strasser, S. & McGovern, C. & Judt, M. eds., *Getting and spending. European and American consumer societies in the twentieth century*, pp. 59-84, Cambridge: Cambridge University Press

de Grazia, V. (1989). Mass culture and sovereignty: The American challenge to European cinemas, 1920-1960, in: *Journal of Modern History*, vol. 61, pp. 53-87

Griffith, R. T. & Bloemen, E. (2002). Resisting revolution in the Netherlands, in: Barjot, D. ed., *Catching up with America*, pp. 113-122, Paris: Presse de l'université de Paris Sorbonne

Grönberg, P.-O. (2003). *Learning and returning. Return migration of Swedish engineers from the United States, 1880-1940*, Umeå: Umeå universitetet

Guasconi, M. E. (2002). Americanisation and national Identity. The case of the Italian labour movement (1947-1955), in Barjot & Lescent-Giles & de Ferrière le Vayer eds. *Américanisation en Europe au XXe Siècle: Économie, Culture, Politique*, pp. 169-178, vol. 1, Lille: Université Charles de Gaulle

Guasconi, M. E. (1999). L'altra faccia della medaglia. Guerra pricologica e diplomazia sindicale nelle relazioni italia-stati-uniti durante la prima fase della guerra fredda (1947-1955), Soveria Manelli: Robbettino

Gui, B. (1996). Is there a chance for the worker-managed form of organization? in: Pagano, U. & Rowthorn, R. eds., Democracy and efficiency in the economic enterprise, pp. 164-162, London: Routledge

Guigeno, V. (2002). What they saw, what they wrote, what they read: the American experience in the reports of the French Marshall-Plan missionaries, in: Barjot & Lescent-Giles & de Ferrière le Vayer eds., *Américanisation en Europe au XXe Siècle: Économie, Culture, Politique*, vol. 1, pp. 196-206, Lille: Université Charles de Gaulle

Hachez-Leroy, F. (2002). The productivity missions for metal assembly work in the building industry, in: Barjot, D. ed., *Catching up with America*, pp. 405-412, Paris: Presse de l'université de Paris Sorbonne

Hachtmann, R. (1996). „Die Begründung der amerikanischen Technik sind fast lauter schwäbisch-allemannische Menschen": Nazi-Deutschland, der Blick auf die USA und die „Amerikanisierung" der industriellen Produktionsstrukturen im „Dritten Reich", in: Lüdtke, A. & Marßolek, I. & von Saldern, A. eds., *Amerikanisierung. Traum und Alptraum im Deutschland des 20. Jahrhundert*, pp. 37-66. Stuttgart: Franz Steiner Verlag

Hall, B. J. & Murphy, K. J. (2003). The trouble with stock options, NBER working paper series No. 9784, Cambridge, Mass.: National Bureau of Economic Research

Hall, P. A. & Soskice, D. W. eds. (2001). *Varieties of capitalism: the institutional foundations of comparative advantage*, Oxford: Oxford University Press

Hallig, K. (1965). *Amerikanische Erfahrungen auf dem Gebiet der Wirtschaftswerbung im Hinblick auf ihre Anwendung im westeuropäischen Raum*, Berlin: Duncker & Humblot

Hampden-Turner, C. & Trompenaars, F. (1993). *The seven cultures of capitalism. Value systems for creating wealth in the United States, Britain, Japan, Germany, France, Sweden and the Netherlands*, New York: Doubleday

Handlin, O. ed. (1949). *This was America*, Cambridge: Cambridge University Press

Hara, T. (2002). Productivity Missions to the United States: the case of Post-War France, in: Barjot, D. ed. (2000). *Catching up with America*, pp. 171-182, Paris: Presse de l'université de Paris Sorbonne

Harms, J. et al. eds. (2003). *Die Ökonomisierung des öffentlichen Sektors: Instrumente und Trends*, Baden-Baden: Nomos Verlags-Gesellschaft

Harris, D. N. (1993). My Job in Germany, 1945-1955, in: Ermarth, M. ed., *America and the shaping of German society, 1945-1955*, Providence: Berg

Hartmann, H. (1963). *Amerikanische Firmen in Deutschland, Beobachtungen über Kontakte und Kontraste zwischen Industriegesellschaften*, Köln: Westdeutscher Verlag

Hartmann, H. (1959). *Authority and organization in German management*, Princeton: Princeton University Press

Hein-Kremer, M. (1996). *Die amerikanische Kulturoffensive. Gründung und Entwicklung der amerikanischen Information Centers in Westdeutschland und West-Berlin 1945-1955*, Cologne: Böhlau

Heinonen, V. & Pantzar, M. (2002). 'Little America': the modernisation of the Finnish consumer society in the 1950s and 1960s, in: Kipping & Tiratsoo eds. *Americanisation in 20th Century Europe*, vol. 2, pp. 41-59, Lille: Université Charles de Gaulle

Heiret, J. (2003). International management strategies and models of industrial relations – a Norwegian experience, in: Fleming, D. & Thörnqvist C. eds., *Nordic management-labour relations and internationalization*, pp. 103-129, Copenhagen: Nordic Council of Ministers

Held, D. et al. (1999). *Global transformations. Politics, economics, culture*, Oxford: Polity Press

Henksmeier, K.-H. (1962). Den Konsumwünschen nachkommen - doch mit der nötigen Vorsicht, in: *Selbstbedienung und Supermarkt*, No. 10, p. 11-112

Hensher, D. A & Button, K. eds. (2001). *Handbook of transport systems and traffic control*, Amsterdam: Pergamon

Herrigel, G. (2000). American occupation, market order, and democracy: reconfiguring the steel industry in Japan and Germany after the Second World War, in: Zeitlin & Herrigel *Americanisation and its Limits*, pp. 340-399, Oxford: Oxford University Press

Hilger, S. (2002). Reluctant Americanization? The reaction of Henkel to the influences and competition from the United States, in: Kudo & Kipping & Schröter eds., *German and Japanese Business in the Boom Years*, pp. 193-220, London: Routledge

Hilton, M. (2002). Americanisation, British consumerism and the international organisation of consumers unions, in: Kipping & Tiratsoo eds., *L' Americanisation en Europe au XXe Siecle, volume 2*, pp. 25-40, Lille: Université Charles de Gaulle

Hobart, D. M. & J. P. Wood (1955) *Verkaufsdynamik*, Essen: Girardet

Hofstede, G. (1991). *Cultures and organisations. software of the mind*, London: McGraw-Hill

Homburg, H. (1991). *Rationalisierung und Industriearbeiterschaft: Arbeitsmarkt, Management, Arbeiterschaft im Siemens-Konzern Berlin 1900-1939*, Berlin: Haude & Spener

Hounshell, D. A. (1987). *From the American system to mass production 1800-1932. The deveolpment of manufacturing technology in the United States*, John Hopkins University Press: Baltimore/London

Hübler, O. (2003). Fördern oder behindern Betriebsräte die Unternehmensentwicklung? in: *Perspektiven der Wirtschaftspolitik*, vol. 4, pp. 379-397

Hübner, J. W. (1981). Worker participation. *A comparative study of The Netherlands, the Federal Republic of Germany and the United Kingdom*, Leiden: Druk Beugelsdijk

Hultquist, C. E. (2003). Americans in Paris: The J. Walter Thompson company in France, 1927-1968, *Enterprise & Society* 4, No 3, pp. 417-499

Hughes, T. P. (1989). *American genesis. A century of invention and technologic enthusiasm. 1870-1970*, Penguin: New York

Huntingdon, S. P. & Harrison, L. E. eds. (2000). *Culture matters. How values shape human progress*, New York: Basis Books

Jain, H. C. ed. (1980). *Worker participation. success and problems*, New York: Praeger

James, H. (2002). Die deutsche Wirtschaft und amerikanische Einflüsse, in: Pohl, M. *Unternehmenskulturen. Deutschland und USA im Vergleich*, pp: 37-48, Frankfurt: FAZ

Jarausch, K. H. & Siegrist, H. (1997). *Amerikanisierung und Sowjetisierung in Deutschland 1945-1970*, in: Jarausch, K. H. & Siegrist, H. eds., *Amerikanisierung und Sowjetisierung. Eine vergleichende Fragestellung zur deutschen Nachkriegsgeschichte*, pp. 11-46, Frankfurt and New York: Campus

Jarausch, K. H. & Siegrist, H. eds. (1997). *Amerikanisierung und Sowjetisierung. Eine vergleichende Fragestellung zur deutschen Nachkriegsgeschichte*, pp. 147-165, Frankfurt and New York: Campus

Jaun, R. (1986). *Management und Arbeiterschaft, Verwissenschaftlichung, Amerikanisierung und Rationalisierung der Arbeitsverhältnisse in der Schweiz 1873-1959*, Chronos: Zurich

Joly, H. (2002). Sociology of the members of the French productivity missions to the USA, 1949-54, in: Barjot, D. ed., *Catching up with America*, pp. 183-196, Paris: Presse de l'université de Paris Sorbonne

Jopp. K. (2000) Insight. The new mixed doubles, in: *agenda*, 1, 2000, 38-40

Kahn, A. E. (1970). *The economics of regulation: principles and institutions*, New York: Wiley

Kane, P. R. (2002) An interview with Milton Friedman on education, *Occasional Paper 67*, National Center for the study of privatization in education, Teacher's College, Columbia University

Kapferer C. (1956). *Market research methods in Europe*, Project No. 261, Paris: OEEC

Karlsen, K. S. (2002). *"Amerikanisering av det norske næringslivet": en undersøkelse av påvirkningen fra amerikanske ledelsesteorier på utvalgte representanter fra det norske næringslivet, 1950-1990*, Universitetet i Bergen: Hovedoppgave i historie

Kaschuba, W. (1995). *Kulturen - Identitäten – Diskurse. Perspektiven europäischer Ethnologie*, Akademie Verlag: Berlin

Katona, G, (1951). *Psychological analysis of economic behaviour*, New York: McGraw-Hill

Katona, G. (1964). *The mass consumption society*, New York: McGraw-Hill

Kiesewetter, H. (1992). 'Beasts or Beagles? Amerikanische Unternehmen in Deutschland', in H. Pohl (ed.), *Der Einfluss ausländischer Unternehmen auf die deutsche Wirtschaft vom Spätmittelalter bis zur Gegenwart*, pp. 165-196, Stuttgart: Steiner

Kindleberger, C. P. (1996). *Manias, panics and crashes: a history of financial crises*, New York: Wiley

King, L. (2002). Tradition and modernity: the Americanisation of Air Lingus advertising, 1950-1960, in: Kipping & Tiratsoo eds. *Americanisation in 20th Century Europe*, vol. 2, pp. 193-206, Lille: Université Charles de Gaulle

Kipping, M. (1999). American management consulting companies in Western Europe, 1920 to 1990: products, reputation, and relationships, in: *Business History Review* 73, pp. 190-220

Kipping, M. (1997). Consultancies, institutions and the diffusion of Taylorism in Britain, Germany and France, 1920s to 1950s, in: *Business History*, vol. 39, no. 4, pp. 67-83

Kipping, M. (1998). *A difficult and slow process: the Americanization of the French steel producing and using industries after WWII*, Discussion papers in economics and management No 378, Reading: University of Reading

Kipping, M. (1998). The hidden business schools: management training in Germany since 1945, in: Engwall & Zagmani eds., *Management education in historical perspective*, pp. 95-107, Manchester: Manchester University Press

Kipping, M. (2002). 'Importing' American ideas to West Germany, 1940s to 1970s: from associations to private consultancies, in: Kudo & Kipping & Schröter eds., *German and Japanese Business in the Boom Years*, pp. 30-53, London: Routledge

Kipping, M. (1998). 'Operation impact', converting European employers to the American creed, in: Kipping & Bjarnar eds., *The Americanisation of European business*, pp. 55-73, London: Routledge

Kipping, M. (2000). A slow and difficult process: the Americanization of the French steel-producing and using industries after the Second World War, in Zeitlin & Herrigel eds. *Americanisation and its Limits*, pp. 208-235, Oxford: Oxford University Press

Kipping, M. & Bjarnar, O. eds. (1998). *The Americanisation of European Business. The Marshall Plan and the Transfer of US Management Models*, London, New York: Routledge

Kipping M. & Engwall, L. eds. (2002). *Management consulting. Emergence and dynamics of a knowledge industry*, Oxford: Oxford University Press

Kipping & Tiratsoo eds. (2002). *Americanisation in 20th century Europe: business, culture, politics, L'américanisation en europe au XXe siècle: entreprises, culture, politique*, vol. 2, pp. 7-23, Lille: Centre de Recherche sur l'Histoire de l'Europe du Nord-Ouest, Université Charles de Gaulle

Klautke, E. (2003). *Unbegrenzte Möglichkeiten: "Amerikanisierung" in Deutschland und Frankreich (1900 - 1933)*, Stuttgart: Steiner

Klein, M. (2001). Coming full circle: the study of big business since 1950, in: *Enterprise & Society*, vol. 2, No. 3, Sept., pp. 425-460

Kleinschmidt C. (2002). America and the resurgence of the German chemical and rubber industry after the Second World War: Hüls, Glanzstoff and Continental, in: Kudo & Kipping & Schröter eds., *German and Japanese Business in the Boom Years*, pp. 161-174, London: Routledge

Kleinschmidt, C. (1998). An Americanised company in Germany: the Vereinigte Glanzstoff Fabriken AG in the 1950s, in: Bjarnar & Kipping eds., The Americanisation of European Business, pp. 171-189, London: Routledge

Kleinschmidt, C. (2004). Driving the West German consumer society. The introduction of US style production and marketing at Volkswagen, 1945-1970, in: Kudo & Kipping & Schröter eds., *German and Japanese Business in the Boom Years*, pp. 75-92, London: Routledge

Kleinschmidt, C. (2002). *Der produktive Blick. Wahrnehmung amerikanischer und japanischer Produktionsmethoden durch deutsche Unternehmer 1950-1985*, Berlin: Akademie Verlag

Kleinschmidt, C. (2000). Unternehmensstrategien, Unternehmenserfahrung und amerikanische Leitbilder: Paul Baumann und Hüls 1923-1964, in: *Westfälische Forschungen*, 50, pp. 109-127

Kleinschmidt, C. & Welskopp, T. (1994). Amerika aus deutscher Perspektive. Reiseeindrücke deutscher Ingenieure über die Eisen- und Stahlindustrie der USA, 1900-1930, in: *Zeitschrift für Unternehmensgeschichte* 39, pp. 73-103

Knox, B. & McKinley, A. (2002). Bargained Americanisation: workplace militancy and union exclusion, 1945-1974, in: Kipping & Tiratsoo eds. *Americanisation in 20th Century Europe*, vol. 2, pp. 389-404, Lille: Université Charles de Gaulle,

Knudsen, H. (1995). *Employee Participation in Europe*, London: Sage

Kochan, T. A. & Katz, H. C. & Mower, N. R. (1984). Worker participation and American unions, threat or opportunity? Kalamazoo, Mich.: W. E. Upjohn Institute for Employment Research

Kogut, B. & Parkinson, D., (1992). The diffusion of American organizing principles to Europe, in: Kogut, B. (ed.), *Country competitiveness. technology and the organizing of work*, pp. 179-202, New York, Oxford: Oxford University Press

Kogut, B. (2000). *The transatlantic exchange of ideas and practices: national institutions and diffusions*, Paris: Ifri

König, W. (2000). *Geschichte der Konsumgesellschaft*, Stuttgart: Steiner

König, W. (1990). Massenproduktion und Technikkonsum, in: König, W. & Weber, W., *Netzwerke. Stahl und Strom 1840-1914*, pp. 265-552, Berlin: Propyläen

Kostov, A. (2002). La Bulgarie face a l'américanisation au XXe siècle, in: Barjot & Lescent-Giles & de Ferrière le Vayer eds., *Américanisation en Europe au XXe Siècle: Économie, Culture, Politique*, pp. 329-336, vol. 1, Lille: Université Charles de Gaulle

Köttgen, C. (1925). *Das wirtschaftliche Amerika*, Berlin

Kreis, S. (1992).The diffusion of Scientific Management: the Bedaux Company in America and Britain, in Nelson D. ed., *A mental revolution. Scientific Management since Taylor*, Columbus

Kroeber-Keneth, L. (1953). *Menschenführung - Menschenkunde. Ein Brevier für Vorgesetzte*, Dusseldorf: Econ

Kudo, A. (2000). *Trends in a globalizing Japanese economy: Americanization vs. Europeanization and the impact of deregulation*, Berlin: Freie Universität

Kudo, A. (2001). Americanization or Europeanization? The globalization of the Japanese economy, in Hook, G. D. & Hasegawa, H. eds. *The political economy of Japanese globalization*, pp. 120-136, London: Routledge

Kudo, A. & Kipping, M. & Schröter, H. G. eds. (2004). *German and Japanese business in the boom years, transforming American management and technology models*, Routledge: London

Kudo, A. & Kipping, M. & Schröter, H. G. (2004). Americanization: historical and conceptual issues, in: Kudo & Kipping & Schröter eds., *German and Japanese business in the boom years, transforming American management and technology models*, pp. 1-29, Routledge: London

Kuisel, R. F. (1993). *Seducing the French. The dilemma of Americanization*, Berkeley: University of California Press

Lamberg, J.-A. (2002). The effects of regulationmarch 1989 and American retail models to Finnish retail sector, in: Barjot & Lescent-Giles & de Ferrière le Vayer eds. *Américanisation en Europe au XXe Siècle: Économie, Culture, Politique*, pp. 281-300, vol. 1, Lille: Université Charles de Gaulle

L'américanisation du droit (2001). Paris: Dalloz

Lammard, P. (2002). Worldwide phenomenon and transfer of technology: Swiss and French watch making in the face of the centennial exhibition of Philadelphia (1876), in: *ICON, Journal of the International Committee for the History of Technology*, vol. 8, pp. 33-42

Lanthier, P. (2000). L'évolution des techniques et des enterprises: le cas de l'électricité en France, in: Hau & Kiesewetter eds., *Chemins vers l'an 2000*, pp 221-244, Zurich: Peter Lang

Lanthier, P. (2002). France and US industrial know-how: the case of electrical engineering, 1945-60, in: Barjot, D. ed., *Catching up with America*, pp. 301-314, Paris: Presse de l'université de Paris Sorbonne

Lanthier, P. (2002). 'Twenty years after': were the big French industrial enterprises still following American patterns in the mid 1970s?, in: Kipping & Tiratsoo eds. *Americanisation in 20th Century Europe*, vol. 2, pp. 243-258, Lille: Université Charles de Gaulle

Lederer, W. J. (1959). *The ugly American*, London: Victor Gollantz LTD

Lehmann, A. (2000). *Der Marshall-Plan und das neue Deutschland : die Folgen amerikanischer Besatzungspolitik in den Westzonen*, Münster: Waxmann

Leroux-Calas, M. (2002). The influence of the productivity missions on R&D in France: the case of AFC-Péchiney, in: Barjot, D. ed., *Catching up with America*, pp. 395-404, Paris: Presse de l'université de Paris Sorbonne

Lescent-Giles, I. (2002). The Americanisation of food retailing in Britain and in France since the 1960s, in: Kipping & Tiratsoo eds. *Americanisation in 20th Century Europe*, vol. 2, pp. 291-308, Lille: Université Charles de Gaulle

Levy, B. and Spiller, P.T. eds. (1996). *Regulation, institutions and commitment: comparative studies of telecommunications*, Cambridge: Cambridge University Press

Lewchuck, W. (1987). *American technology and the British motor vehicle industry*, Cambridge: Cambridge University Press

Lewchuk, W. (1992). Fordist technology and Britain: The diffusion of labour speed-up, in: Jeremy, David
    J. ed., *The transfer of international technology. Europe, Japan and the USA in the Twentieth
    Century,* pp. 7-32, Edward Elgar: Aldershot
Lipartito, K., (1995). Culture and the practise of business history, in: *Business and Economic History* 24
    (Winter 1995), pp. 1-52
Lipartito, K., (1999). Culture business history and business culture, in: *Business History Review* 73
    (Spring 1999), pp. 126-128
Lipartito, K. (2000). Failure to communicate: British telecommunications and the American model, in:
    Americanisation and its Limits, pp. 153-179, Oxford: Oxford University Press
Locke, R. R. (1985). "Business education in Germany: past systems and current practice", *Business
    History Review,* pp. 232-253.
Locke, R. R. (1996). *The collapse of the American management mystique,* Oxford: Oxford University
    Press
Locke, R. R. (1984). *The end of the practical man: entrepreneurship and higher education in Germany,
    France and Great Britain, 1880-1940,* JAI Press, London.
Locke, R. R. (1994). Management education and higher education since 1940, in: Engwall, L. &
    Gunnarson, E. eds., *Management studies in an academic context,* pp. 155-166, Uppsala: Uppsala
    University Press
Locke, R. R. (1989). *Management and higher education since 1940: The influence of America and Japan
    on West Germany, Great Britain and France,* Cambridge University Press, Cambridge.
Locke, R. (1998). Mistaking a historical phenomenon for a functional one: Post War management education
    reconsidered, in: Engwall & Zagmani eds., *Management education in historical perspective,* pp.
    145-159, Manchester: Manchester University Press
Locke, R. R. & Schöne, K. E. (2004). *The entrepreneurial shift: Americanization in European
    management education in the high technology era,* Cambridge: Cambridge University Press
Loeber, H. ed. (1992). *Dutch-American relations 1945-1969, a partnership, illusions and facts,* Assen:
    Van Gorcum
Lundén, R. (1988). *Business and Religion in the American 1920s,* New York
Lundén, R. & Asard, E. eds. (1992). *Networks of Americanization : aspects of the American influence in
    Sweden,* Stockholm: Almqvist & Wiksell: 1992

Macey, J. R. (1997). Italian corporate governance: one American's perspective, in: *ICER Working Papers*
    7/1997
Macshane, D. (1992). *International labours and the origins of the Cold War,* Oxford: Oxford University
    Press
Maddison, A. (2001). *The world economy: a millennial perspective, Development Centre Studies,* OECD
Maier, C. S. (1970). Between Taylorism and technocracy: European ideologies and the vision of
    industrial productivity in the 1920s, in: *Journal of Contemporary History,* vol. 5, No. 2, p. 45-67
Maier, C. S. ed. (1991). *The Marshall Plan and Germany. West German development within the
    framework of the European Recovery Program,* New York: Berg
Maier, C. S. (1975). *Recasting bourgeois Europe: stabilization in France, Germany and Italy in the
    decade after World War II,* Princeton: Princeton University Press
de Man, H. & Karsten, H. & Karsten, L. (1994). Academic management education in the Netherlands, in:
    Engwall, L. & Gunnarson, E. eds., *Management studies in an academic context,* pp. 84-115,
    Uppsala: Uppsala University Press
Mandell, B. & Kohler-Gray, S. (1990). Management development that values diversity, in:
    Personnel, vol. 67, March 1990, pp. 41-47
Mankell, H. (2003). Drømmen om Amerika, in: *Dagbladet* October 25, 2003
Marginson, P. & Sisson, K (2003). *Europeanisation or Americanisation?: industrial relations in the
    single European market,* Basingstoke: Palgrave Macmillan
Marin, S, A. (2002). «L'Américanisation du monde»? Etude des peurs allemandes face au «
    danger américain » (1897-1907) in Barjot & Lescent-Giles & de Ferrière le Vayer eds.
    Américanisation en Europe au XXe Siècle: Économie, Culture, Politique, pp. 71-92, vol. 1, Lille:
    Université Charles de Gaulle
McCreary, E. A. (1964). *The Americanization of Europe. The impact of Americans and American
    business on the uncommon market,* New York: Doubleday
McGlade, J. (2000). Americanisation: ideology or process? The case of the United States Technical
    Assistance and Productivity Programme, in: Zeitlin and Herrigel eds., *Americanisation and its
    limits,* pp. 53-75, Oxford: Oxford University Press

McGlade, J. (1998). The big push: The export of American business education to Western Europe after the Second World War, in: Engwall & Zagmani eds. *Management education in historical perspective*, pp. 50-65, Manchester: Manchester University Press

McGlade, J. (1998). From business reform programme to production drive: the transformation of US technical assistance to Western Europe, in: Bjarnar & Kipping eds., The Americanisation of European business, pp. 18-34, London: Routledge

McGlade, J. (2002). The US Technical Assistance Program: From revolutionary vision to productivity drive, in: Barjot, D. ed., *Catching up with America*, pp.67-86, Paris: Presse de l'université de Paris Sorbonne

Meran G. & Schwarze, R. (2004). Pitfalls in the restructuring the electric industry, in: *German Economic Review*, vol. 5, No. 1, February 2004, pp. 81-101.

Messner, S. (2003). *Die Kostenrechnung im Spannungsfeld internationaler Entwicklungen: über die Amerikanisierung des Rechnungswesens und ihre Bedeutung für die interne Unternehmensrechnung in Österreich und Deutschland*, Wien: Facultas

Meyer, G. W. (1920). *Die Amerikanisierung Europas: kritische Beobachtungen und Betrachtungen*, Bodenbach: Technischer Verlag

Mioche, P. (2002). The mistakes of productivity missions to the United States: the case of the French steel industry, in: Barjot, D. ed., *Catching up with America*, pp. 265-275, Paris: Presse de l'université de Paris Sorbonne

Miskell, P. (2002). British responses to the cultural influence of American films, 1927-48, in: Kipping & Tiratsoo eds., *L'Americanisation en Europe au XXe Siecle: Economie, Culture, Politique*, volume 2, pp. 145-160, Lille: Université Charles de Gaulle

Moen, E. (2002). The American productivity gospel in Norway: a matter of politics, in: Barjot, D. ed., *Catching up with America*, pp. 99-112, Paris: Presse de l'université de Paris Sorbonne

Moen, E. (1998). Oligopoly and vertical integration: the reshaping of the pulp and paper industry, 1950-1970, in: Schröter, H. G. & Moen, E. eds., Une Américanisation des entreprises? *Entreprise et Histoire* No. 19, 1998, pp. 85-97

Mustad, J. E. (2004). Universitetsfinansieringen i England. Et være eller ikke være for engelske universiteter, in: *Forskerforum* No. 4, vol 36, pp. 20-21

Nandrup, F. (1998). Stromhandel will gelernt sein, in: *Standpunkt, Zeitschrift für Energie- und Umweltfragen*, vol. 11, No. 9, pp. 23-27

Nelson W.H. (1968). *The Volkswagen Story*, Fischer: Frankfurt

Newspapers: *Aftonbladet, Berlingske Tidende, The Business, Businessweek, Corriere della Sera, Dagbladet, Dagens Naeringsliv, Dagens Nyheter, The Economist, Financial Times (FT), Financial Times Deutschland, Frankfurter Allgemeine Zeitung (FAZ), The Guardian, Handelsblatt, The Independent, The International Herald Tribune (Trib), Le Monde, Neue Zürcher Zeitung (NZZ), The New York Times, The Times, Süddeutsche Zeitung, Svenska Dagbladet, USA today, De volkskrant, Wallstreet Journal, Die Welt, The Washington Post, Die Zeit*

Niebuhr, R. (1952). *The Irony of American History*, New York: Scribner

Nieschlag, R. (1962). Strukturwandlungen im Handel, in: König, H. ed., *Wandlungen der Wirtschaftsstruktur in der Bundesrepublik Deutschland*, pp. 493-524, Berlin: Duncker & Humblot

Noam, E. (1992). *Telecommunications in Europe*, New York, Oxford: Oxford University Press

Nolan, M. (1994). *Visions of modernity. American business and the modernization of Germany*, New York: Oxford University Press

Norström, C. J. (1995). Die Entwicklung der Betriebswirtschaftslehre in Norwegen unter besonderer Berücksichtigung des deutschen Einflusses, in: *Schmalenbachs Zeitschrift für betriebswirtschaftliche Forschung*, vol. 47, H 5 1995, pp. 408-424

North, D. C. (1990). *Institutions, institutional change and economic performance*, Cambridge: Cambridge University Press

North, D. C. (1997). *The Process of economic change*, Helsinki

Obelkevich, J. (2002). Americanisation in British consumer markets, 1950-2000, in: Kipping & Tiratsoo eds. *Americanisation in 20th Century Europe*, vol. 2, pp. 61-74, Lille: Université Charles de Gaulle

O'Brien, T. E. (1996). *The revolutionary mission : American enterprise in Latin America, 1900 - 1945*, Cambridge: Cambridge University Press

Oksholen, T. (2003). Fra forskning til fri marknad? In: *Forskerforum* 5/2003, pp. 18-

Pagano, U. & Rowthorn, R. eds. (1996). Democracy and efficiency in the economic enterprise, London: Routledge

Passerini, L. ed. (2000). *Across the Atlantic. Cultural Exchanges between Europe and the United States*, Brussels: Peter Lang

Pells, R. (1997). *Not like us. How Europeans have loved, hated, and transformed American culture since World War II*, New York: Basic Books,

Pentzlin, K. (1952). Das Geheimnis des Erfolgs führender amerikanischer Unternehmungen, in: *Rationalisierung*, No. 3, pp. 13-17

Petri, R. (2002). Opting for methane: Italian synthetic rubber, Western European developments and American technology, in: Barjot, D. ed., *Catching up with America*, pp. 315-336, Paris: Presse de l'université de Paris Sorbonne

Pfister, C. ed. (1996). *Das 1950er Syndrom. Der Weg in die Konsumgesellschaft*, Bern: Paul Haupt

Pfoertner, A. (2001). *Amerikanisierung der Betriebswirtschaftslehre im deutschsprachigen Raum*, Engelsbach: Dr. Hänsel-Hohenhausen

Pförtner, A. (1999). Amerikanische "Business Administration" und deutsche Betriebswirtschaftslehre, in: Teichova, A. & Mathis, H. & Resch, A. eds., *Business History, Wissenschaftliche Entwicklungstrends und Studien aus Zentraleuropa*, pp. 211-226, Wien: Verlag Manz

Pieper, R. (1994). Division and unification of German business administration and management education, in: Engwall, L. & Gunnarson, E. eds., *Management studies in an academic context*, pp. 116-137, Uppsala: Uppsala university press

Pohl, M. (2002). *Unternehmenskulturen. Deutschland und USA im Vergleich*, Frankfurt: FAZ

Prahalad, C. K. & Ramaswamy V. (2004). *The future of competition. co-creating unique value with customers*, Cambridge, Mass.: Harvard Business School Press

Puig, N. (2002). The Americanisation of a European latecomer: transferring US-management models to Spain, 1950s – 1970s, in: Kipping & Tiratsoo eds. *Americanisation in 20th Century Europe*, vol. 2, pp. 259-276, Lille: Université Charles de Gaulle

Puig, N. & Alvaro, A. (2003). *International and national entrepreneurship: a comparative analysis of pro-American business networks in Southern Europe, 1950-1975*, Madrid, manuscript

Ranieri, R. (1998). Learning from America; the remodelling of Italy's public-steel industry in the 1950s and 1960s, in: Kipping & Bjarnar eds., *The Americanisation of European business*, pp. 208-228, London: Routledge

Ranieri, R. (2002). The productivity issue in the UK steel industry, 1945-1970, in: Kipping & Tiratsoo eds. *Americanisation in 20th Century Europe*, vol. 2, pp. 357-374, Lille: Université Charles de Gaulle

Ranieri, R. (2000). Remodelling the Italian steel industry: Americanization, modernization, and mass production, in: Zeitlin & Herrigel *Americanisation and its Limits*, pp. 236-268, Oxford: Oxford University Press

Ranieri, R. (2002). The wide strip mill in Western Europe: transferring American technology, in: Barjot, D. ed., *Catching up with America*, pp. 251-263, Paris: Presse de l'université de Paris Sorbonne

Rappaport, A. (1986). *Creating shareholder value: the new standard for business performance*, New York: Free Press

Reilly, P. A. (1978) *Employee financial participation*, London: Management Survey Report No. 41

Ritzer, G. (1995). *Expressing America. A critique of the global credit card society*, Thousand Oaks: Pine Forge Press

Ritzer, G. (1998). *The McDonaldization Thesis. Explorations and Extensions*, London: Sage publishers

Robert-Hauglustaine, A.-C. (2002). How do they weld? A study of US-welding technology through one French productivity mission in 1951, in: Barjot, D. ed., *Catching up with America*, pp. 413-426, Paris: Presse de l'université de Paris Sorbonne

Rönning, A. (1997). *Innföring av divisjonsstruktur I Norsk Hydro*. Hovedoppgave, Olso: Universitetet i Oslo

Röper, B. (1955). *Die vertikale Preisbindung bei Markenartikeln. Untersuchungen über Preisbildungs- und Preisbindungsvorgänge in der Wirklichkeit*, Tübingen: J.C.B. Mohr

Rostgaard, M. (2002). Kampen om sjælene. Dansk Marshallplan publicity 1948-50, in: Jysk Selskab for Historie ed. Historie 2002, Århus: Aarhus universitetsforlag

Rostow, W. W. (1960). *Stages of economic growth*, Cambridge, Cambridge University Press

Sanchez, E. (2002). French technology or US technology? Spain's choice for modernization (1953-1970), in: Barjot & Lescent-Giles & de Ferrière le Vayer eds., *Américanisation en Europe au XXe Siècle: Économie, Culture, Politique*, pp. 215-230, vol. 1, Lille: Université Charles de Gaulle

Sandelin, B. (1997). Internationalization or Americanization of Swedish economics? in: *The European journal of the history of economic thought*, vol. 4, 2, pp. 284-298

Saül, S. (2002). Américanisation et américanisasions: une mise au point, in: Barjot, D. (ed.), *L'américanisation de l'Europe occidentale au XXe siècle. Mythes et réalités*, pp. 253-264, Paris: Presses de l'université de Paris Sorbonne

Scarpellini, E. (2003). *American style supermarkets abroad: imitation or adaptation? The Case of Italy*, Milano, manuscript

Scarpellini, E. (2001). *Comprara all'americana. Le origine della rivoluzione commerciale in Italia, 1945-1972*, Bologna: Il Mulino

Schaaf, P. (2004). *Sports Inc.: 100 years of sports business*, Amherst, N.Y.: Prometheus Books

Schildt, A. & Sywottek, A. eds. (1998). *Modernisierung im Wiederaufbau. Die westdeutsche Gesellschaft der 50er Jahre*, Bonn: Dietz

Schildt, A. (1996). Die USA als "Kulturnation". Zur Bedeutung der Amerikahäuser in den 1950er Jahren, in: Lüdtke, A. & Marßolek, I. & von Saldern, A. eds., *Amerikanisierung. Traum und Alptraum im Deutschland des 20. Jahrhundert*, pp. 257-269, Stuttgart: Steiner

Schildt, A. (1999). *Zwischen Abendland und Amerika : Studien zur westdeutschen Ideenlandschaft der 50er Jahre*, München: Oldenbourg

Schmid, S. (2003). *Blueprints from the U.S.? Zur Amerikanisierung der Betriebswirtschafts- und Managementlehre*, Berlin: Europäische Wirtschaftshochschule

Schnitzer, M. (2003). Privatisierung in Osteuropa: Strategien und Ergebnisse, *Perspektiven der Wirtschaftpolitik*, vol. 4, 359-397

Schröter, H. G. (1998). Advertising in West Germany after World War II. A case of an Americanization, in: Schröter, H. G. & Moen, E. eds., *Une Américanisation des entreprises? Entreprise et Histoire* No. 19, 1998, pp. 15-33

Schröter, H. G. (1996 a). Die Amerikanisierung der Werbung in der Bundesrepublik Deutschland, in: *Jahrbuch für Wirtschaftsgeschichte*, H. 1, pp. 93-115.

Schröter, H. G., (1996 b). Cartelization and decartelization in Europe, 1870 - 1995: rise and decline of an economic institution, in: *Journal of European Economic History*, vol. 25, No. 1, pp. 129-153

Schröter, H. G. (1995). Erfolgsfaktor Marketing: Der Strukturwandel von der Reklame zur Unternehmenssteuerung, in: Feldenkirchen, W. & Schönert-Röhlk, F. & Schulz, G. eds., *Wirtschaft, Gesellschaft, Unternehmen*, vol. 2, pp. 1099-1127, Stuttgart: Steiner

Schröter, H. G. (1997). European integration by the German model? unions, multinational enterprise and labour relations since the 1950s, in: Olsson, U. ed., *Business and European integration since 1800. Regional, national, and international perspectives*, pp. 85-99, Gothenburg

Schröter, H. G. (1987). Kartelle als Form industrieller Konzentration: Das Beispiel des internationalen Farbstoffkartells von 1927 bis 1939, in: *Vierteljahrschrift für Sozial- und Wirtschaftsgeschichte*, vol. 74, pp. 479-513

Schröter, H. G. (1994). Kartellierung und Dekartellierung 1890 - 1990, in: *Vierteljahrschrift für Sozial- und Wirtschaftsgeschichte*, vol. 81, H. 4., pp. 457-493

Schröter, H. G. (1992). The International Dyestuffs Cartel, 1927 - 1939, with special reference to the developing areas of Europe and of Japan, in: Hara, T. & Kudo, A. eds., *International cartels in business history*, pp. 33-52, Tokyo: Tokyo University Press

Schröter, H. G. (1997 a). Marketing als angewandte Sozialtechnik und Veränderungen im Konsumverhalten: Nivea als internationale Dachmarke 1960 - 1994, in: Kaelble, H. & Kocka, J. & Siegrist, H. eds., *Europäische Konsumgeschichte. Zur Gesellschafts- und Kulturgeschichte des Konsums (18. bis 20. Jahrhundert)*, pp. 615-647, Frankfurt and New York: Campus

Schröter, H. G. (2000 a). Modifications scientifiques et techniques structurantes dans l'industrie chimique allemande au XXe siecle, in: Hau & Kiesewetter eds., *Chemins vers l'an 2000*, pp. 47-67, Zurich: Peter Lang

Schröter, H. G. (1990). Nivea and the globalization of the German economy, in: *Entreprises et Histoire*, No. 16

Schröter, H.G. (1996 c). Perspektiven der Forschung: Amerikanisierung und Sowjetisierung als Interpretationsmuster der Integration in beiden Teilen Deutschlands, in: Schremmer, E. ed., *Wirtschaftliche und soziale Integration in historischer Sicht*, pp. 259-289, Stuttgart: Steiner.

Schröter, H. G. (2004 a). "Revolution in trade": The Americanization of distribution in Germany after WW II, in: Kudo & Kipping & Schröter eds., *German and Japanese business in the boom years*, pp. 246-267, London: Routledge

Schröter, H. G. (1997 b). Small European nations and cooperative capitalism in the twentieth century, in: Chandler & Amatori & Hikino (1997). *Big business and the wealth of nations*, pp. 176-204, Cambridge: Cambridge University Press

Schröter, H. G. (2000 b). Der Verlust der "europäischen Form des Zusammenspiels von Ordnung und Freiheit". Vom Untergang der deutschen Konsumgenossenschaften, in: *Vierteljahrschrift für Sozial- und Wirtschaftsgeschichte,* vol. 87, H. 4, pp. 442-467

Schröter, H. G. (2002). What is Americanisation? Or about the use and abuse of the Americanisation-concept, in: Barjot & Lescent-Giles & de Ferrière le Vayer eds., *Américanisation en Europe au XXe Siècle: Économie, Culture, Politique,* pp. 41-58, vol. 1, Lille: Université Charles de Gaulle

Schröter, H. G. (2004 b). Was unterscheidet Europa von Amerika? Europäische und amerikanische Modelle, das Verhältnis von Kapital und Arbeit 'richtig' zu ordnen, forthcoming

Schröter, H. G. (2004 c). Zur Geschichte der Marktforschung in Europa im 20. Jahrhundert, in: *Vierteljahrschrift für Sozial- und Wirtschaftsgeschichte,* vol. 91, no. 4 (forthcoming)

Schröter, H. G. (1997 c). Zur Übertragbarkeit sozialhistorischer Konzepte in die Wirtschaftsgeschichte. Amerikanisierung und Sowjetisierung in deutschen Betrieben 1945-1975, in: Jarausch, K. H. & Siegrist, H. eds., *Amerikanisierung und Sowjetisierung. Eine vergleichende Fragestellung zur deutschen Nachkriegsgeschichte,* pp. 147-165, Frankfurt and New York: Campus

Schüler, A. (1990). *Erfindergeist und Technikkritik. Der Beitrag Amerikas zur Modernisierung und zur Technikdebatte seit 1900,* Stuttgart: Steiner

Schwarz, H. (2000). Europe goes capitalist, in: *SAS-magazine,* Fall 2000, pp. 16-18

Schwarzenbach, R. J. F. (1917). *The Schwarzenbach Enterprises,* New York: private print

Seidensticker, W. sen. (1964). Globales Disponieren im wachsenden Markt, in: *Morgen verkaufen - was und wie.* Bericht über den 2. Kongress für Vertrieb und Marketing, pp. 112-127, p. 114, Düsseldorf

Segereto, L. (2002 a). Changing a low consumption society. The impact of advertising methods and techniques in Italy, in: Kipping & Tiratsoo eds. *Americanisation in 20th Century Europe,* pp. 74-91, vol. 2, Lille: Université Charles de Gaulle

Segreto, L. (2002 b). The impact of the US productivity philosophy in Italy after the Second World War, in: Barjot, D. ed. *Catching up with America,* pp. 135-147, Paris: Presse de l'université de Paris Sorbonne

Segreto, L., Models of control in Italian capitalism from the mixed bank to Mediobanca, 1894-1993, in: Business and Economic History, vol. XXVI, No. 2, pp. 649-661

Sejersted, F. (1997). The so-called 'autonomy' or 'independence' of central banks – reflections on the Norwegian case of minimal formal autonomy, in: Basberg, B & Nordvik, H. W. & Stang, G. eds. *I det lange løp. Essays I økonomisk historie tilegnet til Fritz Hodne,* pp. 207-218, Bergen: Fagbokforlaget

Servan-Schreiber, J.-J. (1967). *Le défi américain,* Paris: Denöel

Siegfried, A. (1927). *America comes of age,* New York: Harcourt Brace

Shearer, R. J. (1997). The Reichskuratorium für Wirtschaftlichkeit: Fordism and Organized Capitalism in Germany, 1918-1945, in: *Business History Review* 71 (Winter 1997), pp. 569-602

Shirley, M. M. & Walsh, P. (2000). *Public versus private ownership: the current state of the debate,* Washington D.C.: World Bank

Shpotov, B. M. (2002), Russia and the Americanisation process (1900-1930s) , in: Barjot & Lescent-Giles & de Ferrière le Vayer eds., *Américanisation en Europe au XXe Siècle: Économie, Culture, Politique,* pp. 303-314, vol. 1, Lille: Université Charles de Gaulle

Sirevåg, T. (1999). *Westerners: six reasons why Americans are different: a view from Northwest Europe,* Oslo: Gyldendal

Sirianni, C. ed. (1987). *Worker participation and the politics of reform,* Boston: Temple

Slater, D. (1999). T*he American century: consensus and coercion in the projection of American power,* Oxford: Blackwell

Sluyterman, K. (2002). Following the American lead: Dutch firms, 1945-1965, in: Kipping & Tiratsoo eds. *Americanisation in 20th Century Europe,* vol. 2, pp. 207-224, Lille: Université Charles de Gaulle

Søilen, E. (2002). Hvorfor gikk det galt? statens rolle i utviklingen av norsk næringsliv etter 1945, Oslo: Gyldedal akademisk

Soskice, D. (1999). Globalisierung und institutionelle Divergenz: die USA und Deutschland im Vergleich, in: *Geschichte und Gesellschaft*, vol. 25, 2, pp. 201-225

Soskice, D. (1999). Divergent production regimes: coordinated and uncoordinated market economies in the 1980s and 1990s in: Kitschelt, H. ed., *Continuity and change in contemporary capitalism*, pp. 101-134, Cambridge: Cambridge University Press

Staley, E. ed. (1952). *Creating an industrial civilization*, New York: Harper & Brothers publishers

Stead, W. T. (1902). The Americanisation of the world or the trend of the twentieth century, London: The "Review of Reviews" Office

Steinherr, A. (1998). Universal versus specialized banks, in: Black, S. W. & Moresch, M. eds., *Competition and convergence in financial markets. The German and Anglo-American models*, pp. 181-190, Amsterdam: Elsevier

Stokes, B. (1978). Worker participation - productivity and quality of work life, *Worldwatch Paper*, No. 25, December 1978

Stokes, R. (1994). *Opting for oil; the political economy of technological change in West German chemical industry, 1945-1961*, Cambridge: Cambridge University Press.

Strauf, H. (1959). *Die moderne Werbeagentur in Deutschland*, Essen: Wirtschaft & Werbung Verlags-Gesellschaft

Suleiman, E. (2003). *Dismantling democratic states*, Princeton, N.J.: Princeton University Press

Swedberg, R. ed. (2000). *Entrepreneurship : the social science view*, Oxford: Oxford University Press

Sywottek, A. (1993). The americanization of everyday life?: early trends in consumer and leisure-time behavior, in: Ermarth, M. ed., *America and the shaping of German society*, pp. 132-152, Providence: Berg

Taylor, F. (1911). *The principles of scientific management*, New York

Temin, P. & Galambos, L (1987). *The fall of the Bell system. A study in prices and politics*, Cambridge: Cambridge University Press

Tiratsoo, N. (1999). High hopes frustrated: the British Institute of Management as an agent of change, 1947-1963, in Amatori, F. & Colli, A. & Crepas, N. eds. *Deindustrialization and reindustrialization in 20th century Europe*, pp. 143-156, Milan: Franco Angeli

Tiratsoo, N. (1998). Management education in postwar Britain, in: Engwall & Zagmani eds. *Management education in historical perspective*, pp. 111-127, Manchester: Manchester University Press

Thorsrud, E. (1984). The Scandinavian model: strategies of organizational democratization in Norway, in: Wilpert, B. & Sorge, A. eds., *International perspectives on organizational democracy*, pp. 337-370, Chichester: John Wiley & Sons

Tolliday, S. (1999). American multinationals and the impact of the Common Market: cars and integrated markets, 1954-1967, in Amatori, F. & Colli, A. & Crepas, N. eds. *Deindustrialization and reindustrialization in 20th century Europe*, pp. 383-393, Milan: Franco Angeli

Tolliday, S. (2000). Transplanting the American Model? US automobile companies and the transfer of technology and management to Britain, France and Germany, 1928-1962, in Zeitlin & Herrigel eds., *Americanisation and its limits*, pp. 76-119, Oxford: Oxford University Press

Tomlinson, J. & Tiratsoo, N. (2002). The American productivity gospel in Britain, 1948-60, in: Barjot, D. ed., *Catching up with America*, pp. 149-156, Paris: Presse de l'université de Paris Sorbonne

Tomlinson, J. & Tiratsoo, N. (1998). Americanisation beyond the mass production paradigm: the case of British industry, in: Bjarnar & Kipping eds., The Americanisation of European business, pp. 115-132, London: Routledge

Toninelli, P. A. (2003). The rise and fall of state-owned enterprise in the Western world, in: *Journal of economic literature*, vol. 41, 3, pp. 931-932

Toninelli, P. A. ed. (2000). The rise and fall of state-owned enterprise in the Western world, Cambridge: Cambridge University Press

Touchelay, B. (2002). L'etat, l'INSEE, le CNPF et l'américanisation entre 1945 et 1961, in: Barjot, D. (ed.), *L'américanisation de l'Europe occidentale au XXe siècle. Mythes et réalités*, pp. 227252, Paris: Presses de l'université de Paris Sorbonne

Trompenaars, F. & Hampden-Turner, C. (1998). *Riding the waves of culture: understanding cultural diversity in global business*, New York: McGraw Hill

Ullenhag, K. (2002). Företagsledarutbildning och samhällsomvandling, in: Isacson, M. & Morell, M. eds, *Industrialismens tid*. Stockholm: SNS Förlag

Ullenhag, K. (2002). Globalization, management education and management practice. The case of IFL, Sweden, manuscript

Ullenhag, K. ed. (1993). *Nordic business in the long view: on control and strategy in structural change*, London: Frank Cass

Ullenhag, K. (1998). I takt med tiden: SNS åren 1948-1998, Stockholm: SNS Förlag

Varaschin, D. (2002). The Americanisation of France's public work firms: a case study of the Tignes dam, in: Barjot & Lescent-Giles & de Ferrière le Vayer eds., *Américanisation en Europe au XXe Siècle: Économie, Culture, Politique*, pp. 201-213, vol. 1, Lille: Université Charles de Gaulle

Vasilieva, M. (2002). Americanisation in the USSR nuclear field, in: Barjot & Lescent-Giles & de Ferrière le Vayer eds., *Américanisation en Europe au XXe Siècle: Économie, Culture, Politique*, pp. 315-28, vol. 1, Lille: Université Charles de Gaulle

Vaubel, L. (1952). *Unternehmer gehen zur Schule. Ein Erfahrungsbericht aus USA*, Düsseldorf: Droste

Verg, E. (1988). *Meilensteine*, Leverkusen: Bayer

Vershofen, Wilhelm (1954). Marktforschung in Deutschland heute, in: *FAZ*, January 30, 1954

Vuillermot, C. (2002). EDF à la Recherche d'une modèl de gestion de personel? Le Role des missions d'études (des orginines à la fin des années 1960), in: Barjot & Lescent-Giles & de Ferrière le Vayer eds., *Américanisation en Europe au XXe Siècle: Économie, Culture, Politique*, pp. 231-245, vol. 1, Lille: Université Charles de Gaulle

Wagnleitner, R. (1999). *"Here, there and everywhere": the foreign politics of American popular culture*, Hanover: University Press of New England

Welch, J. with Byrne, J. A. (2001). *What I've learned leading a great company a great people*, London : Headline

Wellhöner, V. (1996). *'Wirtschaftswunder', Weltmarkt, Westdeutscher Fordismus. Der Fall volkswagen*, Münster: Westfälisches Dampfboot

Wend, H. B. (2002). "But the German manufacturer doesn't want our advice': West German labour and business and the limits of American technical assistance, 1950-1954, in: Barjot, D. ed. *Catching up with America*, pp. 123-134, Paris: Presse de l'université de Paris Sorbonne

Wessel, H. (without year – (1990)). *Kontinuität im Wandel, 100 Jahre Mannesmann 1890 - 1990*, without place (Düsseldorf): Mannesmann

Whaples, R. & Betts, D. C. eds. (1995). *Historical perspectives on the American economy*, Cambridge: Cambridge University Press

Wilkins, M. (1974). *The maturing of multinational enterprise. American business abroad from 1914 to 1970*, Cambridge/Mass: Harvard University Press

Willet, R. (1989). *The Americanization of Germany, 1945-1949*, London and New York: Routledge

Windolf, P. (2003). Korruption, Betrug und 'Corporate Governance' in den USA – Anmerkungen zu Enron, in: *Leviathan*, vol. 31, No. 2, pp. 185-217

Wischermann, C (2000). *Advertising and the European city: historical perspectives*, Aldershot: Ashgate

Without author (1958). *Vom Vertrieb zum Marketing*; 1. Kongress für Vertrieb und Marketing in Deutschland, (without place, without publisher)

Without author (1974) *Worker participation and collective bargaining in Europe*, London: Her Majesty's Stationary Office

Whitley, R. ed. (1996). *The changing European firm: limits to convergence*, London: Routledge

Whitley, R. ed. (1992). *European business systems: firms and markets in their national contexts*, Sage: London 1992

Whittington, R. & Mayer, M. (2000). *The European corporation. Strategy, structure and social science*, Oxford: Oxford University Press

Wolters, T. (2000). "Carry your credit in your pocket": The early history of the credit card at the Bank of America and Chase Manhattan, in: *Enterprise & Society*, vol. 1, No. 2, pp. 315-354

Wood, J. et al. (1974). *Worker participation in Britain, SPR-Study*, London: The Financial Times Ltd

World Bank (1996). *World development report*, New York: Oxford University Press

Wright, G. (1995). The origins of American industrial success, in: Whaples, R. & Betts, D. C. eds. *Historical perspectives on the American economy*, pp. 451-467, Cambridge: Cambridge University Press

Zeitlin, J. (2000 b). Americanizing British engineering? strategic debate, selective adaptation, and hybrid innovation in Post-War reconstruction, 1945-1960, in: Zeitlin & Herrigel, eds. *Americanisation and its limits*, pp. 123-152, Oxford: Oxford University Press

Zeitlin, J. (2000 c). Introduction: Americanisation and its limits: reworking US technology and management in Post-War Europe and Japan, in: Zeitlin & Herrigel eds., *Americanisation and its limits*, pp. 1-50, Oxford: Oxford University Press.

Zeitlin, J. & Herrigel, G. eds. (2000 a). *Americanisation and its limits*, Oxford: Oxford University Press

Zeitlin, J. & Trubek, D. M. eds. (2003). *Governing work and welfare in a new economy: European and American experiments*, Oxford: Oxford University Press

Zieger, R. H. & Gall, G. J. (2002). *American workers, American unions: the twentieth century*, Baltimore & London: The John Hopkins University Press

Index